# THE DAIRY HOLLOW HOUSE
# COOKBOOK

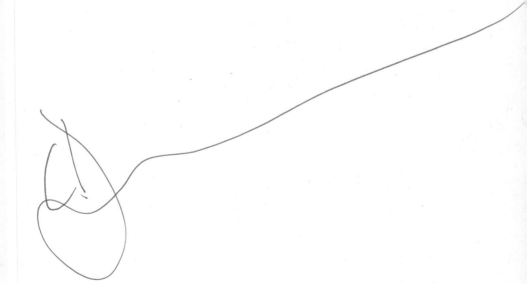

Also by Crescent Dragonwagon

CHILDREN'S BOOKS

*Home Place*
*The Itch Book*
*I Hate My Sister Maggie*
*Half a Moon and One Whole Star*
*Always, Always*
*Jemima Remembers*
*I Hate My Brother Harry*
*Will It Be Okay?*
*Katie in the Morning*
*Coconut*
*Your Owl Friend*
*If You Call My Name*
*When Light Turns Into Night*
*Wind Rose*

NOVELS

*The Year It Rained*
*To Take a Dare*

POETRY

*Message from the Avocadoes*

COOKBOOKS

*Dairy Hollow House Soup and Bread Cookbook*
*Putting Up Stuff for the Cold Time*
*The Bean Book*

# THE
# DAIRY HOLLOW HOUSE
## COOKBOOK

## CRESCENT DRAGONWAGON
### *with*
### JAN BROWN
*Illustrations by*
### JACQUELINE FROELICH

Cato & Martin Publishers
Eureka Springs, Arkansas

Cato & Martin Publishers
P.O. Box 613, Eureka Springs, Arkansas 72632

Library of Congress Cataloging-in-Publication Data

Dragonwagon, Crescent.
    The Dairy Hollow House cookbook.

    Includes index.
    1. Cookery, American—Southern style. 2. Cookery—
Ozark Mountains. 3. Dairy Hollow House (Inn : Eureka
Springs, Ark.) I. Brown, Jan, 1946 . II. Title.
TX715.D7622   1986        641.5        86-5142
ISBN 0-9632569-0-4


10  9  8  7  6  5  4  3  2  1

*Designed by Laura Hough*

Printed in the United States of America

*To our Dairy Hollow House guests, with heartfelt appreciation*
*for the innumerable and individual ways*
*they continue to enrich our lives;*
*and*
*To our husbands, Ned Shank and Blake Clark,*
*for loving us so thoroughly.*

# CONTENTS

# CORRECTIONS FOR THE SECOND EDITION:

Page 61:      *Persimmon Bran Bread, add 1/2 cup butter*
Page 85       *Whole Wheat Butterhorns, bake for 15-20 minutes.*
Page 299:     *Fruit Kuchen, add 1/2 cup additional milk or fruit juice.*
Page 329:     *Fallen Angel Bars, add 6 oz. chocolate chips to topping.*

# ACKNOWLEDGMENTS

Friends, family, and business associates without number have given unstintingly to this project. Many are mentioned throughout. But we must say a special thank you to the following:

*Dorothy Arnof*
*Ruth Eichor*
*Jean Elderwind*
*Elsie Freund*
*Bill Haymes*
*Jim and Sherree Smedley*
*Marcia (Choo-Choo) Yearsley*
*Charlotte Zolotow*
*Maurice Zolotow*
*Stephen Zolotow*

And our stellar lineup of Dairymaids—Peggy, Victoria, Donna, Marianne, Mary, Gina, Ninah, Diana, and Victoria again!

*Grant us a common faith*
*That man shall know bread and peace.*

—*Stephen Vincent Benét*, Prayer

◆————————————————————————————◆

*we will sit around the table*
*hold hands before we eat*
*and for a second the people-place will be quiet*
*but alive with feeling*

*then we will pass the bread, the butter, the milk,*
*the other good food*
*people will be ladling things out*
*and tell what happened in their day*
*and I will be home, I will be home, I will be home*

*wherever I am, I am home, anytime, I am home*
*I am home, I am home, I am home.*

—*Crescent Dragonwagon*,
When Light Turns Into Night

◆————————————————————————————◆

*I trust a good deal to common fame, as we all must. If a man has*
*good corn, or wood, or boards, and pigs to sell, or can make better*
*chairs or knives, crucibles, or church organs than anybody else, you*
*will find a broad, hard-beaten road to his house, though it be in the*
*woods.*

—*Ralph Waldo Emerson*, Journals

# THE DAIRY HOLLOW HOUSE
## COOKBOOK

# Welcome to
# Dairy Hollow House

Starting Dairy Hollow House—a small bed-and-breakfast country inn in a lovingly restored 1888 Ozark farmhouse—has been like sending out a party invitation to the world and then waiting to see who comes. Who will arrive to sip the iced tea afloat with fresh mint, waiting chilled in the refrigerator in August, with the red and yellow zinnias in their white pitcher on the pine table? Who will cup one hand around a mug of hot cider with a cinnamon stick in December, in the other hand a crisp gingerbread heart with white icing from the tree, the white pitcher now filled with pine boughs?

We didn't know who when we opened the inn five years ago, but now we do: warm and special people, as distinctive as this place they've been drawn to (and, since we are ²/₁₀ of a mile down a lumpy bumpy dirt road and have never spent a dime on advertising, one must assume that "drawn to" is the correct phrase). Over the past years, we have had more than two thousand guests, their kindness and individuality the only thing they have in common. We have never had a bad experience—never had a single bounced check or so much as one stolen ashtray. Our guests have included doctors, movie stars (Mercedes McCambridge, since you asked; Stacy Keach did have a reservation here but canceled), as well as horticulturalists developing disease-resistant fruit trees and IBM executives. We've had publishers and psychologists, veterans and veterinarians, peace activists and retired Air Force personnel, defense contractors and theosophists, bank presidents and civil libertarians, writers, artists, and firemen. We've had retired people driving across country staying exclusively in B-and-B's; we've had honeymooners just beginning their journey. We've had a senator's wife, a number of mayors, and the doyenne of American Country, Mary Emmerling. We've had guests from as far away as New Zealand and Kenya, and as close as Berryville.

"We" started out six years ago as three friends—novelist/children's book writer Crescent Dragonwagon; her husband, then-preservationist-now-architectural-services-marketer Ned Shank; and musician Bill Haymes. We shared the fairly common dream of leaving a metropolitan area, moving to a quiet and lovely place (although Ned and Crescent had already lived in Eureka for years), and opening a country inn. "We" has since grown to include many truly exceptional people who have joined in the work of the inn, becoming cherished friends in the process and adding their particular magic.

One of those people is Crescent's brother, Stephen Zolotow, about whom more later. Another is Jan Brown, who joined the Dairy Hollow House staff in December of 1982. A former schoolteacher and exquisite quilter, Jan is an excellent, experienced, and loving cook, and the inn's culinary evolution really soared when she joined us. Jan and Crescent are the authors of this book, and although the "I" in most cases throughout is Crescent, much work has also been done by Jan, in terms of concept, recipe development, and pick-and-shovel stuff. Occasionally Jan speaks as the "I" here, either quoted by Crescent or under the heading, "A note from Jan." Whichever one of our voices you are reading at any given point, you can be sure that we have had some fun doing this book, working on the IBM PC between getting up to toss another log onto the wood stove, in that mixture of high tech and low tech that, we think, also extends to our happily conjoined cooking styles.

Much was also contributed by Dairymaid Marianne Fulton, a fine and innovative cook. (The Dairymaids—at any given time we have two or three—are the women who come in to make breakfast for the guests and to tidy the house; we have had some great Dairymaids over the years!)

All these goings-on would probably astonish dairy farmer Daniel McIntyre, who built what is now the inn's Rose Room as a one-room cabin in 1888. (Although Ruth Eichor, a friend of ours who has done a great deal for the cause of preservation and local history, to say nothing of the cause of us, had an Aunt Mary who was a McIntyre and lived in the house that's now DHH, and Ruth has told us often that she's sure Aunt Mary would approve of the house's present incarnation.) Additions were put on the cabin in 1890 (that room is now the Iris Room) and 1923 (the kitchen/parlor when we first started out, now part of the dining room). It was a plain, functional, solid little farmhouse, unpretentious and down to earth in a town of glamorous and elaborate Victorians. It was about food and shelter and warmth, hard work and family. We loved those things about it; they spoke to us and still do.

Nearly a hundred years after the first room was built, we bought the home from McIntyre descendants, with the idea of turning it into a bed-and-breakfast inn as special as Eureka Springs' indescribable ambience and history. The three of us embarked on a massive "interpretative restoration" that lasted two years. We lavished loving attention on every detail of the house, every single square inch, inside and out. Floors and doors were refinished, two bathrooms plus a new heating/cooling system were added, windows were doubled and tripled (but we used the same type of "barn-sash" style windows that were original to the house), a small old-fashioned flower garden was designed and dug in, old stone retaining walls were restacked and extended. The furnishings, all appropriate to an older Ozarks farmhouse, were carefully chosen from antiques dealers, estate sales, and country auctions.

But throughout all this, even before we opened in 1981, even while we were still sanding and pulling old wallpaper nails, was—the food. Crescent *loves* to cook, and Ned and Bill *love* to eat, so, while Crescent did do her share of hands-on dirty work in restoring the inn (and had the calluses to prove it), she was also excused, often, to instead restore "the boys," via a timely breakfast, lunch, dinner, snack, and cup of coffee. "Would this be good, do you think, to serve at the inn?" "Oh, yeah, sure, this is great!" Ned and Bill were enthusiastic about everything, which made them fun to cook for but frustratingly indiscriminate in terms of analyzing why something was good or how it could be improved. Crescent longed for fellow cooks who understood "food talk." She was to get them, too, when Jan and Marianne joined the staff in later years.

When the inn actually opened, we started out doing just breakfasts, the bounteous offerings that from the first have been part of a night's stay here. Right away guests started saying, "When are you going to write a cookbook?" and so, early on, Jan and I began keeping notes, talking about it, planning it. But while the recipes herein mainly have Jan and Crescent as an immediate source, no recipe is ever purely original. We draw from our families, from our friends, from present and past Dairymaids, from hunting down the maker of that particularly delicious something at the pot-luck dinner, from mulling over cookbooks and magazines for ideas and adapting from them to suit our tastes, our ingredients and our context: the inn, the Ozarks, the season. We have recipes from a few of the other B-and-B's in Eureka Springs that have opened in the last couple of years, and recipes from some very very fine Eureka home cooks, like Elsie Freund, whose vocation as an artist (she is a watercolorist and jewelry designer) shows in her avocation as a cook: every dish she makes is as beautiful to look at as it is perfect to eat. Occasionally a guest sends us a wonderful recipe, like the swooningly rich Chilled Caraway Squash Bisque from Marlene Sapinsley. We have tried, always, to give credit where credit is due.

In 1982, we began to serve dinners. This started unofficially that winter because guests would show up plaintively at our door and say, "Could you feed us? There isn't anything *open*." Of course we did. Officially, though, in a planned and promoted way, we began to serve dinners in 1983, and, as we began to receive requests for picnics as

well, and wedding cakes, and other special orders, we did those, too. Probably that is when the idea for a restaurant first began to percolate seriously in our minds. As with the cookbook, we began to talk about it, think about it, take notes, keep files . . .

All our dishes were and are custom-made, by reservation only; each is lovingly, carefully prepared, generally around seasonal ingredients, taking some regional elements and mixing them with other influences to make that style we call Nouveau'zarks. Also, most important, each dinner was and is made by those who are not only proficient cooks technically but who really *care* about what they are doing and who they are doing it for: we all feel, here, that while a dish prepared without that extra element of love and respect (for the ingredients, the process, and the eventual consumer) may taste excellent, it will still leave the eater hungry.

Most of our cooking is done by Crescent, Jan, or Marianne (with an occasional guest appearance by Shawn Bible, a wonderful home cook, dedicated gardener, and true Eureka-phile). We have, over the past five years, cheerfully swapped notes, recipes, and samples, talked food talk. How does a particular recipe look, taste? What changes would we ring on it were we to make it again? Is it not just good but special, festive in some indefinable way? Does it seem to us, either in ingredients or method of food preparation or origins, "Ozark-y"? Sometimes two or even three of us have collaborated on a particular meal, sneaking off between the courses to sample our own handiwork gleefully at the Innkeeper's House just across the way. And just as people kept saying, "When are you going to do your cookbook?" so guests began to say, "When are you going to open a restaurant?" (Two separate sets of guests from Dallas both offered to finance us; we demurred but were flattered.)

But by 1985, we felt ready for more. We wanted to take on a restaurant.

"We" did not include Bill Haymes this time around. He was ready to reinvest his capital in his musical career, to record a third album. So, enter Stephen, Crescent's brother and a financial analyst. The expansion—a plan as I write these words, a reality as you read them— took place when Bill Haymes left the partnership and Stephen Zolotow entered it. Stephen took one look at our books and said the word that all of us had been thinking: *Expand.* The transition took place entirely amicably, notably missing the rancor that people always say accompanies business upheavals, buy-outs, and partnership changes. We all still like each other as much as we ever did, only more so.

And so: as you read these words, we will have added a small, by-reservation-only restaurant onto the inn, as well as a few more guest rooms, a larger parlor/living room/lodge room/meeting room with a fireplace, a pool, and more. "Oh, that sounds great!" say guests to whom we've described these coming changes. And then they add, cautiously, "Just—not *too* big, okay?" We agree totally. To own a country inn of this type is to be committed to tending the flame of a certain sweetness and romance. And that commitment has to do with being small and personal and caring, the inimitable qualities that simply cannot be faked and that make a business like ours what it is.

But being receptive to change and innovation has also been a Dairy Hollow House trait from the beginning. We were, after all, the Ozarks' first B-and-B and the second, by two weeks, in the state of Arkansas (the first is Williams House, in Hot Springs). Five years later, the state can now boast of about fifty-six B-and-B's, with approximately fifteen in Eureka Springs alone! As with any successful long-

term endeavor in life, there is a dynamic of continuity side by side with change. The continuity keeps the dream strong and alive and faithful, braced with the sturdy spine of history and experience. The changes keep it fresh and interesting for all involved, keep it able to respond to outside forces, challenges, and demands.

This pattern of change and staying the same touches every phase of Dairy Hollow House. We have favorite recipes that we make over and over again; but as the season, the particular yield of vegetables from the garden, what's in the market, what our mood is, moves us, we experiment with new combinations of flavors and textures and colors. The same is true of our flower arrangements and of our flowers themselves: the tiny first-year perennials we planted in the garden are now large, lush, flowering beauties, big enough to need dividing (occasionally, when the timing is right, a newly divided plant has gone home to a guest's garden). And our guests themselves, too, change but stay the same: often people who stayed with us on their honeymoon come back on their anniversaries . . . sometimes with their new babies.

And so we change, and Dairy Hollow House changes, too. Daniel McIntyre added on; we will, too.

A few words here about the fecund soil from which the inn sprang: that is, the Ozarks in general and Eureka Springs specifically. Chances are, if you are reading this book in Dallas or Memphis, Wichita or St. Louis, Houston or New Orleans, you already know a little about our area, which is one of the mid-South's favorite vacation places. Our town hosts 1 to 1½ million visitors annually. But to a Chicago, New York, or Los Angeles reader, Arkansas in general and Eureka Springs in particular may evoke a blank stare and a "Hunh?" despite the empirically proven fact that our town *is* at the center of the universe. So for those of you not yet in the know, Eureka Springs, whose year-round population is about two thousand, is a quirky and indescribable town, long a haven for visitors and in many respects (not all!) the crown jewel in that bright diadem that is the Ozarks.

The oldest mountain range on the continent, the Ozarks span some four hundred square miles. These heartbreakingly lovely wooded contours and steep valleys, washed by creeks, dotted with springs, and studded with limestone bluffs, bless the corners of three states: northwest Arkansas, southwest Missouri, and northeast Oklahoma. The Ozarks (which, like all of Arkansas, were once part of the Louisiana Purchase) got their name from the early French settlers, who found two kinds of *arcs*, or bows, here. One was rainbows, which arch the sky here with stunning frequency. And the other were the Indians' bows and arrows, made from the strong and flexible wood of the Osage orange tree, called by the French *bois d'arc* ("tree of bows"). That name has long since been bastardized to bodark, and the French name for this area, Aux Arcs (which means "at the place of bows"), became Ozarks.

Before the French arrived, however, the Eureka Springs area had a special significance to several different tribes of Indians who used the land in common. The Dakota, Crow, Cheyenne, Arapaho, and Osage Indians all shared the mineral springs which bubbled from the ground (in particular, the one sited in what's now Basin Park in downtown Eureka Springs) to heal their sick and injured. Because the area was looked on as sacred, there was no intertribal warfare here. Much later, after the advent of the white man, Eureka Springs again was a healing refuge from fighting: Dr. Alvah Jackson, a hunter and trapper as well as a physician and Eureka Springs' official first settler/founder, operated a Civil War hospital in a stone cave just up and behind some of the shops in present-day Eureka. The wounded from both North and South were treated here.

7

In the mid-1880s, the well-to-do of cities as far away as Chicago and St. Louis discovered the community, and Eureka began in earnest its century-plus as a resort town. People came to take the waters, leaving behind the ornate Victorian "cottages" which stand to this day, a present-time tourist attraction.

What else draws the visitors to Eureka? Well, there is excellent antiquing, and many very special artist- and craftsperson-owned and -operated shops. There are also extraordinarily lovely lakes (for swimming, fishing, boating, picnicking, or just admiring) only a few minutes' drive away. There is the general natural beauty of the area, the way the architecture settles sweetly into the hillsides and ledges, another early Eureka precedent. A. J. Kalklosch, who recorded his observations of "The Great Mountain Queen" in 1881 in a book entitled *The Healing Fountain*, noted that "Everywhere that a human abode could be constructed, houses of every description sprang up all over the mountain tops, hanging by corners on the steep sides, perched upon jutting boulders, spanning the gulches or nestling under crags and grottoes. It is a most peculiar-looking place, presenting an apparent disregard to anything like order or regularity, with its 'two story' streets, its winding thoroughfares, and circular paths." This pleasing disorder still captivates the visitor—and the long-time resident as well.

Kalklosch also hit the nail on the head with an accuracy that rings true a century later when he described the town's first residents. "People of all classes could be seen assembled at the Basin Spring. No other place upon the continent was ever made up of a heterogenous conglomeration of humanity as was this. It was as if a cyclone had passed through all nations, taking up some of the natives and landing them at the Health Resort . . . We see men, women, and children of all persuasions of color, and castes of religion and politics, coming to the Fountain to receive the boon of health offered by its waters."

In fact, this heterogeneity is what allowed one of Eureka's more notorious townspeople, the American Fascist Gerald L. K. Smith, to live here until his death. Smith was the founder of the pro-Hitler, pro-Mussolini Christian Nationalist Crusade and a devotee of Huey Long. He was also the founder of the "Sacred Projects," which employ, directly and indirectly, hundreds of Eureka residents and are also probably Eureka's greatest present tourist draw in sheer numbers— a sixty-five-foot "Christ of the Ozarks" statue and a prerecorded voice-over pageant in an open-air amphitheater depicting Christ's last week on earth, "The Great Passion Play," attract a large percentage of the town's visitors.

For, as Kalklosch noted, all castes of religion and politics flourish here—especially the more extreme. There are fundamentalist Christians of every imaginable denomination here, but you may also be waited on at the local pharmacy by an ordained Buddhist nun. While the fascists (like Smith until his death) thrive, so do the artists, writers, retirees, natives, late-Sixties refugees, gay men and women. Do we squabble? You bet! Most who live here love the town passionately; each is *convinced* she or he knows what's best for it, and there is always some juicy litigation or scandal going on. That is part of what makes life here interesting; no one is apathetic, and apparently no one who's lived here has ever been apathetic. The town's motto since the 1880s has been, "Where the misfit fits." And in general, on a day-to-day level, the misfits practice live-and-let-live, the differing groups getting along fairly affably: tolerance is the rule, intolerance the occasional and painfully glaring exception.

It is this diversity, I think, that is a large part of the attraction of Eureka Springs; it makes for a captivating dynamic tension as rugged and compelling and beautiful a psychological terrain as the mountains are a physical one. And it is this, I think, that makes it so enticing a place to come and take the risk of living out your dreams. As we have.

Like many dreams lived, Dairy Hollow House has been both much more work and much more joy than we imagined. Unlike many dreams lived, the living did not make us cynical or destroy our friendships. The changes that the life of the business required we make (I mean the expansion) were all compatible with our original ideals and goals and sense of what we are and what Dairy Hollow House is. Innkeeping is also the closest known career to professional fairy godmotherhood. It is a rare privilege to be able to offer something that is *better* than people had imagined, to watch them melt on the floor with pleasure and surprise that such a thing can *be*, is not advertising or hype. We feel delighted with the whole thing, including this, our cookbook. In it, we hope to give you both a literal and a metaphorical taste of what a stay with us is like.

Dairy Hollow House is an open invitation to the world. That invitation is now engraved on the pages of this book. We still can't wait to see who will arrive next. It might be you. In a way, it *is* you. Welcome!

◆————————————————————◆

*Who'er has travell'd life's dull round,*
*Where'er his stages may have been,*
*May sigh to think he still has found*
*The warmest welcome at an inn.*

*—William Shenstone*
*(1714–1763),*
Written on a window
of an inn at Henley

# Old-Time Ozarks Country Cooking vs."Nouveau'zarks" Country Cooking

$M$ost of the recipes in this book are not what you could call traditional Ozarks country cooking.

There are two simple reasons for this. One is that little traditional Ozarks food is available today in its original form; instead, there is a degenerated version which is all too often served at commercial establishments: mashed potatoes from potato flakes, gravy from powder, corn bread from a mix, greens from the deep-freeze or, worse yet, a can, instead of a garden. It just doesn't taste good.

The other is that we feel many, though not all, Ozarks dishes, even when well prepared, do not always make the best use of their ingredients, sometimes excellent ones, in terms of taste or nutrition.

However, there are *some* Ozarks dishes that are the exception to this rule, dishes we are crazy about: light, flaky biscuits; fresh strawberry shortcake; corn bread; huckleberry pancakes; cobblers of apple, huckleberry, or blackberry; to name a few. All these and more do find a place at our table, and I'll get back to them after I discuss the ones that don't and *why* they don't.

Ozarks cuisine, like all native cuisines, grew out of locally available ingredients and cooking methods compatible with area people's heat sources and schedules. For example, in much of China, meat and

11

cooking fuel were both scarce, hence a largely vegetarian cuisine, of ingredients diced into small, quick-cooking pieces, developed.

In the Ozarks, the opposite was true. Meat and wood for wood cook-stoves were both abundant. Virtually every farm family, no matter how poor, raised a hog or two for butchering. Chickens were kept as a matter of course, as was a milk cow; a beef cow was more unusual, a greater luxury. The woods were full of wild game: bear, deer, squirrel, groundhog, possum, raccoon, turkey, and, of course, the fierce and legendary wild razorback hogs. The waterholes were full of catfish, the rivers of bass. The woods and hedgerows yielded plenty of wild fruits and vegetables, free for the gathering: tender, delectable, asparaguslike poke in the spring, then tiny wild strawberries, then huckleberries and later black raspberries and blackberries. Greens like lamb's-quarter and watercress were available all spring and summer and into the autumn; autumn also brought the small, remarkably sweet persimmon, orange with a frosty, slightly purple sheen when dead ripe— which is the only time it can be eaten. The morel mushroom and the puffball were also collected by some, and black walnuts, staining the fingers a deep purple-brown when shelled, were used in desserts and for snacking, along with hickory nuts and the now seldom-seen chinquapins. Added to these wild fruits, nuts, and vegetables were the cultivated ones: just about everybody in the Ozarks had and still has a vegetable garden, and in the old days, a small orchard was also universal. Tomatoes, okra, sweet potatoes, summer squash, and cucumbers were enjoyed all summer and put up for the winter. Potatoes, turnips, and onions would keep at least part of the winter in a root cellar, as would beets, pumpkins, and some varieties of carrots and cabbage. Corn was used fresh, treated with lye to make hominy, and dried and ground for meal. Most farm families, according to everything I've read or heard from the older Ozarks people still living, visited the gristmill surprisingly often—about once every two weeks or so— bringing only a bushel or two of corn at a time to be ground, just enough for immediate use. Fresh-ground meal and flour are far sweeter and more flavorful—and much more nutritious—than meal and flour that've been sitting around awhile: one case in which we copy the original Ozarks method, grinding our own grains when possible, or buying the freshest ground we can find, sometimes from historic War Eagle Mill, which is not far from us. Beans were eaten fresh in the summer, but some were grown to maturity, stripped of their pod, and sun-dried to make beans such as black-eyed peas for winter use. Apples —the Ozark's combination of soil and climate produces some of the best-flavored apples in the world—were also enjoyed both fresh and dried. Cane syrup, from home-grown cane, and honey were available for sweeteners.

So much for what the Ozarks people had. They were and are an incredibly hearty group, long isolated geographically, reputed to be suspicious of outsiders, but in our experience extremely kind, tolerant, and warm under a veneer of flintiness, with a long history of live-and-let-live. What Ozarkers didn't have was access to a wide choice of ingredients from outside their region. Sugar, salt, flour, baking soda, and coffee (bought green, oven-roasted and ground back at the farm, right before breakfast) were the only ingredients regularly traded for from the outside, although Christmastime would see the purchasing of oranges, raisins, and hard candies, all great treats, for the children's stockings, in every family that could afford them. Ozarks people didn't have vegetable oil; lard was used for frying and baking. Butter, something of a luxury (for butter could be made only when the cow was "fresh," that is, giving milk), was used as a table spread when available. Eggs, like milk, were a seasonal treat; present in the spring and summer, gone in the cold weather when the hens stopped laying.

People in the Ozarks also lacked access to different ways of cooking, to foreign or cosmopolitan influences. They didn't have many spices; cinnamon and vanilla extract might be traded for, but that was about it. Though herbs could easily have been grown and used (we do at Dairy Hollow House), apparently they were not employed to any extent, at least not in cooking. Medicinally, herbs and roots were very commonly used (wild "sang"—ginseng, sassafras root, catnip and peppermint leaves, and wild cherry bark are but a few of the Ozarks' countless folk-cure ingredients). But for culinary purposes, the only herb seen with regularity is sage, used in poultry dressing and, with home-grown hot red pepper, in sausage. Garlic was not often used as a seasoning, nor of course wine (the preferred home brew was moonshine) or savory sauces like soy or Worcestershire. There was no lemon for added zip, though apple cider vinegar was easily made and widely available.

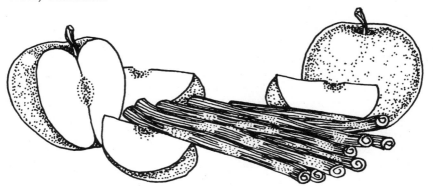

Ozarks food was pretty plain.

It also, where vegetables are concerned, tended to be far over-cooked. I can only guess at the reasons for this.

Wood, both for cooking and heating, was the near-universal fuel source in the Ozarks. Wood heat cannot be precisely regulated; neither can it be simply turned off and on . . .

An old and cantankerous country woman I used to work with years ago in a large hotel kitchen (not Dairy Hollow House's) arrived each morning at seven to begin preparations for lunch. One large pot would already be sitting out, filled with the five or ten pounds of dried beans she'd left to soak overnight. She'd put the beans on to cook and then she'd fill a second large pot with water. Into it she'd chunk three or four five-pound boxes of chopped, commercially frozen greens— turnip or collard. She'd turn the heat on under them, too, then toss a hefty piece of salt pork into each pot, and let them both cook until noon: *five hours.* This was about right for the beans, but hardly so for the greens. Even to call the greens "green" by then was a misnomer; they were black and evil and soggy and redolently bitter. Nobody in the dining room much cared for them; they were consistently left untouched, the only pan on the steam table to be returned to the kitchen full. There, she'd have a spoonful of them with her corn bread (she made excellent corn bread), and then they'd be thrown out (this kitchen, as you can see, was not particularly well managed). I can only guess that she grew up watching her mother cook, that this was the only way of cooking greens she knew, and that her mother learned it from *her* mother, and somewhere down the line it had just developed out of the convenience of simply leaving a pot be on a back corner of the wood stove. You wouldn't need to fuss with it, it could just sit there and cook as you did your chores in and around the house.

Now what of that chunk of salt pork, and the ubiquitous fried chicken and chicken-fried steak and even fried cornmeal dough (hush-puppies), fried okra, and fried pies?

As we have seen, the Ozarks cook didn't have a lot of seasonings to choose from. What she *did* have was pork, which could be smoked (and the home smokehouse didn't have any of the nitrates, nitrites, and other preservatives routinely added to hams and bacon today), salted, and rendered for fat. A piece of salt pork or smoked ham or bacon could add flavor and fatty richness to any number of dishes. And a piece of chicken could be deliciously dressed up by being breaded and fried to a turn in a couple of inches of home-rendered lard. Frying varied the texture of everyday foods; of chicken, fish, and steak; of okra, corn bread, and even fruit pastries.

Today most of us tend to blanch at the thought of all that saturated pig fat. And for good reason: we're cholesterol conscious, and lard has 95 milligrams of cholesterol per 100 grams. We're calorie conscious, and lard has 126 calories a tablespoon. Too, we know that most commercially cured meats are treated with preservatives, and that we live in a world where pesticides are used with alarming frequency. Animals that ingest pesticide residues, either through eating sprayed food or drinking contaminated water, tend to store these residues in their livers and body fat. When we eat lard today, we are getting a concentrated dose of accumulated pesticide poisons. Also, tastes have changed widely in America over the last few years, and many of us find the taste of lard-fried foods too heavy or greasy for our liking. No wonder lard-heavy foods have little appeal to us now.

But Ozarks people a century or even thirty or forty years ago led vigorous, hardworking lives. They could well afford the extra calories; they burned 'em off. They didn't know about cholesterol and saturated fats; no one did. And because their hogs were raised on food that was "organically grown"—there was no other way—and never treated with preservative chemicals after slaughter, their meat was much more healthful than ours, today, could possibly be. Utilitarian men and women, the Ozarks people made great use of what they had, for as many purposes as they could.

And it is this spirit we admire, respect, and emulate in our own way at Dairy Hollow House, even while our cooking style is very different in many respects.

Like them, we at Dairy Hollow House like to use seasonal, especially local, produce whenever we can. Our huckleberry cobblers and coffee cakes, our strawberry shortcakes, our persimmon breads and persimmon puddings, our biscuits and corn breads, our steamed poke, sweet potato pie and apple pie are right out of traditional Ozarks cooking, though our cooking fat is vegetable oil or butter or, when we really have to have it for the texture, hydrogenated vegetable fat such as Crisco rather than lard. We, too, use garden-fresh produce, relying heavily on it all summer long; but when winter comes, we have the option of fresh flown-in produce at market, including many "exotic" vegetables and fruits unknown to earlier Ozarks people. Too, we—and I use *we* here in a collective sense, to mean people in our society generally—know far more about nutrition than any of our ancestors, Ozark or otherwise, knew. And we know that often the cooking methods that preserve the most nutrients also preserve the most flavor. Our greens *are* green at the end of cooking, and there are rarely leftovers. Our vegetables are generally steamed or stir-fried rather than boiled, and they are served tender-crisp. Lastly, we have access to a literal world of cuisines, herbs, ingredients, and spices. We know about them, we draw on them, and we use them, accepting gladly the many different influences we were exposed to, just as, when Italians moved into the Ozark community of Tontitown, grapes began to be grown here, wine made, and pasta enjoyed. My sense is that people here embody most of all the ethos of using what you have—and what Jan and Marianne and I have as cooks is the knowledge about and access to many more foods and cuisines than the Ozarks people who lived here before us.

Because of the changes in the way animals are raised for slaughter, we do not believe that meat is a healthful food. Two of the partners are comparatively strict lacto-ovo vegetarians; one partner, plus our innkeeper, leans heavily in that direction but still enjoys seafood and occasionally chicken. That is why, in this strictly personal cookbook, you will find no beef or pork recipes (although we do note when a recipe could easily be adapted that way). We do have plenty of chicken and fish recipes, though, as well as virtually everything else we cook, enjoy, and love. Our cuisine is not one of denial or fanaticism; if much of it is healthful, that is *almost* incidental: whole grains and the freshest caught fish taste better and *are* better nutritionally.

We aim for a sense of style and sensuality: abundant, original, fresh, light, filling, sometimes rich but not heavy, based not on the absence of anything but rather on the presence of many lovingly chosen ingredients from the world over, prepared carefully and attentively, with imagination and taste. The visual sense is extremely important to us—but we are not so "nouveau" that we feel a beautifully presented plate can inherently overcome miniscule portions, underseasoning, and a dearth of textural contrasts. Of course food should be beautiful; that is inherent in good quality and attentive preparation. But visuals should never become the only recommendation for a food, any more than healthfulness should.

Besides the aspects of healthfulness and good taste, a diet low in meat or free of it altogether is ethically sound, also, first from the point of view of sensitivity to animals and prevention of their needless suffering, and second from the standpoint of sensitivity to the other, less materially fortunate human beings with whom we share this planet. As has been well documented in many books, starting with Frances Moore Lappé's *Diet for a Small Planet*, in wealthier meat-eating nations like ours, large quantities of vegetable protein which could be directly eaten by people are "shrunk" into animal protein. For example, it takes 16 pounds of corn and legumes fed to a cow to produce one pound of dressed-out beef, which then shrinks further during cooking. It is said that 90 percent of the world's protein deficiency could be made up now, on the spot, were the United States alone to stop this shrinkage of vegetable protein into meat. And when a way of eating is available which is not only healthful and ethical but delicious and fully sensually gratifying as well, people who are unaware of this option deserve to know about it and, if possible, to experience it firsthand, done well.

More and more people are. We find many of our guests share our feelings about food, and even those who do not are intrigued. We have yet to have a request for (or a complaint about the lack of) red meat on our menu. Everywhere, it seems, there is a burgeoning interest in lighter foods, and we are pleased to be part of that.

We also owe some allegiance to the natural foods movement, not only in healthful cooking styles (such as steaming and stir-frying rather than boiling vegetables), but in ingredients as well. We prefer to use whole-grain whole wheat or whole-wheat pastry flour or cornmeal whenever possible; when only white flour will work in a particular recipe, we opt for unbleached white. When time permits, Jan grinds our flours and meals immediately before use. We often, though certainly not always, use honey, maple syrup, or molasses as a sweetener. As mentioned earlier, we rely heavily on fresh seasonal foods rather than on canned or frozen ones wherever possible. We do have some digressions: not only white flour, but sugar, coffee, and chocolate (both Jan and I consider carob, which natural foods cookbooks sometimes cite as a replacement for chocolate, a travesty when so billed, though an occasional carob recipe, if not passed off as chocolate, is very good). In some recipes, we use altogether more butter and/or cream than can be condoned on any but sensual grounds (and, of course, we *are* Dairy Hollow House, and so we do have a certain nostalgic affinity for such delectable dairy products).

The main thing to remember is, we are sensual cooks. Ideological consistency is not our prime goal; preparing fine, voluptuous food which pleases and delights our guests is. At Dairy Hollow House, in a sense, we are always hosting a party; we are always cooking for guests.

As our friend Louis Petit, the French maitre d' at Jacques and Suzanne's, Little Rock's finest restaurant, once said to me, "People sink I eat like zis every day. No, no! I do zat and I become fat like pig!" Our food is a bit richer than "everyday" food; it is special-occasion food, for we want our guests to feel pampered, indulged, and that their visit to Dairy Hollow House is a special occasion (in fact, many people who stay with us are on honeymoons, anniversaries, or birthday trips). Bear this in mind as you browse through these recipes, many of which are rich and/or elaborate.

One can, however (and we frequently do), create and serve some lighter meals around many of the recipes included here, and we frequently offer suggestions for "lightening" particular recipes by careful substitutions (such as low-fat milk slightly thickened with cornstarch instead of heavy cream in some soup recipes). For a simple yet sumptuous repast, take a selection from our soup section, team it with an appropriate homemade bread and a really good generous salad, fruit for dessert—and there you have it. In private life, we have such a dinner several times a week and find it always satisfying and infinitely variable.

What do our soup-and-salad-and-bread meals, our breakfasts, and our knock-your-socks-off elegant terrines and tortes and mousses have in common? What is the link between our straightforward honey-sweetened apple pies in whole wheat crusts and our decadent chocolate wonders? Simple: everything is done attentively and with care, from scratch; no shortcuts, no convenience foods, the freshest and best possible seasonal ingredients.

And in this aspect, traditional French haute cuisine, nouvelle cuisine, real old-time Ozarks country cooking, well-done natural foods cooking, and good food preparation from many lands the world over all come together.

We like to think of Dairy Hollow House, small though it is, tucked into an obscure little Ozark hillside, down and up a lumpy bumpy dirt road, as perched happily at this particular intersection.

# A FEW IMPORTANT COOKING NOTES

Please read these few notes over before trying any recipe in the book; they simplify and explain some of our basic frames of culinary reference.

- On herbs and spices: When we specify an herb, such as parsley or sweet basil, *unless otherwise stated* we mean the *dry* version. If *fresh* parsley or basil is called for, we'll explicitly tell you. We also mean the so-called leaf or whole or flake version of the dried herb, not ever the ground or powdered kind: powdered herb leaves quickly lose their savor. Spices, however, such as cinnamon and cloves, maintain a good strength in powdered form, so with them we *do* generally mean the ground or powdered kind, and we will specify "whole cloves," "stick of cinnamon," and so on when we don't. Ginger we use about as often fresh as dried, and vice versa, so we always specify which form we mean in a specific recipe.

  To get the most in flavor from dried herbs in the leaf form, always, *always* crush them between your thumb and forefinger as you add them to a dish. This bruises them slightly, bringing out their aromatic essential oils (the reason powdered herbs are often so sawdusty-tasting is that the essential oils have vamoosed by the time you use them). Doing this is also highly pleasing to the senses and will ultimately teach you a great deal about what goes with what and which flavors and aromas go together. We won't tell you in every recipe to do this, but we think you should.

- On salt and "Taste, and correct the seasonings": We generally undersalt dishes, both in real life and in the cookbook. This is not for reasons of health, though too much salt is definitely linked to heart disease, but because it is always easy to add salt later—and impossible to take it out. This is one reason so many of our recipes say "Taste; correct the seasonings." Another is that personal preferences vary and that *ingredients* vary. Has your oregano been on the shelf the same period of time that ours has? We have no way of knowing, of course, so we approximate—and then leave it up to the individual cook's discrimination.

- On calories: As mentioned earlier in this chapter, we are in a sense always cooking for company here at the inn, and we go all out, no holds barred, pour on the whipping cream, melt the butter, heat

19

the olive oil. We do make these same basic dishes for ourselves at home, but we keep an eye out for calories. We use less or no fat when sautéing a dish for ourselves, for instance, instead spraying the cookware first with a nonstick spray release coating such as Pam, which, in the pump-spray bottle, is our first choice of brands. It's made from lecithin, a component of soybeans, and is not artificial in any way. It is also tasteless; we have done fine omelettes with it, and even stir-fries (they take close watching, though, if no oil whatsoever is used). While dishes made with it will not have the richness that only butter or oil can give, the calorie savings are tremendous and over a period of time really add up.

We use lightly salted butter here, because the unsalted butter available in this country has, to us, a slightly rank "off" taste. If we had the divinely fresh unsalted butter we've tasted in rural France, we'd feel differently.

Another calorie-watching trick is to substitute evaporated skim milk for heavy cream in recipes (though we balk totally at chilling it, whipping it, and using it as a substitute for whipped cream. *Nothing* is a substitute for whipped cream, one of the most sublime foods known to man or woman, and we find all imitations obscene). We also sometimes replace cream cheese with ricotta at home and substitute plain, unsweetened yogurt for sour cream.

- Unusual ingredients: From time to time, you will see an ingredient listed that may not be familiar to you. Generally this will be something that is either of foreign origin (as toasted sesame seed oil or miso) or from the natural foods store (as Morga cubes or nutritional yeast). Check the Glossary in the back of the book if an ingredient is unfamiliar.

- Last but not least: If you get into a real fix over something, call us at the inn! Our number is 501-253-7444.

◆————————————◆

*As aromatic plants bestow*
*No spicy fragrance while they grow;*
*But crush'd, or trodden to the ground,*
*Diffuse their balmy sweets around.*

—Oliver Goldsmith,
The Captivity, *An Oratorio, Act I*

# Beautiful, Bountiful Breakfasts

Breakfast is the first meal of the day and the first meal we served here regularly, so we think it is only logical to make it the first chapter of our cookbook.

In our prerestaurant days, perhaps a third of our guests ordered a dinner at Dairy Hollow House, but *everyone* had breakfast and still does. Breakfast comes with a night's stay, and we have been known for great breakfasts from the first. One journalist called our breakfasts legendary; another said that they were unmatched anywhere; and our visitors' register, which we ask guests to sign just after they finish breakfast, is filled with rhapsodies of praise to our German Baked Pancake, our omelettes, our breads, and to the sweet Dairymaids who cook and serve them as well.

With this in mind, here are some of our morning favorites, as well as a few notes on breakfast.

● Because it is the first meal of the day, breakfast should be worth waking up for. It should delight all the senses, yet there must be something *there* to it nutritionally. We feel very keenly that every breakfast worthy of the name should contain, in one form or another, three basic elements:

fresh fruit or juice in season

protein: eggs, milk, cheeses, nuts, yogurt, etc.

starch, often one that is whole grain

- For special occasions—and of course we try to make every guest's breakfast at DHH a special occasion—some sort of sweet roll or bread or coffee cake is not out of place, provided the three basics are first provided.

- Some people wake up ravenous; others have no interest in food until they've been up for an hour or two. Both types will be pleased with basically light breakfasts that rest on the three cornerstones just listed, if you offer ways for the parameters to expand for more solid morning eaters: a bottomless breadbasket, plenty of preserves, butter, and hot beverages. (For hints on the composition of a delightful, satisfying breadbasket, see our Breads chapter, page 59).

- Morning entertaining is well and good, and, having done it professionally for five years and unprofessionally for almost more than we can (among us) count, we can say that we like doing it a lot. But be forewarned: besides the obvious—that not all guests are morning people—we've found that tastes are most conservative in the morning. A highly adventurous eater by night may blanch at the thought of something that deviates only mildly from his accustomed breakfast fare. Bear this in mind before you plan any dishes even faintly unusual. By brunch hour, however, you have a little more leeway and can certainly get away with, let's say, garlic in the scrambled eggs or whatever morning exotic your taste runs to. If you do mimosas—fresh-squeezed orange juice cut fifty–fifty with champagne—you can probably get away with anything.

- Feed the visual senses, too. Many people who go to great lengths to set an elaborate dinner table, with fresh flowers and gleaming silver and carefully garnished plates, for some reason never consider doing anything special for breakfast. Single people also tend to shortchange themselves this way, making the effort for guests but not for themselves. Try setting the table for breakfast the night before, especially if it's just you eating. This is doubly true if it is the Sunday night before a week that you anticipate will be difficult. Use cheerful napkins and place mats and good china, and a small vase of flowers or a potted plant or even just some fresh or dried weeds stuck in a pitcher, and see if your day or week isn't better. Make a good breakfast; garnish the plate. By such small steps—of self-appreciation, of close-at-hand aesthetics—a life is gently revolutionized.

# EGGS

Most people's first breakfast thought is eggs, and a good thought it is. Versatile, healthy, delicious, satisfying, we do them many different ways. Although a guest's first morning's fare here is generally the German Baked Pancake for which we are famous, a second-day breakfast, and alternate mornings' meals after that, are usually centered around eggs in one form or another, most often:

## OMELETTES

*(Directions given are per individual omelette.)*

A perfectly done omelette (to us, one that is mottled golden brown on the outside and cooked to creamy softness on the inside) is a glorious envelope for any number of fillings: sweet or savory, hearty or light, subtle or assertive. This classic French way with eggs is simple, adaptable, and truly not hard to master.

Much more time consuming to explain than to do, omelette making will be easier for a novice if she or he is first shown the steps that follow by a more experienced cook. But one *can* learn from a book. I did . . . a Betty Crocker cookbook, when I was still in grade school, and had decided to fix my parents a surprise breakfast in bed. Oh, the agony of waiting to see if the eggs would really coagulate! They did, of course, as eggs will. (And, to be fair, and avoid misrepresentation of the event, I had seen my mother make them many times, often with fresh dill, an herb she loves with eggs.)

Anyway, it isn't difficult.

For each serving, whip together briefly with a fork

*2 or 3 eggs*
*1 tablespoon light cream or milk; a bit more for 3 eggs*
*a dash or two of salt*

Do not overbeat. Spray Pam on a pan—a small (5- or 6-inch) skillet with slightly curving sides is the classic omelette pan, but we have made perfectly good omelettes in good old black cast-iron skillets. And no, Pam is neither essential nor traditional, but we find it adds an extra measure of ease and security to the whole process, besides offering the option of saving calories and keeping the omelette from being excessively, greasily oozy with butter.

Have ready the plate you wish to serve the finished omelette on, and if the plate is warm, so much the better. Also have close at hand the prepared filling for the omelette, and some butter at room temperature.

Turn the heat up to medium-high, place the pan on the burner, and scoop into the pan some

*butter—1 teaspoon to 1½ tablespoons per omelette*
*(you can go with the lesser amount, or even none, if you used Pam)*

After the butter has melted, it will first get bubbly and slightly sizzly, and then the bubbles will die down a little. This is the perfect moment to add the eggs.

Pour 'em in, all at once; they'll sizzle slightly going in if your pan is hot enough. From this point on, keep an exceedingly close eye on the omelette, raising the pan instead of lowering the burner heat to control heat. Almost immediately you will see that the underneath and edges of the omelette are starting to set, while the upper part remains runny.

Now, with one hand gripping the handle of the skillet (the left hand, if you are right-handed) and a spatula in the other (the right hand, for right handers), carefully tip the skillet toward you, lifting the edge of the omelette with the spatula as you tip, which allows the uncooked part to run underneath. Repeat, tipping the skillet away from you. Do this until the omelette is cooked as you prefer it. At this point, fill the omelette in one of the following ways, beginning in the middle of the pan and extending out. In other words, your omelette is circular, your filling a half-circle which lies on the opposite side from the pan's handle.

Now, lift the pan just over the serving plate, tipping the filling side toward the plate. With your spatula, lift the upper edge of the

24

omelette, now near the handle, and fold it over onto itself, in a motion which will continue, till the omelette has practically rolled itself out and onto the plate. Garnish and serve the omelette immediately.

Easy. Come into my kitchen sometime and I'll show you.

Errors in omelette making are eminently edible (unless you burn them, of course), and with each try, you come closer to perfecting the skill. Don't give up! As we mentioned, it's far easier to do than to describe, and the infinitely variable technique, once mastered, can take you through every meal of the day, every course of the meal, for that matter (well, not soup and salad, but hors d'oeuvres, entrée, and dessert—though not all at the *same* meal, one hopes). Plunge on fear-lessly!

A delectable, very simple omelette filling is this: little dabs of garlic-and-herb Boursin cheese, dotted on the interior of the omelette before folding it over. Heavenly! Or try:

## Apple—Brie Cheese Omelette

*Apple sauté makes enough for 4, assembly and Brie is described for*
*1 omelette but easily quadrupled*

A Dairy Hollow House specialty that collects raves, even from those who start out skeptical about the combination.

Sauté together in a small skillet

*1 tablespoon butter*
*1 thinly sliced cored cooking apple, peeled or not,*
*as is your preference*

Cook, stirring often, until the apple has softened but is not mushy. Remove from heat and set aside.

Make an omelette as directed. When omelette has started to set and is done around the edges and underneath but soft in the center, arrange apples on one half of omelette, and top apples with

*sliced ripe Brie cheese, the equivalent of about 2 to 4 tablespoons*

Fold omelette over and slide onto serving plate. Garnish with a raw apple slice and a sprig of mint. Or try

*Gina's Great Apple Peel Garnish:* From Dairymaid Gina Meadows. You won't believe how pretty this looks. Using a sharp knife or vege-table peeler, begin peeling apple at the top of the stem, moving carefully around in a spiral, not breaking the peel. You don't have to go all the way down, just about a third of the way. Arrange the spiral on the plate with the Apple–Brie Cheese Omelette, or with almost any breakfast, and tuck in a sprig of fresh mint at the center.

# Omelette Jardinière

*Filling sufficient for 4 omelettes*

A very springtime-tasting vegetable omelette. I first made it up years ago out of refrigerator odds and ends but was so pleased with the combination I've made it ever since, often.

Sauté together in small skillet until slightly softened

*1 to 2 tablespoons butter*
*½ onion, finely diced*
*½ green pepper, finely diced*
*1 small carrot, in small dice*

Continuing stirring in butter. Then add

*5 or 6 large mushrooms, stems diced, caps sliced*

Stir-sauté a minute or two more, then remove from heat. Make omelette(s), following basic recipe but adding a drop of Pickapepper sauce to the beaten eggs. Place filling in omelette(s) with

*a generous sprinkle of grated Swiss or Jarlsberg cheese*
*1 tablespoon finely chopped parsley*
*a drop of Pickapepper or Tamari soy sauce (optional)*

Serve and garnish with more parsley.

*And in the morning when she wakes*
*Susan will eat breakfast cakes*
*And breakfast breads, at breakfast hour,*
*The morning glories full in flower,*
*Her summer nightgown light and loose,*
*Her parents drinking orange juice.*

—Crescent Dragonwagon,
Half a Moon and One Whole Star

# Mushroom and Swiss Omelette

*Filling for 2 omelettes (but easily doubled);*
*assembly and cheese for 1*

A classic combination. It became classic for a reason.

Sauté together in small skillet

*6 to 8 mushrooms, sliced*
*1 tablespoon butter*
*¼ teaspoon Tamari soy sauce*

If you wish, you can also add a little

*white wine* or *sherry*

Stir and cook over medium heat for 2 minutes. If you added wine, you may raise the heat near the end of the cooking to evaporate any excess liquid. Set this filling aside while you make an omelette, sprinkling it with

*¼ cup grated Swiss or Jarlsberg cheese*

After cheese melts distribute filling over omelette. Roll and serve. Garnish with 1 slice of raw mushroom and a bit of additional cheese sprinkled on the exterior of the rolled omelette. Repeat with remaining filling.

A fresh-tasting springtime variation:

## Asparagus–Mushroom–Cheese Omelette

Add leftover steamed or freshly stir-fried asparagus, cut in ¾-inch lengths, to the mushrooms. If you want, go all-out and use only the asparagus tips. Also consider

## Italian Artichoke–Mushroom–Cheese Omelette

*A jar of artichoke hearts, with mushrooms,*
*makes enough filling for 4 omelettes*

Rich and good, perhaps more suited to brunch than breakfast (though we've never had any complaints!). Use, instead of butter, 1 tablespoon liquid from a jar of bottled artichoke hearts. Use white wine in the sauté. When mushrooms soften, remove them from heat and add to them 4 or 5 of the marinated hearts, well drained and sliced into fourths. Instead of Swiss cheese, try fontina with a sprinkle of Parmesan and sweet basil.

## Festive Winter Solstice Brunch for a Crowd

*Fresh Orange Juice with or without Champagne*
*Cucumber Mousse surrounded by Crudités*
*Lemon-Pepper Marinated Chicken Wings*
*Crepes with Ratatouille, Broiled with Parmesan-Cream*
*Gingerbread Muffins à la Elsie, Angel Biscuits,*
*Crescent's Favorite Whole Wheat Butterhorns*
*Assorted Jams • Butter*
*Platter of Homemade Assorted Cookies*
*Hot Coffee • Hot Spiced Cider*

## Farmer's Omelette

*Filling sufficient for 4 omelettes*

Heartier than most of our omelettes, this old-fashioned combination is a winner every time. Eggs and potatoes have a natural affinity, and the green pepper (in summer, straight from our garden) adds a good touch. Male persons seem to have a special fondness for this. A nice lunch, too.

Have ready

*4 to 6 small cooked potatoes, sliced*

Sauté together

*1 tablespoon butter*
*1 onion, slivered into small crescents*
*1 green pepper, likewise*

Add cooked potatoes when onions are soft, along with

*a couple of drops of Pickapepper sauce*

Fill each omelette, prepared as directed, with a quarter of the potato-onion mixture and

*2 tablespoons grated sharp Cheddar cheese*
*a few thin slices of fresh tomato*

*Garnish:* a tomato slice and fresh parsley on the plate, additional cheese on the omelette. Serve with buttermilk biscuits or a good hearty rye bread, toasted and buttered.

# Omelette Torte

*Serves 6, beautifully and synchronistically*

It can be difficult to serve perfectly prepared omelettes simultaneously to more than two hungry breakfasters. We've solved that dilemma by simply making all four omelettes and stacking them on top of each other, one at a time, unfolded, on a warmed plate. The filling is placed between each layer, and one omelette is allowed per person.

When the last omelette has been stacked and the whole thing appropriately garnished, carry to the table and show it off whole and beautiful. Slice into wedges, layer-cake style, and serve, lifting out onto the individual plates with a spatula. (Individual plates should be ready and waiting, each with a substantial garnish of its own, for this to continue to work visually, since, though it's the identical quantity of an individual rolled omelette, it looks a little smaller cut in wedges.)

This beautiful solution to omelette serving was invented by Jan. When used at home, it allows the cook to eat with the family. Omelette Torte can be layered with any of the fillings we use for Dairy Hollow House omelettes—Jardinière, Farmer's, Apple Brie, and so on. Here is one more variety we dreamed up especially for the torte: a different sautéed vegetable goes between each layer, with a specially seasoned sour cream filling to boot. We call it Whole Garden Omelette Torte.

## Filling and Assembly
## for Whole Garden Omelette Torte

*Serves 6*

Sauté lightly

*1 tablespoon butter*
*1 bunch scallions, derooted and finely chopped*

When tender but a little crispy, remove from heat. Set aside. Again, in

*1 tablespoon butter*

*(continued)*

29

sauté

*1 green pepper, finely diced*

Set aside. And again, sauté

*1 tablespoon butter*
*1 cup sliced mushrooms*
*½ teaspoon Tamari soy sauce*

Now comes the fillip that lifts this filling to the skies. Blend together until smooth in blender or food processor

*½ cup sour cream*
*½ cup cottage cream*
*¼ teaspoon Tamari soy sauce*
*1 teaspoon chopped chives*

Set aside. Now begin preparing 6 omelettes and stack as for Omelette Torte. Place first omelette on serving plate. Spread over it the reserved green onions. Add second omelette and one-third of sour cream mixture. Add third omelette spread with green pepper mixture. Add fourth omelette and another third of sour cream mixture. Add fifth omelette and top with mushroom mixture. Add sixth omelette and remaining sour cream mixture. Garnish with

*black olives, sliced*
*fresh parsley, finely minced*

and serve immediately.

We ourselves like this served hot with fresh hot biscuits and homemade jam. It would also make excellent picnic fare by chilling the entire torte and serving wedges with a good antipasto.

## Breakfast Tartlets

*Serves 6*

An oven-poached egg nestled cunningly in its own prebaked pastry basket. Baking eggs is tricky; watch closely to make sure that the white firms while the yolk remains on the liquid side. Just a little overbaking and your egg can turn out rubbery, but worth the risk till you get it right.

Preheat oven to 400°. Prepare a single pie crust, as on page 337. After you form the dough into a ball, divide the ball into six equal parts. Roll out each into an ⅛-inch-thick round, and trim the edges with a knife, to make them smooth and perfectly circular.

Fit each little pie crust round into a 6-ounce custard cup, tucking and folding if necessary (irregularities are part of their charm). Place in each tartlet shell, filling it loosely, a loosely crushed wad of aluminum foil. This helps shape the shell as it bakes, preventing it from collapsing on itself. Place custard cups on a baking sheet and bake for 15 minutes. Remove cups from oven. Let cool for 2 minutes. Remove tartlet shells from custard cups; remove aluminum foil from shells. This much can be done the night before.

Reduce oven temperature to 350°, or, if you have baked the tart shells earlier, preheat oven to 350° about a half hour before breakfast-time. Into each tartlet put

*¼ cup shredded sharp Cheddar cheese*

This cheese is essential, not only because it tastes wonderful, but because it forms a barrier between the egg you are about to add and the crust, keeping the latter nice and crisp. Break into each tartlet, on top of cheese

*1 whole egg, being careful not to break the egg*

Top each egg with

*1 tablespoon heavy cream*
*½ teaspoon butter*
*a dot of Tabasco sauce (if desired)*
*a sprinkle of paprika*

Place tartlets on baking sheet and bake for 15 to 20 minutes in 350° oven, or until eggs reach desired doneness. Remove from oven and let sit for 1 minute before serving. If desired, sprinkle with

*scallions, chives, or other fresh herbs, finely chopped*
*(parsley or dill for Charlotte!)*

Serve on a pretty plate garnished with alfalfa sprouts and a thin slice of tomato.

# Eggs James the Piedmont House

*Serves 6*

Jim and Sherree Smedley are among the kindest people we know. They're also house restoration miracle-workers. To create Piedmont House, at 165 Spring Street here in Eureka, they took on a full *5,500* square feet in the form of a large and dignified turn-of-the-century boardinghouse, which had provided lodging continuously since the 1880s but had fallen on hard times. By early 1982, when the Smedleys began work on the inviting, porch-encircled house—with its distinctive simplicity among the many gingerbread Victorians Spring Street is famous for—it had reached the point where if it was not attended to, it would be lost.

The Smedleys Sheetrocked, painted, papered, stenciled, added bathrooms, sanded floors. While the house is not yet where they want it to be—is any house, to its loving owner/restorers?—it is already a before-and-after miracle. Returned to its original name, closer than it has been in decades to its original self, Piedmont House opened as a seven-bedroom B-and-B in 1984. This treat is one of Jim and Sherree's regular offerings.

Preheat oven to 325°. Melt

*1 tablespoon butter* or *margarine*

over low flame, and in it sauté

*1 tablespoon finely sliced onion*

Add

*4 to 8 small mushrooms, sliced*
*2 tablespoons sliced black olives*
*¼ cup small shrimp, fresh or frozen (optional)*

Season lightly with

*salt, pepper, cayenne, to taste*

Continue cooking "until the mushrooms give up their vital juices," as Jim says, and remove from heat. Spoon this sautéed mixture into the bottom of 6 custard cups. Grate

*Cheddar cheese*

into the custard cups until they are about two-thirds full. Top cheese with

*1 green pepper ring*

and then press cheese gently away from center to form a shallow cradle for

*1 egg per custard cup, 6 eggs in all*

Break each egg and ease into its cradle in the cheese-lined custard cup. Bake for 20 to 25 minutes.

# A Spring Breakfast

*Fresh Strawberries and Blueberries with Cream*
*Breakfast Tartlets with Parsley and Alfalfa Sprout Garnish*
*Miniature Apricot Danishes*
*Hot Coffee or Tea*

# Hashed Brown Quiche

*Serves 6*

This hearty country favorite is served in a cast-iron skillet and sliced into pie-shape wedges. Golden hashed brown potatoes form a crust for a delicate quiche custard topped with cheese that is always —always—popular with guests.

Preheat oven to 350°. Scrub and grate

*5 medium white potatoes (peel and all)*

You may wish to let the grated potatoes soak in water as in Potato Latkes, page 38, before proceeding, to prevent discoloration. If you do that, be sure to squeeze them dry, again as in Latkes, before using them. In any event, heat in a 9-inch cast-iron skillet

*2 tablespoons vegetable oil*
*(not butter, which would burn in this case)*

Sauté

*1 medium-size onion, finely chopped*

When onion is tender, add grated potatoes, squeezed dry if necessary. Cover the potato-filled skillet with a lid and cook over low heat until potatoes are clear and slightly browned (about 5 minutes).

*(continued)*

As the potatoes cook, prepare filling as follows: Blend in food processor or blender

*3 eggs*
*1½ cups heavy cream* or *a 12-ounce can evaporated milk (excellent and creamy in this recipe, and a considerable caloric saving— though what can ever match pure heavy cream!)*
*½ teaspoon Tamari soy sauce*
*½ teaspoon dry mustard*
*a couple of grinds black pepper*

Blend until smooth. Meanwhile, when the potatoes are done, remove from heat. Press the cooked grated potatoes to the bottom and edges of the skillet with the back of a wooden spoon, shaping into a crust. Pour filling into crust, and sprinkle with

*1 cup sharp New York Cheddar cheese, grated*
*3 tablespoons fresh parsley*
*paprika, evenly over the top*
*Parmesan cheese*

Place in oven and bake for 35 to 40 minutes, or until filling is set, potato crust is browned, and cheese is bubbly. Cut into wedges and serve. Garnish the plate with a slice of tomato and a large sprig of parsley.

# PANCAKES AND WAFFLES

## Elsie Freund's Rice Flour Waffles

*Makes 6 waffles*

Wonderfully crisp waffles from the redoubtable Elsie, watercolorist, jewelry designer, and superb cook. Her recipes add almost as much to this book as her graceful and cheering presence adds to our lives. She developed these because her husband, Louis, also a fine artist and muralist, is highly allergic to gluten, a protein found in almost every grain except corn and rice. The rice flour gives an extra crispness to these light, marvelous waffles.

Preheat waffle iron. Combine in a mixing bowl

> *1 egg, lightly beaten*
> *1 scant cup milk*
> *1 tablespoon honey*
> *2 tablespoons mild vegetable oil*

Sift together

> *1 cup rice flour, available at health food stores*
> *¼ teaspoon salt*
> *2 teaspoons baking powder*

Gradually add dry ingredients to moist ones and stir until fairly smooth. Bake in hot waffle iron. Serve with honey-butter or strawberry butter (see Strawberry Bread, p. 63) or pure maple syrup or a smear of homemade jam. Or have one waffle with each!

---

*FLOWERS AT DAIRY HOLLOW HOUSE: THE SOURCES*

*As with our cooking, we draw on a variety of resources when we create a flower arrangement here at the inn. Of course, we use flowers from our own, lovingly cultivated garden, but we often combine these with the treasures the natural world offers us: weeds and wildflowers, foliage and branches from the woods and fields and hedgerows. And throughout the year, but most especially in the winter, we have the precious luxury of florist's flowers; even on icy days, Nancy of Eureka Flowers has been known to mount our hill with a green-wrapped, ribbon-tied bouquet. Too, we occasionally use fruits and vegetables in our arrangements. Our most beautiful bouquets draw on flowers from two, or sometimes three, of these sources.*

---

# Lazy October Sunday Brunch for Family at Home with the Paper

*Fresh-squeezed Orange Juice*
*German Baked Pancake with Sautéed Fall Apples*
*Hot Tea, Indian-Style, or Coffee*

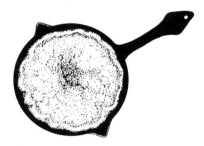

## Dairy Hollow House German Baked Pancake

*2 to 4 servings, depending on what it is served with*

Okay, this is it! The famous Dairy Hollow House specialty you may have heard about if you've ever had a friend who stayed here. Not unrelated to a popover or Yorkshire pudding batter, it's a delectable, versatile breakfast delight—a single pancake baked in a skillet that comes out puffed and golden and fragrant, hot from the oven, in no time. We have received raves on this from countless guests, in inn guides, magazines, and newspaper articles. But it really is almost embarrassingly simple to make, as many of our visitors, who've copied the recipe by hand, have discovered to their pleasure. We confess setting it down here in the book gives us a bit of a twinge—will every other inn owner in the world make it, too? Well, we suppose that would be okay—just serve it with a copyright line. That's © D-A-I . . .

Preheat oven to 450°. Beat together

> *3 large eggs*
> *¾ cup unbleached white flour*
> *¾ cup milk*
> *½ teaspoon salt*
> *½ teaspoon vanilla or lemon extract*

When very smooth, set aside while you melt

> *1½ tablespoons butter*

in a 12-inch heavy cast-iron skillet. When skillet is quite hot, pour in batter and put skillet in oven. Bake for 15 minutes at 450°; lower oven temperature to 350° and bake for another 10 minutes. It will have puffed dramatically but will soon settle down a bit, so show it to your guests quickly so they can exclaim with delight. Also, the edges end up higher than the middle, making a crater perfect for any one of the following delightful toppings, or fillings, that follow. Enjoy!

*Lemon Topping:* When pancake is done, squeeze over it

*juice of ½ lemon*

and sprinkle amply with

*sifted powdered sugar to taste.*

Garnish with lemon twist.

*Fruit Fillings: A General Recipe Followed by Specifics:* Apple, banana, blueberry, strawberry—take your pick of any one (combining several fruits, we think, dilutes the impact). No matter what your choice, you will always be pleased with the results. (If you're using any of these variations rather than the lemon version, prepare filling while pancake bakes.)

In a heavy skillet (*not* the one the pancake is baking in, obviously) melt

*4 tablespoons butter*

Lightly sauté in butter

*prepared fruit in season, peeled, if necessary (specifics follow)*

Drizzle over fruit as it softens

*¼ cup honey (or to taste), or brown or white sugar if you prefer
a dash each of cinnamon and nutmeg*

Cook fruit until just heated through: tender, not mushy. When pancake is done, spoon fruit preparation, hot, over the center of the pancake. Sprinkle with

*sifted powdered sugar to taste*

And present—whole, puffed, fruited, sugared, glorious. Then slice into pie-shape wedges and serve.

- Apple: Use 4 or 5 washed, peeled, sliced tart apples (reserve peel for Gina's Great Apple Peel Garnish, p. 25), and allow about 7 to 10 minutes' sautéing time. Tart apples, like Granny Smiths or Stayman Winesaps, are best, but Golden or Red Delicious will do in a pinch. Some people like an Apple German Baked Pancake served as a dessert, as one would an apple pie, hot, with either ice cream or whipped cream to accompany it.

- Peach: Use 4 to 6 washed, peeled, pitted, sliced fresh peaches, allowing 4 to 6 minutes of sauté time, depending on how ripe they are, and adding a tiny drop of almond extract to the peaches as they're taken from the stove. We think brown sugar is a delectable sweetener with peaches—not too much, though. This, too, can serve delightfully as a dessert.

- Banana: Use 4 bananas, slightly underripe, peeled, cut lengthwise and then halved (you end up with 4 pieces per banana). Sauté them gently for 2 to 4 minutes only.

- Strawberry: Wash, pick over, and slice strawberries to equal 2 cups, sliced. Heat them in the butter, stirring with extreme gentleness so as not to mush them, for 2 minutes only.

- Blueberry: Follow the directions for strawberries but leave blueberries whole and give them 4 to 5 minutes.

*A Note to Pancake Lovers:* See also Crepes, page 224, and the many ways we offer them, with various savory fillings ideally suited for brunch, in the Vegetarian Entrées chapter. We have often served them for breakfast with a dot of vanilla and a teaspoon of sugar added to the basic white flour or whole wheat crepe batter, and a filling/ topping of slightly crushed, slightly sweetened raspberries, strawberries, or blueberries, or banana slices, folded into whipped cream. And buckwheat crepes, with butter and maple syrup, are ambrosial!

Also, check out Potato Latkes, page 38. These are a luscious, very special breakfast (though not one that the cook can hope to sit down long enough to eat with her/his guests! Get someone to spell you at the stove). It's a New Year's Day tradition with us to serve these.

*June 1, Sunday.*
*Rain in the night—sweet mild morning.*

—*Dorothy Wordsworth,*
*Grasmere Journals, 1800–1803*

## Potato Latkes

*Serves 4 to 6 as an accompaniment, 3 to 4 as an entrée*

A delicious Jewish dish, these are tiny, very light, crisply fried pancakes of grated potatoes. This could as well be in the Hors D'oeuvres chapter (for, done in very small rounds and served with a dab of sour cream and a delicate spoonful of caviar or minced scallions, they are a totally elegant starter) or the Vegetarian Entrées chapter (a perfect meatless dinner is these with sweet and sour red cabbage, applesauce, and sour cream). As an accompaniment, they do almost any entrée proud, provided it is not swimming in a creamy sauce. They're traditional with pot roast or sauerbraten, but we also like them with any simply done fish dish. Because the Jewish holiday Hannukah commemorates the miracle of the day's worth of sacred oil lasting for eight days in the temple, these oil-fried delights are traditional at that time.

Grate in a food processor

*6 fist-size potatoes, well washed and scrubbed but not peeled*

*Quickly,* the second they have been grated, dump the potatoes from the food processor bowl into a large bowl of cold water, and swish the potatoes around therein. Let the potatoes stand in the water for about 10 minutes. Though this does rob the potatoes of some nutrients, it is also one of the secrets of perfect potato pancakes: it prevents their common postgrating discoloration and removes some of the starch, making extreme thinness, lightness, and crispness possible later on.
Beat in a bowl

*1 large egg (or 2 small ones)*
*½ teaspoon salt and several grinds of fresh black pepper*
*½ onion, finely chopped or grated*

Please note secret number two: *no flour or baking powder!*
Now, the potatoes having had their soak, remove them from the water a handful at a time, squeezing each handful dry and stirring it into the egg mixture. The batter should be mostly potato, with a little beaten egg hiding in the bottom of the bowl, which you will stir up into the potatoes often. (The nutrient-rich potato water makes a wonderful liquid in a bread, but don't try making soup stock out of it; the potato starch will thicken the whole stock pot.)

Now heat till not quite smoking but quite hot about

*4 tablespoons vegetable oil*

in a large cast-iron skillet. Drop the prepared potato batter into the hot oil, a tablespoon at a time (use a teaspoon if doing hors d'oeuvre–size ones). Immediately mash the potato latkes down, pressing with a fork or spatula, to thin them. The oil, by the way, should sizzle as you drop in the batter. Once the potato batter is added, however, you may turn the heat down to a medium slightly on the high side rather than a flat-out high—you don't want these to burn.

After about 1 minute, turn the latkes over—they should be beautiful browned. Brown the other side and remove from oil, draining well on paper towels and immediately serving. Repeat, adding more oil and adjusting heat as necessary.

What to serve with them is a topic of hot debate. Meaty gravy is a natural, and traditional, accompaniment. Unsweetened applesauce is also traditional, and perfect. But sour cream people argue over— "Never, never!" exclaims Bert Greene, author of *Greene on Greens* and other fine cookbooks—and many others, my father among them, concur. "Sour cream on potato blintzes, on cheese blintzes, on any kind of blintzes—even on other types of pancakes, like those matzoh meal pancakes. Yes!" opines Maurice, father of the author. "But not on latkes. No. It's wrong. I don't mean that the Talmud says, 'Thou shalt only eat applesauce on latkes,' it just *tastes* wrong." Familial dissent notwithstanding, at the inn we love latkes with *both* applesauce and a dish of sour cream and unsweetened yogurt, mixed together 50–50.

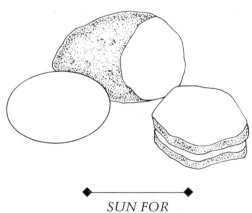

◆————————◆

*SUN FOR*
*BREAKFAST*

*Night now is gone*
*Morning upon*
*her silver tray*
*is serving day.*
*All you who wake*
*up hungry: take!*

—*Norma Farber*

# CEREALS

And now, as we near the end of our breakfast bounty, two spectacular cereals—actually four, if you count variations.

## Bircher-Muesli

*Serves 6 to 8 for breakfast, or 5 to 6 for dessert*

A Swiss doctor, Dr. Bircher-Benner, who ran a naturopathic clinic in the Alps many years ago, was the originator of this delicious *muesli*, or cereal. Bircher-Benner's theories—about the importance of whole grains and fresh fruits in the diet—were ahead of his time. But this soaked-fruit-and-nut cereal has been popular since its inception: it tastes so good.

We offer two versions: a country style, which is closer to Bircher-Benner's simple, strictly natural foods original, and a very dressed-up, elegant city style, which is as good for dessert as it is for breakfast, and which we have run into at very tony hotels in Zurich and Berne. We ourselves eat the country style often, for breakfast in the summer months, and have served it to guests who were strict natural foods lovers. The city style we save for special occasions, such as Ned's Birthday Breakfast Surprise Party, some years back.

*City Style:* Over

*2 cups oatmeal*

pour

*1½ cups milk*

(continued)

41

Let the mixture stand, covered, overnight in the refrigerator. Also soak overnight

*6 each pitted prunes and dried apricots*

by pouring over them to just barely cover

*boiling water*

In the morning, combine the soaked oatmeal and the dried soaked fruits (quartered). Mix the following ingredients

*2 apples, grated (unpeeled, unless peel is tough)*
*2 to 4 tablespoons honey or maple syrup, to taste*
*3 tablespoons lemon juice*

Stir the apples to coat them with the honey and lemon juice, and stir them into the oat mixture with any or all of the following fresh fruits, saving a few whole or especially pretty pieces for garnish

*½ cup seedless green grapes, halved*
*½ cup fresh pineapple, diced*
*¼ cup each ground toasted almonds, hazelnuts, and sesame seeds*
*1 to 2 cups sliced fresh strawberries*
*1 sliced perfectly ripe banana*

Just before serving, whip

*1 cup chilled heavy cream*

adding, when almost stiff

*1 tablespoon honey and 1 teaspoon vanilla*

Finish beating cream to stiffness, then gently fold two-thirds of it into the cereal. Serve the cereal in glass cereal bowls, each portion garnished with the reserved fresh fruit pieces, a puff of whipped cream put through a piping tube with a large star tip (or simply dolloped, if you can't bear fussiness in the morning), and a

*fresh mint leaf*

Serve at once. Fresh orange juice to start, hot herb tea or coffee to follow.

*Country Style:* Follow the proportions for City Style, but soak oatmeal in water instead of milk and omit the whipped cream treatment. Add raisins with the ground nuts, about ⅓ cup. Serve with a dish of good, thick, plain very fresh yogurt to be passed at the table, along with additional maple syrup or honey for those who want it.

Vary the fresh fruits according to what's in season, but strawberries and bananas are fairly essential.

# Breakfast After a First Night Together

*Melon Boats with Strawberries*
*Omelette Jardinière*
*Blueberry Muffins • Butter • Blueberry Jam*
*Café au Lait*

# Edna's Crunchy Granola

*This recipe yields about 3 quarts dry granola, or about 20 servings*

This delicious breakfast treat changes with ease: it's based on an infinitely variable number of grains and nuts. (Starred items are available from your local health food store.) Experiment with a little more of this and less of that to create a granola that is entirely to your taste. From our friend Edna, a wonderfully feisty woman who's an old teaching compadre of Jan's.

Preheat oven to 325°. Mix together in a very large bowl

*4 cups rolled oats (the quick-cooking kind)*
*1½ cups shredded unsweetened coconut\**
*1 cup wheat germ\**
*1 cup raw hulled sunflower seeds\**
*½ cup raw sesame seeds\**
*½ cup wheat bran\**
*1 cup ground roasted soybeans\**
*1 cup raw cashews, almonds, pecans, or peanuts\**

In a saucepan, heat together until well blended but not boiling

*½ cup oil (vegetable, sesame, or corn oil)\**
*½ cup honey*
*1 tablespoon cinnamon*

Remove saucepan from heat and stir in

*1½ teaspoons vanilla*

*(continued)*

Stir hot honey mixture well and pour slowly over dry ingredients in large bowl. Stir all ingredients together, coating all the grains and nuts and seeds lightly with the honey mixture. Spread one-fourth of the mixture onto a shallow baking sheet. Bake, turning as suggested just following, for about 15 minutes—until light golden brown.

*Most important:* You don't just slide this into the oven for 15 minutes and forget about it. Just as a garden takes continual tender loving care, so does granola as it bakes, and in much the same way: you need to turn the granola with a spatula, much as one turns the soil to plant. The granola-turning schedule: place in oven, bake for 5 minutes, turn; turn after 4 more minutes; turn after 3 more minutes, toast 3 more minutes and remove from oven. Repeat entire baking procedure for each fourth of the untoasted mixture.

When entire batch is removed from the oven, stir in

*1 cup seedless raisins*

Let toasted crunchy granola cool thoroughly on trays. Place in glass gallon jar or tightly covered tin. Enjoy in a bowl with a generous pouring of milk or country cream, topped with your choice of fresh fruits. Someone we know (hint: her initials are J. B. and she has worked like crazy on this book) eats her granola with fresh orange juice poured over the top; another (C. D.) loves to put plain yogurt in her breakfast bowl and sprinkle it with granola and fruits and maybe a drizzle of fresh maple syrup or, on less indulgent days, a packet of artificial sweetener.

*Crescent's Granola Notes:* I, too, am a granola fan, and I use this basic recipe but:

1. Substitute maple syrup for the honey, or add a tablespoon or two of molasses to the honey; omit cinnamon and add an extra teaspoon of vanilla.

2. Omit the ground soybeans and sunflower seeds and use a cup or so each of raw cashews and almonds and pecans, with a cup more oatmeal and a half cup of whole wheat flour; substitute oat bran for wheat bran.

3. Cook it at 275° for an hour or so, thereby cutting down on the chance of its burning, though it does, indeed, take watching and stirring always. To really crisp it up, I leave it in the turned-off oven after it's done.

4. Substitute chopped dates and apricots for the raisins.

44

Typing this recipe, Jan and I felt the room slowly fill with friends: Edna; Billy Haymes, with whom I once made a huge batch of this years ago as joint Christmas gifts for mutual friends; Fran Henderson, at whose home we made it. . . . What evocative power a beloved recipe has! Cooking is memory's sorcerer as nothing else is.

◆————————————◆

*COFFEE POEM*

*Love and Victory,*
*    these days,*
*Has the flavor of coffee beans.*

*Our spoons,*
*one by one, buy use of*
*are turning Silver.*
*Our mugs Gold.*

*—Blake Clark, 1984*

◆————————————◆

# FRUIT AT BREAKFAST

## Broiled Maple Grapefruit Sunshine

*Serves 2*

I freely admit I was totally prejudiced against this until Jan fixed it for me and more or less forced me to try it (I had had an unpleasant experience with broiled grapefruit some years back; I will spare you the tawdry details). Well, the maple syrup makes all the difference, and I am a happy convert. (She will never convince me on steamed radishes, though.)

*(continued)*

Cut in half and lay open

*1 grapefruit*

Run a grapefruit knife or sharp paring knife around the grapefruit rim and between the whites of the grapefruit, leaving sections loose but still inside grapefruit peel. Over each half, pour

*1 tablespoon maple syrup*
*a sprinkle of cinnamon*

Place under broiler for 5 minutes, or until lightly browned and bubbly. Remove from heat, garnish with 1 walnut half in center of grapefruit half. Serve. We think it is as wonderful for a light late-night snack as it is at breakfast.

## Breakfast with the Visiting Nieces from Iowa

*Sliced Oranges and Strawberries*
*Scrambled Eggs*
*Marianne's Cinnamon Bow Knots*
*Hot Chocolate*

## Winter Fruit Compote

*Directions for four servings, plus a large jar of soaked fruit base, which keeps well for up to three weeks and is sufficient for perhaps twelve to fifteen compotes*

This seasonless, luscious, and titillating compote was first served to us by Elsie—yes, her again. First, make up this larger quantity of soaked fruit, which keeps, refrigerated, quite well for several weeks (note from Jan: "If you don't eat it all!"). Later on in the recipe, you'll make up individual servings out of the soaked fruit, reserving most of it for future breakfasts.

## Soaked Fruit Base

Place in large enamel, pottery, or glass bowl

> *¼ to ½ pound each dried apricots and prunes*
> *1 cinnamon stick*

Pour over them

> *boiling water to barely cover*

Let soak overnight. In the morning, stir in

> *¼ cup brown sugar*

Now, from this point on, one mixes up day-to-day servings out of this soaked mixture. To make four servings of the completed winter compote, proceed as follows: In each of four individual serving dishes, preferably glass, place 2 each of the soaked apricots and prunes. In a separate bowl, combine

> *¼ cup soaking liquid*
> *¼ cup orange juice, preferably fresh*
> *2 or 3 tablespoons orange marmalade*

Whisk until smooth. Add to this

> *assorted fresh fruit*

We like, again for four, 1 sliced banana; 1 crisp apple, such as a Granny Smith, diced; 1 good orange, peeled and sectioned; and a bit of grapefruit, diced. We also sometimes add a few fresh grapes, halved— or, really, whatever looks good (and sometimes, when not much did, we've been known to resort to canned pineapple chunks in juice).

Toss the fruit gently in the liquid. Spoon a fourth of the fruit mixture into each serving dish and sprinkle with

> *chopped English walnuts*

and serve.

This is one of Jan's two or three personal favorite recipes from this entire collection. "I could eat this *every* day," she told me contemplatively the first time I, fresh from breakfast with Elsie, made it and served it to her. It has since become a DHH standby.

*She lives alone, and, at least sometimes, revels in it. She always leaves out the most beautiful breakfast setting for herself the night before, in her favorite blues and whites, place mat and crisp napkin and shiny, deeply glazed Arabian china. In the summer, there is always a pitcher of flowers from her own garden on the table; in the winter, a small potted plant or perhaps some small pine branches. The setting faces the window where she had a bird feeder placed some years back, so she can watch the birds at their breakfast while she has hers. She's my mother.*

# FRUIT PLATES

Other than Winter Fruit Compote, we do not generally serve what one could really call a fruit cup in the morning. What we do offer, in the summer, as fruit and berries come into joyful season one after another, are Fruit Plates—carefully arranged, beautiful still-lifes of seasonal fruit. The plate, a salad plate, is chilled in the freezer before we arrange on it, per serving, let's say

*3 thick, glistening circular slices of a peeled orange, overlapped*
*a couple of just-washed cherries, dried with a towel so they gleam,*
*piled together, stems and all*
*5 perfect strawberries, leaves left on*
*1 slice of kiwi fruit (the kiwi peeled before slicing)*
*a small bunch of grapes on the stem*
*a sprig of fresh mint from our ever-abundant mint patch*

We hope you get the idea. A tiny bunch of perfect grapes on the stem is always a lovely addition, and grapefruit rounds can substitute for the orange, and a spear of fresh pineapple, if it's a good ripe one, is superb. The important thing is arranging with care and beauty.

A major subspecies of our Fruit Plates is our

## Melon Boats

*One cantaloupe supplies boats for 4 to 6*

These are lovely, and much simpler to do than explain. Cut a wedge of perfect melon in season: cantaloupe, honeydew, Crenshaw, Persian, Santa Claus, any but watermelon. At its widest point, the melon slice should be about 2½ inches across. Insert a sharp knife at the point, the tip, of one end of the melon wedge, where the edible part of the melon ends and the greenish part of the rind begins. Carefully sail the knife down, across, and back up to the other tip, following the contour of the rind. You now have a wedge of melon that fits into perfectly but is no longer attached to its shell of rind. Now, make cuts in the melon about 1 inch apart, across the flesh. Set the melon on a chilled plate, and gently push the cut pieces out partway from the rind, alternating sides.

After the melon boat is perfect, scatter along it and on the plate around it a few other fresh fruits, either cut into pieces (like pineapple chunks or banana slices or pieces of a contrasting melon, cut into small globes with a melon baller) or left whole (blueberries, strawberries, wild black raspberries from Dairy Hollow Road . . .).

## Other Fruit Ideas for Breakfast

- Blueberries and banana slices in a goblet. A pitcher of cream and/ or a dish of sour cream and/or a dish of unsweetened yogurt, with a dish of brown sugar on the table (and artificial sweetener, for those who want it)

- Nectarine and banana slices, as above

- Strawberries and banana slices, with the same accompaniments

- Or strawberries and blueberries, with same

- Or strawberries, blueberries, and raspberries, with same

- Or—heaven—just raspberries. Serve with crème fraîche. Oh, don't bother to wrap it, we'll take it as is.

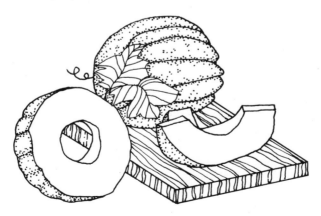

*A note on orange juice:* We like our orange juice fresh, fresh. That means our Dairymaids freshly press juice from the orange, to the juicer, to the frosted champagne glass, to you, delicious pulp and all. We garnish each glass with a fresh orange slice.

We think fresh orange juice is so perfectly delicious, so ambrosial, that we can't imagine drinking the kind made from concentrate (though we sometimes cook with it or use it in punch). If we can't have fresh-squeezed, none for us, thanks. If vitamin C is the issue, we'd rather take a pill than drink the stuff.

### FOGGY'S CORN DODGERS

*. . . is really my Missouri Mama's recipe. And it isn't every boy or girl who has had the Mom I had nor the chance of adventuring in Woods that are a mix between Twain's Woods and Burroughs' jungles and then come home to, or start out with Mom's Corn "Mush" Dodgers. Here's how to cook it.*

*When you've got a good amount of cornbread left over from the Beans and Cornbread that you had the night before, meaning everyone ate as little cornbread as they could, well knowing that the less they ate now, the more for the corn mush the next morning, you crumble it up in a frying pan, pouring milk into it as you go. When it all gets good and hot and has a texture that allows the eater to cut shapes into it with his fork as he eats it, then it's ready. Flatten the corn dodgers into each heated plate with a fork. Put lots of butter on it and lots of pepper on it. Serve with hot tea. Lipton's is fine. I suggest watching someone make it who really knows how, before making it yourself.*

*—Blake Clark (alias "Foggy")*

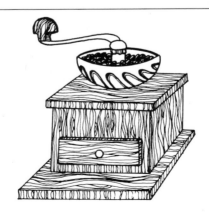

# BREAKFAST BEVERAGES

Because we always serve our guests their choice of hot drink at breakfast, we have chosen to put beverages in the breakfast section. In fact, some are appropriate at any time of the day, and some—like the iced tea and iced tea variations—we never serve at breakfast. Or haven't yet—you never can tell what someone will ask for.

In the winter months, we often offer arriving guests a cup of hot spiced apple cider or herb tea; in December (and sometimes, if the guests' timing has been lucky, at other times), with a plate of cookies to go with it. In the hot months, we usually have a pitcher full of one of the iced teas chilled and ready in the fridge . . . Or maybe lemonade . . . maybe with sugar cookies . . . Maybe.

*I like my coffee with sugar,*
*I like my sky filled out with clouds,*
*I like conversation to linger*
*While the autumn sun goes down.*

*—Bill Haymes,*
*"Blue Willow Autumn"*

## COFFEE

Our house coffee is French Market, a lusty New Orleans coffee with a touch of chicory and a dark European-style roast. We brew it strong and dark (it can always be diluted—though we've never seen anyone do it—but it can't be made stronger once brewed). Although we use a Melita drip pot in private life, we do use an electric drip machine at the inn. We allow, placing in the filter-lined basket, 1 to 2 level tablespoons per cup of water run through the machine. Were we using a less potent blend of coffee, we'd invariably use the classic proportions—2 tablespoons of ground coffee per cup of water—but with French Market, for many guests, 1 does the trick.

I can't tell you how many guests have told us that coffee done this way makes them *very* happy.

We should add that Dairy Hollow House partner Bill Haymes is so fond of coffee that he has a calligraphed sign on his kitchen wall which reads, Better far throw pearls before swine than pour good coffee into the cups of the indifferent.

*On the Care and Upkeep of Coffee Machine: Periodically one must clean the coffee machine's inner mechanism in order to dissolve mineral deposits that build up from the water. You can tell it's time to do this when the coffee machine begins making loud, obscene noises as the water drips through. Silence it by adding 2 tablespoons of vinegar to 1 quart of water and running this through the coffee maker, being sure to use a filter. Follow by running plain water through.*

## Cinnamon Coffee

Brew coffee as directed, but add a cinnamon stick to the ground coffee in the filter before pouring through the water. We feel this is more suitable for an evening or late-afternoon coffee than a morning one.

## Brewed Decaffeinated Coffee

An interesting cultural phenomenon. For our first three years, no one—not one guest—asked for brewed decaf. One, in that period, requested Sanka. Halfway through our fourth year, we got our first brewed decaf request, and since that time, probably one out of four guests asks for it. We use a Tanzanian decaf, which we'd never heard of either but were introduced to by our local coffee-tea-and-tobacco dealer, Eureka Springs Tobacconist (you better believe that is one sweet-smelling shop!). We love this tangy coffee, plenty flavorful despite the removal of the caffeine, and all our decaf-drinking guests comment favorably on it.

## Café au Lait or Decaf au Lait

The simple treat from French cafés and brasseries, and, of course, Café du Monde at the waterfront in New Orleans, where it is served with beignets at any hour of the night or day.

Have ready good hot strong coffee (or good brewed decaf). Have ready hot milk. Combine equal parts of the two together, in the cup.

The French waiter (show-off-y) way is to pour starting right at the cup, from the two containers, the coffee and the milk, simultaneously, raising them both aloft quickly and then back down to the cup, resulting in (a) a nice froth on top of the Café au Lait and (b) a large tip for the waiter. We could never manage this—though our Dairymaids have received some amazingly generous tips over the years despite this failing.

## Mocha

Pure, delicious indulgence; kind of like the best parts of being little *and* being a grown-up, combined. This is simply equal parts good strong coffee or decaf and hot chocolate, following, combined in the cup.

◆————————————◆

*A cup of hot chocolate,*
*A book that's good,*
*Little lamp beside my bed—*
*Stay up later than I should*
*Then I'll lay down my head.*

—*Bill Haymes,*
*"Sleepytime"*

◆————————————◆

## Hot Chocolate

Per generous serving (actually this is two servings, but we call it one because everyone wants a refill, and why not?), put on to heat

*2 cups milk*

and grate or chop

*½ ounce semisweet chocolate*
*(you may also use a heaping tablespoon of chocolate chips)*

Drop the chocolate into the heating milk, giving it a stir once in a while with a whisk and keeping an eye on it (milk boils over suddenly and easily). Meanwhile, stir together to a smooth paste

*1 tablespoon unsweetened cocoa*

and

*2 tablespoons each sugar and cold milk and 1 drop vanilla*

*(continued)*

When the milk on the stove is hot and the semisweet chocolate is melted, stir in the chocolate paste, beat altogether with the whisk, and serve.

If we have any on hand, it always tickles us to offer the classic and ultimate lily-gilding hot chocolate treatment: real whipped cream!

*The milk was boiling on the blue-tiled charcoal stove. Nearby, a bar of chocolate was melting in a little water for my breakfast, and, seated squarely in her cane armchair, my mother was grinding the fragrant coffee which she had roasted herself.*

—*Colette,*
My Mother's House

## TEA

I am as fond of hot tea as Billy is of coffee and consider it, these days, my "work drug." A pot of it, good and strong and well made, gives one the lift that coffee does, but without the stomach discomfort that the acid in coffee can sometimes cause. Besides its salutory effects, good tea is also delicious and, depending on where and how it is grown, blended, and roasted, totally versatile in flavor; coffee is, too, of course, but tea has an even wider range of flavors and aromas, I think.

The proper way to make tea: warm the teapot before you start, pouring in very hot water and capping with the lid. Let the teapot warm as you bring to a boil in a teakettle freshly drawn water (true tea fanatics will use only spring water, not water from the tap) and prepare a tea ball—wire mesh, porcelain, or perforated stainless steel —by filling it with tea. How much tea? We allow 1 teaspoon per cup plus 1 for the pot. The tea may also be put directly in the pot instead of in a tea ball, if you plan on drinking off the whole thing fairly quickly after it has brewed, as at an afternoon tea with friends, for instance. When the water in the teakettle has come to a boil, quickly dump out the water that has been warming the teapot and just as quickly place the tea ball in the now-warm pot and pour the freshly boiled water immediately over it. Dangle the tea ball by its chain up and down a few times, or, in the case of loose leaves, give a couple of

stirs with a spoon. Put the teapot lid on, and, if you wish, wrap the teapot in a towel or tea cozy. Let brew for 3 to 5 minutes, and then either remove the tea ball or strain the leaves.

If you are doing individual portions, of course, it is simplest to use tea bags, one per person.

I am especially fond of Indian-grown teas—Darjeeling, from high in the Himalayas, Ceylon from Sri Lanka, Assam from a middle province of India. Two parts Darjeeling to one part each Assam and Ceylon are the best choice for the spiced Indian tea, Chia, which follows. And, although we despise most flavored teas (hard to believe but there is even a *chocolate-mint* flavored tea available now! Ugh! The tea lover shivers at the thought!), we do love both Twining's Black Currant tea and the more classic bergamot-scented Earl Grey tea.

## Chia

A delicious Indian-style spiced tea with hot milk. Prepare a good hot Darjeeling-Assam-Ceylon tea as directed, perhaps using 2 teaspoons or even 1 tablespoon for the pot instead of the usual 1. For four generous servings: To 4 cups of steeping tea, heat 2 cups whole milk (or half-and-half, to go all out) in which you've placed a slice of fresh ginger root, a few whole peppercorns, a healthy dash of cinnamon, a smaller dash of cloves, and a trace of nutmeg, and, most important, 6 to 8 whole cardamom seeds. Take the milk from the heat just before it comes to the boil. The way they do it in India is to strain the spices and then prepare, in the individual cups, hot milk and tea mixed Café au Lait style—pouring from a height, making a froth, and so on. We just mix the hot spiced milk right in with the hot brewed tea and serve it like that and *boy* is it good. In India they serve it presweetened, very, very sweet; we don't, but we do supply sugar and low-cal sweetener with it. It really should be taken sweetened to fully appreciate it.

## Herb Teas

Herb teas, called *tisanes* by the French, are available both made from individual herbs (peppermint and chamomile are the two most popular) and as blended mixtures (Mellow Mint is a Celestial Seasonings blend of several kinds of mint, for instance). Some of our guests are longtime herb tea lovers; some think it is quite an adventure to partake of herb tea and do it for the first time in the spirit of, "Well, it's my vacation, I'll try something new!" I have enjoyed herb teas for over sixteen years now, and Jan for more than a decade. It still delights us that they are now available in every supermarket, where once you had to go to a health food store or herb shop to find them. Celestial Seasonings, a so-called New Age business that began in Colorado, has been largely single-handedly responsible for popularizing herb teas; our hats are off to them!

We do herb teas by the cup or small pot, using tea bags. Place tea bag in cup, pour boiling water over, and let steep to taste, generally 3 to 5 minutes. Here are some of our favorites:

Peppermint or spearmint: Clear-flavored and familiar, these clean-tasting teas are ideal after a dinner, as they help settle the stomach. A good choice for those new to herb teas.

Chamomile: A sweet, flowery-tasting golden-colored tea, very mild. Said to be mildly conducive to sleep.

Sassafras: The pungent-tasting, deliciously spicy flavor many people remember from root beer or sarsaparilla, this is taken from the roots of the sassafras tree, which is as common as stones are in the Ozarks. Brew briefly. Old-time Ozarks people drank this as a matter of course to "thin the blood" each spring.

Rose hips: Mild fruity-tasting reddish-pink tea, high in vitamin C.

Hibiscus: From dried tropical flowers, bright red and tart, pungent, good. Tangy.

Lemon verbena: A delicious lemony-fruity-flowery taste, one of our favorites. An intoxicatingly summery fragrance. We grow fresh lemon verbena in the garden and love to float it in fruit punches, and we also make the most exquisite apple jelly flavored with it.

And a few of our favorite blends, all from Celestial Seasonings, our favorite brand:

Mellow Mint: A combination of mints and other herbs.

Lemon Mist: Lemon verbena plus lemon grass plus lemon this and that. An excellent tea, mild and fragrant.

Almond Sunset: A provocative combination of orange peel and blossoms, carob, and almond flavors, this reminds us of Chinese almond cookies. It's not really an herb tea as such but our guests love it; it's our most frequently requested tea.

Red Zinger: People love or hate this bright red tea with the citrusy sharp tang to it. Blended from hibiscus, mint, and other herbs.

Sunburst C: It may remind you a bit of Hawaiian Punch, but it's delightful; a blend of hibiscus, blackberry leaves, chamomile flowers, chicory, orange, licorice, and more.

And last, a non–Celestial Seasonings herb tea everyone should try occasionally: Mu Tea, an Oriental blend that includes ginseng and licorice and tastes to us like gingerbread you sip. Said to promote longevity. We like it on those strange, mysterious winter days peculiar to the Ozarks where it is cold, but not too cold, and very, very foggy.

◆——————————————————◆

*I'm a little teapot, short and stout*
*Here is my handle and here is my spout*

*"Polly, put the kettle on*
*and we'll have some tea!"*
*Grandma used to say.*
*Though since then our taste has changed*
*In so many ways*
*Yet to the pot we cling!*

*—Traditional Nursery Rhyme*

Most herb teas are subtle in taste unless you brew them for a long time. But they grow on one, these infusions of the most aromatic plants on earth, each with its own mythology. Herbs, whether for cooking, medicinal purposes, or brewing tea, are magic plants.

# HOT APPLE CIDER OR JUICE

A wintertime treat for our guests, we simply heat cider or apple juice with a cinnamon stick and a few whole cloves in it.

# ICED TEA

Susan Carr Hirschman, a distinguished children's book editor at Greenwillow Press, told me the secret of good iced tea years ago. "Use the cheapest you can find." Lipton, plain old Lipton, is great for iced tea; Luzianne is excellent too. We brew it double or triple strength, and pour it, hot, over plenty of fresh mint, and chill the whole thing in the fridge in a big glass pitcher so one can see the floating mint, still on the stem. Serve, with fresh lemon, sugar or low-cal sweetener, and more fresh mint, over plenty of ice. Nothing, but nothing, is more refreshing than icy iced tea on a summer's day.

## Iced Herb Tea with Fruit Juices

Make a quart of triple-strength Sunburst C or Red Zinger tea, following the package directions but using triple the amount of tea suggested per cup of water. Let steep for 15 minutes; remove bags. Sweeten if desired. Pour tea into the bottom of a glass gallon jug and add a couple of slices of fresh lemon and orange, and some fresh mint. Fill the jug with a combination of apple juice, fresh orange juice, pineapple juice, what have you. We love making this for work parties, where everyone gets together to paint or paper a room or hang Sheetrock or whatever. A wonderful summer drink, it can be made sparkling by adding either Perrier or low-cal ginger ale. Kids love this and usually want it sweeter than the adults.

# The Bottomless Breadbasket

The staff of life, the stuff of life—
we've proudly served sweet breads, yeast breads, rolls, muffins, and
more at Dairy Hollow House from the first. Nothing smells so sublime
as the aroma of baking yeast bread; nothing makes the cook feel more
wholly connected to life and the earth as the timeless and relaxing
rhythms of *mix* and *knead* and *punch* and *rise,* as the tiny yeast organ-
isms multiply and work their magic yet again, as they have for millen-
niums, all over the world.

Sweet breads, too, weave a spell of connection for their baker;
loaded with the harvest of the season, aromatic with spices from India
and Zanzibar and the Far East (the very spices so prized that the dis-
covery of America was a mere by-product of the search for them), they,
too, evoke a world of associations.

Our guests love to eat these wonders almost as much as we love
to bake them, so it's no wonder that this chapter kept doubling in bulk
no matter how many times we punched it down! Here are some of our
many favorites: breads simple and elaborate, hearty and delicate,
earthy and ethereal. You will find a bread to match your every mood
and your every meal. We'll start with sweet breads, move on to other
quick (i.e., baking powder or soda leavened) breads and muffins, plunge

into yeast breads, and finish with some spectacular exceptions to the rule.

# QUICK SWEET BREADS

On paper, the following quick sweet breads may read very similarly; their ingredients are nearly identical (though some use sugar and others are honey sweetened). They are each put together in much the same simple way: dry ingredients are combined with or without sifting, wet ingredients are combined in a separate bowl, then the wet and dry mixes are quickly combined.

But one crucial ingredient individualizes the tone and taste of each. These breads, with their sweet surprises of fruits both fresh and dried, nuts, and even grated vegetables, are each distinctive in flavor. They also mark the seasons at the inn. Zucchini breads find their way to our table in the summer, pumpkin or persimmon breads in the fall and winter, and strawberry breads—yes!—in the spring and first days of summer. Carrot and coconut breads are all year-round treats for us.

Timing on quick breads is variable; much depends on the size of the loaf pans, how accurate the oven heat is, how moist the batter is. A quick bread is done when the edges are deeply browned and the center, which will be cracked in most cases, is a lighter golden brown and firm to the touch. A toothpick inserted in the crack will come out clean.

Most of our quick-bread recipes have a fairly large yield. This is because (1) quick breads are great gifts from the kitchen and (2) virtually all of them freeze very well.

## Victoria's Pumpkin Bread

*Yield: three large loaves, or five or six small ones*

Victoria, one of our first two Dairymaids, is a wonderful cook, a charming hostess, an extremely sharp dresser, and just generally a kind and bright and warm person. We lost her to the bright lights and big city: a salaried job that paid roughly fifteen times what we could. I see her whenever I go to New York, and she always swears she'll come back to us someday (the first time I called her office in New York and asked to speak to Victoria, I was told, rather curtly, "Ms.

Desoff is in a meeting right now . . ."). This pumpkin bread is one of Victoria's legacies; I believe she told me she got it from her aunt, and one autumn we made a ton of it, due to the gift of an extremely large pumpkin that had graced a shop window, Beau Troutt's fantastical Sidereal Jewels, in Eureka Springs.

Preheat oven to 350°. Into a large bowl, sift together

*2 teaspoons* each *cinnamon and baking powder*
*1 teaspoon* each *nutmeg, baking soda, and salt*
*½ teaspoon cloves; ¼ teaspoon ground ginger; dash of allspice*
*6 cups unbleached white flour*

In a separate bowl, mix the following until smooth

*1 cup mild vegetable oil*
*½ cup water* or *yogurt*
*4 eggs*
*3 cups sugar*
*2½ cups unsweetened pumpkin puree*

Combine the two mixtures, beat till smooth, and fold in

*1 cup chopped nuts*
*(the flavor of black walnuts blends nicely with pumpkin, we think)*

Pour batter—it will be thinner than usual for a quick bread—into Pam-ed loaf pans. This batter rises quite a bit, so be careful not to fill the pans more than two-thirds of the way. Bake for about an hour, testing for doneness at 45 minutes.

## Persimmon Bran Bread

*Yield: one large or two small loaves*

This sweet and delicious bread is quite solid textured. It is excellent served with cream cheese or whipped honey-butter.

Preheat oven to 350°. Beat together

*2 eggs*
*½ cup honey*

*(continued)*

61

In a separate bowl blend

*3½ cups whole wheat flour*
*2 teaspoons baking powder*
*1 teaspoon baking soda*
*½ teaspoon salt*
*2 cups bran*

Gently add egg-honey mixture and dry ingredients. Stir in

*2 cups seeded, stems removed, mashed dead-ripe persimmons*
*1 cup chopped walnuts*

Turn into Pam-ed bread pans. Bake for 50 minutes.

---

*DAIRY HOLLOW HOUSE FLOWERS: MEDITATIVE HOSTESSING*

*Some of the most sweetly peaceful moments Jan and I have known at the inn are in arranging flowers in preparation of a guest's arrival. The cider may be ready for heating or the iced tea chilling, the porch and steps swept, the registration card filled out; but in that final moment of fussing with the flowers, getting the colors just right for the room in which they will go, carrying them from the kitchen to the guest rooms, setting them down upon the marble-topped or oak bureau, fussing with them a bit more, pulling a bloom out a little farther, removing it, adding a bit of greenery, stepping back to survey it with satisfaction—all the while with the guests-to-be in the back of our minds—this is a very special kind of welcoming, from the heart. The kind of welcome we'd like to have if we ever left Dairy Hollow.*

## Waioli Tea Room Carrot Bread

*Yield: four small or two large loaves*

What and where the Waioli Tea Room is I have no idea; neither do I know how its recipe for Carrot Bread fell into the hands of Vince and Ramona, a "host home" couple Ned and I stayed with once through Bed and Breakfast Atlanta. What I do know is that this is a scrumptious bread: very sweet, dark, dense, rich, moist.

Preheat oven to 350°. Sift together

> *4 cups unbleached white flour*
> *1½ teaspoons* each *baking powder and baking soda*
> *1 teaspoon* each *salt, cinnamon, and nutmeg*

Beat together

> *2 cups mild vegetable oil*
> *6 eggs*
> *2¼ cups brown sugar*
> *2 teaspoons vanilla*

Combine the wet and dry ingredients together with

> *1½ cups chopped walnuts*
> *4 cups grated carrots*
> *½ cup chopped dates* or *diced dried pineapple*
> *½ cup flaked coconut*

Turn the mixture into Pam-ed pans. Bake for about 30 minutes for small pans, 40 to 45 for large.

## Strawberry Bread

*Yield: one large or two small loaves*

I first experienced Strawberry Bread at the Little Rock wedding rehearsal dinner of our dear friends Starr Mitchell and George West in May of 1984. The dinner was held at the Arkansas Museum of Science and History, where a large stuffed grizzly bear presides at the front door. As Starr is a preservationist/dulcimer player/writer and George is a folklorist/fiddle player/video documentary maker, a grizzly bear as maitre d' seemed perfectly appropriate. With the excitement of the pending marriage, I forgot to ask who had made the Strawberry Bread, let alone track down a recipe for it, but when cool-headed back at home, I was able to reconstruct this reasonable and delicious facsimile.

*(continued)*

63

350°. Sift together

*1½ cups unbleached white flour*
*1 teaspoon cinnamon*
*½ teaspoon baking soda*
*⅛ teaspoon salt*

Beat together in large bowl

*1 cup sugar*
*2 eggs*
*⅔ cup vegetable oil*

Combine the two mixtures till just barely blended, then fold in

*a pint basket (12 ounces) of fresh strawberries that have been washed, sliced, and slightly mashed (not pureed; they should still have texture to them)*
*1 teaspoon vanilla*
*½ cup chopped walnuts or pecans*

Pour into Pam-ed pan(s) and bake for 45 to 55 minutes, testing for doneness.

This is quite excellent served with a Strawberry Butter made by creaming together a stick of butter and a medium-size package of cream cheese, both at room temperature, with ¼ cup honey and ½ cup mashed strawberries. Yum! And, though we haven't tried this yet, we suspect a Blueberry Bread with Blueberry Butter would also be excellent, and we intend to see next June.

## Esther's Coconut Bread

*Yield: one large or two small loaves*

In the summer of 1975, I worked for a season as the kitchen manager of Eureka's venerable Crescent Hotel dining room, the Crystal Room (an experience I later drew on in my first novel, *To Take a Dare*). One of the best cooks was Esther, tiny, feisty, dark-haired, dark-eyed, and energetic. Her wedding, to Spencer, several years later, was catered by Jan. The marriage feast was held outdoors near Lake Lucerne on a bright April day, and one of the nuptial treats was this bread, baked by Jan, according to Esther's recipe, and consumed in joyful abundance. Jan has made it ever since. It has a moist, almost but not quite puddinglike quality, and a sweet flavor reminiscent of coconut cream pie yet very much its own.

Preheat oven to 350°. Combine

*1 cup milk*
*2 eggs*
*½ cup melted butter*
*1 teaspoon vanilla*

Mix together

*3 cups unbleached white flour*
*2 cups dried, unsweetened shredded coconut*
*1 cup brown sugar*
*1 tablespoon baking powder*
*1 teaspoon salt*
*1 teaspoon nutmeg*

Blend wet and dry ingredients. Pour into Pam-ed loaf pan. Sprinkle with

*¼ cup coconut*
*½ teaspoon nutmeg*

Bake for 1 hour, testing for doneness.

# QUICK COFFEE CAKES

Actually there is only one quick coffee cake we make with regularity, and this is it, in its infinity of fine variations.

## Blueberry—Sour Cream Coffee Cake

*Yield: one 9- × -13-inch cake*

Sweet and buttery, this is our favorite summer coffee cake when made packed with delectable locally grown fresh sweet-tart blueberries. We like it pretty well year-round, though, with other fruits as they come into season or—luxuriousness!—chopped dried apricots and prunes. The crunchy-crumbly streusel topping, whose recipe follows, makes this even better.

Preheat oven to 350°. Pam a 9- × -13-inch rectangular pan. Combine

*2¼ cups sifted flour, either unbleached white or whole wheat pastry*
*2 teaspoons baking powder*
*½ teaspoon each salt and baking soda*

Set aside. Cream

*¾ cup butter*
*¾ cup sugar*
*1 teaspoon vanilla*

Beat in, one at a time, till fluffy

*2 eggs*

Add flour mixture alternately to creamed butter-egg mixture with

*1 cup sour cream*

Make Streusel (see following) and set aside. Now spread half the batter in pan. Sprinkle with

*1 cup fresh blueberries*
*½ Streusel mixture*

Spoon on remaining batter and sprinkle with the reserved half of the Streusel mixture. Bake for 40 minutes. Cool for 10 to 20 minutes before serving.

*Streusel:* Simply combine, tossing lightly with fingers till crumbly, ¼ cup *each* butter and flour, 1 teaspoon cinnamon, and ⅔ cup packed light brown sugar. Stir in ⅔ to 1 cup chopped pecans or walnuts. Use as directed in recipe.

*Fruit Variations:* Instead of blueberries, use 2 sliced, peeled peaches or apples. Or try ⅔ cup fresh cranberries, chopped and tossed with 2 tablespoons sugar. Two small bananas, diced, work well, and so do well-drained halved sour pie cherries, about a cup. Or, for a delicious Lemon–Sour Cream Coffee Cake, omit fruit altogether but add a tablespoon each fresh lemon juice and freshly grated rind to batter. After cake is cool, drizzle with a thin icing made of sifted powdered sugar and fresh lemon juice.

---

### The Perfect Breadbasket: Interior

*Fold back the clean napkin lining of the breadbasket at breakfast time here at Dairy Hollow House and you will find the source of the sweet smell that woke you up or drew you from the other room or back from an early morning walk—our homemade breads, usually (though not always) an assortment of two contrasting types.*

*Ideally, we think, any breadbasket for a special breakfast should contain a plurality. The contrast can be made in any one of three ways: one bread can be yeast risen, while the other, a quick mix, differs in texture. One can be a simple, plain bread or roll or biscuit and the other a sweet, flavorful, fruity one. And one can be a hearty, healthy whole grain delight, while the other is a lighter, more traditional white flour offering. Here are some nice contrasting pairs we like to use:*

*Angel Biscuits and Hefty Bran Muffins*

*Crescent's Favorite Whole Wheat Butterhorns and Strawberry Bread (or Waioli Tea Room Carrot Bread)*

*Scones and Victoria's Pumpkin Bread (or Persimmon Bran Bread)*

*Dairy Hollow Oatmeal Bread Supreme and Waioli Tea Room Carrot Bread*

*Dairy Hollow House Dinner Rolls and Blueberry–Sour Cream Coffee Cake*

*Any of these combinations would make an exceptional breadbasket: fulfilling, soon emptied.*

---

# MUFFINS

*A Muffin Note:* Muffins are the quickest of all quick breads. They *must not be overmixed* or the consequences are disastrous: flattened, tough, weird-looking muffins with odd holes in them. Mix the wet and dry ingredients of muffins with as few strokes as possible; the dry ingredients should barely be moistened. On no account beat a muffin batter! I am so vehement on this point that I once got a letter from

Ned when I was here in Eureka and Ned was in Atlanta, in which he mentioned making bran muffins. "And," he wrote, "I could almost hear you saying, 'Don't overbeat the batter!' "

## Jan's Corn Muffins

*Yield: one dozen*

For a peasant's feast with a bowl of hot soup, one can't beat a good corn muffin. Pioneer Ozarks kitchens always had a pan of corn bread or muffins on the stove. This, with the variations that follow, is a Dairy Hollow House evening staple.

Preheat oven to 375°. Blend

*1 egg*
*¼ cup honey*
*¼ cup mild vegetable oil*

Combine

*1 cup water, preferably spring water*
*1 tablespoon apple cider vinegar*

Pour water-vinegar mixture into egg-honey-oil mixture and blend thoroughly. Mix

*½ teaspoon salt*
*3 teaspoons baking powder*
*1 cup cornmeal*
*1 cup whole wheat flour*

Add dry ingredients to moist ones; stir just enough to blend. Fill twelve Pam-ed muffin cups about two-thirds full. Bake for 25 minutes.

## CORNMEAL MUFFIN VARIATIONS

### Buttermilk Corn Muffins

Substitute buttermilk for water and add ½ teaspoon baking soda to the dry ingredients. Replace oil with melted butter. This is Crescent's favorite. Or go all out: substitute sour cream (with 2 tablespoons extra) for buttermilk!

### Carrot Corn Muffins

This makes a slightly sweet, very moist corn bread or muffin. To corn bread batter, add 1 cup finely grated carrots. Stir lightly and pour into a Pam-ed loaf pan or muffin tins. Yummy.

### Pumpkin or Sweet Potato Corn Muffins

Here our old friend takes on a cakelike texture and most delicious sweetness. To moist ingredients, add 1 cup pureed pumpkin or baked mashed sweet potato, ¼ cup molasses, 1 teaspoon cinnamon, ¼ teaspoon ground cloves. Stir together and pour into Pam-ed baking pans.

### Jalapeño Corn Muffins

We love this very spicy bread with a crunchy slaw and a bold bean soup such as Downtown Black Bean Soup (p. 101), or simply with a baked sweet potato. Our friend Choo-Choo, whose Buttermilk Pie recipe, among others, appears later on, makes this often. She is a fan of all dishes Mexican and once asked for nachos for a birthday present. Anyway, to the basic corn muffin batter add ¼ cup chopped green pepper, ¼ cup chopped green onion, 2 tablespoons pimento, and 2 finely sliced jalapeño peppers. Stir ingredients into batter. Pour batter into Pam-ed muffin tins. Sprinkle muffin tops with paprika, and bake. A further subvariation is to add grated sharp Cheddar cheese to this batter and sprinkle the muffins with additional grated cheese 5 minutes before they are to come out of the oven.

### Sesame Corn Muffins

Sesame seeds add a very special nutty flavor and crunch to corn bread, as well as improved nutrition. To the batter, add ½ cup sesame seeds. Pour into Pam-ed baking pans. Sprinkle tops with additional sesame seeds. Bake.

### Double-Corn Corn Muffins

Somehow this version of muffins pleases every eater. The corn makes them even more moist. First, cut the kernels from three or four ears of corn and steam the kernels for a few minutes, perhaps three. Measure; there should be 1 to 1½ cups corn. Into corn bread batter, stir these steamed corn kernels. Bake as directed. This is not half bad made with frozen corn kernels, either, and is even acceptable with the canned "niblets."

## Janice Carr's Mixed Grain Muffins

*Yield: one dozen*

For many years, Dr. Carr, who has since semi-retired out near Beaver Lake, worked his magic on the sore backs and necks of much of the Eureka Springs population. Janice, in turn, worked her culinary magic on him—and occasional lucky guests. Her almond soup was the first I ever tasted, and I remember she once served me a delicious custard—at breakfast. These infinitely variable muffins of hers are simple and great, and very easy and inexpensive to boot. They work well with almost any meal. Try them once and they'll be a standby forever.

Preheat oven to 400°. In a bowl, stir together with a fork

*¾ cup unbleached white flour*
*1¾ cups your choice of assorted whole grain flours, as many or as few as you like (whole wheat, rye, cornmeal, triticale, oatmeal ground coarsely in a food processor, rice flour)*
*2 tablespoons baking powder (yes, this is the correct amount)*
*1 teaspoon salt*

In another bowl, beat together till creamy

*⅓ cup shortening (solid white or softened butter)*
*⅓ cup sugar*
*1 egg*

Add the shortening mixture to the flour mixture with

*1 cup milk*

Quickly stir with a few strokes till wet and dry ingredients are combined. Depending on which flours you have used, you may need to add more—perhaps up to a ½ cup more—to achieve the correct muffin consistency: moist but quite thick. Scoop the batter into Pam-ed muffin tins and bake till browned and fragrant—about 15 to 20 minutes. Serve hot. Best fresh from the oven; they don't reheat that wonderfully.

## Bountiful Blueberry Muffins

*Yield: one and a half dozen*

All blueberry muffins are good, and everybody has a favorite recipe for them. What sets this one apart from the crowd? Well, this most delicious batter contains, among other things, *pureed blueberries!* Whole blueberries are incorporated, too, along with other good things. We got this innovative idea from *The Political Palate,* an excellent cookbook put out by a feminist-run vegetarian restaurant called Bloodroot. We think this double whammy of berries raises an always popular treat to the ultimate heights of blueberry-ness.

Preheat oven to 400°. Combine

*2 cups plus 2 tablespoons whole wheat pastry flour*
*2 teaspoons baking powder*
*½ teaspoon salt*
*¼ teaspoon cinnamon and a dash of nutmeg*
*(optional; good with or without)*

Set this aside while you clean

*a pint basket of blueberries*

Measure them. Puree about one-quarter of them in a blender or food processor. Toss the remaining whole berries with about 2 tablespoons of the flour-spice mixture and

*¼ cup chopped pecans*

*(continued)*

Now mix the blueberry puree with

*2 eggs*
*½ cup honey or brown sugar*
*1 teaspoon vanilla*
*⅓ cup butter, melted*
*½ cup milk*

Combine the wet and dry ingredients with a few strokes. Before the flour has been completely moistened, fold in the floured berries. Turn into Pam-ed muffin tins and bake for about 20 to 25 minutes.

## Hefty Bran Muffins

*Yield: one and a half dozen large muffins*

In the galaxy of bran muffins that have appeared since fiber came into vogue, we think these stars shine brightest. Moister than most bran muffins, they are rich, flavorful, substantial, and, quite incidentally, good for you. For years, I made these with wheat bran, until one day I heard on good old "All Things Considered," National Public Radio's great afternoon news show, that oat bran had been found not only to contain fiber like wheat bran but to actually lower one's cholesterol level as well. Ned came home pleased as punch one day shortly after that with a bag of oat bran in tow. We tried it with this old favorite and found our dearly beloved Hefty Bran Muffins tastier and moister than ever.

Preheat oven to 350°. Stir together

*2 cups whole wheat pastry flour*
*1¼ cups bran, preferably oat bran*
*¼ teaspoon salt*
*1¼ teaspoons baking soda (sift in if lumpy)*

In a separate bowl, beat together

*1 egg*
*2 cups buttermilk or sour milk (or 2¼ cups plain yogurt)*
*4 tablespoons melted butter*
*½ cup honey*
*2 tablespoons blackstrap molasses*

Combine the wet and dry ingredients with a few quick strokes only, and before dry ingredients are completely moistened, fold in

*¾ cup chopped English walnuts*
*½ cup chopped dates*

Bake in Pam-ed muffin tins for about 25 minutes.

*Variation:* Add 1 finely chopped apple or a mashed banana.

These are great eaten hot from the oven with plenty of melted butter soaking into them; enough to undo any cholesterol-sparing benefits the oat bran might have netted you. Cream cheese, too, is excellent on these. And although we always serve them as part of a full breakfast at the inn, in private life, we have found that one or two, with a glass of milk, make a great morning send-off in themselves.

## Gingerbread Muffins à la Elsie

*Yield: one and a half dozen*

We so love Elsie's Gingerbread, page 354, that we have devised a muffin out of it by cutting the sugar and adding nuts and raisins.

Preheat oven to 350°. Combine

*1½ cups unbleached white flour*
*¾ cup sugar*
*2 teaspoons ground dried ginger*
*1 teaspoon cinnamon*

Cut in

*½ cup butter or shortening*

*(continued)*

Set aside a quarter of the resulting crumbly mixture, tossing this reserved portion with

*¾ cup chopped walnuts*

To the remaining shortening-flour mixture, add

*1 egg, beaten*
*3 tablespoons molasses*

In

*¾ cup buttermilk*

dissolve

*1 teaspoon baking soda*
*¾ teaspoon salt*

Stir this quickly into the batter, being careful not to overmix, also adding

*a good handful of raisins*

Spoon the batter into Pam-ed muffin cups, halfway full (they rise a bit more than ordinary muffins). Sprinkle with the nutted topping, and bake for about 20 minutes.

These are just delicious, and a great success at a buffet brunch. Also they're a boon for morning entertaining: the dry ingredients can be combined, the shortening cut in, and the topping set aside the night before, so all that's necessary in the A.M. is the addition of the liquid ingredients and the raisins, the mixing and baking.

# BISCUITS AND NONSWEET QUICK BREADS

In this category, we do quite a few corn breads, adding ¼ cup extra liquid (usually buttermilk) with the baking soda dissolved in it. The method is given under Jan's Corn Muffins, page 68. For biscuits, scones, and the like, read on. (For another corny treat, possibly to be served in place of corn muffins, see Wanda's Soft Corn Tortillas, page 227.)

# CUSTOM-MADE BISCUITS AS YOU LIKE 'EM: TIPS

- For the *flakiest* of biscuits, handle the dough as little as possible. After the liquid is added to the flour-shortening mixture, stir dough till it just barely comes together and leaves the sides of the bowl. Turn out on lightly floured surface and knead a very few strokes—just enough to make the dough handleable. Roll the dough out if you must; many fine biscuit cooks simply pat it out gently with their palms.

- For *high-rising, tall* biscuits with a bit of soft doughiness in the center, roll or pat to about a half-inch. For *thinner*, crusty biscuits, roll or pat to ¼-inch thickness. Rule of thumb: biscuits double in size as they bake; oven-ready biscuit dough should be approximately half the thickness you want the finished biscuits to be.

- For *level tops* on your biscuits, cut out with a floured biscuit cutter, with a definite straight-down motion. Do not twist the cutter (or knife, if you are doing square biscuits). Square biscuits have the great advantage of using every scrap of dough so no re-rolling is necessary. If you must use a cutter, cut biscuits out as close together as possible, to avoid unnecessary rerolling and re-cutting of the scraps. Each rerolling slightly toughens the dough. When you do reroll the scraps, press them together gently—don't knead—before rolling. Biscuits thus rolled will look a little bumpy on top, but they will be far more tender than those of neatly kneaded and rerolled dough. .

- For *soft-sided* biscuits, place the cut biscuit dough rounds close to each other in a shallow baking pan. For *crusty* biscuits, slightly crisp on the outside, the dough rounds should have at least an inch between them, and they should be baked on a flat (no-edged) cookie sheet.

- No matter how you like your biscuits, remember: *use a light touch!*

## Angel Biscuits

*Yield: two dozen large or four and a half dozen small biscuits*

An often-requested, very special, very Southern biscuit—light, flavorful, high rising, meltingly flaky. It is one of the few baked goods we use white shortening in, but nothing works better. A high percentage of shortening, plus buttermilk, plus a triple leavening of yeast *and* baking powder *and* baking soda, is what give these their sublime qualities. The triple sifting is essential, too.

Ned and I first enjoyed these at an inn called the Randolph House in Bryson City, North Carolina, where they're made tiny—not much bigger than a quarter. Ruth, the innkeeper/cook, gave us the recipe. Hers used self-rising flour; we've substituted unbleached.

Let soak

>*1½ teaspoons yeast*

in

>*¼ cup warm water*
>*1 tablespoon honey*

Meanwhile, sift together three times

>*2½ cups* sifted *unbleached white flour*
>*2 tablespoons sugar*
>*1½ teaspoons baking powder*
>*½ teaspoon baking soda*
>*¼ teaspoon salt*

Quickly cut into this, using two knives

>*⅓ cup white shortening*

Cut in this shortening only to the point that it resembles coarse cornmeal. Then quickly stir in, at the same time, the reserved yeast and its soaking water and

>*1 cup buttermilk*

Stir just till batter comes together, and turn out of bowl onto lightly floured surface. Knead lightly, gently, quickly—30 seconds at most—and then place in a greased bowl. Cover and refrigerate for at least 1 hour (but the dough can be refrigerated successfully for as long as three or four days at this point).

When ready to bake, preheat oven to 400°, remove dough from refrigerator and roll out on a very lightly floured board. Cut out to a ½-inch thickness and place biscuits on Pam-ed cookie sheet, about ½ inch apart. Bake the little angels until golden—about 12 minutes. Serve hot, with plenty of butter and jam.

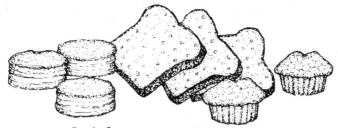

## Quick Buttermilk Biscuits

*Yield: one dozen good-size biscuits*

Classic. Very good. We use them often as a counterpoint to a sweet loaf in a breadbasket. There are many delicious variations.

Preheat oven to 450°. Combine

*2 cups unbleached white flour (you may use whole wheat pastry*
*flour here, if you like, instead)*
*1 teaspoon salt*
*1 tablespoon baking powder*
*½ teaspoon baking soda*

Cut in, preferably with a pastry blender

*⅓ cup shortening (can be white shortening or butter or half of each)*

Add, with a few deft strokes

*just enough buttermilk to make a soft dough—about 1 cup*

Turn out on floured bowl, knead with a couple of strokes till dough just comes together, pat or roll it out, cut the biscuits, and bake them on an ungreased cookie sheet for 15 to 20 minutes, or till golden. Brush tops with

*melted butter*

when you first take 'em out.

### Whole Wheat Sour Cream Biscuits

Meltingly rich, hearty with the good whole wheat flavor. We love these. Follow the recipe for Quick Buttermilk Biscuits, substituting whole wheat pastry flour for the unbleached white and using sour cream instead of buttermilk. It'll take more sour cream than buttermilk; perhaps as much as 1¾ cups to achieve proper biscuit texture.

### Biscuit Variations

Start with either of the above and . . . For *Sweet Milk Biscuits*, omit baking soda and use milk instead of buttermilk or sour cream. For *Cheese Biscuits*, use only ¼ cup shortening and cut in with it ½ cup very finely grated sharp Cheddar cheese, and, just before they're done, shake Parmesan over them and return to oven for the last few minutes (excellent with many soups). For *Sweet Biscuits*, add 3 or 4 tablespoons sugar to the dry ingredients and a drop of vanilla to the wet; brush tops of biscuits before baking with melted butter and then dust with cinnamon and sugar (this biscuit is fine for use in a short-cake or cobbler, about which more is in the Fruitpoem chapter). For *Herb Biscuits*, combine 2 tablespoons chopped fresh parsley with 2 teaspoons to 2 tablespoons other assorted fresh herbs of your choice: basil, sage, thyme, rosemary, and so on. Use the lesser quantity if the herbs you've chosen are particularly dominant in flavor. Add this when you cut in the shortening. For *Savory Biscuits*, in addition to the herbs just listed, add to the dough a small, finely chopped onion that has been sautéed in butter and one or two pressed raw cloves of garlic, plus a drop of Pickapepper or Worcestershire sauce in the liquid. Herb or Savory Biscuits are great with chicken; if made small, they make a great base for hors d'oeuvres.

## The Perfect Breadbasket: Exterior

*We love baskets of all kinds. Our very favorites are those local vine baskets whose makers gave them "provenance": a small tag attached explaining the specific history and origins of the piece. A tag on a basket, thus, might read, "Breadbasket of raspberry vine, grapevine, and spicebush, gathered at Beaver Creek, 1984, woven by Ninah Kessler." Definite knowledge of an antique or a new quality craft piece (who made it, when, how, out of what, for what purpose) almost always adds to its financial value (particularly in the case of older furniture and quilts and paintings). But, much more important, it adds to its emotional value; it gives an object a weight, a substance, a connection of past and present, of the object's one-time creator and its current user and enjoyer. When objects intended for daily use, like breadbaskets, have such a meaning, the timeless and the everyday merge; the present brushes eternity.*

# Scones

*Yield: three dozen very small scones*

Simply this: a richer, egg-and-cream-enriched version of a biscuit. A classic at teatime. I dedicate this recipe with great fondness to Lyn Littlefield Hoopes, a fellow children's book writer and dear friend, who has asked me for it at odd intervals for years, but somehow we just start talking about our work, kids, husbands, philosophies, living in the country versus living in the city, and on and on and we never get around to it.

Preheat oven to 450°. Sift together

> *2 cups already-sifted cake flour (such as Swansdown) or*
> *1¾ cups already-sifted unbleached white flour*
> *2¼ teaspoons baking powder*
> *1 heaping tablespoon sugar*
> *½ teaspoon salt*

Cut into this, using a pastry blender

> *¼ cup butter, firm, which you've cut into eight pieces*

Stop when the butter particles are pea-size, and beat, in a separate bowl

> *2 eggs*

Scoop out 2 or 3 tablespoons of the egg and set it aside for later. To the remainder, add

> *⅓ cup half-and-half or, to go all-out, heavy cream*

Pour the wet ingredients into the flour-butter mixture and stir together with a few strokes. Pat it out on a floured board, handling it as little as possible, until it is ½ to ¾ inch thick. Dough will be stickier than for biscuits. Brush the biscuits with the reserved egg and bake for about 15 minutes.

If you come to the inn, buy some of our sweet basil jelly and try it on a buttered scone, with a dab of ricotta cheese. Sublime!

To achieve true excellence, scones must be piping hot. When serving scones at a large tea (and, frankly, what is a tea without scones?), make up and cut the dough a few hours ahead of time and refrigerate it. When the guests start to arrive, pop a *small* batch of scones into the oven, set the timer so you don't forget them, race out and greet your guests, bing goes the timer, race back into the kitchen, place the hot scones on a napkin-covered plate or biscuit, race back out, offer them around, and watch them disappear (especially if your tea table is properly laden with jam and marmalade and thick Devonshire cream or crème fraîche and butter), and do the whole thing again.

It makes you understand why the English had butlers.

# YEAST-RISEN BREADS AND ROLLS

When you make a yeast bread, consider making a thick, long-cooking soup at the same time. The rhythms in making both are much the same; attention, not constant but occasional, is needed over a period of several hours' duration. Bread and soup making are natural companions on a snowy afternoon when you have other at-home work to do. By evening the house will be warm and fragrant, and the two foods, perfect with each other, will sit on bread board, steam in pot, waiting and welcoming those who've been out and about in the world back to the place that could only be home.

## Land of Milk and Honey Whole Wheat Bread

*Yield: three large loaves*

This is the first whole wheat bread I ever made, and I still think one of the best. I learned it in a Brooklyn brownstone, in 1969.

Preheat oven to 400°. Scald

*2 cups milk*

Pour this over

*1 tablespoon salt*
*3 tablespoons nutritional yeast*
*¼ cup each honey and oil (or butter)*

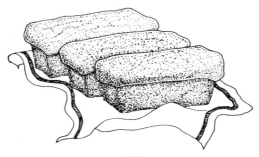

Let this cool to lukewarm, meanwhile dissolving

*2 tablespoons yeast*

in

*1 cup warm water or vegetable stock (p. 91)*
*1 tablespoon honey*

When yeast is bubbly, combine it with the lukewarm milk mixture, beating in

*3 eggs, at room temperature*

Add and beat in thoroughly

*7 cups whole wheat bread flour*
*(hard whole wheat, not pastry flour)*

Let the dough stand for 10 minutes while you clean up the mess that has accumulated so far. Then add to the dough

*enough additional whole wheat flour (about 3 cups)*

so that the dough begins to come away from the sides of the bowl and becomes easily kneadable. Turn the dough onto a floured board and knead vigorously for 8 to 10 minutes. Then oil the dough, place it in a clean bowl, cover with a towel, and let it have its first rise till double in bulk. Punch down and let it rise a second time. Punch down; shape into three loaves. You may do the loaves rounded or freeform on Pam-ed cookie sheets, or do them in Pam-ed loaf pans, as you prefer. Let rise for the third time, until loaves are doubled in bulk. If you like, you may slash the tops with a very sharp knife, brush with oil, and sprinkle with sesame seeds.

Bake at 400° for 15 minutes; lower heat to 375° and bake for about 30 minutes more. If using small pans, bake at 400° for 10 minutes, 375° for 25.

## Dairy Hollow Oatmeal Bread Supreme

*Yield: two large loaves plus one small loaf*

Out of milk one day, with a picnic basket to which I'd been planning to add oatmeal bread, I improvised with heavy cream—and have been making this heavenly bread ever since. It has a supremely crisp crust and the best of flavors, somehow both hearty and delicate. It's so good as is, it doesn't require a drop of butter over it. It's a great sandwiches-or-toast bread; its aroma while baking is sublime.

*(continued)*

81

Preheat oven to 375°. Place in a large bowl

*3 cups oatmeal*
*1 tablespoon salt*
*⅓ cup mild honey*

Heat together till the butter melts

*1¾ cups heavy cream (no substitutes, if you want true greatness)*
*¼ cup water*
*¼ cup butter*

Pour the hot mixture over the oatmeal and let stand till lukewarm. Meanwhile, combine in a small bowl

*⅓ cup lukewarm water*
*2 tablespoons yeast*
*2 tablespoons honey*

By the time the oatmeal-milk mixture has reached lukewarm, the yeast-honey mixture should be bubbling exuberantly. Combine the two, and stir in, a cup at a time

*2 cups unbleached white flour*

Continue adding unbleached white flour till dough is stiff enough to knead, and do so, for 5 or 6 minutes, on a floured board, until dough is smooth and elastic. Place in a clean greased bowl and let rise till doubled in bulk—about an hour. Punch down dough, shape into two large and one small loaves (or three medium), and place the loaves into greased bread pans to rise a second time. Let rise again, this time about 45 minutes, and bake for about 50 minutes, less for the smaller loaf.

## Two Sisters Russian Black Rye Bread

*Yield: two medium loaves*

As Jan and I worked on this chapter, Jan said, "Oooh, we have *got* to use my recipe for Russian Black Rye Bread, it's too good." I said, "Well, *I* have one that's really really really good too." Somewhat petulantly, we each got out our specific pet recipes, figuring to compare them and then combine what was best in each, which is what we've done throughout this book. Our great Russian Black Ryes were identical!

This is them—a dark, heavy, serious peasant bread, chewy and delectable. It's a must with borscht, and very good with any substantial soup. Try it, too, toasted in thick slices with Gruyère cheese melted over it. Rye flour is a low-gluten flour; breads made with it will take longer to rise, will never be as light as all-wheat breads, and will be a bit more challenging to knead as well as to slice when done.

Preheat oven to 350°. Melt

*4 tablespoons butter*

in

*2½ cups water*

Cool to lukewarm and in it dissolve

*2 packages yeast*
*1½ teaspoons honey*

When bubbly, stir in

*2 tablespoons caraway seeds*
*2 teaspoons instant coffee granules*
*¼ cup apple cider vinegar*
*2 teaspoons salt*
*½ teaspoon anise seeds*
*2 tablespoons cocoa*
*2 tablespoons honey*
*½ cup dark molasses*

Gradually beat in

*2 cups unbleached white flour*
*1 cup whole wheat flour*
*3 cups dark rye flour*
*½ cup bran*

Beat 3 minutes, then stir in

*additional unbleached, whole wheat, and rye flours*

until kneadable. Let rest for 10 minutes. Knead for 10 minutes. First rise: 1½ hours. Second rise (after shaping): 1½ hours. Bake for about 45 minutes.

## Sweet-Sour Rye Bread

*Yield: two large loaves*

A most enjoyable bread developed by a long-ago friend, Diane Wienerman, and me, way back in 1969. Sweet-Sour Rye Bread is lighter in color and texture than the previous rye. The orange rind—which does not come across to the taste buds as orange but as an indefinable sweetness—is essential, and a Scandinavian touch. The pan of water in the oven makes for a steamy baking environment, which, in turn, helps the crust become thick and deliciously crusty. People always ask for the recipe for this delicious and very healthy bread. Diane, if you read this, hello, how are you?

Dissolve

*2 tablespoons or packages yeast*

in

*2 cups warm water*
*¼ cup honey*

Set aside while you heat together

*1¼ cups sour milk, buttermilk,* or *yogurt*
*¼ cup butter*
*1 to 2 tablespoons cider vinegar*
*3 tablespoons blackstrap molasses*
*1 tablespoon caraway seeds*
*1½ tablespoons salt*

Heat till the butter melts. The milk will curdle, but that has no ill effect at all on the bread. Remove this from the stove and let cool to lukewarm. Then add to it

*the very finely grated rind of 1 orange*

When the yeast is bubbly and the sour milk mixture lukewarm, combine the two and beat in, a cup at a time, the following flours

*3 cups dark rye flour*
*3 cups whole wheat flour*
*1 cup unbleached white flour*
*½ to 1 cup soy flour*

Mix well; add whole wheat flour till dough reaches a kneadable consistency; turn out of bowl and knead for a few minutes. Rye flour is always a bit sticky in the kneading; oiling and/or flouring the hands

84

helps some, but basically you just have to get in there and do it. After kneading for a few minutes, turn out the dough into a greased bowl, turn to coat dough, and let rise, covered, in a warm place, for 1 hour and 15 minutes.

Turn out onto a floured board and knead a few times, then shape into two or three loaves. Place in Pam-ed bread pans, and let rise a second time, for about 45 minutes. Preheat oven to 350°. When the loaves have risen, place the bread pans on a larger cookie pan or baking dish. Fill the larger pan with water, coming part of the way up the outside of the loaf pans. Place the whole thing in the oven. (The water allows the bread to bake in a moist, steamy environment, part of what gives this bread its special texture.) Bake for about an hour.

This is divine with any kind of cheese, particularly Gjetost (an odd but delicious Scandinavian cheese with an unusual texture and color and an almost caramellike taste). Or try Sweet-Sour Rye with egg salad, or simply toast it and slather with butter.

## Crescent's Favorite Whole Wheat Butterhorns

*Yield: approximately two dozen butterhorns*

A delicious DHH classic. We also offer a convenient do-ahead freeze method that works perfectly. Look for the * to spot it. When Dairy Hollow House was mentioned in the September 1983 issue of *SELF* magazine, one of the accompanying photographs showed our Dairymaid par excellence, Marianne Fulton, removing a pan of these beauties from the oven.

These work well with any meal.

Soften

*1 tablespoon yeast*

in

*1¼ cups previously scalded, then cooled to lukewarm, milk*
*½ cup honey*
*¼ cup melted butter*
*1½ teaspoons salt*

When yeast is bubbly, beat in

*3 eggs, at room temperature*
*2 tablespoons nutritional yeast*
*5 to 6 cups whole wheat flour*

*(continued)*

Keep adding flour till dough is of a kneadable consistency. Knead till elastic. Oil; place in bowl. Cover and let rise. Punch down. Let rise a second time. Punch down. Divide dough into two balls and roll out into a circle. Dot with butter. Cut circle into pie-shape wedges and roll each wedge up, starting from wide end. Place on greased cookie sheets * and let butterhorns rise a third time.

Preheat oven to 400°. When butterhorns are again doubled, bake for 40 minutes. Remove from oven and brush with

*1 egg yolk, diluted and beaten with*
*1 tablespoon milk or water*

Bake for another 5 to 10 minutes, or till golden and crusty.

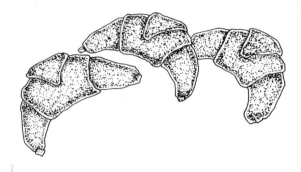

## Dairy Hollow House Dinner Rolls

*Yield: one dozen dinner rolls*

These very light and airy whole wheat rolls often appear in the breadbasket for our "Nouveau'zarks Haute Country Cuisine" dinners. They're a Jan Brown specialty. We think the vinegar is largely responsible for their remarkable texture.

---

* For freeze-ahead baking, freeze at this point, on cookie sheets. You can transfer the butterhorns to plastic bags after they have frozen solid. The night before you want to serve them, remove as many as desired from freezer. Place on cookie sheet, cover, and let thaw overnight, *refrigerated.* In the morning, let them rise unrefrigerated for an additional 15 minutes in a warm place. This takes the place of the third rise. Proceed as directed post third rise.

Dissolve

*1 tablespoon yeast*

in

*1 cup warm water*
*1 tablespoon honey*

Sift together

*1½ cups whole wheat flour*
*1 cup unbleached white flour*
*¼ teaspoon baking soda*
*1 teaspoon baking powder*
*½ teaspoon salt*

Mix dry ingredients with yeast. Add

*1 tablespoon cider vinegar*
*3 tablespoons safflower oil*

Knead together. Place in a Pam-ed bowl. Cover and let rise in warm place about 1 hour. Punch dough down. Shape into dinner rolls or bread.

Preheat oven to 425°. Let rise again until double in size. Bake for 15 to 20 minutes.

❖

# EXCEPTIONS TO THE RULE

For one reason or another, the breads that follow are each in a class of their own. We have assembled a collection here of outstanding, very different, memorable, and delicious breads and pastries that we hope will please you as much as they have our guests.

# Incredible From-Scratch Danish

*Yield: three dozen*

A lovely sweet pastry from my childhood, remembered fondly from the now-defunct Steinburg's Restaurant and re-created about ten years later. Making these is a big, big, almost all-day deal, so we don't make them often, but it is a happy day when we do. Totally worth the time and the expense of all that butter, those eggs, almonds, succulent dried fruits—mmmmm.

All ingredients should be at room temperature. Beat well

*2 eggs*

Add

*¾ cup lukewarm water (or milk if you like)*

and beat again. Dissolve in this mixture

*1 cake, tablespoon, or package of yeast*

Refrigerate this for about 15 minutes while you get together

*3½ cups sifted whole wheat flour*
*1 teaspoon salt*
*1½ tablespoons sugar*
*½ cup butter*
*2 teaspoons ground cardamom (this is one of its secrets—it gives a*
*lovely smell and a slightly lemony taste)*
*1 teaspoon grated lemon or orange rind*

Mix until smooth. The butter must be well incorporated into everything else. Now make a well in the ingredients and pour in the chilled egg-yeast mixture. Work this in well and knead lightly on a floured board for 2 minutes. The dough should be light and soft as a baby's cheek. Form into a smooth ball and refrigerate for 20 minutes.

Remove dough from refrigerator. Roll out very very lightly into a rectangle about ½ inch thick. Have ready

*1 to 1½ cups butter, beaten until creamy*

Divide butter into four lumps. Dot one of these lumps of butter over the rolled-out dough and fold it over itself in thirds. Turn dough slightly and roll out again. Repeat butter treatment four times in all. Let dough rise for another 2 hours, chilled.

Preheat oven to 375°. Roll out, cut into squares, and place about 1 tablespoon filling on each. Pull two of the corners opposite each other. Secure, using water as glue. Brush these Danish with

*1 egg, beaten (and a little water)*

Sprinkle with

*a bit of sugar*
*a few slivered almonds*

Place on a Pam-ed cookie sheet, spaced well apart. Bake for 15 minutes.

*Filling:* Cook together

*1 cup dried pitted prunes* or *apricots*
*¼ cup water*

until fruit is thick and soft. Mash a little and add

*honey, cinnamon, and grated lemon peel to taste*

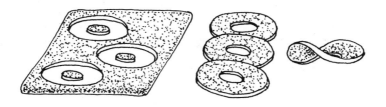

## Marianne's Cinnamon Bow Knots

*Yield: one dozen*

A breakfast treat from our Dairymaid Marianne, these yummy breakfast confections are an almost-biscuit dough dressed up with cinnamon and other good things and twisted into little bowtielike figure eights. A lovely choice for a child's birthday breakfast. Adults like them, too.

Preheat oven to 450°. Combine

*1 cup each unbleached white and whole wheat pastry flour*
*1 tablespoon baking powder*
*1 teaspoon salt*

(continued)

Cut in, till crumbly

*2 tablespoons butter*

Add all at once

*⅔ cup milk (or use 2 teaspoons baking powder, add ¼ teaspoon*
*baking soda, and use ⅓ cup each yogurt and water)*

Form ball, and knead lightly about twenty-five times. Roll out ½ inch thick. Cut with 2½-inch doughnut cutter. Twist each ring to form a figure eight, and re-form and reroll leftover dough, handling as little as possible. Place on ungreased cookie sheet, bake for 12 minutes, remove from oven, and dip into the following, combined

*¼ cup melted butter*
*¼ cup sugar*
*1 teaspoon cinnamon*
*¼ cup finely chopped almonds or walnuts (optional and great)*

Excellent with café au lait.

---

### HEARTH SONG

*Here at the inn, we sit and sing,*
*the flames are brightly dancing;*
*Here at the inn we sit and sing,*
*and winter has no calling.*
*What better reward on snowy eve, than sitting with good company?*
*What better reward on snowy eve, than conversation light and gay?*
*And winter has no calling, here as we sit close by the fire;*
*And winter has no calling, everyone has his heart's desire.*

*—Bill Haymes, 1978*

# Soups for All Seasons

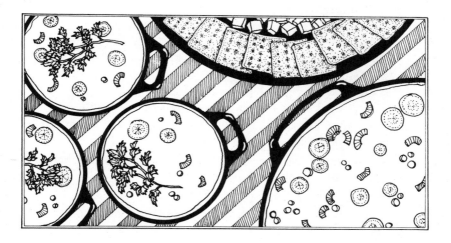

## SOUP NOTES

Jan and I are inveterate soup makers. We think you will be pleased with this selection, which includes many of our favorite vegetable soups, creamy soups, and legume soups, soups from all over the world, and soups for every season.

## Basic Golden Vegetable Stock

*Makes about 5 cups*

A good soup stock is the culinary equivalent of a good pair of basic black pants; perhaps not inherently exciting, but, with a few accessories, it can be dressed up or down and will carry you through all the seasons. Any decent cookbook can teach you how to make a respectable chicken or beef broth, but recipes for a good solid vegetable broth are few and far between. Here is one. Besides tasting very good, much like a chicken broth (which the uninitiated assume it is), this Basic Golden Vegetable Stock has much to recommend it. It is simple to do. It does not need to go through the process of being chilled so that the fat rises and congeals and can be removed, for the simple reason that it has no fat, thus no cholesterol, thus no grease to clog your sink. It will also make any vegetarian friends you have very, very happy.

Don't be put off by the entire head of garlic called for; it simmers and mellows to a gentle richness. Don't be alarmed, either, by the skin left on the onion; it adds a brown color to the stock and a good flavor, and it does get strained out at the end.

Simmer together in a large pot

*1 large onion, skin on, quartered*
*1 large carrot, 1 sweet potato, and 1 white potato,*
*treated the same way*
*1 whole head of garlic, papery skins left on*
*2 teaspoons salt*
*1½ quarts water*

Bring to a boil, turn down heat to a simmer, and simmer gently for 45 minutes to 1 hour. Let cool; strain.

Into lukewarm vegetable stock, whisk

*½ cup Good Tasting or Red Star brand nutritional (not baking) yeast*
*(see Glossary, p. 383), available at natural foods stores*
*1 tablespoon golden miso, sometimes called white miso*
*(concentrated bean paste, delicious and very salty, used for making*
*many stocks in Japan, also available at natural foods stores)*

For a *Dark Vegetable Stock*, follow the basic recipe but omit sweet potato, using instead an additional onion and white potato. Omit salt and season with 1 tablespoon Tamari; after straining, use only ¼ cup yeast and use dark instead of golden miso.

## A Third Vegetable Stock—From Scraps

The previous vegetable stocks are delicious and predictable, and their ingredients are strictly planned for and intended. But Jan and I make yet another kind of vegetable stock, which is made simply from vegetable scraps, the parts of vegetables that one would usually discard. Carrot tops, onion peels, the pods of fresh peas, the stem ends of squash and green beans and tomatoes, the innards of green peppers, the cores of apples, ad infinitum. You simply accumulate such throwaways for a week or so in a plastic bag in the refrigerator. When your soup bag is full, combine your bounty in a large pot, cover with cold water, add 2 teaspoons or so of salt. Five or 6 cloves of garlic and a couple of bay leaves also never hurt such a stock. At any rate, bring the mixture to a boil. Turn down the heat to a simmer, and simmer for 45 minutes or so. Cool. Strain.

This is generally quite good, but because its ingredients vary, the end product varies. We use stock made in this manner in dishes where its flavor will not predominate, since it is an uncertain element. In most cases this "found stock" is excellent, adding an extra dimension of flavor to such dishes as breads, beans, or grains, the liquid for which would often otherwise simply be water. But for a soup where the flavor of the stock takes a starring role, we generally make up one of the stocks mentioned first.

*Caution:* In making a stock from scraps in this manner, avoid using scraps from vegetables in the cabbage family. These are cauliflower, broccoli, Brussels sprouts, and cabbage itself; these don't belong in your soup bag. The cruciferous vegetables, delicious in and of themselves when lightly steamed, take on an objectionably strong flavor and odor when simmered for as long as it takes to do a good stock justice.

# HOT SOUPS

## Dairy Hollow House Supreme of Vegetable and Olive Soup Eureka

*Serves 6*

Possibly the best, most elegant soup we make. White wine, both black and pimento-stuffed green olives, light cream; felicitous flavors year-round, any time, always a knockout. It can be made with or without chicken, is always impressive. Don't miss this!

In a skillet, in

*4 tablespoons butter*

(continued)

sauté

*¼ cup each finely diced onion, carrot, and celery*

When vegetables have softened, sprinkle them with

*5 tablespoons unbleached white flour*

Gradually whisk in

*4 cups either rich defatted homemade chicken stock or
Basic Golden Vegetable Stock (p. 91), lukewarm*

Stir vigorously with the whisk as you raise the heat to medium, to prevent lumps from forming. When stock is smooth and slightly thick, transfer it from skillet to a Pam-ed heavy soup pot. Add

*1 cup white wine*

and simmer for 20 minutes. Then, stir in

*1½ cups half-and-half*

Lower heat; from this point, the soup must not be permitted to boil. Add

*½ cup cooked white rice*
*¼ cup each large black and pimento-stuffed olives, sliced into circles*
*¼ cup peas, fresh or frozen*
*meat and skin picked from the bones of 1 cooked chicken, if you
used chicken to make your stock*

Heat through. Taste, and correct the seasonings; you'll need

*salt and white pepper*

Serve very hot, with finely chopped parsley floating on top. The chicken variation makes this more of a full meal type of soup, but either version is just unforgettably delicious. For a lower calorie version, substitute low-fat milk for the light cream. Whenever I serve this to guests, they always say, "Now, is *this* going to be in the cookbook?"

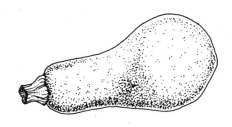

# Valentine's Day Luncheon

*Dairy Hollow House Supreme of Vegetable and Olive Soup Eureka*
*Tiny Angel Biscuits ● Butter*
*The Salad with Artichoke Hearts*
*French Strawberry Shortcake with the Season's First Berries*

## Butternut Squash and Apple Soup I and II

*Serves 6 to 8*

Two delectable, full-bodied harvest soups with the voluptuous smoothness of pureed butternut squash and the sweetness of apples in four forms: cooked and pureed, cooked and in chunks, raw, and as concentrated juice. If fall had a taste, either of these would be it. Though both are very rich, the first does not contain cream and it has very few seasonings, relying on the fruits and vegetables themselves to carry the show (they do, brilliantly). The second contains cream and curry powder, which make it literally a soup of a different color. Both are very good. Either makes a wonderful first course for virtually any dinner at which poultry is the entrée; the first is lighter and less caloric.

Butternut Squash Soup, either way, is one potage that absolutely does *not* work cold; it can, however, be made in advance, chilled, and reheated; actually this even improves the flavor by allowing the ingredients more time to celebrate their marriage. If you do go this route, remember to reheat either version over an extremely low flame: this scorches easily.

There are five basic steps: making the stock, steaming and peeling the squash, preparing the apple-onion sauté, combining and assembling the whole shebang, and, last, garnishing and serving it. Several of these steps can take place concurrently, however, so this is not as fussy as it sounds.

*(continued)*

First, the stock. Core and cut off stem ends of

*3 cooking apples*

Reserving the apples for later in the recipe, put the core, seeds and all, in a stockpot with

*2 heads of garlic (yes, entire heads, peel and all)*
*1 large onion, quartered, with peel*
*1 large potato, in eighths, with peel*
*rind from ½ orange*
*1½ teaspoons salt*
*1½ quarts water*
*the scooped-out seeds from 1 very large, 2 medium,*
*or 3 very small butternut squashes*

Reserve the squashes themselves for the next step. Now, bring the ingredients to a boil, cover, turn down heat and simmer for 45 minutes. After mixture has cooked, let it cool and then strain it. Discard the solids; reserve the liquid.

As the stock simmers, you can easily do the next two steps. The Butternut Squash Puree: Steam until tender, about 10 minutes, the deseeded butternut squash(es), cut into chunks. After squash is tender, let it cool and peel it.

As the squash is steaming and the stock simmering, you can easily do the next step, which is the Apple-Onion Sauté. In

*4 tablespoons butter*

sauté

*1 large onion, cut into thin crescents*

till soft and transparent. Then add

*2 apples, chopped (2 of the 3 apples whose innards are now*
*simmering in the stock)*

Stir-fry until the apples, too, are softened. Now, if your stock has been strained, your squash cooked and peeled, you are ready for the next step: assembly.

Puree, in the food processor or blender, half of the apple stir-fry with

*3½ cups of strained stock*
*the steamed, peeled squash chunks*
*½ cup thawed but not diluted unsweetened frozen*
*apple juice concentrate*

Pour this puree of squash and apple and stock into a nice thick-bottom soup pot, along with the remaining reserved raw apple, chopped. Reheat all this (or stop at this point and cool, for later reheating) and serve piping hot, in heated bowls, with one of the following garnishes:

1. a circle of raw apple, skin on, cut across the center, so the star-flower pattern of black seeds shows, and a sprinkle of a few chopped English walnut pieces

2. a thatch of raw apple pieces, preferably some with red peels and some with green or yellow, cut in small, thin, crisp matchsticks (use a very sharp knife), with the peel left on

### Butternut Squash and Apple Soup II: A Curry-Cream Variation

A richer, more highly seasoned version. Follow directions as in the basic recipe, except that when sautéing the apples, add

*1 tablespoon curry powder, sprinkled over the apples*

Continue as in the original until you get to the point at which everything is combined and reheated. Then use 3 cups stock instead of 3½ and add 1 cup heavy cream. Reheat carefully; do not allow to boil. If you wish, garnish with a spoonful of sour cream or crème fraîche, as well as the apple, sliced or julienned.

*Nowhere is the temperature of food more important than in soup. Hot soups should be served really hot: piping, steaming. It helps if bowls or cups are heated or at least warmed ahead of time. Similarly, a cold soup must be very, very cold—icy cold—not lukewarm, and served in a chilled bowl. If the chilled bowl can be set in a larger bowl of crushed ice, so much the better.*

# Almond Soup Dairy Hollow House

*Serves 10 to 12*

A very special, very rich soup, an ideal starter for an elegant dinner. Natural foods cuisine at its best.

Sauté in a large saucepan

> *2 tablespoons butter*
> *1 medium-size onion, finely chopped*
> *½ Jonathan apple, finely chopped (can substitute another good cooking apple)*
> *1 stalk celery, finely chopped*
> *½ teaspoon anise seed*

Cook until onion and apple are tender. Add

> *5 cups Basic Golden Vegetable Stock (p. 91)*
> *½ cup raw brown rice*
> *2 cups blanched almonds*
> *¼ cup white raisins*
> *2 teaspoons Tamari soy sauce*

Cook over medium heat until rice is tender—about 45 minutes. Cool slightly and puree in a blender or food processor. Add

> *1 cup heavy cream*
> *½ slice whole wheat bread, torn into small pieces*

Blend until soup is perfectly smooth and golden brown. Pour soup into saucepan and heat thoroughly, stirring frequently, being careful not to boil. Serve immediately, garnishing each bowlful with a raw apple slice and 1 raw almond.

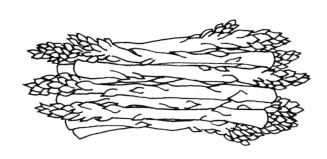

# Asparagus-Cheese Soup with White Wine

*Makes 4 small servings*

A soup that says spring to us as clearly as Apple-Butternut Squash says fall. After a big pile of plain, steamed asparagus with butter and lemon, this is the first thing we make when we find the premier scaled shoots poking up in the garden or lying in state at the market.

Combine and bring to a boil

*½ cup each water and dry white wine*

Into it, drop

*2 dozen or so asparagus spears, tough ends trimmed*

Cover and cook asparagus *just* till tender—no longer. Meanwhile, melt

*2 tablespoons butter*

and whisk into it

*1 tablespoon unbleached white flour*

Whisk in next

*1 cup milk*

Cook, stirring often, till thick and smooth. Don't let it boil. Then stir in

*⅔ cup finely grated very sharp Cheddar cheese*

When cheese has melted, remove pot from heat. Now, back at the asparagus, drain it, reserving the liquid, and, on a cutting board, slice off the little pointy tips of the asparagus. Set the tips aside; puree the stalks in the food processor with their cooking liquid. Now combine this puree with the cheese-milk mixture. Heat through, but, again, avoid a boil. Taste; correct the seasoning. Use only

*salt and pepper, preferably white pepper*

No herbs, or Tabasco, or anything else should interfere with the inherent flavor of this soup's lovely ingredients. Now, stir in

*1 cup heavy cream*

Again, heat with care. Last, just before serving, stir in the asparagus tips, which have been sliced into pieces ½ inch or so long.

*(continued)*

Serve very hot. I myself have never found a garnish that I consider appropriate to this soup, one that is not distracting in flavor or color, so I serve it as is, pristine and delectable, with a homemade whole grain bread dripping with butter as an accompaniment.

If you discover the perfect Asparagus-Cheese Soup garnish, please let me know.

By the way, when cooking this at home for myself, to save calories, I have often used all milk, no cream at all, with a little cornstarch (say 2 teaspoons) dissolved in the milk as a nominal replacement for the textural heft heavy cream adds. Even this way the soup is superb.

---

*FLOWERS AT DAIRY HOLLOW HOUSE: SEASONAL
LOVE LETTERS*

*Fresh flowers in every room are an important part of what makes the inn so special. Their form, color, and scent, their aliveness, the way they reflect the changing seasons, the way they quietly communicate the time of year and the mood of each month—flowers subtly enliven, freshen, and update our rooms and our lives. Month to month, they connect us with the changing natural world of which we are part. The languorous pink Grand Commander lily says "July" to us and our guests as clearly as sunburns and chilled Cascadilla in an iced bowl do; and what could be more "early spring" than lipstick-red Darwin tulips combined with branches of flowering dogwood, the white, peculiarly squared blooms a lovely flattened cup against the spring-green leaves—with Asparagus-Cheese Soup with White Wine to start!*

---

# Supper Before the Opera at Inspiration Point

*Asparagus-Cheese Soup with White Wine
Land of Milk and Honey Whole Wheat Bread • Butter
Salade Parkhurst
Lemon Mousse with Whipped Cream and Blueberries*

# Downtown Black Bean Soup

*Serves 6 to 8*

Simple can be good, even great, even elegant. This is one legume soup, even in this downtown version, that's highbrow enough to be at home as a starter at the most formal dinner party; a *small* cup (more would be too filling) seems to us especially suited to a meal featuring an egg-based entrée: a soufflé, an omelette or roulade, a quiche. Yet Downtown Black Bean Soup is also hearty enough to serve as a full meal with a salad and bread.

While most beans, peas, and legumes are delicious when given plenty of help, black beans, the most inherently flavorful of all the legumes, almost stand on their own. These are soups everyone loves; Ned and I loved this one so much we served it as a first course at our wedding. Keep it in mind, too, as a good hot winter soup to take along in a Thermos on a winter hike, picnic, or cross-country ski trip.

By the way, our friends Louis and Elsie, who've been to Cuba, swear that this downtown version is identical to the dark potage Havana used to be famous for.

Bring to a boil

*2½ quarts water* or *vegetable stock made from scraps (see p. 92)*

Stir into it

*2 cups black beans*
*2 bay leaves*

Turn down heat and let simmer for a couple of hours until the beans start to get tender. Then heat

*¼ to ¾ cup olive oil (how much will your conscience allow?)*

and cook in it until tender but not browned

*3 onions, chopped*
*2 green peppers, chopped*
*1 fresh jalapeño pepper, chopped (optional)*
*4 to 6 cloves garlic, pressed*
*1 to 3 teaspoons salt, maybe more—start with the
lesser amount and taste it*

Stir this mixture into the simmering black beans and let cook until quite tender and flavorful. More salt may be needed, and if you have a chance to let the soup sit overnight at this point, it will be even better. If desired, puree half or all of this to smoothness; we like it half-pureed, half-chunky. If you do puree it, be sure to reheat it before serving it, either as is or Cuban-style: bowls of steaming hot white rice and dishes of chopped raw onions are on the table, and each person stirs as much or as little rice and onions as they wish into their soup.

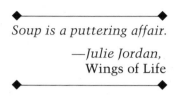

*Soup is a puttering affair.*

—*Julie Jordan,*
Wings of Life

## Uptown Black Bean Soup

*Serves 6 to 8*

Another tune from Black Bean's Greatest Hits.

Follow the same proportions of beans and water (or stock) as given for the Downtown version, but when beans are nearly tender, forgo the olive oil treatment. Instead, add to the simmering soup

*½ teaspoon each thyme, sage, and savory*
*a large handful of fresh chopped parsley*
*a good dash of nutmeg or mace*
*½ teaspoon crushed red pepper flakes*
*salt to taste*

Then, in

*2 tablespoons each peanut oil and butter*

sauté

*1 carrot, sliced*
*2 onions, chopped*
*1 stalk celery (with leaves)*

Add these to the herbed beans and continue simmering till the beans are quite tender.

Again, puree all or part of the soup if you like. Return soup to the pot, reheat, and add

*⅓ cup dry sherry*

When piping hot, serve. A super garnish for this version

*a rosette of unsweetened whipped cream and a half-slice of lemon*

# Ozark-Style Tuscany Bean Soup

*Serves 12*

This is a sublime Italian vegetable and bean soup, regionalized by the use of very Ozarks navy beans instead of imported cannellini beans. We think it's even better than the more famous minestrone. The preparation is fussy, the ingredients and steps many, and you may have to substitute dried herbs for the fresh ones called for. Plunge onward—this soup is worth it! Served, as it should be, over toasted French or Italian bread, flavory with garlic and onions and a bit of barely detectable tomato and white bean puree, this makes a swooningly delicious full meal when served with a good salad with some bite to it, like The Salad made with arugula.

Start this soup the night before, or even earlier. Soak overnight in water to cover

*2 cups dried navy beans*

In the morning, place the soaked beans, which will have absorbed most of their water, in a large stockpot with

*4 quarts water*
*1 large red onion, coarsely chopped*
*a few sprigs of parsley, preferably Italian (large-leaf)*
*3 cloves garlic, peeled, whole*
*1 large stalk celery with leaves, diced*
*2 tablespoons chopped fresh sweet basil (substitute 1½ teaspoons dried if absolutely necessary)*

Simmer until beans are tender enough to mash easily when you press against the side of the soup pot with a spoon, but still retain some shape. This should be 1½ to 2 hours. Toward the end of that time, in a skillet, heat

*¼ cup olive oil*

*(continued)*

103

In it sauté till softened

*1 red onion, finely chopped*

As the onion sautés, puree in a blender or food processor

*3 large fresh tomatoes, preferably garden ripe, skin and all*
*1 teaspoon fresh thyme (if you must, ½ teaspoon dried)*

Add the tomato puree to the sauté and simmer for 5 to 10 minutes with

*2 teaspoons honey*
*salt and pepper to taste*

Set the tomato mixture aside while you scoop out about half the cooked beans. Puree them, measure, and add water to equal a total of 4 quarts. Bring this mixture to a boil. Meanwhile, slice into thin ribbons

*1 small cabbage, preferably Savoy*

Steam it quickly above boiling water for 8 to 10 minutes, then add to the simmering bean puree along with the sautéed tomato-thyme mixture. Simmer for 5 minutes, correct the seasonings, and add the reserved whole beans. Serve the soup very very hot, over

*French or Italian bread slices*

which have been toasted slowly in an oven at about 300° for 15 to 20 minutes, or until dry, crisp, and slightly browned. Garnish with

*chopped raw red onion, chopped Italian parsley, and a liberal*
*sprinkle of freshly grated Parmesan cheese*

## Italian Soup Supper in December

*Ozark-Style Tuscany Bean Soup over Toasted Bread*
*with a garnish of*
*Parmesan Cheese, Red Onion, Italian Parsley*
*The Salad*
*Three Golden Fruits Italian Ricotta Tart*

# Jan's American Borscht

*Serves 6 to 8*

I thought, being of Russian-Jewish descent, that I knew all about borscht, a beet-and-vegetable soup from the country my grandparents were born in. I also thought I could not abide turnips in any shape or form. Jan's version—lighter, simpler, fresher tasting then mine—taught me a thing or two on both counts. This is more summery tasting, well suited as a starter. Mine, more substantial and a bit more assertive, is a dish for winter, and one large bowl is a meal in itself. Try both!

Puree in the blender

*6 small freshly cooked beets with ½ cup of their cooking liquid or 2
cups canned beets and their liquid
2 cloves garlic
1 lemon slice, seeded, but rind included
1 tablespoon Tamari soy sauce*

Add this pureed mixture to

*8 cups good vegetable stock*

and bring to a boil. Turn down heat and simmer during this next step. In a separate pan, steam

*5 or 6 new potatoes, sliced*

After giving the potatoes a 5-minute head start, add to them

*5 or 6 carrots, thinly sliced
1 turnip, in small dice*

Give all that another few minutes and add

*2 stalks celery, with leaves, thinly sliced
2 cups red cabbage, cut in fine slivers*

Steam for only a minute or so after this last batch is added. Now add these steamed vegetables to the simmering beet stock along with

*1 tablespoon chopped fresh sweet basil*

The minute all is good and hot, with the steamed vegetables still retaining a touch of crispness, ladle into soup bowls. Garnish with a dollop of sour cream or yogurt and top with a sprig of fresh dill.

# Crescent's Winter Borscht à la Vieille Russe

*Serves 6 to 8*

Unlike most borscht recipes, this one starts with *baking,* rather than simmering, the beets. This results in brightly colored, firmer beet pieces that have a more pronounced beet flavor, rather than watery pieces of beet that have given up most of their flavor to the broth in which they float. A rich, thick, wonderful soup with an intriguing march of flavors in each spoonful.

Scrub well, after removing tops and tails

*a bunch of fresh beets (3 or 4)*

Rub their skins lightly with

*vegetable oil*

and wrap them well, individually, in aluminum foil. Put them in the oven to bake at 350° for about an hour. Meanwhile, in a heavy Dutch oven or soup pot, preferably cast iron, melt

*4 tablespoons butter*

In it, sauté

*2 large onions, chopped*
*4 or 5 cloves garlic, pressed*
*2 carrots, diced*
*1 parsnip, very thinly sliced*

When onions have softened, add

*1 large can tomatoes in juice, which you have pureed in a blender or*
*food processor beforehand*
*4 cups dark vegetable stock or beef stock or water plus 4 unsalted*
*vegetable cubes*
*2 bay leaves*
*1 teaspoon each leaf oregano and basil*
*⅔ bunch fresh dill (the kind of bunch that is young enough to be*
*bright green, whose stalks are still tender, and which has not yet*
*begun to form seed-head flowers), chopped fine*
*2 tablespoons honey*
*1 teaspoon salt*

Simmer all this gently for about 40 minutes.

Meanwhile remove the beets from the oven; unwrap them and give them a poke with a fork: they should be barely fork-tender. Let them cool to where you can handle them, *quickly* run them under cold water, and slip off their skins. Discard skins. Dice beet insides and add to the soup along with

*½ head cabbage, sliced into fine ribbons*

Allow the soup to continue to simmer, or, if you wish, remove it from the heat at this point to let it sit overnight, refrigerated, to the end of getting even better. In any case, about 20 minutes before serving, reheat the soup, and, in a separate pot, steam

*about a dozen smallish red-skinned potatoes,*
*preferably new potatoes*

When the potatoes are completely tender and the soup is good and hot, place 1 or 2 whole small potatoes in each bowl, and ladle the soup over them. Top with a liberal amount of

*sour cream, crème fraîche, plain yogurt,* or *tofu sour cream*

on which you rest a large frond of fresh dill. Wonderful!

*Note:* Cooked kasha, about ½ cup per bowl, can replace the boiled potato in this dish.

# Garden Vegetable–Cheese Chowder

*Serves 6 to 8*

Jan has served this countless times, with countless combinations of vegetables, to countless delighted guests at the inn as well as at many workshops and retreats she's cooked for over the years. In fact, she served it at the very first dinner she ever fixed at Dairy Hollow House, to a couple who had eloped to Eureka and gotten married in our parlor on the first day of the New Year. She still recalls with some amusement how, when she tried to leave the inn to return to the innkeeper's house, soup pot in hand, James, the new groom, who'd had several helpings already, said in alarm, "Hey, wait a second, where are you *going* with that?"

Sauté

*1 onion, chopped*

in

*1 tablespoon butter*

After a minute or so, add

*3 tablespoons* each *fresh chopped parsley and Tamari soy sauce*
*½ teaspoon dried or 1 tablespoon fresh chopped basil*

Cook and stir till the onions are clear. Then add

*5 or 6 washed, scrubbed potatoes, cut in ½-inch pieces*

with

*enough water* or *vegetable stock to cover*

("Don't peel those potatoes!" says Jan vehemently. "Use that fiber and those nutrients!") Simmer, partially covered, until potatoes are tender. Whirl this entire mixture till smooth in the blender or food processor with

*1 cup heavy cream (or a 12-ounce can evaporated milk)*

Return to a heavy soup pot you have first coated with Pam or similar spray, and add enough additional

*cream* or *milk*

to make mixture a chowderlike consistency. Place on very low heat while you meanwhile wash, chop, and lightly steam *separately* your favorite assortment of fresh vegetables, such as

*carrots, celery, broccoli, corn cut from the cob, green beans, green onions, peas—a total of 4 or 5 cups' worth*

When vegetables are steamed, add them to the cream-potato-onion mixture and heat through, stirring frequently (at this point one could also add chopped cooked ham, sausage, bacon, chicken, or seafood; shrimp and mushroom chowder is delicious, especially with a dollop of sherry added just before serving). Thin again, if necessary, with more

*cream* or *milk*

And taste to correct the seasonings. Spoon into heated bowls, topping each serving abundantly with

> *a handful of grated sharp Cheddar cheese*

and a sprinkle each of

> *minced fresh parsley*
> *paprika*

Serve immediately. And watch your guests savor every bite.

---

*Throughout the book, we have suggested garnishes with each recipe. Always important, they are essential in the soup world, because many soups look a little pallid without them. Thin soups should be garnished at the table because their toppings have a tendency to migrate; on thicker soups, the garnish will stay put.*

*Some of the most beautiful summer garnishes are flowers: nasturtium blossoms, borage blossoms, spring violet petals, tiny fairy rosebuds, a special variety of orange-flavor marigold, geranium blossoms (any portion of the geranium blossom is lovely, and we particularly like to separate the large blossom, which is made up of a number of smaller flower buds, and remove one of the tiny unopened buds, which resembles a tiny rosebud). And, yes, each of these garnishes is edible!*

---

## ON POTATO SOUP

Few dishes are as comforting as good, made-from-scratch potato soup, a food that people of all ages tend to say, "Ahhhh . . ." at the very mention of. It's a welcoming potage; when you make a pot of it, you find yourself wanting to invite friends over to share it with.

Potato soup can be as mediocre as it can be sublime, for the two basic ingredients, potatoes and milk or cream, are themselves quite bland. Seasoning is therefore all-important, for these same two ingredients, given a bit of help, can reach magical heights of flavor and texture. At Dairy Hollow House, that help is given in several different ways: sometimes with cheese and beer, sometimes with sour cream, always with onions, herbs, and spices. Space does not permit the inclusion of all our favorite potato soups; here is one that is sublime.

*(continued)*

*Note:* Always make potato soup well in advance of when you intend to serve it. Making it the day before is best, but even a sit of several hours vastly improves any potato soup, heightening the flavors. Do not, therefore, correct the seasoning until right before serving; a potato soup that seems undersalted at noon may well have reached perfection by evening.

Potato soups, like anything with cooked potatoes, do *not* freeze well. Freeze a cooked potato, thaw and reheat it, and no matter what the dish, it will be undesirably mushy and half disintegrated. Why, then, you may wonder, can one purchase reasonably acceptable commercial frozen potatoes? Because, according to the good old *Joy of Cooking* (where would any American cook be without it?), commercial frozen potatoes are treated with a "quick vacuum partial dehydration," followed by instant freezing, "to which," notes Rombauer succintly, "home freezing equipment does not lend itself."

## Potato-Cheese Soup with Beer

*Makes 6 to 8 large servings*

Hearty, voluptuous, full flavored; a very distant cousin of Welsh rarebit. The beer adds an indefinable and delicious piquancy. Make sure the Cheddar is sharp and aged, so it will melt smoothly as well as add the requisite flavor.

In a large, heavy soup pot which you have Pam-ed, place

*6 to 8 large all-purpose sliced potatoes, peeled or not as you prefer*
*(we prefer not; we also prefer the larger red-skinned potatoes*
*for soup)*
*3 bay leaves*
*½ teaspoon each leaf basil and oregano*

Pour over these ingredients

*2 cups beer* or *ale*
*additional water* or *vegetable or chicken stock to just barely come*
*level with potatoes*

Bring to a boil, turn down heat, and let simmer, covered, while you sauté

*1 large onion, sliced*
*3 cloves garlic, pressed*
*2 carrots, sliced*

in

*4 tablespoons butter*

When onions are soft, sprinkle over them

*2 tablespoons flour*

Whisk vigorously; add gradually, as you continue whisking

*2 cups half-and-half*

Cook, stirring, till smooth and thick, then season with

*1 teaspoon Tamari soy sauce*
*several vigorous shakes of Tabasco or hot pepper sauce*
*½ teaspoon dry mustard*
*a couple of grinds fresh black pepper*

After the potatoes have simmered for about 20 minutes, add this sauce to them, stirring well. Then stir in

*12 ounces grated sharp Cheddar cheese*

Cook, stirring often, over very low heat, for another 20 minutes or so. Test the potatoes for doneness. If possible, remove from heat and allow soup to sit meditatively for at least several hours. Just before serving, reheat it gently, taste and correct for seasonings, and serve, very hot, in hot bowls, with a sprinkle of

*finely chopped parsley, paprika, additional grated sharp Cheddar*

## Déjà Food: Leftover Potato Soup

What a nice leftover to have on hand, even though you can't freeze it! A couple of cups of it make a fine basis for *Vegetable Pot Pie:* simply steam some sliced carrots and broccoli florets, add them with a handful of mushrooms that have been sliced and sautéed, and some peas, to the soup. Heat, correct the seasoning, pour into a baking dish, and cover with a top crust of either biscuit dough rolled thin, or Angel Biscuit dough, also rolled thin, or either of our two basic pie crusts. Bake at 400° for 10 minutes and 350° for another 20 minutes.

And just a few tablespoons of potato soup mixed with sautéed mushrooms and/or onions makes a dandy omelette filling.

## First Lighting of the Wood Stove or Fireplace Fall Supper

*Potato-Cheese Soup with Beer*
*Garlic Slaw*
*Baked Apple and Elsie's Gingerbread*

# COLD SOUPS

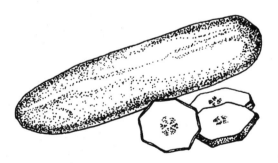

## Cascadilla (pronounced kass-kah-DEE-ah)

*Serves 6*

This, like Garlic Spaghetti (p. 241), is one of those dishes whose commonplace ingredients defy the spectacular end results. I'd read recipes for Cascadilla for years without being impressed at all, but after tasting it at a now-defunct Atlanta restaurant, I raced home to re-create it and have been doing so ever since. It's excellent summer food. Keep a jar of it in the refrigerator during the months when it is too hot to cook.

Combine

*4 cups good bottled tomato juice (from the health food store; we like
the Caliente brand, which is pleasantly hot)
1 cup each plain yogurt and sour cream
1 chopped cucumber, peeled unless from your garden or unwaxed
3 to 6 chopped scallions or 1 small mild red onion, finely minced
2 cloves garlic, pressed
½ cup chopped green pepper
½ cup chopped sweet red pepper
2 red-ripe garden tomatoes, chopped
1 tablespoon honey
fresh dill to taste
salt and pepper to taste*

Chill thoroughly. Serve garnished with finely chopped parsley.

## Chilled Strawberry Soup with Mint

*Serves 4 to 6*

A minted refresher, delicious, not too sweet, an early summer—late spring treat. Unlike many fruit soups, it is not too sweet to serve well as a first course. It's unusual enough so that it might be off-putting to the more conservative in taste, but the mildly adventurous love it. Make it the night before.

First, heat together in an enamel or nonaluminum pan

*¾ cup hearty red wine, such as a Beaujolais or Burgundy
¼ cup honey
dash each cinnamon and cloves*

As this heats, smush together with fingers until lump-free

*2 tablespoons cornstarch
¼ cup additional red wine*

Stir the cornstarch paste into the simmering wine, and whisk till smooth and thick. Remove from heat and let stand till lukewarm. Meanwhile, puree

*2½ cups sliced hulled strawberries*

(continued)

Measure the puree; you'll need about 1⅓ cups of it. Whisk about 1 cup puree into the thickened wine with

*1 cup* each *heavy cream and sour cream*
*3 tablespoons fresh mint, cut fine into thin ribbons*

The easiest way to chop mint: strip leaves from the stem; stack leaves; slice first lengthwise several times, using a long, sharp knife. Then grasp the leaves and snip them crosswise (the short way) directly into the bowl, using scissors. This method, which can also be used for cutting sweet basil or any other fresh herb with fairly good-size leaves, makes lovely small, delicate ribbons of mint.

Chill the minted strawberry soup deeply. An hour before serving time, whisk in

*1 or 2 tablespoons thawed, undiluted apple juice concentrate*
*1 or 2 tablespoons brandy*

When this is smoothly combined, stir in

*¾ cup sliced fresh strawberries*

Serve this lovely soup in chilled cups or bowls; glass bowls would be perfect, especially if set in larger bowls of crushed ice. Now garnish as follows: In each bowl, atop the pale pink soup, float a spoonful of the reserved strawberry puree. You may allow it to remain in one scarlet pool, or draw a toothpick through it a few times to marble it. Then add a dab of plain sour cream, crème fraîche, or unsweetened whipped cream. Then form a half-circle around the sour cream by carefully sprinkling on about a teaspoon additional finely chopped mint leaves.

Admire your handiwork. Doesn't it look like it could be a *Gourmet* or *Bon Appétit* centerfold?

# Chilled Caraway Squash Bisque

*Makes 2 quarts; about 12 servings*

This recipe comes to us from Marlene Sapinsley, one of the Dairy Hollow House guests we have most enjoyed. She loved our cooking, and we love this soup of hers. We regularly correspond about recipes.

Sauté together in a large saucepan

> *¼ pound butter*
> *1 onion, sliced*
> *1 rib celery, diced finely*
> *1 carrot, diced*

When vegetables are tender, add

> *1½ pounds acorn squash, cubed*
> *1 potato, cubed*
> *1½ quarts soup stock*
> *1 teaspoon to 1½ tablespoons caraway seeds*
> *1 teaspoon salt*
> *freshly ground white pepper to taste*

Cook together until vegetables are soft. Cool completely. Puree the soup in a blender or food processor. Add

> *1 cup heavy cream*

Serve well chilled with a slice of squash and parsley for garnish. We have not yet tried this, but suspect it would also be good done with zucchini and golden summer squash.

# Salads:
# The Green Art

When is a good salad ever out of place? With soup and thick bread, salad makes a simple but totally satisfying meal, as rounded sensually as it is nutritionally. As one course of a more elaborate meal, a straightforward salad is an unaffected grace note, pure and palate clearing. For lunch, a good big salad, well and interestingly made, dressed with care but not too richly, perhaps with cheese added, or meat or fish, is the thing itself.

Ah, you say, but not a salad at *breakfast*. Well, while we certainly wouldn't spring one on an unsuspecting guest at the inn, we *have* been known, in the dog days of summer, to wander out desultorily into the garden here at Dairy Hollow, pick a bit of this and that, wander back into the house and get out the olive oil, slice open a lemon, go into the front yard for herbs, and eat a green, green breakfast.

Anybody can make anything taste reasonably good with enough cream, butter, melted cheese, and other enrichments. But a dish that, to be perfect, is the freshest essence of itself, whose natural flavors must be heightened but never disguised, whose elegance is the elegance of simplicity, not elaboration: that is where you see real caring and knowledge on the cook's part. This is a knowledge of restraint, not embellishment; of knowing when to stop; of caring enough to pay attention to small and not always interesting or show-off-y details. This knowledge reaches its pinnacle in The Salad; not complex or difficult, but exacting in its parameters.

A guest from Dallas, here with her husband and son, had a dinner that included The Salad. After a few bites she put down her fork and said to us solemnly, "This is the best salad I have eaten in twenty-five years." (What was the salad she had had twenty-five years ago? Where she had eaten it, and with whom? Her utter seriousness made me wonder.)

At an "Excellence in Dairymaiding" luncheon we did last December as a thank-you to Gina and Marianne, both stellar Dairymaids and fine cooks themselves, The Salad again played a part; both Gina and Marianne wanted the recipe. I gave it, glad, as always, to spread the gospel. A few weeks later, doing a New Year's Eve dinner for two couples, a dinner at which Gina (elegant in a long black skirt, white tuxedo shirt, black tie) was serving, one of the members of the party said, "*What* is in this salad, *what* makes it so good?" and I had the pleasure of hearing Gina enumerate to the guests the secrets of The Salad, secrets I had shared many times, as they had been shared with me; secrets which cannot be told often enough—though, it seems, relatively few people have the restraint and discipline to carry them out.

Oh, yes, we make less demanding salads than The Salad here that are very good; we make salads that keep better, that look more decorative. We make very special marinated salads. We make salads that have the wonderful quick fillips of avocado and orange and grapefruit and olives and cheeses in them; memorable salads, interesting salads, good salads. We like them all, we like them a lot, and we wouldn't want to prejudice you against them.

But nothing comes close to the pristine, virginal purity and the perfectly balanced clarity of flavor of The Salad.

Listen closely to the secrets; this is your initiation. And for heaven's sake, read the recipe through before you start; it is long because it is detailed, and while it is exacting, it is simple. After a first read, assemble your ingredients before you and have at it.

# THE SALAD: THE MOST IMPORTANT RECIPE IN THIS BOOK

The Salad recipe consists of nine secrets.

## SECRET 1: THE BEST INGREDIENTS

Choose the freshest lettuces and/or greens you can find, preferably at least two different kinds: romaine, spinach, buttercrunch, oakleaf, arugula, raddichio, red leaf, curly. A bit of finely shredded green or red cabbage, interestingly enough, is not out of place here, and you may wish a red-ripe, perfect garden tomato (anything less would be sacrilegious here). Allow the equivalent of one head of lettuce for every four people. Avoid iceberg lettuce: it was bred not for flavor but to keep well and ship well, and those hard, firm heads, though pleasantly crisp, are essentially tasteless.

In addition to good greens, you will need the following: olive oil, a fresh lemon, fresh garlic, salt, black pepper. Optional, but so good as to almost be necessary, are good grainy mustard, a savory sauce such as Worcestershire or Pickapepper, finely minced fresh parsley, a selection of dried herbs. There are many, many other truly optional ingredients with which to gild the lily, but we will discuss them after the basic recipe for The Salad is completed, and we suggest you try it once straight, simple, Spartanly unembellished.

## SECRET 2: A THOROUGH WASHING

It would seem no secret at all that salad greens need a thorough washing, but the number of times we have encountered grit in salads has convinced us otherwise. Lettuce washing is not difficult but it is boring, and it requires real diligence and dedication to do the job as it should be done. It is an ideal job for the serious cook to delegate to a patient assistant who wants to help, and Jan and I have been lucky to often have such assistants. Ned has regularly been the salad greens washer at our house, and Blake, Jan's husband, has done quite a few lettuce heads and spinach bunches for her over the years. I would also like to commend, in print, the Cooneys of Aurora, New York, who provided invaluable lettuce-washing assistance to me, above and be-

118

yond the call of duty, when I was involved in cooking on a volunteer basis for a large group of people attending a special conference in Austin, Texas, last summer.

Here is how to do the thankless job.

Separate the lettuces into individual leaves. Survey the general dirt situation while you're at it. Rinse each leaf quickly under cold running water. That *may* do it, but it's not too likely. Stack the once-rinsed leaves in a colander, and rinse the whole batch a couple of more times. Does that do it? Maybe; maybe not. Examine the leaves. Bite one. Do grains of sand crunch against your teeth? If so, go into phase three, serious lettuce-washing technique: Fill a large bowl with *luke-warm*—not hot—water. Add the leaves and swish them around in the water. Lift them from the water, being careful not to stir up the bottom of the bowl, to which the grit is sifting down. Transfer leaves to a colander. Empty bowl. Rinse bowl, noting the amount of grit left. Repeat. Keep repeating until there is no grit left in the bottom of the bowl. Diligence and persistence are your watchwords.

At no point should the lettuce and greens actually soak in the water, which will rob them of vitamins and flavor and crispness. It should be a quick matter of in—swish—out.

After their final bath in the lukewarm water, run a blast of cold water over the greens in the colander. Let them drain in the colander set into the sink while you undertake:

## SECRET 3: A THOROUGH DRYING

This is the first step we have mentioned that is not widely known and that is all too rarely practiced. A salad made with leaves to which even the faintest hint of water clings may be okay, even good—but it will never, ever be great. Why?

1. Wet leaves become soggy leaves.

2. Moisture dilutes the dressing you apply.

3. Moisture prevents the magic workings of Secret 8, which has to do with application of the oil.

So, the lettuce must be dried *impeccably.* How? You can do it:

1. Leaf by leaf, very carefully with a paper towel.

2. In a plastic centrifugal salad spinner, a very clever device which many salad-loving households possess.

3. In the forerunner of a centrifugal salad spinner, the Ozark version, the totally silly-looking but more totally effective than either of the above, to say nothing of cheaper, the New Age miracle device that should be part of every household and generally is: a pillowcase.

A pillowcase? Yes.

Put the dripping wet greens into a clean, clean pillowcase. Go outside. Hold the pillowcase about halfway down, closing it tightly with one hand. Whirl it around and around and around, over your head or to the side or in front of you, whatever is most comfortable. We lean over the porch and let fly and hope no guests see us (now, thank God, it is in print, so we will have a logical explanation at hand). You will see the drops of water exiting the lettuce as quickly as they can, flying off in all directions.

The sense of sheepish embarrassment, the certainty that one will be hauled off if observed in this activity, is a clear indication that one is doing it correctly.

Open the pillowcase, which should be quite damp. Pull out the lettuce, which should be quite dry. If it isn't, whirl again and open the bag again. Don't worry about a few—a very few—last remaining drops of moisture. They will be absorbed when you undertake:

## SECRET 4: PROPER STORAGE
## OF WASHED GREENS

Lay out a length of either paper towel or clean cloth towel(s). Lay over it (them) the washed greens. (By the way, you may well be wondering whether all this rinsing and swishing and whirling won't completely destroy the greens. Now you can see that it hasn't.) Roll the greens into the towels, jelly-roll style. Put the towel-covered mass of greens into a bowl and cover tightly or, alternately, into a plastic bag, which you secure with a twist-tie. At this point, the greens will keep quite well for at least twenty-four hours, and we have sometimes known them to keep perfectly for as long as three days.

## SECRET 5: UNABASHED YET SUBTLE USE
## OF GARLIC

Some suggest merely rubbing the salad bowl with a clove of garlic and then discarding the clove. We call that wimpy.

120

We press the entire clove of garlic into the salad bowl, rub it around a bit, and leave it there. Which brings to mind:

## SECRET 6: THE CORRECT SIZE OF THE SALAD BOWL

You are going to toss this salad, and you need a bowl big enough to be able to do so uninhibitedly. Think large. Think small bathtub. Big, big, big—the bigger the better.

You do not need to concern yourself with what the salad bowl is made of. It was once in vogue to use only wooden salad bowls and never to wash them. This, with the repeated rubbings and discardings of garlic, was said to add more flavor to salads with each passing year. We think it added a disgusting patina of rancidity. If you do have a wooden salad bowl, by all means wash it after each use. The other item on the equipment agenda is:

## SECRET 7: SALAD PLATES

Chill them in the freezer now. A salad on a chilled plate always tastes better.

## SECRET 8: IN WHICH WE GET INTO SERIOUS SALAD CONSTRUCTION—THE PROPER USE AND TIMING OF THE OIL

Begin this step only when your guests are already at the table. Remove the lettuce from the refrigerator and tear (never cut with a knife) the greens into bite-size pieces, not too small. Into a large, garlicky salad bowl pour, for a salad for 4 to 6 people

*4 tablespoons good, fruity, aromatic olive oil*

Now understand the logic of what is going to happen. You will put the bone-dry, washed, chilled lettuce into the bowl on top of the olive oil and garlic. With nothing else added, you will toss the salad greens repeatedly (clean hands make the best salad tossers, but if you are squeamish about this sort of thing, use a salad fork and spoon). You will toss the greens, gently yet with vigor, until each leaf glistens with olive oil.

The reason? The olive oil seals in the leaves' own moisture and flavor, keeping each leaf in that state of distinctive crispness which the careful washing, drying, and storage has brought about. Thus, when the next ingredients are added, they will not immediately penetrate the oil-protected leaves, and, for a few moments, the salad will exist in a sublime state—the leaves crisp and flavorful, ever so lightly covered with their dressing, a dressing so light it is like the most delicate lingerie, the leaves more undressed than dressed, not penetrated, not sodden, not soggy. This is the essence of the whole thing, the bottom line: the olive oil acts as a sealant.

Do it, now. If you wish, a few chopped scallions may be added with the lettuce before tossing.

## SECRET 9: THE SPEEDY AND AROMATIC COMPLETION

No longer than a minute after you have added the olive oil, quickly—quickly—sprinkle the following over the oil-glistening greens. These are imperative.

*the juice of ½ lemon, squeezed directly into the bowl
(pick out seeds) (If lemon is small, or you have a whole lot of greens, you may wish to use the entire lemon; start with a half, though, and taste later)
½ to 1 teaspoon salt
several vigorous grindings of fresh, coarsely ground black pepper*

Now comes the list of optional ingredients, any or all of which will heighten, but not disguise, the perfection of this salad

*1 teaspoon Dijon mustard
a dash of Tamari, Worcestershire, Pickapepper, or Tabasco sauce, or all four
1 tablespoon or 2 of very, very finely chopped fresh parsley
(this is a wonderful, very French touch)
any other minced fresh or dried herb you like—sweet basil, oregano, thyme, dill, chives, and so on . . . we also love using whole fresh chive blossoms, small and beautifully lavender*

Now toss again, vigorously but gently, until you feel that these ingredients have been well distributed among the lettuce leaves. Taste. Correct the seasonings—you may well need a bit more lemon or salt or pepper, but probably not much else. Don't stand there swooning with delight! Grab those salad plates from the freezer! Plunk the salads down on them! Eat, now!

You may well be heady with delight over what you have created. You will wonder why this simple technique, so easy to do if time-consuming to describe, is not more widely understood and practiced. You will experience a moment of sheer revelation.

You may even feel called, as we have, to initiate others into The Secrets of The Salad.

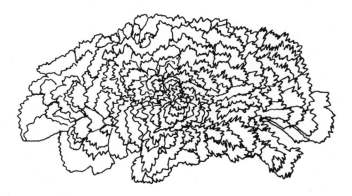

## FINE POINTS AND VARIATIONS

- We vastly prefer lemon juice for the touch of tartness every salad requires, for it imparts a special freshness. However, vinegar has its devotees, and the herb, balsamic, and various wine and fruit vinegars now available do add many interesting and subtle variations. Since one has a lifetime in which to enjoy salads, they are worth experimenting with.

- The Salad need not be made as austerely as described. Other ingredients may be added—though we think never too many at any one time, or the wonder of the thing is lost. Hard, crisp, *nonmoist* ingredients can go in with the lettuce at the time of the first tossing, with just the olive oil. Those ingredients include:

  celery; broccoli or cauliflowerets; carrots (sliced but not grated. Grated is too moist for inclusion at this point; we think carrots for salad are best done in tiny, tiny julienne slivers); thin half-slices of red onion; red or green sliced cabbage; well-scrubbed raw Jerusalem artichoke (which is delicious in a salad, very crunchy and sweet and surprising)

The next set of ingredients goes in after the olive oil toss, with the seasoning toss. They are less firm than the first round of ingredients just listed but still on the sturdy side, and, again, not too moist:

> sliced fresh mushrooms; sliced firm cheeses (for example, Cheddar, provolone, mozzarella; again, we like julienne pieces better than grated); alfalfa seed sprouts; any leftover chilled and sliced meat or fish (chicken, roast beef, what have you); whole green grapes; fresh peas, cooked and chilled, or any cooked leftover diced vegetable if it is still tender-crisp and not too moist; raisins or dried fruit chunks (these have their devotees but I am not one); slivers or chunks of fresh apple; radishes; olives; sunflower seeds or nuts; croutons (but don't feed them to my father!)

The third time to add ingredients is after the salad is, for all practical purposes, complete. The ingredients added then are those which are very delicate or crumbly (chopped hard-boiled egg, for instance) or soft (ripe avocado chunks) or juicy (tomato slices, most fresh fruit pieces). Add them, toss just once or twice, and serve. Here's a list of such add-ins:

> marinated artichoke hearts, well-drained; avocado; tomato; hard-boiled eggs; soft cheese crumbles (blue, some goat cheeses); citrus fruit chunks; grated carrot

There is one last time and place at which to embellish The Salad, and that is after it is completed and scooped onto its chilled plates. At that point, if you have waiting any marinated morsels, carefully lift them from their dressing onto the bed of The Salad, and serve. (We think The Salad is so perfect, though, that we would almost rather not adulterate its delicacy with the stronger flavors and textures of a marinated something and would serve the marinated something instead over a plain, straightforward, un-dressed bed of lettuce and sprouts.)

Here are a few more specific variations on The Salad. Actually, they cannot really be called variations as such, because they are each distinctive, delicious salads on their own and not much like The Salad. Most of them could, perhaps, be called more interesting than it is, and every one of them is very good, if lacking the intense purity of flavor that makes The Salad The Salad. But they do use the basic oil-first, then-the-other-elements-of-the-dressing method, and in that sense they are a variation. Since we think everyone should eat salad at least once or twice a day, there is plenty of time to dally deliciously with them all—and still return lovingly to The Salad.

# "Excellence in Dairymaiding" Luncheon

*Potato-Cheese Soup with Beer*
*The Salad*
*Angel Biscuits • Butter*
*Deluxe Ambrosia*
*Pipparkakut*

## Spinach, Orange, and Avocado "The Salad"

*Serves 4*

A magic blend of flavors and textures: lush fresh spinach; juicy oranges; smooth, creamy avocado; the bite of scallions and garlic with the tang of vinegar and a touch of sweetness. A popular and unusual salad, very good with chicken and some vegetarian entrées.

Wash, dry, and wrap in towel as directed

*6 to 8 cups fresh spinach*

Shake in a jar

*⅓ cup fresh orange juice*
*3 tablespoons red wine vinegar*
*1 tablespoon lemon juce*
*1 tablespoon sugar or honey (heat the honey under hot water*
*so it will thin and blend into the other liquids)*
*or a half envelope of artificial sweetener*
*½ teaspoon Tamari soy sauce*
*½ to 1 teaspoon grated orange rind*
*several good grinds of fresh black pepper*

Set this aside. Now, in a lightly garlicked bowl, pour

*⅓ cup vegetable oil*

Olive is fine but a bit heavy; you may wish to use peanut oil here. Toss in it the prepared spinach. Then add, working quickly

*1 or 2 navel oranges, peeled, sectioned, and seeded*
*1 ripe avocado, peeled and diced into good-size chunks*
*4 sliced scallions, green tops included*
*(or use thin half-slices of red onion)*

*(continued)*

Shake the contents of the jar vigorously one more time, pour over the salad, toss once or twice, and serve immediately.

### Oriental Spinach, Avocado, and Orange Salad

A few changes make a big difference. Try both versions. Use peanut oil to which you've added

*1 teaspoon toasted sesame seed oil*

And, to the mixture shaken in the bottle, add

*½ to 1 teaspoon grated fresh ginger root*

Sprinkle a few toasted sesame seeds over the top of this. Or turn it into a light summer lunch that's a vegetarian's delight by tossing in a few cubes of firm tofu. Delicious!

# Crescent's More-or-Less Greek Salad

*Serves 4*

My favorite lunch, with—sometimes in—half a toasted pita. Follow the basic The Salad recipe, using 2 or 3 cloves of garlic in the olive oil. Toss in, with the seasonings (omit salt from among them, as several of the following ingredients are quite salty)

*crumbled feta cheese, to taste (feta is available made from
cow, goat, or sheep's milk; they're all good,
but the sheep's milk kind is extraspecial)
fresh dill weed
a little dried oregano
1 sweet red bell pepper, slivered
¼ red onion, in thin slivers
a few Kalamata olives—the large moist purple-y black kind, or those
other delicious dried, oil-cured, wrinkly black Greek olives
¼ ripe avocado half, diced (not Greek at all, of course, but, oh my,
don't the avocado flavor and texture blend perfectly
with the other ingredients here?)*

Toss. Taste for seasonings and correct, if necessary.

Although they have different national origins, this makes a very good and surprisingly rich meal served with Ozark-Style Tuscany Bean Soup, page 103, or really any bean soup. It also works well as a prelude to almost any vegetarian meal, or to almost any tomato-y chicken or fish dish: Chicken Marengo Our Way (p. 180), for instance, or Baked Fish Provençal (p. 208).

# Dinner for the Library Board

*Cascadilla*
*Italian Spinach Torte*
*The Salad with Artichoke Hearts, Tomato, and Olives*
*Sliced Oranges with Chilled Honeyed Zabaglione Napoleon*

# House Salad à la Dairy Hollow

*Serves 4*

If we have a House Salad besides The Salad, this is it—a wondrous combination that Blake, Jan's husband, created. We serve it frequently in our Haute Country Cuisine dinners, accompanied by buttery hot whole wheat dinner rolls, after the hors d'oeuvres and soup, before the entrée. Spectacularly festive.

Wash, dry, and tear as directed for The Salad

*1 bunch romaine lettuce*

When the lettuce has been rolled in its towels and refrigerated, prepare and set aside

*a fresh grapefruit, peeled, deseeded, sectioned, cut in pieces*
*4 green onions, sliced*
*¼ cup sliced black olives*
*1 or 2 dozen sweet pea blossoms, washed (in season, of course)*

They grow like crazy all over the Ozarks—our hillside—and gathering them is a moment's work, and yes, naturally they're edible! Need you ask? They have a sweet, soft, and tender mild crunch to them, pleasant and nonassertive, and their pink color adds a beautiful visual surprise.

*(continued)*

Now, set the salad plates to chill, and remove the romaine from the refrigerator. Tear into serving-size pieces. Into the salad bowl, pour

*4 tablespoons olive oil*

Add the romaine and toss. Then add

*juice of 2 lemons*
*½ teaspoon Tamari soy sauce*
*½ teaspoon freshly chopped parsley*
*black pepper to taste*

Toss again. Add the grapefruit, the sweet pea blossoms, the olives, the scallions, and toss one or two more times. Divide evenly among the four chilled plates, making sure each gets a fair allotment of some of each special ingredient. Garnish each serving, if desired, with a generous sprinkle of

*Parmesan cheese*

P.S.: Jan and I are in accord down to this last ingredient. She and Blake love the Parmesan touch; to me, it's a little funny with the grapefruit. Try both, and you decide!

We have also sometimes gilded the lily on this wondrous creation by adding either ripe avocado or well-drained marinated bottled artichokes (in this case, save the liquid for future salad dressings).

# ARRANGED SALADS

As much as we love The Salad, as much as we find it the pinnacle of salad making, we must admit that there is one way that it falls short, and that is visually. Oh, it's pretty enough, the greens vivid and a-glisten with olive oil, but it is, well, tossed and tousled, of casual mien. An arranged salad, however, can be a still-life on a plate, each ingredient carefully placed for color and form, for contrast, for surprise and pleasure. It has a visual elegance that The Salad cannot match. And if we have stated that The Salad is on a whole other plane as far as taste goes, we mean no disrespect to the other salads we make and enjoy. Arranged salads can be tempting, provocative, delicious, and wholly as worthy of eating as looking at. Here are some of our favorites.

---

*FLOWERS AT DAIRY HOLLOW HOUSE: SPRING*

*Spring arrangements: flowering dogwood branches and red Darwin tulips; forsythia and daffodils with daisy mums from the florist's; tiny pitchers of dwarf iris (the iris* Reticulatas *are the most incredible shade of indigo blue, and they bloom here at the same time as the perennial vinca, whose pale lavender flowers make a beautiful backdrop); tiny pitchers of violets; red-bud blossoms and flowering quince branches with early narcissus.*

---

## Jan's Pleasures of Summer Salad

*Serves 4*

Delightfully cool and refreshing, this lovely salad features cucumbers, scallions, and green beans marinated in an unusual vinaigrette. We find it will work practically with *any* meal and, in fact, with some julienned Swiss cheese, it works very nicely as a meal—a summer luncheon, particularly.

Wash and dry

*1 head red leaf lettuce*

Wrap up in towels and refrigerate it till needed. Also put the salad plates in to chill. Prepare

*1 recipe Gingered Vinaigrette (p. 140)*

Into vinaigrette place

*4 green onions, finely sliced*
*1 medium-size cucumber, seeded and unpeeled, coarsely grated*

Let vegetables marinate while preparing the rest of the salad. Wash and steam for 3 minutes.

*1 pound green beans*

Rinse immediately in cool water. Drain, dry, and chill the beans. Just before serving, drain vinaigrette from cucumber mixture. Remove reserved red leaf lettuce from fridge and tear into serving-size pieces. Arrange on individual chilled salad plates. Place one-fourth of the chilled green beans on lettuce, arrange one-fourth of cucumber mixture over beans, sprinkle with

*borage flowers*

(continued)

(Pluck these beautiful little blue stars from the borage plants in your herb garden. Gently rinse them and add to any food you want to sparkle. They have a delicate flavor you simply must taste: faintly cucumbery-flowery. Borage blooms mid- to late summer.)
Serve immediately.

# Saturday Lunch After Working in the Garden

*Jan's Pleasures of Summer Salad*
*Two Sisters Russian Black Rye* ● *Butter*
*Iced Red Zinger Herb Tea*

## Salade Parkhurst

*Serves 4 to 5*

A salad we created in honor of Ted and Liz Parkhurst, founders of August House, an Arkansas publishing company that did my book of poetry, *Message from the Avocadoes.*

Salade Parkhurst has its origins in Paris, where every little charcuterie offers an array of freshly made, always beautifully presented, prepared salads, many of which are of some form of raw or cooked vegetable that is grated or sliced and then bathed in vinaigrette. When, shortly before the Parkhursts' arrival, I went shopping at Hart's, our local supermarket, I was thrilled to the gills to find fresh baby beets there, and in December, no less! (This is rural Arkansas; we just don't *have* things like baby beets at Hart's in the middle of the winter very often. But then again, Hart's has recently astonished us by offering phyllo dough in the freezer and feta cheese in the dairy case.)

Anyway, some very nice fresh broccoli, in addition to the baby beets, clinched it. I immediately had a vision of the salad I wanted to prepare. This is it, and it's good.

First, prepare

*1 recipe Sharp Classic Vinaigrette with a Bite (p. 139)*

Reserve it. Then steam till tender

*4 to 6 small baby beets, unpeeled, tails intact
and tops cut down to ½ inch of stalk*

Separately, steam just until barely tender, still a bit crisp

*the stems (peeled and julienned) and florets of 1 stalk of broccoli*

When each vegetable is done, run it quickly under cold water to stop the cooking, drain, and, in its own private dish, cover with the prepared vinaigrette. Also, grate

*2 carrots*

and cover them, raw, with vinaigrette too. Let all marinate, refrigerated, as you wash and dry

*1 head red leaf lettuce*

Wrap in towels till serving time, and put plates in to chill. At serving time, arrange lettuce on the chilled plates and, atop the lettuce, place a little pile of each of the three marinated vegetables: the deep red grated beets, the bright green broccoli, the orange carrot. Sprinkle the whole thing with

*very, very finely minced scallion and minced parsley*

and place

*a slice or 2 of ripe tomato*

on each plate, tucking it under the lettuce so that only its edge peeps out. An optional additional garnish is a small puff of alfalfa seed sprouts. Serve.

Variations on such a salad are infinite. I like very much the idea of three piles of marinated vegetables, contrasting in color, flavor, and texture. What about cooked marinated tiny new potatoes, fresh asparagus spears, and raw red pepper slivers? Or snow peas, steamed for a few seconds only and marinated; raw marinated cucumbers; and sliced raw marinated mushrooms—all on a bed of spinach? Or whole steamed baby carrots marinated, and raw cherry tomatoes marinated, and green peas, barely steamed, marinated? Corn cut from the cob, thick slices of raw fresh tomato, and, again, cucumber? Or the baby new potatoes again, this time with half an artichoke, cooked and marinated, and cherry tomatoes. And on and on . . . such is the way of arranged salads. Firm cheeses, julienned, and ampler portions make such salads into a full meal.

*Let first the onion flourish there*
*Rose among roots, the maiden-fair*
*Wine-scented and poetic soul*
*Of the capacious salad bowl.*

—*Robert Louis Stevenson,*
*"To a Gardener"*

## Salad Luncheon in the August Dog Days

*Mama Murray's Potato Salad*
*Salade Parkhurst with Julienne of Jarlsberg Cheese*
*San Francisco-Comes-to-the-Ozarks Chicken Salad*
*Dairy Hollow Oatmeal Bread Supreme*
*Peach Ice Cream Topped with Fresh Peach Slices and Berry Puree*

# SLAWS AND HEARTIER SALADS

We enjoy several nonlettuce salads, heartier cold dishes that travel beautifully to picnics and potlucks, keep well in the fridge until you want them, and, in general, wait, obliging you with no fussiness or temper tantrums. Try *that* with a prepared The Salad and you'll have a fine soggy mess!

Within the realm of nongreen salads, we think these are supreme.

132

# Confetti Slaw

*Serves 4*

Cabbage, slivered and crunchy, with a light sweetness, makes this a perfect match for a winter soup in a hearty Peasant's Feast.

Toss together in a large salad bowl

*½ head green cabbage, in finely slivered long strands
1 stalk celery, finely chopped
1 green pepper, diced
1 red apple, unpeeled and finely chopped (try an Arkansas Black
or a Delicious)
½ cup raisins
½ cup sunflower seeds*

Combine, beating well

*½ cup peanut oil
1 teaspoon Tamari soy sauce
2 tablespoons honey
1 clove garlic, pressed
½ teaspoon poppy seeds*

Pour this over the slaw. Stir well, chill thoroughly and serve.

## Crescent's Wonderful Oriental Slaw

Omit apples, raisins, seeds. Use a whole cabbage, a grated carrot, and ½ bunch of green onions, diced. Mix the dressing in a blender or food processor, increasing Tamari to 1 tablespoon, honey to ⅓ cup, and garlic to 2 cloves. Add, in addition, 2 teaspoons toasted sesame seed oil; a thumb-size piece of fresh ginger root, peeled and diced; 4 tablespoons rice wine vinegar; and ¼ to ½ teaspoon hot red pepper to taste. This is just incredibly refreshing; a most delicious, piquant change from many slaws. Since there are no Oriental restaurants to speak of in Eureka Springs, we make it whenever we have a Chinese food craving.

## Garlic Slaw

*Serves 6 to 8*

No kidding, we love garlic. And we love cabbage. The combination, mellowed by a creamy dressing, is unbeatable with either of our black bean soups and a corn muffin.

Mix until well blended in food processor or blender

*½ cup mayonnaise*
*½ cup sour cream*
*2 tablespoons heavy cream*
*5 cloves garlic, peeled and minced*
*½ teaspoon Tamari soy sauce*
*½ teaspoon paprika*
*½ teaspoon celery seed*

Pour this dressing into the bottom of a large mixing bowl. Add

*1 head cabbage, finely grated (reserve large outer leaves*
*for "serving bowls")*
*2 carrots, finely grated*
*1 stalk celery, finely grated*

When grated vegetables are added to bowl, stir well and chill. Serve each portion nestled in a cabbage leaf with a sprig of parsley and a sprinkle of paprika.

## A Light Supper for a Hot Summer's Night

*Cascadilla*
*Crescent's Favorite Whole Wheat Butterhorns and/or Angel Biscuits*
*Chilled Poached Trout and/or Cheese Board*
*The Salad with Fresh Lightly Steamed Peas*
*Fresh Pineapple Marinated in Kirsch*

## Slaw à L'indienne

*Serves 4 to 6*

Not too long ago I visited India for an extended period of time. I was staying in a rural village, one that did not cater to foreign tourists, and the food was delicious but limited in diversity. If you get tired of a big heap of steaming fresh rice (from the paddy just outside the door) and five or six assorted smaller piles of various kinds of spiced, seasoned, sweet, chopped, stew-y, stir-fried vegetables, each very different from the other and very different day to day, you can't just say, "Well, let's call out for pizza."

The single food I missed most was salad. The climate is too hot to grow those tender greens, for one thing, and, for another, Indians just don't care much for raw vegetables other than tomatoes or in Raita (see the following). Finally, from the available vegetables which were all of enviable, picked-that-morning freshness, I devised the following salad. It was delicious—though at the time I thought the attraction must be just that it was raw and crunchy and fresh-tasting. But the simple, clean, refreshing flavors stayed with me, and I still make it at home.

Shred finely

*½ head green cabbage*

Toss with it

*⅓ cup finely chopped red onion or shallot*

(In India, at least the part I visited, the available onions are tiny, rather mild onions, much like our shallots.)

*2 carrots, scrubbed very well and diced into tiny squares*
*½ teaspoon salt*

Sometimes I added (and still do) and sometimes not

*a teaspoon or so finely grated fresh ginger*

Sprinkle over all this

*the juice of 1 or 2 fresh limes*
*1 tablespoon—no more—of light sesame oil (optional)*

Toss. Add

*2 red ripe tomatoes, chopped*

Toss again, and serve.

◆————————————————◆

*My salad days, when I was green in judgement.*

—*William Shakespeare,*
Cleopatra, *Act I*

## New Wave Carrot-Pineapple Salad

*Serves 4*

Remember that wonderful cool sweet salad that (if you were lucky) your mama used to make, that refreshing carrot-pineapple congealed salad made with packaged gelatin? We've discovered a new version we like, with all the delicious flavors and none of the color and preservative artifice of prepared gelatin. Chill well before serving. This keeps quite well.

Wash and grate

*3 large organic carrots (or about 1 pound of any kind
of carrots, fresh and raw)*

Place in mixing bowl. Open and pour over

*1 can crushed pineapple (in its own juice) and the juice*

The juice tastes wonderful, marinates the carrots, and keeps them from turning dark. Stir these together well. Sprinkle with

*¼ cup finely diced green pepper
½ cup raw pepitas (pumpkin seeds—available at your health food
store; you could also use raw sunflower seeds,
English walnuts, or pecan halves)*

Stir together well, refrigerate, and serve a portion (well drained) on a curly lettuce leaf. *Variation:* Add the juice of an orange as well as ½ teaspoon grated orange rind.

## Garden Rice Salad

*Serves 4 to 6*

This is a very hearty and nutritious salad, almost a complete meal in itself, excellent served with a light tomato bisque and Parmesan-ed melba toast.

Whirl together in a mixing bowl

*½ cup mayonnaise
½ cup yogurt
1 teaspoon Tamari soy sauce*

Add

*2 cups cooked brown rice, chilled*
*1 tomato, finely chopped*
*3 stalks celery, finely chopped*
*½ medium-size cucumber, peeled, seeded, and finely chopped*
*3 tablespoons minced fresh parsley*
*1 tablespoon minced fresh basil (or ¼ teaspoon dried)*
*½ cup water chestnuts, drained and sliced fine*

Stir together lightly until rice and vegetables are well coated with dressing. Just before serving, toss in

*1 cup salted roasted peanuts*

Give a quick stir and serve immediately, garnished with a tomato wedge and a slice of cucumber.

Although we use this interchangeably with our potato salads, we made the decision to place our Garden Rice Salad here and our potato salads in the picnic chapter. Don't ask us why; it's our book—we can do what we want!

## TOMATO SALADS SEVERAL QUICK WAYS

This brings us to the subject of tomatoes. We do without them in their raw form until we can get them vine-ripened. When they do arrive—full-flavored, luscious, deeply red, plump with the sweet dripping juice they contain—we can't get enough of them. We:

- Slice them, lay out the slices overlapping each other on a romaine-lined chilled plate, and sprinkle with fresh chopped sweet basil, fresh chopped sage, or fresh chopped thyme, or fresh dill and just a few grains of salt.

- Do the same, but alternate thick tomato slices with paper-thin onion slices (either red onions or, when we can get them, sweet Vidalias from Georgia), and drizzle just a bit of Classic Sharp Vinaigrette with a Bite (p. 139) over them.

- Do the same, but use the sliced tomatoes on their romaine as a bed for any marinated green vegetable: broccoli, green beans, etc. Top with a little sliced or crumbled feta and a sprinkle of basil and oregano.

- Chop the tomatoes coarsely, place in a bowl with a bit of chopped red onion (say, 1 level tablespoon chopped onion for every 1½ tomatoes), add a bit of salt, toss well, let stand for a few minutes, and serve. (This simple way is from south India, and it is far more delicious than it sounds—pure, fresh, intense flavors. Don't even think about it with inferior tomatoes.)

- Do the same, but add a bit of grated ginger.

- Make a *Raita Salad* by following either of the two chopped tomato variations, adding a finely diced cucumber, and spooning on just enough fresh, thick, plain yogurt to "stick" it; toss lightly, and serve. (You won't believe how good this is—simple and refreshing, a natural with anything spicy yet, interestingly, it also adds a bit of tang to a bland meal. Also, very low calorie!)

## Birthday Dinner Among Good Friends

*Mushrooms Diablo*
*Spinach, Orange, and Avocado "The Salad"*
*Lemon-Pepper Chicken*
*Rice ● Stir-Fry of Broccoli ● Butternut Squash Puree*
*Whole Wheat Sour Cream Biscuits ● Butter*
*Dairy Hollow House Mocha Dream Torte*
*Cinnamon Coffee*

# DELECTABLE DRESSINGS

You might suppose, after all our carrying-on about The Salad, whose dressing, such as it is, is mixed right in the bowl, that we wouldn't have much use for made-up salad dressings. But we do. The Salad doesn't travel; yet we often bring a salad—a good green one—to parties, picnics, and potlucks. The Salad doesn't adapt to those who like a salad un-dressed (like Bill Haymes, former Dairy Hollow House partner) and to those who like it very dressed (like Ned Shank, Dairy Hollow House partner), or to those who intermittently watch their calories and use just a bit of some sort of luscious dressing, spelled out by the juice of a freshly squeezed lemon (like Crescent, third partner). Dressing-on-the-side—especially when it's as good as these that follow—settles all differences deliciously. Too, every cook needs a couple of good vinaigrettes up her/his sleeve, to marinate firmer vegetables as they come into season.

## Sharp Classic Vinaigrette with a Bite

*Makes scant 2 cups*

This is the salad dressing I make most often, a good basic one for any salad lover's repertoire. Don't stint on the mustard or garlic.

In a food processor, whirl

> *½ cup cider vinegar (or tarragon, herb,*
> *balsamic—whatever you fancy)*
> *¼ cup good grainy mustard—Dijon or any of the*
> *French country mustards*
> *½ teaspoon salt*
> *4 to 6 good-size cloves garlic, more if cloves are small*
> *1 to 3 leaves fresh basil (optional, but great)*
> *several solid grinds of coarse black pepper*

Buzz quickly, and turn off machine. Then, with machine running, pour in slowly

> *1 cup olive oil*

Turn off machine when all oil is added and vinaigrette is thick, creamy, aromatic, and pungent. This keeps quite well, refrigerated.

## Gingered Vinaigrette

*Makes scant ¾ cup*

A French vinaigrette receives new life and interest with the addition of ginger. Use it in Jan's Pleasures of Summer Salad (p. 129) or to freshen any green salad, particularly one with spinach.

Whirl in blender container

*½ cup olive oil*
*juice of ½ lemon*
*1 tablespoon red wine vinegar*
*1 tablespoon candied ginger*
*½ teaspoon Tamari soy sauce*
*dash of black pepper*

◆————————————————◆

*Q: What is a honeymoon salad?*
*A: Lettuce alone, without dressing.*

◆————————————————◆

## Spinach Dressing Brenda & Lana's in Quantity

*Makes about 1½ quarts (see Note)*

Brenda Evans and Lana Lloyd opened the café that bears their name in March of 1982. Tucked in unprepossessingly on tiny Center Street, which branches off behind Spring, Brenda & Lana's Center Street Café was an immediate hit with locals (any guests we've sent have also enjoyed it). We love to go there for breakfast midweek, when and if we have a day off from feeding our guests. B & L's does wonderful omelettes, and a great poached egg on spinach-on-English-muffin-with-cheese-sauce, and decadently gooey homemade cinnamon rolls. They do a fine job of catering to the totally diverse tastes of a totally diverse local population that includes an unusually high percentage of vegetarians cheek to jowl with the good ol' biscuits-and-gravy fans.

We also like B & L's salads. They always use fresh, interesting greens: red leaf lettuce or curled loose-head. In fact, Mary Romano, who waitresses there and was a very good Dairymaid for us for a season, was once asked by a visitor how the kitchen curled the lettuce. And their salad dressings are spectacular. Lana, who runs the kitchen, and Brenda, who takes care of the front, have contributed two very special dressing recipes.

*Note:* This recipe, as given to us, yields about 1½ quarts. It's always handy to have a few quantity recipes on hand, so we have left the original proportions but *added parenthetically the amounts needed to make an average home-size batch.* We know you'll enjoy this cool, creamy, refreshing pale green delight as much as we do.

Combine in a blender or food processor

> *32 ounces sour cream (8 ounces sour cream)*
> *½ cup buttermilk (2 tablespoons buttermilk)*
> *full bag washed spinach (1 handful)*
> *½ cup mayonnaise (2 tablespoons)*
> *1 teaspoon Vege-Sal (¼ to ½ teaspoon)*
> *1 teaspoon Spike (¼ to ½ teaspoon) (Both Spike and Vege-Sal are herb blends that are available at health food stores; we like 'em both on popcorn!)*
> *½ teaspoon celery seed (dash)*
> *½ teaspoon garlic powder (dash; we use 1 small clove fresh garlic when we make this at home)*
> *¼ teaspoon white pepper (dash)*
> *½ teaspoon nutmeg (2 dashes)*
> *2 tablespoons honey (1 teaspoon)*

Whirl till smooth. Keeps about 4 to 5 days in fridge.

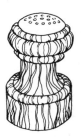

## Buddy's Boston Mountain Poppy Seed Dressing as Given to Lana

*Makes about 1 quart*

Another of our favorite B & L dressings was given to Lana by Buddy of the Boston Mountain Bakery in Fayetteville. This is a wonderful poppy seed dressing, sweet and tangy, yet not overpoweringly sweet as most poppy seed dressings are. We love this on green salads and—green onions omitted—on fruit salads. Although this, too, makes a fairly good-size quantity, it keeps well, so we generally just go ahead and make it up as is.

Whirl together in a blender or food processor

*1½ cups honey*
*½ cup water*
*2 cups oil (safflower or peanut)*
*½ cup apple cider vinegar*
*¼ cup lemon juice*
*1 bunch fresh green onions, cleaned and diced*
*4 teaspoons dry mustard*
*salt to taste*

After mixture is well blended, stir in

*⅓ cup poppy seeds*

## Crescent's Blue Cheese–Herb-Garlic Dressing

*Makes about 2¼ cups*

Most blue cheese dressings are way, way too mayonnaise-y and heavy for our taste. This lighter, refreshing one has the smooth richness of sour cream, the tang of yogurt, and the wonder of herbs, garlic, lemon, and black pepper.

Stir together with a whisk

*1 cup each yogurt and sour cream*

Scoop out half of this and combine it in the blender with

> *3 cloves garlic, crushed*
> *several sprigs fresh parsley*
> *assorted fresh herbs, a tablespoon or two's worth—basil, oregano,*
> *and thyme are perfect, with a tiny bit of rosemary added (or, if you*
> *must, a teaspoon of assorted dry herbs)*
> *the juice of 1 lemon*
> *several grinds of black pepper*
> *2 or 3 onions, diced*

Whirl this till smooth and stir back into the unblended yogurt–sour cream mixture with

> *crumbled blue or Roquefort to taste—use 3 tablespoons to ½ cup,*
> *depending on the cheese's sharpness*

Keeps about 1 week.

## Lemon Tahini Dressing

*Makes 2½ cups*

One last favorite dressing, one I have been using for years. It is rich and smooth, with a salty-sharp tang and an exotic flavor that comes from tahini, a ground-up "butter" of sesame seeds, used in many Middle Eastern dishes and available at natural foods stores (we like the A. H. Sahadi brand). This is one of those recipes that started scribbled on a paper napkin—in this case, the napkin, and the dressing, were from a Golden Temple Restaurant in Los Angeles, California, sixteen years ago. I've rung some changes on it over the years, but its delectable, surprising flavors are still as much of a pleasing taste revelation as they were to me the day I copied it from a chef who kept shrugging and saying, "And, well, you know . . ."

In a blender or food processor, buzz till smooth

> *1 cup tahini*
> *1 cup vegetable oil (not olive)*
> *¼ cup Tamari soy sauce*
> *⅓ cup lemon juice, preferably fresh*
> *1 stalk celery*
> *1 green pepper, seeded and chopped*

Keeps 1 week. Despite its health-foody sound, this has been one of my most often requested recipes over the years.

# Hors D'oeuvres: Superior Starters

Hors d'oeuvres literally means "outside the meal." Sometimes ours are—as when we do a cocktail buffet without a dinner to follow. More often they are part of the meal, a delectable first course designed to titillate and whet the appetite, not dull it, to prepare the palate for the feast to come. Sometimes, though, they make up the meal itself; many of our hors d'oeuvres work well as delicious, savory meatless entrées, perfect for our vegetarian guests.

We serve hot starters and cold, we serve finger foods and those that require a fork, we serve some that are "gift-wrapped" in pastry (phyllo dough, perhaps, or wonton wrappers or a from-scratch pastry shell) and some that are pastry themselves, as in Jean Gordon's Rocquefort Wafers or Parmesan Olive Balls, and some that are straightforward and completely free of even a hint of pastry—our array of hot and cold artichokes, for example. Many of our appetizers are built around that most festive and infinitely variable of foods, cheese: we heat it, we chill it, we combine it with an array of delicious ingredients, we stuff it into vegetables, we spread it on crackers.

But all our hors d'oeuvres are irresistibly savory.

# CHILLED HORS D'OEUVRES
## Stuffed Pea Pods

*Makes enough filling for 50 to 60 pea pods*

In our gardens each summer, we grow plenty of delectable sugar-snap peas. They're perfect eating absolutely any way: fresh from the vine, tossed into green salads, ever so lighly steamed. If you're not yet familiar with this variety, give it a try—its main virtue is its edible pod, as tasty as the sweet little peas inside. We developed these morsels to serve on our hors d'oeuvres trays. A single stuffed pod makes a nice garnish, too, to many other starters: a Jenelle's Tomatoes Rockefeller (p. 155), for instance, or a slice of Terrine (p. 169).

Pick and wash

*about 2 quarts edible-pod peas*

Set them aside. In a blender or food processor, cream together

*one 3-ounce package cream cheese*
*1/2 cup cottage cheese*
*1/4 cup watercress, washed and patted dry*
*1/4 cup almonds*
*1 tablespoon chutney*

We use our homemade Peach Chutney, for sale at the inn, an ambrosial stuff. Blend until smooth. Add

*3 tablespoons chopped freshly snipped chives*

Stir well and chill mixture for 30 minutes.
With pastry bag, pipe cream mixture into opened pea pods. Garnish each with

*3 radish slices*

Serve these dainties, which themselves look like flowers, with fresh flower garnishes.

◆───────────────────◆

*He that is of merry heart hath a continual feast.*

—*Proverbs VIII: 15*

# DIPS WITH CRUDITÉS

This, with its variations, is an all-time favorite dip for freshest garden vegetables. Nothing makes so beautiful an array at any big do as a table absolutely laden with the bounty of the garden; a lovely way to get a large group started.

Place vegetables of the same kind together for the most visual impact, and do as little to them as possible. Some—green beans, for instance—should be very lightly steamed before being put out; others —like cherry tomatoes—need nothing but a good wash, and if a little water is still glistening on them, so much the better. There are lovely pictures of such arrays in Martha Stewart's glamorous book, *Entertaining*. For a smaller number of people, of course, a platter of assorted vegetables will suffice.

But, however lovely they look, most people simply will not eat raw vegetables without something lovely to dip them into. Here is an assortment of such lovelies.

---

### DAIRY HOLLOW HOUSE FLOWERS: COLCHICUM

*Our favorite least-known flowering bulbs are the colchicum, an autumn-blooming beauty that is like a very large, vaselike crocus, six to eight inches tall, pink or white. Plant colchicums anytime in the summer, up till late August, and they will bloom for you obligingly that same fall. Sprinkle them in groups of three throughout the garden, a scoop of bonemeal in each colchicum hole. They look especially splendid with white and wine-red chrysanthemums, among the bright green of the out-of-bloom-season creeping phlox. We have been very happy with colchicums ordered from Van Bourgondien Brothers, Box A, Babylon, New York 11702.*

# Savory Onion and Herb Dip

*Makes 2½ to 3 cups*

In a skillet, sauté

*1 large onion, diced*

in

*2 tablespoons butter*

After onions are slightly cooked, pour in

*2 teaspoons Tamari soy sauce*

Cover and cook until onions are soft. Into a blender or food processor, put the onion mixture and

*1 cup mayonnaise (or ½ cup each sour cream and plain yogurt)*
*1 cup cottage cheese (or ricotta)*
*one 3-ounce package cream cheese*
*2 drops each Tabasco and Pickapepper sauce*
*2 tablespoons each chopped freshly snipped chives, parsley,*
*and basil*

Whirl in blender, chill, and serve.

### Spinach Version:

To blender container, add 1 cup fresh spinach, washed and dried. After whirling in the blender, chop finely and add 1 small can water chestnuts.

### Watercress Version:

Pick and wash 1 cup watercress. Pat dry and add to blender with other ingredients.

### Moscow Version:

Wash, steam until tender, and slice 6 to 8 beets. Add to blender container with 1 tablespoon Dijon mustard.
Eliminate Tabasco for this version.

## Natural Food Lovers' Delight

Substitute 1 cup plain yogurt for mayonnaise, 1 cup aduki bean sprouts, and 1 tablespoon peanut butter. Add sprouts to other blender ingredients. They give this dip a delicious crunchy flavor, along with a great nutritional bonus.

Crescent's Blue Cheese–Herb-Garlic Dressing (p. 142) as well as Lemon Tahini Dressing (p. 143) also make excellent dips.

*Note:* Any of these dips may be beautifully served in a pumpkin, or vegetable, "bowl." Make one by hollowing out the seeds and pulp of the prettiest little pumpkin you can find and then filling it with the dip—surrounding the bowl, of course, with a veritable garden of fresh vegetables. One can also remove most of the innards from half a large cabbage and use the cavity to hold dip. When Jan ran Moonflower Catering, such vegetable displays were one of her hallmarks, and she has served them, with assorted dishes, in assorted vegetable bowls, at countless picnics, weddings, dinners, and other festivities.

## Ramu's Tuna Pâté

*Makes about 6 cups*

This smooth, not-too-stiff pâté is excellent served in a crock, with sesame crackers and crispy vegetable slices. The blend of flavors is terrific—tuna, pistachios, cream cheese, dill.

Dissolve

*1 envelope unflavored gelatin*

in

*¼ cup cool water*

In blender or food processor, blend the gelatin-water mixture and

*2 cups tuna (two 7-ounce cans, water-packed, drained)*
*1 cup vegetable broth (see p. 91 for soup stocks and broths)*
*2 hard-boiled eggs*
*1 cup pistachios, hulled*
*one 8-ounce package cream cheese*
*juice of 1 lemon*
*¼ cup fresh parsley*
*1 teaspoon dill weed (either fresh or dried, though fresh is best)*

Whirl together until very well blended. Chill for at least 6 hours, or overnight. Served garnished with

*cucumber slices, very thin*
*plenty of fresh dill*

We also do a wonderful *Lentil Pâté*. We would love to give you the recipe, but it is done totally by tasting; we've never quite gotten the measurements even approximated on paper. But natural foods cooks, familiar with these unusual ingredients, will understand the putting together of it.

You do it in a food processor, beginning with 1 pound of dry lentils, cooked till soft. Into this, you process onions and mushrooms which have been sautéed in butter with garlic, as well as a good dollop of peanut butter, a couple of tablespoons dark miso, and a good handful of nutritional yeast. Seasonings: black pepper, garlic, herbs and spices to taste. Buzz, buzz. Taste, taste. This is almost identical to a very fine chicken liver pâté, though, dear knows, from reading the ingredients list, there's no reason it should. We like to finish this with a few drops of brandy. Of course, salt to taste. No kidding, this is great!

# A Midsummer's Night Buffet Feast at Which a Special Announcement Is Made

*Cold Hors D'oeuvres Tray:*
*Stuffed Pea Pods, Asparagus Vinaigrette,*
*Whole Baby Beets Vinaigrette, Crudités, Dips*

*Cold Soups in Chilled Mugs:*
*Chilled Caraway Squash Bisque, Cascadilla*

*Chilled Poached Trout*
*Middle Eastern Vegetables*
*Meringues with Vanilla Ice Cream, Fresh Raspberry Sauce,*
*Whipped Cream*
*Asti Spumante • Iced Tea • Hot Coffee*

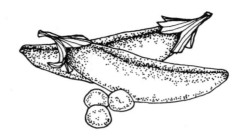

## Jean Gordon's Cucumber Mousse

*Serves 6 to 8, more if part of an hors d'oeuvres buffet*

Jean Gordon—wonderful potter, relaxed and easygoing hostess, lifelong peace activist—is one of our favorite people in Little Rock. She is also a fine and interesting cook. We love her Cucumber Mousse and enjoy it in several incarnations.

*Original Recipe:* Grate

*3 large peeled and seeded cucumbers*

Let stand 10 minutes and then squeeze out juice. Also grate

*1 medium onion*

Mix onion and cuke together while you soften

*1 envelope unflavored gelatin*

in

*½ cup fresh lemon juice*

Heat together till gelatin dissolves, and blend in food processor with cucumber and onion and

*1 cup heavy cream*
*1 cup mayonnaise*
*1 teaspoon salt*
*cayenne pepper and dill weed to taste (the dill is essential;*
*it and cucumber are flavors made for each other)*

Buzz quickly, and pour into a Pam-ed ring mold. Chill deeply, unmold, and garnish with cucumber slices. "Good with salmon," notes Jean. Good with anything, we think!

Actually, though, we have rarely eaten Jean's mousse this way because, like almost everyone, she sees no reason to load things unnecessarily with calories if there are wonderful substitutes. So she generally uses low-fat plain yogurt to replace mayonnaise. Sometimes, too, she substitutes ½ cup of cottage cheese for half the heavy cream. With these deviations, she uses a little extra gelatin—about 1½ envelopes.

## Theda's Chilled Stuffed Artichokes

*Makes enough filling for 4 artichokes*

Wonderful and pungent and refreshing, a great first course filled with the flavors of Greece and Provence and any sunny Mediterranean place you can imagine.

Have ready

*4 cooked artichokes*

Prepare for stuffing by opening each artichoke after it is cooked and gently scooping out the "choke" with a spoon, as well as the thornier inside leaves, making a cavity; also cut off the stem even with the base (reserve stem) so the artichoke can stand upright. Prepare and set aside

*1 recipe Lime Vinaigrette (see end of recipe)*

Combine in bowl and toss gently the soft portion of the cooked stem, diced, with

*6 ounces mozzarella cheese, cut into tiny dice*
*½ cup sliced black olives, preferably the purple-black Greek*
*Kalamata type*
*1 or 2 tablespoons feta cheese, crumbled*
*½ small red onion, sliced in half, then sliced crosswise*
*in paper-thin slices*

*(continued)*

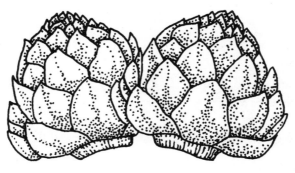

151

*1 or 2 ripe summer tomatoes, peeled, seeded,*
*and very finely chopped*
*¼ each red and green peppers, slivered finely (or 1 red pepper roasted*
*in oil, the bottled kind, finely diced)*

Shake or stir the waiting vinaigrette. Spoon about 4 tablespoons of it over the vegetable-olive-cheese mixture. Toss again, and taste. Season to taste with any or all of the following:

*1 or more cloves garlic, pressed*
*oregano and/or basil (if you can get fresh herbs and chop them fine,*
*so much the better)*
*perhaps the juice of ½ lemon*
*freshly ground black pepper*
*a few tablespoons finely chopped parsley*

Toss yet again; taste yet again. When mixture is savory, stuff into prepared artichoke cavities. Serve these artichokes deeply chilled on a romaine- or curly lettuce–lined plate, with a few cherry tomatoes and a scallion brush for a garnish, as well as a small dish of the remaining vinaigrette, one dish per diner, on each plate, for dipping the leaves into. Don't forget to provide a dish for the discarded artichoke leaves.

### Lime Vinaigrette

Follow Sharp Classic Vinaigrette with a Bite, page 139, but do a half-recipe. Use fresh lime juice instead of vinegar, omit mustard, and use only 1 small clove of garlic.

◆————————————————————◆

*I'm sitting in this courtyard,*
*My hands wrapped around this blue willow cup,*
*I'm watching the change in the seasons,*
*Letting those changes fill me up.*

*—Bill Haymes,*
*"Blue Willow Autumn".*

◆————————————————————◆

## Simple Chilled Summer Artichokes

*Serves 4*

We often eat artichokes this way in private life. They couldn't be easier or more delicious, and they are very low in calories.

Prepare by steaming and chilling

*4 artichokes*

Shortly before dining, mix the following delicious dipping sauce by whipping together

*½ cup plain yogurt*
*2 tablespoons coarsely ground French mustard, Pommery-type*
*(it comes in a small stoneware crock), or more, to taste*
*½ teaspoon grated horseradish (optional)*
*1 teaspoon each mayonnaise and sour cream (optional)*

Taste. If desired, season further with mustard or horseradish, as well as

*salt, freshly-ground black pepper, and perhaps a drop*
*of Tamari soy sauce*

Serve each artichoke on a chilled plate, quite cold, garnished with a sprig of fresh dill and a couple of thick, juicy slices of ripe tomato. Serve accompanied by a saucer of the mustard sauce.

A variation of this is to cut down on the mustard, omit the horseradish, add a crushed clove of garlic and 2 to 4 tablespoons of chopped fresh dill.

# HOT HORS D'OEUVRES

To get your party off to a hot start!

## "Hollow-Mades," or Stuffed Grape Leaves Our Way

*Makes 12 to 15*

In Greece, these little specialties are called *dolmades*, or "Stuffed Grape Leaves." We have developed our own Hollow-Mades by gathering wild grape leaves very close to home—right from our own Dairy Hollow House hillside.

First, take your basket and gather grape leaves, wild or tame, those lovely serrate-edge, round dark green leaves, getting the ones that are at least as big as your hand, the ones with hardly any holes in them. Gather lots, because they freeze very well. We keep a winter's supply well wrapped in the freezer. Wash the leaves thoroughly and pat dry.

*(continued)*

Tear off the tough stem. Stack, wrap well, and freeze. (This freezing process is important, as it softens the leaves. They can also be steamed lightly, if you use them fresh.) When ready to use, thaw the leaves and separate them, again patting them dry if necessary.

*Filling:* Cook according to package directions but without salt

*1 cup rice (brown rice, Uncle Ben's, basmati, and wild rice are all good)*

Meanwhile, in

*3 tablespoons butter*

sauté the following, all finely diced when necessary:

*5 or 6 green onions*
*1 green pepper*
*1 stalk celery*
*1 teaspoon fennel seed (optional but good; people are funny on fennel, though)*

When tender, add to cooked rice. Mix in

*½ cup finely chopped parsley*
*¼ cup finely chopped fresh mint leaves (the mint makes this, we think)*
*½ teaspoon cinnamon*
*¼ cup sunflower seeds*
*one 6-ounce can tomato paste*
*2 tablespoons Tamari soy sauce (more or less, to taste)*

Stir together well, and stuff grape leaves by placing a large spoonful in center of grape leaf, folding sides over and rolling loosely. Place, seam side down, in baking dish. Melt

*¼ cup butter*

with

*1 cup water*

Pour over grape leaves. Sprinkle with juice of

*2 lemons*

Bake at 325° for 1 hour.

### Crescent's Version

Omit cinnamon, tomato paste, sunflower seeds, and fennel. Use a bit more mint. Add a few raisins, and some oregano and dill. Use olive oil instead of butter, and simmer, very gently, over low heat, covered, for about 40 minutes, instead of baking in the oven.

## Jenelle's Tomatoes Rockefeller

*Serves 5*

I remember distinctly when I first discovered these morsels: it was at a potluck party in the back of Kay and Lonnie Powers' home in Little Rock. I went ape over these savory stuffed tomatoes and spent nearly an hour circulating among the guests and saying, "Excuse me, did you bring those little tomatoes with the sort of crusty, cheesey stuffing and I think spinach?" The bringer of tomatoes turned out to be none other than my friend Jenelle. I have made this ever since, using full-size tomatoes to make a vegetarian entrée of it and tiny cherry tomatoes to make an hors d'oeuvres.

Prepare

*about 20 cherry tomatoes or 4 to 6 full-size tomatoes*

for stuffing by cutting off blossom end, scooping out pulp (reserve for other use), and turning upside down to drain. Scooping out the tomato innards is easier if you have a serrate-edge grapefruit spoon. Leaving the tomatoes draining, in

*4 tablespoons butter*

sauté

*1 small onion, diced*
*2 cloves garlic, pressed*

*(continued)*

155

When onions soften, add

*½ cup soft whole wheat breadcrumbs*
*1 teaspoon oregano*
*½ teaspoon sweet basil*
*⅛ teaspoon dried rosemary*
*salt and pepper to taste*
*one 10-ounce box frozen chopped spinach, thawed well and drained*
*(I've also used fresh spinach, cooked and chopped,*
*and couldn't tell the difference, so why not?)*

Remove from heat and stir in

*1 well-beaten egg*
*¼ cup Parmesan cheese*

Preheat oven to 400°. Let spinach mixture cool until it can be handled, then stuff into prepared tomato shells. Bake stuffed tomatoes for about 20 minutes, or until the tops are slightly browned and crunchy. (For cherry tomatoes, bake for 10 to 12 minutes.) Ooh, so good!

## October Anniversary Dinner

*Mushrooms Diablo in Phyllo*
*Butternut Squash and Apple Soup II*
*Charlotte's Chicken Breasts French-Asian Grandmother*
*(For Vegetarians: Large Jenelle's Tomatoes Rockefeller )*
*Rice ● Stir-Fry of Zucchini, Green Beans, Onions*
*Honeyed Tarte aux Poires*
*Cinnamon Coffee*

## Hot Stuffed Artichokes Rockefeller

*Makes enough for 4 stuffed artichokes*

Preheat oven to 450°. Make

*1 batch of the breadcrumb stuffing in Jenelle's Tomatoes*
*Rockefeller, preceding recipe*

Stuff this into the cavities of

*4 artichokes, prepared for stuffing (see Theda's Chilled Stuffed Artichokes, p. 151)*

Bake the stuffed artichokes for about 15 minutes, or until fragrant and slightly brown. Serve each artichoke, very hot, with

*lemon wedge*
*small dish of melted butter per diner, for dipping leaves into*

---

### DAIRY HOLLOW HOUSE FLOWERS: BASKETS OF BOUNTIFUL BLOOMS

*Although we admire starkly simple Japanese arrangements, they're not our style, any more than single-buds-in-single-vases are. We like a generous, full, overflowing bouquet. Sometimes we do such a bouquet in a vase or pitcher, but often—particularly as a centerpiece for a buffet or as a room decoration—we do a basket of flowers. Of course, we have the best possible source of wonderful handmade baskets—a downtown store here in Eureka, Baskets and Such.*

*Here's how to do it: Line a good-size basket, preferably the kind with an arched handle, with thick plastic, the black kind from which heavy-duty trash bags are made. Gather together all the flowers you plan to use, and more. Soak florist's oasis until dripping wet, let drain, and press into basket, cutting to fit until basket is solidly filled.*

*Along the outer perimeter of the basket, place a ring of dense plant material, or, if you wish, line the entire edge with any sturdy, shiny leaf that has a good stout stem (magnolia leaves, for example). Then, place a central branch or stalk, the one that will be tallest in your arrangement, just off center to one side or the other of the basket's handle. Then, start filling in, grouping the flowers by type: three daffodils here, another three there, three more here; three irises, carefully positioned; a cloud of baby's breath; five white tulips; a branch of forsythia, and so on. Add and add and add. When you get finished, the basket should be a beautiful, generously overflowing mass of flowers. Check from every angle to make sure no oasis or plastic is visible.*

# Mushrooms Diablo

*Serves 4 to 6 as an appetizer, 2 or 3 as an entrée*

Hot, sweet, spicy, dark, and malevolent-looking, these mushrooms always thrill our guests. Judge Tom Glaze finished off a whole batch of them at a dinner, leaving his wife Phyllis only one teeny tiny portion. Of course he *did* later on write me a letter, on his official letterhead and all, thanking me and saying, "If there's ever anything I can do for you . . ." A letter like that from a judge could be very handy in the future!

These do very well as part of a lineup at a cocktail buffet, placed in a chafing dish after their savory sauce has been reduced.

In

*⅓ cup butter*

sauté

*1 large onion, cut into very thin crescents*

When transparent, add

*1 each red and green bell pepper, finely slivered*
*1 pound mushrooms, wiped with a damp paper towel if dirty,*
*and quartered*

Continue to sauté, over low heat, while you whisk together in a bowl

*⅔ cup red wine vinegar*
*2 tablespoons each Dijon mustard and Pickapepper sauce*
*(if available; if not, substitute a teaspoon of Tamari soy sauce*
*and several dashes of Tabasco)*
*3 tablespoons brown sugar*
*freshly ground black pepper and salt to taste*

When mushrooms have softened, raise the heat and pour over them the red wine mixture, adding

*3 tablespoons golden raisins*

Keep the heat medium high and, stirring often, let cook, uncovered, until the sauce has reduced greatly. Serve hot or at room temperature. Warning: People will be congregating in your kitchen as you cook this, because its aromas are totally tantalizing.

# COCKTAIL NIBBLES

Serve with cheese, with soup, with crudités, with anything.

## Parmesan Olive Balls

*Makes 36*

These crunchy, slightly fiery little nuggets are delightfully received by most guests. A cheese dough surrounds a green olive (try substituting a section of dilled green bean, an almond, or a tiny onion) and they are baked to a golden brown.

Preheat oven to 400°. In a mixing bowl, blend

> *½ cup butter, softened*
> *1½ cups sharp grated Cheddar cheese*
> *½ cup grated Parmesan cheese*

Add and stir until well blended

> *1 cup unbleached white flour, sifted*
> *½ teaspoon salt*
> *1 teaspoon paprika*
> *½ teaspoon cayenne*

Place on paper towel (to remove excess moisture)

> *about 36 olives (or other fillings—once I used ½-inch pieces of dilled green beans in place of the olives)*

With 1 teaspoon dough for each, wrap dough around olive, forming a small ball. Place on a baking sheet (the balls can be frozen at this point; thaw for 15 minutes only before baking) and bake for 10 to 15 minutes.

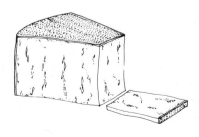

## Roquefort Wafers

*Makes 2½ dozen very thin wafers*

These are unbelievably delicate. From Jean Gordon.

Mix together

*7 tablespoons Roquefort cheese*
*7 tablespoons butter*
*4 teaspoons heavy cream*
*a pinch of salt*
*1 egg yolk*
*cayenne to taste*
*1 cup unbleached white flour*

Roll into a dough and let rest for 20 minutes. Either roll dough thin—about ⅛ inch thick—and cut into oval shapes, or form into an oblong log and refrigerate, slicing very thin later.

When ready to use, preheat oven to 400°. Place on an ungreased cookie sheet, the type that has no sides, and bake for 8 to 10 minutes, watching closely. Remove from sheet with great care, as they are extremely delicate. Serve as is, with any hors d'oeuvres. These are simply too melt-in-your-mouth good to be believed.

# SHOWSTOPPERS

These are hors d'oeuvres for when you want to knock their socks off, dazzle 'em, leave 'em begging for more, melting on the floor—and so on. Some, like the fabulous Vegetable Terrine or the Layered Crepe Torte, are a big deal to make. But some, like the Tidbits in Phyllo Dough, are shockingly simple, though every bit as impressive.

## TIDBITS IN PHYLLO DOUGH

What, you ask, is phyllo dough?

In general terms, it is your easy ticket to any number of absolutely melt-in-the-mouth hors d'oeuvres, entrées, or desserts, all so good that your guests will go into raptures over them, yet all so easy to make that you, their creator, may well feel like a con artist at such raves. For phyllo'd *anything* is delicious, and though people always do rave, the finished product in no way betrays the ease with which it was wrought.

More specifically, phyllo is an incredible pastry of Greek origin. Used correctly (and it is hard to do otherwise), the dough inside will bake up into many, many crisp, golden, crunchy layers, enfolding anything you wrap in them, from a chicken breast to a mushroom cap to an apple filling.

Phyllo is purchased ready-made. Tissue-paper thin, this white dough comes in rectangular sheets measuring about 12 inches by 18 inches. The sheets, 25 to 30 of them in a one-pound box, come stacked, and the stack is then rolled on top of itself in a cylinder and encased in a plastic bag. The bag, in turn, is placed in a box—a distinctively shaped long, narrow box—and it is this box that you may look for in your grocer's frozen food case with every possibility of finding. Believe me, it was not always so easy.

When I lived in New York I used to go to a Greek bakery called The Poseidon, in the sleaziest of neighborhoods—Eighth Avenue, in the mid-Forties—to purchase fresh-made phyllo and other wonderful Greek pastry. You could see the bakers in the next room—swarthy, muscular Greeks in clean white aprons—pulling the dough out, circling around and around a large wooden table with a peculiar light, almost dancing step. Even after I moved to Arkansas, for the next several years, I'd pay a call on the bright, sweet-smelling Poseidon whenever I returned to New York and bring back home to the Ozarks a huge supply of phyllo, which I'd stash in my freezer.

Times change. I do not know if the Poseidon still exists, for I gradually stopped going there as phyllo began to be available in frozen food cases, first in Little Rock . . . then in Rogers . . . then in Berryville . . . and just now, this year, right in our own Hart's Family Center here in Eureka. Phyllo at Hart's! I still can't get over it. But there it is, and the truth, unusual though it sounds, is that frozen phyllo is just as good as, if much less romantic than, the fresh I used to buy in Manhattan.

How does one work with phyllo? To break down the basically simple process into phases, one could say that there is thawing, handling, assembling, and baking. Let's go over these one by one. A choice of fillings and ideas follows.

## Thawing

Three days or so before you plan to use it, remove the phyllo from the freezer and let it thaw in the refrigerator. Two hours before, remove it from fridge and let it come to room temperature, still in its pristine plastic bag inside the box. By this point, hopefully, you have read through this recipe and decided if you are going to bake the phyllo dough as little individually stuffed triangles or as one big pan of pastry cut into diamonds with a very sharp knife. You have also decided which filling you are going to stuff the triangles/diamonds with, and have prepared it.

## Handling

Understand, before you open the bag, that phyllo is so very thin that it *dries out very quickly.* For this reason, you want to expose it to open air as little as possible until it has been brushed with melted butter, at which point it is protected from its former propensity toward drying to brittleness in the time it takes to swat a fly or answer the phone. Before opening the bag inside the box, have ready an adequate clean work surface; the prepared filling; a clean, slightly damp but not wet cloth towel; a clean pastry brush; and a quantity of melted butter. (If you were to make the entire box of dough into triangles, you would probably need about 3 sticks [1½ cups] melted butter. A pound of phyllo yields 40 to 60 appetizer-size triangles; we rarely need that many in a sitting, so we usually use half, rerolling the unused sheets of phyllo back into a cylinder, rebagging them, reboxing them, and refreezing them.)

Lay a sheet of wax paper out on your counter. Open the cellophane bag, unroll the phyllo sheets, and lay the whole stack of them on top of the wax paper, marveling at how thin each sheet is, and quickly covering the stack with the damp paper towel. Let rest, covered, for 5 to 15 minutes.

## Assembly

This goes fairly quickly, so preheat the oven to 350° before you start assembling.

*Triangles:* Remove one sheet of phyllo from the stack, quickly re-covering the stack. Quickly brush the entire sheet with melted butter, and quickly cut the sheet across, the short way, into four or five even strips. Each strip will become a triangle; five strips make smaller triangles, ideal for cocktail buffets or stand-up affairs; four strips make slightly larger triangles more appropriate for sit-down appetizers.

Place a rounded teaspoon of filling in one corner of each of the strips, and, if your recipe so directs, a bit of grated cheese over that. Fold another corner of phyllo over the filling, and continue folding the package over itself, sort of as if you were (a) folding paper for a paper airplane or (b) folding a flag the way they taught you at Girl Scouts. Any excess dough can be tucked in. Although the object is to achieve neat, uniform triangles, in fact, as long as the filling is enclosed securely, it doesn't matter whether the triangles are neat or uniform; they will all taste delicious when baked, and people will be far too busy exclaiming in delight to carp about or even notice your folding technique.

Repeat with the remaining phyllo, keeping the stack covered with the towel as much as possible, and making as many as you wish. Remember, the unused phyllo dough, if rewrapped securely, will keep in the refrigerator for up to a month, and will keep, refrozen, almost indefinitely.

Place the triangles on a Pam-ed cookie sheet.

*Diamonds-in-a-Pan:* This is a bit faster going than the triangles. This is the classic way the Greek pastry baklava is made. You will need a rectangular baking dish, well Pam-ed. You can play around with the pan size by manipulating the phyllo dough leaves, but something in the 10- × -14-inch size is a good bet.

Remove one sheet of phyllo from stack, recovering stack. Place the sheet in the baking dish, draping one side over one side of the baking dish, leaving an overhang of perhaps two inches extra, the rest of the sheet lying flat in pan. Brush with melted butter. Lay in another sheet, draping it so another edge of the pan is covered. Brush with butter. Repeat, with the overhang switching from edge to edge. When you have used up about half the phyllo dough, spread the filling over the dough and then begin stacking sheets one at a time, buttering each, over the filling. Tuck the excess in with the top sheets, and fold in the overhang from the bottom phyllo here and there.

When all phyllo is used up and the whole is well brushed with melted butter, cut diagonally into diamonds with a very sharp knife. If you don't cut the diamonds before baking, you will be unable to cut them, or any other shape, afterward.

## Baking

Preheat oven to 350°. Bake triangles for about 25 minutes. They should be a deep golden brown; a too-pale golden brown means the phyllo layers inside are still a bit underdone and there will be a slight doughy taste. Break one open to check; filling should be steaming, bubbling hot. Serve immediately, on a warm garnished plate. A baking dish of diamonds will take longer—35 to 40 minutes—before the desired deep-golden state is reached.

See how easy it is?

- Although the filled, unbaked triangles *can* be refrigerated for up to 24 hours before baking, we think there is a noticeable loss of quality. We prefer to make up the filling in advance but to do the actual assembly at the last minute.

- Completed unbaked triangles can be frozen and then baked, *without defrosting*, for about 40 minutes. This works better than storing them refrigerated, we think, but the freshly done ones are still superior.

- Occasionally freezer-case phyllo sheets will stick to each other slightly and tear apart when you try to separate them. *Don't worry.* The essential thing about phyllo is, if you work with it one layer at a time, or even one scrip or scrap of a layer at a time, and brush it adequately with butter, even the most ragtag collection of phyllo odds and ends can be rolled around a filling so as to enclose it in some way, and they will still bake into those distinctive, delicious, crisp buttery layers. They may be trapezoids,they may be pyramids, but they will taste fabulous.

### Fillings
Our two favorite mixed fillings are:

## International Stir-Fry

*Filling for 1 pound phyllo*

In

*2 tablespoons butter*

sauté

*½ onion, cut into thin crescents*

Add, tossing in the butter

*1 carrot, sliced in tiny julienne*
*1 broccoli stalk, peeled and sliced in julienne*
*the broccoli florets, in slightly larger pieces*

Cover, steam for 3 minutes, raise cover, and add

*½ zucchini, cut in julienne the size of a smallish French fry*
*3 or 4 mushrooms, sliced*

Toss, stir-frying over medium heat, for about 3 minutes, seasoning with dashes of

*Tamari soy sauce*
*sweet basil*

When vegetables are still on the crisp side, remove from heat and stir in

*a few tablespoons frozen green peas*
*4 or 5 water chestnuts, peeled and sliced, fresh if available,*
*canned if not*

The finished stir-fry should be on the crisp side when done, and also not too juicy. Cool to room temperature. Have ready

*1 cup grated Swiss or Jarlsberg cheese*

Fill each triangle with a teaspoon of the stir-fry and a bit of grated cheese. For the pan diamonds, double the recipe and spread out all the filling on top of the bottom layer of the phyllo, sprinkle with the cheese, and top with remaining phyllo.

## Ratatouille

Everyone has a favorite version of this Provence summer delight in which onions, garlic, zucchini, tomato, eggplant, and occasionally green beans are simmered together in olive oil. For use as a phyllo filling, we like to do a quick-cook version, with everything cut into tiny dice, and a bit of tomato paste added to intensify the tomato flavor. Again, we also add water chestnuts, sliced, to the finished product—we really like that crunch. We do use a sprinkle of cheese atop the ratatouille, usually a Cheddar.

*(continued)*

For other, very good fillings, try

- Mushrooms Diablo, page 158
- The thick tomato filling in Italian Crepe Torte aux Arcs, page 232
- The ricotta-and-zucchini filling in Anne's Chicken with Zucchini Florentine, page 196
- The spinach filling from Jenelle's Tomatoes Rockefeller, page 155

And, lastly

## Asparagus or Poke Salat Cylinders Phyllo

*Makes two dozen*

Steam till tender-crisp

*2 dozen stalks of asparagus or poke, tough ends removed*

Remove from heat, plunge under cold water, and dry well.
Combine the following, mashing to a smooth paste

*½ cup each grated Swiss, Gruyère, or Jarlsberg*
*1 teaspoon Dijon mustard*
*1 tablespoon butter, softened*
*3 cloves garlic, pressed*
*juice of ½ lemon*
*4 green onions, very finely chopped*
*2 tablespoons finely minced fresh parsley*
*fresh ground black pepper to taste*

Have ready

*8 sheets of phyllo*

Working with one sheet at a time, with asparagus and cheese mixture both close at hand, brush each sheet with

*melted butter*

Then cut each sheet into thirds, going the short way. On each third, parallel to the short end of the phyllo and about 1 inch in, lay a stalk of the steamed asparagus or poke. Along the stalk, dab/spread some of the prepared paste. Folding up edges of phyllo to enclose stalk on all sides, roll asparagus up to form a cylinder. Bake as for triangles, though they get done a bit faster.

We also like *Mushroom Cap Packets in Phyllo* done this way: whole mushroom caps, stems removed, are steamed/stir-fried with butter and garlic and Pickapepper sauce and white wine, the liquid completely reduced at the end. Season with salt and black pepper, place on thirds of buttered phyllo, which fold up into a neat square surrounding mushroom (you may also add the cheese treatment, p. 165).

# Publication Party for a Book on the Fall List

*Crepe Torte Mediterranée aux Arcs*
*Jenelle's Tomatoes Rockefeller*
*Assorted Tidbits in Phyllo*
*Spinach Dip in a Pumpkin* • *Ramu's Tuna Pâté* • *Crudités*
*Ample and Interesting Cheese Tray:*
*Brie, Extra-Sharp New York Cheddar, Black Pepper Boursin, Chive*
*Chèvre, Stilton, Jarlsberg, Feta Cheese Slices with a Drizzle of*
*Olive Oil and Fresh Herbs*

*Breadbasket with Two Ryes:*
*Sweet-Sour Rye, Two Sisters Russian Black Rye*
*Butter* • *Assorted Mustards*
*Bowl of Polished Granny Smith Apples*
*Cookies: Viennese Nut Crescents, Chocolate-dipped*
*Oatmeal-Walnut Cookies*
*Cocktails* • *"Mocktails"*
*Hot Coffee*

## Feta Cheese Tartlets in Crepe Cups
## with Fresh Sage and Onions

*Makes 12 small crepe cups*

Silvery green sage grows beautifully in our garden. That, and a love of feta, and a pile of crepes, and a yen for an interesting quiche, combined last summer to give rise to this enchanting savory starter. It's one of those recipes guests are always writing back to us for. We love it as a beginning for almost any summer dinner.

Make

*crepes, page 224*

*(continued)*

After they have cooled, fit one into each of the twelve cavities of a greased muffin tin. Preheat oven to 350°. Set aside the muffin tin while in

*2 tablespoons butter*

you sauté

*1 bunch green onions, chopped*
*½ each red onion and yellow onion, finely chopped*

As these cook, beat together in a smallish bowl

*3 eggs*
*1 tablespoon sour cream*
*⅔ cup half-and-half*
*3 or 4 slivered leaves of fresh sage (1 teaspoon dried if you must)*
*good grind of fresh black pepper*

When onions have softened, let them cool slightly and turn them into the egg mixture with

*¾ cup or so crumbled feta cheese (if feta is extremely salty,*
*you may want to rinse it first)*

Fold all together and spoon carefully into the crepe cups. Bake till set —about 25 minutes. Serve immediately, garnished with, of course, a spray of fresh sage leaves.

## Walnut Wings

*Makes two dozen, from one package wonton wrappers*

This delicious Jan Brown creation always garners raves. It's an inspired combination: melting, creamy cheese and a crisp walnut, encased in a pastry that is simple because it is purchased ahead as—well, read on and you'll see! An example of how Arkansas thinking, culinary creativity, and international flavor blend so well for us here: Jan had intended a phyllo dough hors d'oeuvres; Hart's was out of phyllo but had wonton wrappers. The accompanying illustration above explains the folding described in the recipe.

Purchase a package of 3-inch-square wonton wrappers. For each walnut wing, place

*½ teaspoon cream cheese or ricotta*
*1 walnut half*

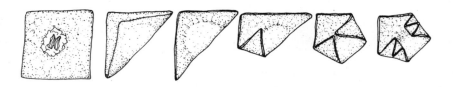

on wonton wrapper. Fold wrapper in half diagonally, moistening tip with a bit of water to seal. Fold sides in to form "wings," also sealing with water. Fry quickly in preheated skillet, using

*½ cup safflower oil*

Fry on each side until golden brown. Drain.

We serve 3 per person on each plate with little "puddles" of our homemade apple butter or our best chutney, and fresh flower garnishes. Ecstasy!

## Vegetable Terrine Wrapped in Romaine

*Yield: one large loaf-shape terrine, makes 10 to 12 servings*

A marvelous creamy pâté, perfect for an all-out or "important" dinner. As beautiful to look at as it is to taste, layers of savory vegetables, alternated with a voluptuous vermouth-drenched creamy cheese mixture, are enrobed in steamed romaine lettuce leaves and baked in a loaf pan. The whole thing is quite a production. The finished terrine *must* chill. We do it a day or two or three before the big event. Also, you don't absolutely have to do *all* the layers; it's smashing with even a few.

*(continued)*

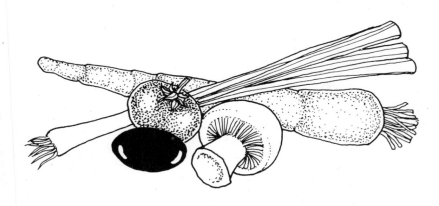

Wash and separate

> *1 head romaine lettuce (about 12 of the large outer leaves)*

Set the washed lettuce aside. Now prepare, one after the other, the Cheese Layer, the Spinach Layer, the Tomato Layer, the Scallion Layer, the Carrot Layer, the Black Olive Layer, and the Mushroom Layer, as follows:

*Cheese Layer:* Mix together in a large bowl

> *one 8-ounce package cream cheese, softened*
> *1 cup ricotta cheese*
> *6 eggs, beaten*
> *1/3 cup vermouth*
> *1/2 cup unbleached white flour*
> *2 to 4 cloves garlic (to taste), pressed*
> *2 tablespoons Tamari soy sauce*
> *1 teaspoon Tabasco sauce*
> *2 tablespoons melted butter*

Set aside. One taste of this, even raw, will give you a hint as to how spectacular the completed terrine is going to be.

*Spinach Layer:* Wash well

> *1 pound spinach, tough stems removed*

Squeeze and place on paper towels to dry. Chop fine, either by hand or with the steel blade of a food processor, and stir in

> *1/2 teaspoon nutmeg*

Set aside.

*Tomato Layer:* Chop

> *2 whole fresh tomatoes*

Place chopped tomatoes in frying pan and cook over medium heat. Add

> *1 teaspoon minced basil (fresh, if available)*

Cook and stir until liquid evaporates and mixture is quite dry—about 30 minutes. Let cool.

*Scallion Layer:* Sauté

> *1 cup chopped green onions with*
> *2 tablespoons butter*

Add to sauté pan

*1 cup heavy cream*

Stir and simmer over very low heat until cream thickens—about 20 minutes. Cool.

*Carrot Layer:* Square

*4 large carrots*

by cutting off the curved outside and the last bit of the tapering tip. Cut each squared carrot into quarters the long way, so you end up with 16 long squared carrot pieces. Steam them for about 3 minutes, and cool them quickly with a dip in ice water. Do not overcook. Drain, dry, and set aside.

*Black Olive Layer:* Just have ready

*1½ cups whole pitted black olives*

*Mushroom Layer:* Sauté

*12 to 15 medium-size mushrooms*

in

*2 tablespoons butter*
*1 teaspoon Tamari soy sauce*

until golden brown and liquid is absorbed.
   Pause. Survey your completed fillings. Take a deep breath. Clean up the kitchen, and continue.

*Assembly and Baking:* Place steaming basket in large canner with about 1 inch of water. Steam romaine lettuce leaves for about 1 minute. Remove lettuce leaves from canner and plunge into very cold water (to retain clear green color). Remove from cold water, rinse a few times, and let drain in colander. Let cool. When it has, line a Pam-ed 9- × -5-inch bread pan with the chilled romaine leaves, leaving edges to hang over sides of bread pan, and overlapping the leaves. Reserve a few of the steamed leaves.
   Soon the vegetable layers you have labored so diligently to prepare will be alternated with the cheese layers in the romaine-lined pan, and the whole shebang will be baked.
   Preheat oven to 450°.
   Spread scallion layer over romaine leaves in the bottom of loaf pan. Then place on top of the scallion layer the olives, laying them

171

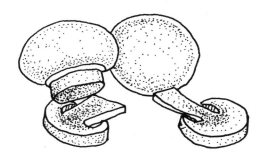

neatly side by side, in little rows like soldiers, all facing with their pit cavities in the same direction. The scallion layer should be completely covered with the lined-up olives.

Spread over this, very carefully so as not to disarrange the olives, 1 cup of the cheese layer mixture, and place atop it the spinach layer, evenly distributed over the cheese. Then another 1 cup of carefully spread-on cheese. Then the carrot layer, all the carrot sticks laid on an angle with their edges touching, so they will float, like little diamond-shape kites, in the middle of the creamy cheese, when the terrine is cut open. Cut the carrots to fit the length of the pan evenly, and leave about ½ inch between each line of carrots. The way the terrine should now look, looking down on it, is a creamy bed of cheese with five strips of joined-together carrot pieces, the cheese visible between the strips of carrots. Cover this with another cup of cheese, pressing in gently so the filling settles in between the carrots. Now spread on the tomato layer. Top with the remaining cheese, smooth carefully, and top with the reserved steamed romaine. Fold the overlapped romaine leaves over the whole thing.

Whew!

Cover the loaf pan with aluminum foil or, if by any chance it has one, its own cover. Set the loaf pan into a larger 9-×-13-inch baking pan. You are going to bake the terrine surrounded by hot water, which helps it bake more evenly. Once the larger pan, with the smaller resting in it, is in the oven, leave the door open and pour 1½ inches of hot water into the larger pan. Lower the oven temperature to 375°, and bake for 45 minutes. Lower the heat to 325°, and bake for another 30 to 45 minutes.

Remove the terrine pan from the water pan and set it on a wire rack to cool, removing the foil or lid. Cool for 30 minutes. Cover with plastic wrap and put terrine (still in its baking pan) into refrigerator and cool thoroughly (at least 4 hours or overnight).

Turn out the thoroughly cooled terrine onto a serving platter; serve in slices, as you would a loaf of bread. Each slice will glimmer with the carrot squares, the round O's of the olives, the tiny green ribbons of spinach, the rosy red tomatoes, the brown and savory mushrooms. Lay the slices on their sides on chilled plates, and garnish with

*Deviled Whipped Cream Sauce:* Whip with electric mixer until light and airy

*1 cup whipping cream*

Fold in

*2 teaspoons grated horseradish*

Whip till stiff. Pipe this through a larger star tip around each terrine slice. Or, if you don't enjoy working with a piping tube, put a dollop of Deviled Sauce beside each slice. In either case, finish the presentation with a raw mushroom slice, an olive slice, and a sprig of parsley. This sauce, by the way, does wonders for many summer dishes. It's great with Boeuf en Gelée, a beef dish any classic cookbook can offer a recipe for.

As for the terrine, amen! We really like layered dishes that are cut in such a way as to reveal the beautiful contrasting fillings inside. It's a trick we exploit to great advantage in our Crepe Torte, which you will find in the Vegetarian Entrées chapter, and which we often serve as an hors d'oeuvres, cold, hot, or lukewarm. This basic terrine, too, we do in lots of ways. We sometimes omit one or two of the vegetable layers to make it a bit simpler, or we use black olives alternated in rows with pimento-stuffed green olives. Asparagus, laid crosswise like the carrots, is a wonderful addition; we think steamed scallions might also be interesting . . .

We have also done terrines that featured purees of seasoned lentils, bound with beaten egg and a bit of cornstarch, for a rich, brown, pâtélike layer, and terrines that had a beautiful golden-orange layer of mashed sweet potato . . .

Terrines are dishes that should only be undertaken by people who really love to cook, for they are a lot of work, and they also lend themselves to innovation, which only kitchen experience can pull off. Well, not *only* kitchen experience, but imagination. And love. And, in the words of Georges Jacques Danton, "Boldness, again boldness, and ever boldness."

# Sunday Chicken
# All Week Long

Chicken is one of the Ozarks main agricultural products, and we would indeed be foolish if we did not take advantage of all this local bounty. Tender, relatively inexpensive, chicken can be beautifully prepared in ways limited only by the cook's imagination. When fresh fish is not available, chicken is our guests' most frequent choice of dinner entrée, and we have eagerly developed and collected many, many interesting ways with it. Some, like so many of our recipes, take a nod from international cooking, particularly French; some have strictly local origins; there are two from Crescent's mother, one from an inn guest, even one from the president of the Bank of Eureka Springs.

Yet whatever their provenance, most of the thousands of chicken recipes the world over amount to one of the following five methods. Either the chicken is simply browned on top of the stove until it is cooked through or it is browned lightly and then covered with savory liquid and braised, either on top of the stove or in the oven, until done, or it is broiled under direct heat (perhaps marinated first), or it is baked (roasted) stuffed or unstuffed, covered or uncovered. Of course, we've also managed to work in a few exceptions to this rule, including that all-time country classic of the South, fried chicken, which Jan makes two or three times a year and makes better than anyone in the world, calories notwithstanding.

Most of our favorite chicken recipes, however, take the brown-and-braise path, which we think as a rule results in the most tender, flavorful chicken, with the extra dividend of lots of delicious sauce. The sauce may be creamy or tomato-y; it may be enlivened with herbs, with Dijon mustard, with garlic or wine; but the chicken is always the better for its sojourn therein, and the sauce benefits from the chicken's presence. Chicken done this way—or these ways, for there are infinite variations on this theme, depending on which liquids are used for braising—can be made in advance and does not mind waiting for late guests. Whole cut-up chickens are often done this way, as in our Marengo or Country Captain recipes, or our country-style old-fashioned fricassee, or a couple of the other good ones that follow.

Still along this line but more elegant—also much more fussy and last-minute—is a chicken-breast-only, quick stove-top variation on this theme: a chicken breast, usually boned, usually pounded thin, perhaps stuffed, is browned lightly, quickly, over high heat and then finished off with a little cream, or sour cream, or brandy, or diced tomato. The technique for any of these versions is almost identical, though being last-minute, somewhat less versatile: it decidedly does not wait well.

If a meal is already on the rich side, though, we may shy away from these rich creations. Chicken is an adaptable fowl, as good simply done as dressed in company clothes. Sometimes, especially in the summer when perfect vegetables are at their peak, we like to build a nonvegetarian meal around two or three really special vegetable prep-arations: a fresh corn soufflé baked in a green pepper half, for instance, and a tomato stuffed with sour cream and green chili, and some sort of glazed carrot, plus a bounteous salad. With this, we serve chicken that has simply been rubbed with garlic and butter and all manner of fresh herbs from the garden and the juice of a half lemon, and then quickly broiled. Or we may marinate the chicken pieces first, again, simply, before broiling them. Simply done chicken with a garden full of perfectly done vegetables, attentively presented on a plain white plate, makes a lovely summer supper. We usually serve a dab of one of our herb jellies—lime-mint, or apple-sage, or sweet basil—with such a plate.

We do roast chicken once in a while, and when we can get Cornish game hens, they too are roasted, with a last-minute browning under the broiler. Roasting is a simple and classic poultry treatment, poten-tially dull—ours is enlivened by extraspecial, fruit-enriched stuffing and, usually, a glaze of peach or apricot jam seasoned with a bit of this and that . . . some ginger, some garlic, a dab of soy sauce. Out of this world—yet very much of it, an earthy harvest-time pleasure.

And our chicken repertoire would not be complete without a recipe for that sublime pairing of chicken breasts with our old friend phyllo dough—tender, meaty chicken, made savory with Dijon, baked in a crispy, crunchy, many-layered wrapping.

## Lemon-Pepper Chicken

*Serves 2 generously, 4 lightly*

Here is our favorite treatment for broiled chicken. Fresh and clean-tasting. Good hot or cold, in a picnic basket.

First, the marinade. Bring to a boil the following

*¼ cup tarragon vinegar*
*2 tablespoons peppercorns, cracked, or 1 tablespoon*
*fresh coarsely ground black pepper*
*1 teaspoon salt*
*¼ cup brown sugar*

Remove from heat and pour into a glass or pottery bowl. Add

*½ cup fresh-squeezed lemon juice*
*1 teaspoon grated lemon rind*
*½ cup mild-flavored vegetable oil (peanut or corn)*

Mixture should now be at room temperature. Add

*one 2½- to 3-pound broiler-fryer chicken, cut into serving pieces*

and marinate overnight or for several hours. Toss chicken pieces occasionally to distribute marinade.

Preheat oven to 325°. Lift chicken from marinade and place on greased baking dish. Bake for about 20 minutes, basting twice with marinade. Then slide the baking dish under the broiler and broil the chicken, turning once, for 10 to 12 minutes per side and basting with marinade every few minutes, until it has browned nicely. Broiling is always a bit dicey to give directions for, as each broiler is so different, and some can get the object being broiled closer to or farther away from the flame than others, so know thy broiler and adapt the timing on this accordingly. Serve this tangy chicken with rice; garnish with a lemon wedge.

*And we meet, with champagne and a chicken, at last.*

——*Lady Mary Wortley Montagu (1689–1762),*
The Lover

## An Ozark Classic: Jan's Country-fried Chicken with Milk Gravy

*Serves 6 to 8*

Jan Brown knows her chicken-frying. A third-generation Kansas farm girl, she grew up on her mother's and grandmother's fried chicken. For this, the chickens were killed directly before preparation, a preparation always simple but attentive to the small details. It's the details—the perfectly fresh oil at just the right temperature, in an iron skillet (never, never a deep fat fryer), the onion added to the pan for just the subtlest flavoring to the dish, the paprika added to the flour mixture for good browning—that make this dish sublime, a world away from the tough, greasy parts that pass as fried chicken at fast-food emporiums. Do not jazz up the breading mixture with crushed cornflakes, herbs, or anything else; leave this classic alone.

Jan remembers the fights that broke out among the nine children in her family over who would get the "crispy" left on the paper towels the finished chicken drained on. She remembers the sweet milk gravy her mother made, and how her Uncle Pete would judge a man by the pieces of chicken he selected from the platter: if he took one good piece, like a drumstick or thigh, and one bad piece, like a back or neck, he was deemed unselfish, kind. But a man who took *two* good pieces was apt to steal from his own mother!

*(continued)*

The wages of fried chicken are living with the smell of fried chicken lingering in your kitchen for days, which is why we don't make it at the inn, and only once or twice a year at home. But it is simply too good, when we do make it, and too deeply Ozark, not to include in this book. Remember, follow directions exactly.

Place in a large shallow dish

*one 2½- to 3-pound frying chicken, cut into serving pieces*

Cover with

*1 cup buttermilk or sweet milk*

Let sit for 10 minutes, while preparing the flour mixture and heating the oil as follows. Preheat in a 10- or 12-inch cast-iron skillet

*3 cups vegetable oil (safflower is Jan's first choice;*
*peanut would be Crescent's;*
*Jan's grandma used Crisco or bacon grease)*

over a medium flame. You want the oil to reach about 375°; use a thermometer. As oil heats, blend together in a large bowl

*2 cups unbleached white flour*
*3 teaspoons paprika*
*1 teaspoon salt*
*½ teaspoon freshly ground black pepper*

Remove chicken from milk and dip each piece of chicken into the flour mixture. Dredge thoroughly.

◆━━━━━━━━━━━━━━━━━━━━━━━━━━━━━━━━━━━━━◆

### DAIRY HOLLOW HOUSE FLOWERS: SUMMER

*Summer arrangements: Queen Anne's Lace, field daisies, wild roses, and honeysuckle sprays; shasta daisies, pink* Achillea *(yarrow), Martha Washington pink-and-white-striated geraniums, pink and fuchsia cosmos, and three long-stemmed wine-red roses; Grand Commander lily with tall wild grasses, field daisies, pink* Achillea *(yarrow), pink nicotiana, and pink zinnias; field daisies, yellow and orange marigolds, and tiger lilies or day lilies; blue salvia, blue iris (from the florist), and white zinnias; red zinnias, yellow yarrow, and a cloud of flowering chamomile; purple lilacs, blue iris (from the florist), blue scabiosas, long trailers of honeysuckle, and pink or lavender alliums.*

When oil has reached 375°, place floured pieces in pan, crowding pieces in until all the chicken has been accommodated. Now cut into quarters

*1 medium-size onion*

Fit it into the pan among the various chicken pieces. Cover the skillet with a lid and cook over medium heat for 12 to 15 minutes. Then turn each piece with tongs or a fork. Fry, covered, for 10 more minutes. Remove the lid and continue frying for 5 more minutes, until golden brown and fork-tender. Drain chicken on paper towels (some old-timers drained theirs on a folded brown paper bag). Let chicken sit while you prepare the gravy.

*Milk Gravy:* Pour off and discard all the oil from the skillet except for about 3 tablespoons. (Be sure to leave all those little crumbles in the skillet—they give the gravy a wonderful texture and flavor.) Blend into the oil

*4 tablespoons unbleached flour*

Stir flour-and-oil mixture until smooth. Place the skillet over medium heat and whisk while gradually adding

*1½ cups milk (if you are cooking potatoes, for mashed potatoes,*
*the classic accompaniment to fried chicken,*
*you may use half potato cooking water and half milk)*

Whisk and stir and stir and whisk until gravy is smooth and thickened and piping hot and completely free of any raw flour taste. Add

*salt and freshly ground pepper to taste (go easy on salt*
*if you are using 'tater water as part of the liquid)*

Pour finished gravy into your favorite gravy boat. Serve with the warm, just-fried chicken. True country feasts' accompaniments—the kind Jan grew up with—would be mashed potatoes with plenty of butter, corn on the cob, buttermilk biscuits, homemade blackberry jam, more butter, freshly sliced tomatoes, cole slaw, and summer peach pie. Yum!

## Old-Fashioned Sunday-in-the-Country Chicken Dinner

*Relish Tray: Olives, Carrot and Celery Sticks, Radishes*
*Thickly Sliced Garden Tomatoes*
*Fresh Corn on the Cob ● Butter ● Maple-glazed Carrots*
*Country Chicken Fricassee or Jan's Country-fried Chicken with*
*Milk Gravy*
*Angel Biscuits ● Assorted Jellies, Relishes, Pickles*
*Lemon Sour Cream Pound Cake*
*Iced Tea ● Coffee*

*On the table:* Daisies in a blue-and-white pitcher

## Chicken Marengo Our Way

*Serves 2 generously, 4 lightly*

The classic version of this is a bit tomato-y for our tastes. We cut down on the tomato as well as the amount of butter and oil originally called for (this is plenty buttery enough!). Then we added a few more herbs and threw in some raisins for that faint contrasting touch of sweetness we like so well in many dishes. This is an excellent casserole for a buffet, since it only profits from being made a day or two ahead and then reheated. It also freezes successfully, so why not double the recipe and put half aside?

This should be served over either rice or lightly buttered noodles, to soak up its good juice. French bread at the table offers additional scooping-up-the-juice options. A simple green salad with a good vinaigrette, a creamy-fruity dessert like Persimmon Mousse (p. 288) or Honeyed Zabaglione Napolean with fresh fruit (p. 296), and you have a wonderful, wonderful company meal, most of which can be done in advance.

In

*2 tablespoons* each *butter and olive oil*

brown lightly

*one 2½-pound frying chicken, quartered*

As the pieces brown, transfer them to a heavy-bottom Dutch oven. Next, in the same pan in which chicken was browned, sauté

*1 onion, chopped*

When onion softens, add and sauté for 1 minute more

*4 cloves garlic, minced*

Then add, whisking in

*an additional tablespoon olive oil*
*⅓ cup unbleached white flour*

Cook for about a minute, over medium-low heat, stirring constantly. Then pour in

*1 cup white wine*
*1½ cups good strong chicken broth*

stirring constantly to deglaze pan and assure the smoothness of the sauce. When sauce is smooth and thick, stir in

*3 fresh tomatoes, peeled and chopped (or about 1½ cups canned,*
*if that's all that's available)*

Pour over the browned chicken waiting in the Dutch oven. Sprinkle the chicken and sauce with

*½ cup golden raisins*
*½ teaspoon or so freshly ground black pepper or 5 or 6 whole black*
*peppercorns that have been crushed*
*¼ teaspoon each crumbled leaf thyme and basil*
*1 bay leaf*
*a few needles of rosemary*

Stir well to combine; bring all to a boil; turn down heat and let simmer for about an hour. Meanwhile, sauté

*a dozen or so small white onions, peeled, left whole*
*½ pound mushrooms (if small, leave whole; otherwise, slice)*
*2 carrots, sliced*

*(continued)*

in

*a little butter (since this already has so much butter and oil in it,
we use the absolute minimum here,
first coating skillet with Pam spray)*

When vegetables are slightly softened, remove them from heat and put
them in a greased ovenproof casserole—the one you intend to serve
from. Sprinkle the vegetables in their dish with

*the juice of ½ lemon
1 cup large pitted black olives, sliced in fat rounds*

Meanwhile, back at the chicken, its hour of simmering should be up.
Remove the chicken pieces from the sauce and lay them in among the
olives, mushrooms, etc., in the casserole. As for the sauce remaining
in the chicken cooking pot, you may strain it or not as you prefer; do
you want it smooth or with a bit of texture to it? (Our personal preference, both for ease and taste, is to leave it chunky, but picking out
the whole bay leaf if we can find it.) In either case, in other words,
after straining or not, return the sauce to the fire and bring it to a boil,
stirring often, for about 5 to 10 minutes, to reduce this slightly savory
liquid. Between stirs, heat oven to 375°.

Pour the reduced sauce over the chicken and vegetables in the
casserole, and lastly sprinkle on

*4 to 6 tablespoons cognac* or *brandy*

Reheat in oven for 10 minutes covered, another 10 minutes uncovered,
and serve, piping hot, with a garnish of fresh chopped parsley.

## Elsie's Chicken Country Captain

*Serves 2 amply, 4 more lightly*

Another dish where the chicken is first browned, then braised in
savory liquid. Another classic from our friend, fine cook and jewelry
designer Elsie Freund. At first glance, this might sound similar to the
Marengo recipe, but the addition of curry powder and the absence of
wine or cognac give it a very different character—deliciously, subtly
spicy; faintly exotic. Double this for a buffet; it stands well and can
easily be made in advance. Delectable, and just-falling-off-the-bone
tender, it's a perfect dish, we think, in very cold weather, like the New
Year's Eve we served it to four Texas guests, one of whom told us a
joke about a three-legged chicken . . . but that's another story.

Preheat oven to 275°. Sauté

*⅓ cup chopped parsley*
*2 green peppers, chopped*
*½ cup finely diced fresh parsley*

in

*2 tablespoons mild vegetable oil*

When tender, add

*2 cups canned whole tomatoes with their juice (one 20-ounce can)*
*2 teaspoons curry powder*
*½ teaspoon mace (or ⅓ teaspoon nutmeg)*
*salt and pepper to taste*

Cook 15 minutes more, stirring often, then add

*2 cloves garlic, pressed*

Pour this sauce into a baking dish while you dredge

*One 2½- to 3-pound broiler-fryer chicken, cut into serving pieces*

in

*flour seasoned with salt, pepper, and paprika*

Brown the floured chicken pieces on all sides in

*additional oil, about 2 more tablespoons*

Remove chicken from skillet as pieces are browned and lay them in the sauced baking dish. Bake, covered very well, for 1 hour and 15 minutes.
Remove cover and stir in

*¾ cup currants or plump black raisins*

Re-cover and bake for another 20 minutes. Remove chicken from sauce and keep warm. Taste sauce and correct the seasonings. We have sometimes added, at this point

*a dash or so of wine vinegar, a few drops Tabasco, a touch of honey, and additional salt and black pepper*

To serve, on each plate, pile a large mound of

*fluffy, steaming hot rice*

To one side of the rice, place a chicken piece; to the other, your choice of simple steamed green vegetable (a broccoli spear is nice) or garnish.

*(continued)*

183

Then ladle the thick aromatic sauce over both rice and chicken and sprinkle with

*toasted almond pieces*

## Chicken for Friends by the Fireplace in November

*Garden Vegetable–Cheese Chowder in Small Cups*
*Fresh Spinach Salad with Thin Red Onion Rings*
*Spinach Dressing Brenda & Lana's, Passed Separately*
*Elsie's Chicken Country Captain*
*Rice • Broccoli*
*Mexican Chocolate Pudding Pie, Whipped Cream*
*Hot Cinnamon Coffee*

*On the table:* Lots of polished brass, yellow chrysanthemums

## Country Chicken Fricassee

*Serves 2 generously, 4 more lightly*

Another brown-and-braise chicken recipe, this one is a country classic. The herbs raise it to distinction, as does the egg-and-cream enrichment at the finish. Made for Sunday-afternoon dinners, and very wonderful served over split buttered biscuits.

Dredge

*One 2½- to 3-pound broiler-fryer chicken, cut into serving pieces*

in

*flour seasoned with salt, pepper, and paprika*

Brown it in

*2 tablespoons olive oil*

then transfer to a large heavy pot. Add

*boiling stock (vegetable or chicken) or even water, just to cover*
*1 bay leaf*
*quite a bit of freshly ground black pepper*
*½ cup finely chopped fresh parsley*
*1 bunch green onions, chopped*
*½ teaspoon each basil and salt (unless cooking liquid is already-salted stock)*
*¼ teaspoon each rosemary, sage, and oregano*
*1 teaspoon summer savory (essential for this dish, and wonderful)*

Cover and simmer over very low heat until chicken is very tender—1 hour and 15 minutes or so. Lift chicken pieces from stock and keep warm. Measure stock—there should be about 3 cups; if not, add water to equal this amount, and taste for seasonings. Put on low heat and let simmer while, in another pan, you melt

*4 tablespoons butter*

and stir into it

*4 tablespoons unbleached white flour*

Cook slowly for a few minutes, then gradually whisk in 1 cup of the simmering stock. Simmer for 1 minute, stirring constantly, then add this thickened broth to the remainder of simmering stock. Simmer gently for about 10 minutes, stirring often. Meanwhile, beat together in a small bowl

*1 cup hot cream*
*2 egg yolks*

Stir this gradually into the thickened simmering stock, then remove from heat and taste again for seasonings. Return chicken to pot and very gradually reheat, but on no account let it boil after cream-yolk mixture has been added.

This succulent dish, which smacks of the farm and its abundance, really contains an unconscionable number of calories. For our own use at home, we sometimes cut them down by using less oil (and Pam-ing

185

the skillets first), and substituting evaporated milk beaten with only 1 egg yolk and 1 tablespoon cornstarch. There's nothing like real, true-blue heavy cream, of course, but this substitute is extremely good. And it can be served, most deliciously, over plain steamed rice, thus avoiding the caloric addition of insult to injury of biscuits.

You can also make it slightly more sophisticated by adding sautéed mushrooms and several vigorous dashes of sherry or brandy to the sauce at the last. When we do this we call it *Chicken Fricassee Parisienne.*

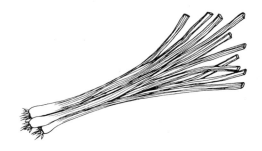

## Chicken Nouveau'zarks

*Serves 2 to 4*

What we have here is a delicious dish that uses a lot of ingredients which, as of this writing, are trendy. We think this winning combination of flavors will outlast the trendiness of Dijon mustard et al., however, and will become a classic, not a cliché.

Combine

> *2 cloves garlic, pressed*
> *the juice of 1 large lemon*
> *several grinds of fresh black pepper*

Rub this into

> *one 2½-pound frying chicken, cut into serving pieces*

Let the rubbed chicken stand for at least 1 hour so these flavors can seep in. Then heat together

> *2 tablespoons butter*
> *2 tablespoons vegetable oil (olive is nice here)*

and in it brown the chicken pieces over medium heat, allowing about 15 minutes. Be careful not to let the heat get too high. After the chicken has been browned on both sides, pour over it

*⅔ cup dry white wine*
*½ cup chicken broth*

into which you've blended

*1 tablespoon Dijon mustard*

as well as

*1 bunch scallions, diced*
*a handful fresh sliced mushrooms*
*5 whole cloves garlic, peeled*
*1 bay leaf*
*½ teaspoon thyme (1 teaspoon minced fresh if available)*
*salt to taste, or about 1 teaspoon unless broth is salty*

Cover and simmer gently for about 25 minutes, or until chicken is quite tender. Remove the chicken from its cooking liquid and keep warm. Remove the bay leaf from the liquid, and mash the whole cloves of garlic into the side of the skillet with a wooden spoon. Raise the heat under the cooking liquid and bring to a boil. Cook uncovered, stirring often, for about 5 minutes, which will reduce and slightly thicken the cooking liquid. Serve with

*hot rice or cooked noodles*

with plenty of sauce for each delectable piece of chicken. French bread is also excellent with this. Garnish with fresh, finely chopped parsley and, if you have it, a nice sprig of fresh thyme on each plate.

## Baked Chicken Supreme with Plenty of Garlic

*Serves 2 to 4*

As you will know from our Garlic Spaghetti recipe, page 241, we are big garlic fans. Both that dish and this are quick and easy, and both use an enormous amount of garlic and some sweet basil, but there all resemblance ceases. Though the chicken recipe here uses much, much more garlic to start with than the spaghetti, its garlic is baked, so the pungency turns to a mellow aromatic sweetness. If you didn't tell your guests what the main seasoning was, they probably wouldn't guess. But in the case of the pasta we love so well, the garlic is left raw—and unmistakable. Don't miss either garlicky delight—the other assertive, this one mild.

*(continued)*

Preheat oven to 350°. In a well-greased baking pan that can go under the boiler, arrange

*one 2½- to 3-pound broiler-fryer chicken, cut into serving pieces*

Sprinkle over the pieces

*juice and grated rind of ½ lemon*
*2 teaspoons dried basil*
*½ teaspoon rosemary needles*
*salt—just a bit, and plenty of freshly ground black pepper*
*½ cup dry white wine*
*⅓ cup vermouth*
*1 large onion, cut into thin crescents*
*a dash, carefully distributed, red pepper flakes*
*2 tablespoons each melted butter and olive oil*

and, the kicker

*2 heads of garlic, which have been separated into cloves and peeled*
*—there should be between 35 and 55 garlic cloves*

Quickly, before you regret this seeming rashness, cover the baking dish and bake for 50 minutes. Uncover it and, when the aromatic steam subsides, mash any visible pieces of garlic into the chicken itself or the cooking liquid, using a fork. Broil for another 5 to 10 minutes, to brown the chicken. Serve immediately, as by now your guests will be climbing the walls with anticipation because of the delicious smells issuing from your kitchen.

This is excellent with a simply cooked bulgur wheat (the chicken pan juices spooned over, of course), and a tomato provençal, and a good classic perfect green salad—with plenty of raw garlic in it!

## Peach- or Apricot-glazed Cornish Game Hens with Rice-and-Apricot Stuffing

*Stuffing for 6 chickens*

A Rock Cornish game hen was the entrée at the first restaurant meal I remember, a meal eaten with my parents overlooking the Hudson River, on a cold, cold day. I have forgotten the name of the restaurant and the specific occasion—a holiday? a birthday? But I remember clearly the hen itself, small and self-contained, stuffed with wild rice. A tomato half, nicely grilled with buttered breadcrumbs on the top, accompanied it. Dubious at first because I was then, like so many children, a diffident eater and because I'd heretofore disliked cooked tomatoes, I ate the entire thing, wondering at this even at the time.

188

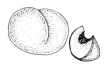

Time knit a circle back to this experience: some twenty-five years later, I prepared a dinner based around such glazed hens for a family of five who stayed at the inn one Thanksgiving. This family, the Mehlburgers, included a little girl of about nine, who eyed the small cunning bird sitting on her plate with initial skepticism and then ate every bit of it, including the tomato provençal that accompanied it.

*Stuffing:* We always make more of this ambrosial mixture than we need, so we can eat it as a side dish with anything. First, you'll need to toast in a preheated 300° oven

*6 slices good whole wheat bread, torn into pieces*

Check the bread pieces every 5 or 10 minutes. You want them very, very dry, but only minimally browned. You'll also need to cook up according to the package directions

*2 cups Uncle Ben's Converted Rice*

Let the rice and the toasted bread cool to room temperature. Then combine them in a large bowl with

*¾ cup melted butter (1½ sticks)*
*1 small onion, very finely chopped*
*2 teaspoons dried leaf sage (or more fresh, to taste)*
*1 to 2 cups diced dried peaches* or *apricots*
*1 small apple, diced*
*2 stalks celery, with leaves, thinly sliced*
*salt and black pepper to taste*
*dash of sweet basil, couple of dashes Tamari soy sauce*
*¼ to ½ cup chopped walnuts* or *black walnuts*

Toss these ingredients. Bring to a boil

*¾ cup water*
*1 unsalted Morga broth cube* or *2 teaspoons golden miso*

Stir till broth cube or miso dissolves, and pour over stuffing mixture. Toss again. Taste. Correct the seasonings. Try not to eat all of it. Set it aside, refrigerated, until you are ready to stuff and bake the Cornish game hens. (Do not ever refrigerate cooked stuffed raw chickens, game hens, or turkeys; the cold cannot penetrate a stuffed bird and spoilage may result.) *(continued)*

*Glaze:* Combine over low heat until butter melts and set aside

*4 tablespoons butter*
*1 cup peach or apricot jam*
*2 teaspoons Tamari soy sauce*
*1 teaspoon grated fresh ginger root*

*Assembly, Baking, and Glazing:* For a roasting hen, wash the chicken, pat it dry, and, of course, remove any giblet packages inside. (We must confess we are *not* giblet gravy fans and tend to feed the innards to our pets, not our guests, but if you feel differently, any good basic cookbook can guide you.) Note how much your roasting chicken weighs, for this will determine cooking time. Place the hen on Pam-ed baking sheet, one with edges. Pack stuffing into cavity rather loosely (as it expands while baking and can easily come cascading out if it has been too firmly stuffed) and fold chicken skin "flaps" over cavity. (Sewing up is another nicety we forgo, except in the case of turkey. Nothing bad happens.) Rub chicken skin with

*1 teaspoon olive oil* or *melted butter*

Bake at 325°, allowing 1 hour for the first 2 pounds of weight and 20 minutes for each pound above 2. Remove chicken from oven and brush with Glaze. Bake for another 15 minutes, until very golden. (If chicken isn't quite golden brown enough, put it under the broiler for a few minutes.)

For Rock Cornish game hens, follow directions for roasting hens, except think smaller. The game hens will hold about ¼ cup of stuffing. Bake the stuffed hens, thoroughly thawed, of course, if you bought them frozen, at 325° for 40 minutes, brush on glaze, and bake for another 10 to 15 minutes, or until lovely golden brown. Test for doneness by wiggling drumstick up and down—it should move with ease and pull away slightly from the bone. Serve with extra stuffing, separately baked, covered, mounded on each diner's plate as a nest in which the game hen sits, regal.

And here is Jan's way with Rock Cornish game hens.

## Cornish Game Hens "Simple Gifts"

*Serves 1*

Everyone raves about these succulent creations. The fruits and spices flavor the chicken delicately while keeping it very moist and tender. And the filling can be scooped out and spooned over the accompanying rice pilaf.

Preheat oven to 325°. Wash each Rock Cornish game hen and place in baking dish or skillet about 2 inches deep. Into the cavity of each game hen, arrange prettily

*¼ Jonathan apple, raw and unpeeled, cored*
*1 small piece of celery stalk, about 3 inches long, including some leaves*
*1 cinnamon stick*
*1 green onion, with some green top, about 3 inches long*
*1 tablespoon raisins*

Sprinkle little hens with salt and pepper. Pour into bottom of Pam-ed baking dish

*½ cup water*
*½ cup dry white wine*

Bake for 50 minutes, or until golden and tender, basting as needed. When done, serve each game hen on a bed of your best rice pilaf, with steamed asparagus spears and carrot slices.

# Thanksgiving Dinner for the Mehlburgers

*Crepe Torte*
*Butternut Squash and Apple Soup I*
*The Salad*
*Angel Biscuits • Butter • Assorted Jams and Jellies*
*Apricot-glazed Cornish Game Hens*
*with*
*Rice-and-Apricot Stuffing*
*Tomatoes Provençal*
*Stir-Fry of Zucchini and Yellow Squash*
*Persimmon Mousse, Whipped Cream*
*Penuche Lace Cookies*
*Brewed Decaffeinated Coffee • Assorted Herb Teas*

# CHICKEN BREASTS NUMEROUS WAYS

If you know exactly when your guests are coming and don't mind a little last-minute work at the stove, you can do many delicious, quick variations on a theme starting with 2 whole chicken breasts, skinned, boned, cut in half and pounded thin, and lightly dredged in seasoned flour. Allow ½ breast per person; this will be plenty in any dinner that includes a starch, a vegetable or salad, and a dessert. Anyway, the breasts are quickly browned in 2 tablespoons butter or oil, depending on the variation you choose. After browning, about ½ cup liquid (see the variations for specifics) is poured over them, along with miscellaneous seasonings, vegetables, etc. Bring to a simmer, cover, and let cook till breasts are tender—7 to 10 minutes, less if you have pounded the breasts thin before dredging them. Overcooking will toughen these—don't do it! Remove breasts from sauce, keeping them warm, and raise heat under skillet. Bring liquid quickly to a boil for just a few minutes, uncovered, to reduce and slightly thicken sauce. There will be just a tablespoon or two of sauce per portion—enough to glaze each breast nicely as you put it, piping hot, on each lucky diner's plate.

For *Chicken Breasts à la Russe*, brown the breasts in butter and use as cooking liquid ⅔ cup chicken broth and ⅓ cup brandy, along with a handful of sliced mushrooms and a tablespoon of chopped onion. After sauce has been reduced, stir in a couple of tablespoons of sour cream, a dash of nutmeg, and plenty of black pepper.

For *Chicken Breasts Piccata*, rub the breasts lightly with garlic before dredging them and brown in equal parts butter and olive oil. After browning, pour over them ½ cup white wine and the juice of 1 lemon. Garnish each breast, after glazing with the reduced liquid, with a thin slice of lemon cut in a twist.

For *Chicken Breasts Scallopini*, follow the Piccata recipe, but instead of white wine use ½ cup vermouth and ¼ cup good chicken broth. My mother used to make this with veal as I was growing up; we all loved it. Excellent!

For *Chicken Breasts Eldred*, a delightful specialty invented by Eureka Springs pharmacist Jerry Stamps, pound the chicken breasts extra thin and fold them in half. Insert a thin slice of mozzarella cheese and a few slivers of good ham, if desired, in the space between the fold, like a turnover. Dredge, brown in equal parts butter and olive oil, and add ½ cup vermouth; 1 tablespoon diced onion; 1 clove garlic, pressed; a couple of sliced mushrooms; and 1 peeled, chopped, fresh tomato. After sauce is reduced and removed from heat, stir in 2 to 4 tablespoons heavy cream. "Oh, you know," says Jerry, "*enough* cream."

For *Chicken Breasts Provençal,* season dredging flour with a pinch of dried sweet basil and brown dredged breasts in straight olive oil. Cooking liquid: ½ cup white wine; 2 peeled, chopped fresh tomatoes; 2 cloves garlic, pressed; ¼ onion, in thin crescents. When sauce has been reduced, add to it sliced black olives. Garnish with a lot of very finely chopped fresh parsley.

For *Chicken Breasts à la Grecque,* prepare the chicken breasts for stuffing as in Chicken Breasts Eldred and fill them with a sprinkle of finely crumbled feta cheese and a bit of oregano. Dredge and brown as in Chicken Breasts Provençal. To the reduced sauce, add sliced Greek olives and, if desired, tiny slivers of sautéed green and red peppers. Fresh dill is nice in this sauce.

The list is endless—try apple juice and cognac for cooking liquid, with a fresh apple garnish, or orange juice and white wine, with a bit of orange marmalade stirred in at the last. For a decidedly Oriental flavor, add ½ cup chicken broth with ¼ cup sherry and a bit of grated ginger and a teaspoon each of Tamari soy sauce and honey. Sautéed mushrooms, finely minced, can serve as a delicious stuffing for chicken breasts done this way; virtually any combination of cheese and fresh herbs is also a good filling, as is herb-and-garlic Boursin cheese . . .

Think about chicken breasts this way, in any of the variations mentioned, when you are in a hurry and need something quick and good and special. Once you get the hang of the basic recipe, you will be amazed at how quickly these go together.

## A Spring Dinner for New Lovers

*Chilled Strawberry Soup with Mint*
*Asparagus Marinated in Gingered Vinaigrette on*
*a Bed of Red Leaf Lettuce, Garnished with Oranges and Grapes*
*Chicken Breasts Eldred over Rice*
*Stir-fried Green Beans with Butter and Lemon*
*Dairy Hollow House Mocha Dream Torte*
*Vouvray, Meurasalt, or Pouilly Fusse*

*On the table:* Old-fashioned roses in a bowl, petals of one scattered randomly on the tablecloth, which is peach damask; white linen napkins, lots of candles; silver (unmatched but polished); white plates

*Later:* Frangelico or Cognac, Fresh Grapes on the Stem

193

# Charlotte's Chicken Breasts French-Asian Grandmother

*Serves 4*

A simple and delicious chicken breast recipe that starts like the previous ones but finishes off in the oven; from my mother, Charlotte Zolotow.

In

*3 tablespoons butter*

sauté

*4 chicken breast halves, boned and skinned, not pounded*

until golden brown, turning them once. Remove from the skillet, place in a greased baking pan, and season with salt and pepper. In the pan in which you browned the chicken, heat

*1½ cups white wine*

Scrape pan to get up any flavor-y brown bits. Pour the hot wine over the chicken breasts, with

*½ to 1 teaspoon grated fresh ginger*

Re-cover the casserole and put it in the oven for about 10 minutes. Lift over and add

*½ pound seedless green grapes, whole*
*½ cup blanched, slivered, toasted almonds*

Re-cover and bake the dish for another 15 minutes. Serve with plain rice, so as not to overwhelm the lovely delicacy of the sauce.

*Variation:* Omit ginger; add a branch of fresh dill.

# Chicken Breasts in Phyllo with Dijon

*Serves 6*

A smashing, show-off chicken dish that, like almost anything in phyllo, always garners raves. Deliciously rich, zinged with the pizzazz of good mustard and sour cream. The accompaniments should be simple and light: a fresh light green salad, say, a tomato provençal and Brussels sprouts, which you've given a quick steaming to and then finished off with a quick stir-fry in butter and a squeeze of lemon. Saffron rice, and later, fresh fruit marinated in liqueur, would complete a glorious meal.

Melt in a large skillet

*4 tablespoons butter*

In it, place

*3 chicken breasts, skinned, boned, and cut in half, but* not *pounded thin*

Cook them, covered, over medium heat for 10 minutes. Remove from skillet. Into skillet drippings, whisk and stir together

*1 cup sour cream*
*3 tablespoons Dijon mustard*
*1 tablespoon fresh basil*

Set aside while you lay out

*1 sheet phyllo dough (for working with phyllo, see pp. 160–164)*

Brush the sheet quickly with

*melted butter*

Preheat oven to 425°. Repeat twice more, so you have three sheets of butter-brushed phyllo dough stacked one on top of the other. Place 1 chicken breast in center of phyllo dough, top with about ¼ cup sour cream mixture, and wrap phyllo dough around the chicken, sealing edges with more melted butter. Repeat with remaining chicken breasts, using three sheets of phyllo, plus melted butter, for each. Place seam-side down on baking sheet. Bake for 15 to 20 minutes.

# Anne's Chicken with Zucchini Florentine

*Serves 4*

Another extraspecial chicken breast recipe, this one from our friend Anne Breedlove. Anne and I agree on the essential things: that every main dish must have garlic, as every dessert must have chocolate, as often as possible and in the same meal.

Although *Florentine* in a dish generally means with creamed spinach, Anne's version replaces the spinach with grated zucchini and the cream sauce with ricotta. You will love the succulent stuffed pillows with their hidden surprise.

Grate

*1 medium-large zucchini*

Squeeze out liquid from zucchini with your hands, saving liquid for soup stock. Set aside while you melt

*4 tablespoons butter*

In it sauté till barely softened

*1 onion, finely diced*

then add the grated zucchini. Stir-fry for a few minutes. Remove from heat and stir mixture into

*6 ounces ricotta cheese*

along with

*salt and pepper to taste*
*2 fresh cloves garlic, pressed*
*½ cup grated Parmesan cheese*
*1 tablespoon fresh basil, finely chopped, or fresh tarragon (or 1 teaspoon dried basil)*

Now, line up this filling, a spoon, a well-greased baking dish, and

*3 chicken breasts, boned but not skinned, cut in half*

Preheat oven to 350°. Carefully separate skin from flesh of chicken breasts, being sure to leave much of it still attached. In the pocket thus formed, between skin and flesh, pat in a good-size handful of the ricotta-zucchini mixture and press skin back down around edges to seal in filling. Place filled breast in casserole. Repeat with remaining breasts, and place on top of each

*a pat of butter*

196

Pour around the breasts

*½ cup dry sherry or white wine*

Bake, covered, for 30 minutes. Uncover and bake for another 15 minutes. Finally, run the breasts under the broiler for 5 minutes to brown them.

*Note:* If you sauté the onions and zucchini "dry," in a Pam-sprayed pan, and use only a thin part of butter at the last, you have a really elegant, entirely party-worthy dish that is relatively low-calorie.

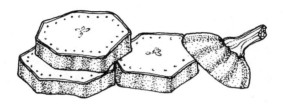

## Mary's Chicken "Shotgun"

*Serves 4 to 6*

Good recipes travel. This one did; from a professional chef nick-named Shotgun, to his friend Mary Creasy, an eighth-grade teacher, ardent cook, bicyclist, and former Dairy Hollow House guest, to us. Here, chicken breasts are laid out in a rectangle, stuffed, and rolled—as *one* unit, not individual breasts—and baked. This delicious dish, which bears some resemblance to Jerry's Chicken Breasts Eldred (p. 192), may be assembled several hours ahead of time and then popped into the oven an hour before serving, so it's especially suited for occasions when you want the elegance of chicken breasts without the last-minute fuss.

Lay out, open, close together but not overlapping

*3 whole boneless skinned chicken breasts*

The breasts form a rectangular base on which you will now arrange small amounts of the following ingredients, in this order

*slivered, sliced ham*
*grated Swiss cheese*
*whole canned pimentos, extremely well drained*
*finely chopped green onions*
*fine breadcrumbs*

*(continued)*

197

Dot this with

*butter, 2 teaspoons in all*

Preheat oven to 350° and begin rolling up the rectangle of chicken, jelly-roll style. When there is only about an inch left unrolled, separate the pieces of

*½ pound good bacon, the kind in long strips*

Lay the strips out, slightly overlapping, and finish rolling the chicken. You now have a cylindrical stuffed chicken roll, from the long edge of which protrude many strips of bacon. Wrap each strip around the outside of the roll, overlapping it when you come to the point where it is folded into the chicken. Carefully transfer the bacon-wrapped chicken roll into a Pam-ed baking dish and bake in the preheated oven for about 1 hour, or until chicken is done and bacon is lightly browned but not crisp. Slice into 1-inch pieces and arrange on plates. Serve immediately.

We have sometimes done this with lightly sautéed mushrooms replacing the ham, and a few water chestnuts, sliced, for crunch, and a blanket of chopped parsley for color. Although the bacon adds a nice fillip, it can be omitted if you use a little sherry in the baking dish, dab the outside of the roll liberally with butter, and baste occasionally.

Like so many chicken dishes, this is excellent with rice, a tomatoes provençal, and a good green vegetable. Jan's "Appl'ava" (p. 272) is the perfect dessert.

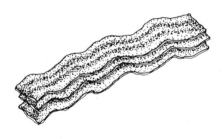

*Went out to milk and I didn't know how,*
*I milked the goat instead of the cow;*
*Turkey in the hay, Turkey in the straw,*
*Roll 'em up and twist 'em up a high tuckahaw,*
*And hit 'em up a tune called Turkey in the Straw.*

*—Traditional American Folk Song*

## Jo Luck's Chicken Maciel

*Serves 6 to 8*

When Jo Luck Wilson, director of Arkansas Parks & Tourism, told us she would like to submit a recipe to this cookbook, we wondered what it would be, and Ned quipped, "Jo Potluck Wilson!" Actually, this luscious chicken casserole is perfect for a pot-luck or covered dish supper. It features two Arkansas products, chicken and rice, and Jo Luck says it's been a favorite of hers since her college days.

Dice

> *2 pounds cold cooked chicken breasts, boneless*

Quickly stir-fry, just long enough to heat the chicken pieces, in

> *6 tablespoons butter*
> *½ teaspoon paprika*

Remove from heat. Meanwhile, heat

> *1 pint heavy cream*

As it heats, blend with fingers till lump-free

> *4 tablespoons sherry*
> *1 teaspoon curry powder*

Whisk this into cream, stir till thick, and remove from heat. Fold in chicken pieces and

> *1 cup cooked rice*

Turn into a well-greased 8- × -10-inch pan and sprinkle liberally with

> *½ pound grated sharp cheese (Jo Luck uses American,*
> *we like Cheddar)*

Brown under broiler and serve.

---

*Better a dinner of herbs where love is, than a stalled ox and hatred therewith.*

*—Proverbs XV: 17*

199

Last but not least,

# John S. Cross's Great Southern Barbeque Sauce

*Makes about 2 cups*

John says, "It's so good you can shave with it." Tangy and pungent, not sweet, the Cross family uses it on chicken, on pork ribs, even on steak, basting it gently when grilling the meats and poultry inside on their Jenn-Air and more vigorously when grilling outside, where the flames flaring up will not singe the ceiling. John loves it so much that when chicken he has been grilling and basting with this is done, he plunges it into the remaining sauce for one last bath of savor before putting it on the serving platter. "Couldn't you marinate chicken in it before?" I asked him. "Put it like this," said John. "The more you can get of the sauce on your meat or chicken, the oftener the better."

Combine the following ingredients in the top of a double boiler:

*½ cup butter (1 stick)*
*1 sour pickle, finely chopped*
*2 tablespoons finely chopped onion*
*2 tablespoons Worcestershire sauce*
*2 tablespoons chili sauce*
*4 slices lemon, rind included*
*1 green pepper, finely chopped*
*1 teaspoon brown sugar*
*1 cup vinegar*

Turn on heat under double boiler and heat, stirring constantly, until butter melts. Keep warm until ready to use on barbequed meats. "I like to cook this for at least two hours before using," notes Ludean Cross, John's wife.

# Behind-the-Scenes Political Backyard Barbeque

*Sausage Fingers*
*Chicken Basted and Grilled with*
*John S. Cross's Great Southern Barbeque Sauce*
*Fresh Corn on the Cob, Grilled*
*Garlic Slaw*
*Mama Murray's Potato Salad*
*Watermelon • Dairy Hollow House Sweet Potato–Black*
*Walnut Pie*

# Fish,
# Fresh and Fine

The Ozarks are studded with springs, crisscrossed by creeks and streams and rivers, and, in the last twenty years or so, enriched with huge and lovely man-made lakes, often edged by stupendous, curving limestone bluffs. In these waters live trout, walleye, large and smallmouth bass, tiny lobster-tasting crawdads, and catfish (which are also "farmed" commercially in the area; and we think the day is coming when we'll see commercial crawdad hatcheries). When we can buy fresh fish legally (there are all sorts of restrictions about the resale of fresh-caught fish, designed to avoid depletion of the waters), we do. And sometimes we are given some by Jan's in-laws, Jack and Mary Clark, who fish a few yards from their porch at Table Rock Lake. Too, there is a fish hatchery we sometimes make a run to in Cassville, Missouri, just across the state line. Unfortunately there is no regular, dependable source for fresh-caught saltwater fish, shrimp, and lobster. For a while, there was a good fresh seafood market in Fayetteville, but that has closed, so we are dependent on the occasional person who makes a run to the Gulf and brings back a supply. We also have a friend who sometimes brings in salmon from the Northwest.

We also have, sometimes, guests who fish. We leave them a breakfast basket instead of our usual morning fare so they can get a good early start, and when they return with their catch in the afternoon, we prepare it for them. While they nap, shower, etc., we're busy in the kitchen, at work on one of the offerings that follow, chosen according to what they've caught, which we serve that same evening as part of an elegant dinner in the parlor.

## Tenth Anniversary Dinner in June

*Theda's Chilled Stuffed Artichokes*
*Jan's American Borscht*
*Breadbasket: Dinner Rolls, Sweet-Sour Rye*
*The Salad*
*Oven-poached Rainbow Trout with Cucumber-Dill Cloud*
*Tomatoes Provençal*
*Steamed Baby Potatoes in Jackets, Parsley-Buttered*
*Geranium Cake with Raspberry Whipped Cream*
*A Good Moselle, such as Schloss Johannesburger*
*Coffee or Brewed Decaffeinated Coffee*

*On the table:* Low bowl of field daisies and old-fashioned roses, with blossoming honeysuckle vines trailing; votive candles in yellow glass holders

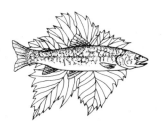

## Oven-poached Rainbow Trout with Cucumber-Dill Cloud

*Serves 4*

Rainbow trout is one of our guests' all-time favorite entrées. Partly this is because we serve it only when we can get it really fresh-fresh. There are those who still like their trout dipped in milk, rolled in cornmeal and pan-fried, a classic Ozark treatment, but we prefer the sweet and delicate flavor of this oven-poached trout. With white wine for a poaching liquid and a grated cucumber and fresh dill garnish, this recipe fairly sparkles.

Preheat oven to 325°. Wash and pat dry

*4 small rainbow trout, about 10 ounces each*

Place them in a buttered baking dish, and pour over them

*½ cup white wine*
*1 cup water*

Sprinkle with

*the juice of 2 lemons*
*paprika*

Bake for 35 to 40 minutes, or until fish is firm to the touch and flakes easily with a fork. Gently spoon Cucumber-Dill Cloud over each trout and serve, garnished with a large sprig of fresh parsley. A tomato provençal and a heap of tiny steamed and buttered new potatoes works very well with this, as with so many fish dishes.

*Cucumber-Dill Cloud:* Blend together well, preferably several hours in advance so flavors have a chance to marry

*½ cup sour cream*
*¼ cup plain yogurt*
*1 teaspoon Tamari soy sauce*
*¼ cup finely grated cucumber*
*1 tablespoon minced fresh dill (or 1 teaspoon dried)*

◆———————————◆
*This Bouillabaisse a noble dish is—*
*A sort of soup, or broth, or stew.*

*—William Makepeace Thackeray,*
The Ballad of Bouillabaisse
◆———————————◆

## Ozark Bouillabaisse

*Serves 8 to 10*

There is a ridiculous amount of argument about this justly famous hearty saffron-scented fish stew from France, which food fanatics insist cannot be made correctly in this country because we don't have all the proper and authentic fish. What silliness! Bouillabaisse is peasant food, humble of origin, made from whatever was caught that day, so no one ingredient can be called authentic. What *is* authentic about it is the spirit of: Use what you have, use what's fresh, and combine it artfully and with cunning.

In this spirit, we present our wonderful Ozark Bouillabaisse, which, every time we've made it, has had guests swooning with delight—despite the fact that we have no rockfish, no shrimp, no clams, mussels, or lobsters (though crawfish are almost identical in flavor and texture)—in fact, nothing at all from the sea. What we do have is a wonderful variety of freshwater fish, the traditional seasonings (saffron, a tomato-onion-garlic-olive-oil-sauté, white wine, herbs), and some nontraditional bounty from our vegetable garden (corn—which the French think is only fit for cattle fodder anyway, peas, zucchini, acorn squash, and that most Ozark of vegetables, okra, albeit in small quantities). We also add a handful of ground almonds—a Jan Brown innovation that adds texture and is somehow, mysteriously, just made for the assorted tomato-drenched fish. Of course, there's certainly nothing to prevent you from adding fresh seafood if you have a good source for it, but do try it this way and see if it doesn't knock your socks off.

Begin by shelling

*1 pound crawdads*

Set the crawdads themselves aside for the stew. Place their shells in a stockpot; they will be used to prepare the flavorful fish stock that gives body and intensely delicious fishiness to this aromatic brew. Next, wash and debone (reserving heads, bones, skin, and other scraps for the stockpot)

*2 pounds assorted fish (catfish, perch, bass, walleye, carp)*

The fish should be in assorted varieties and sizes, some left whole, some cut into steaks, some cut into bite-size pieces. Set the prepared

fish aside. Into the stockpot place the reserved bones, heads, etc., along with

*2 quarts water*
*1 cup dry white wine*
*juice of 1 lemon*
*2 teaspoons salt*
*1 bay leaf*
*1 tablespoon fresh oregano (or 1 teaspoon dried)*
*1 teaspoon each dill weed and thyme*

Bring to a boil and cook over medium heat for 15 minutes, uncovered. While fish stock is cooking, sauté together until golden and tender

*2 medium-size onions, finely chopped*
*5 cloves garlic, minced*

in

*¼ cup olive oil*

Puree in blender

*4 medium-size tomatoes, peel and all*

Add this to the sautéed onions, and set the mixture aside. When the stock has simmered, strain it. You should have about 6 cups liquid. If there is not enough, add water or white wine to make the full 6 cups. Pour fish stock back into the cleaned stockpot or into your favorite soup pot—this is the pot from which you will be serving.

To the stock, add the sautéed tomato-onion mixture and

*1 bay leaf*
*4 tomatoes, quartered*
*4 tablespoons minced fresh parsley, preferably Italian*
*2 tablespoons finely chopped fresh basil (or 1½ teaspoons dried)*
*1 tablespoon finely chopped fresh oregano (or 1 teaspoon dried)*
*1½ teaspoons saffron, crushed (do not omit)*
*¼ cup raw almonds, ground in blender or food processor*
*1 whole stalk fresh fennel (omit if fresh is not available)*

Simmer this over medium heat for 1 hour, covered. Add the assorted fishes and the crawdads you prepared earlier and simmer for another 20 minutes. During these last 20 minutes, in a separate pot, steam for 5 minutes

*1 acorn squash, chopped into ½-inch cubes*

After 5 minutes, add

*3 zucchinis, thinly sliced*

(continued)

and steam for 3 minutes. Then add

*2 cups corn, cut fresh from the cob (or frozen kernels, if you must!)*

and steam for 2 minutes. The last steamer addition is

*2 cups fresh green peas (or frozen, if necessary)*

After the peas are added, steam for only 1 minute more. Remove the steamer from heat, and reserve vegetables. (This matter of steaming the vegetables separately and timing them closely rather than just throwing them into the main pot is an instance of our pickiness—we are fervently dedicated to the proposition that even in soup or stew, vegetables ought to be tender-crisp, and intensely colored, with a little bite to them, not overcooked and of depressing gray-green hue. Of course, if such fine points don't matter to you, you can just whomp 'em directly into the bouillabaisse . . . but don't say we didn't warn you.)

After the final 20 minutes of the bouillabaisse simmering, add the steamed ingredients to the bouillabaisse with

*half a dozen or so thinly sliced fresh okra pods (omit if fresh are not available; frozen or, God help us, canned will not do!)*

Stir. Let cook a scant 3 minutes more. Remove fennel stalk and bay leaves. Ladle into soup bowls and serve.

---

*I never lost a little fish—yes, I am free to say*
*It always was the biggest fish I caught that got away.*

—*Eugene Field (1850–95)*

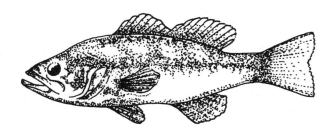

206

# Supper in a Cabin at Beaver Lake

*Ozark Bouillabaisse*
*Breadbasket: Warm French Bread, Corn Bread Squares*
*The Salad*
*Lemon Mousse with Fresh Fruit Garnish*
*Penuche Lace Cookies*
*Coffee*

*On the table:* Vervain, Queen Anne's lace, field daisies in a pitcher

## Jankowski's Souffléed White Bass

*Serves 4*

Of course, we have many memorable guests at Dairy Hollow House, and often they visit us again and again. The Jankowskis started coming to Eureka Springs to play golf, golf, and more golf, and part of their love affair with this area began over this elegant Souffléed White Bass, named in their honor. White bass is one of the area's favored catches, and the fluffy soufflé makes this dish supreme beyond words.

Wash and pat dry

*4 small white bass, 10 to 16 ounces each, cleaned*

Place fish on Pam-ed broiler pan. Blend together

*3 tablespoons dry white wine*
*4 tablespoons melted butter*

Brush butter mixture over fish and broil 5 to 8 minutes on each side, basting frequently, until fish is done and firm to the touch and flakes easily with a fork. Meanwhile, beat until stiff

*4 egg whites*

Fold in gently

*⅓ cup mayonnaise*
*1 teaspoon Dijon mustard*
*3 tablespoons Parmesan cheese*
*2 tablespoons finely chopped fresh parsley*
*1 tablespoon finely chopped fresh chives*

*(continued)*

Pile one-quarter of soufflé on each fish. Broil fish with soufflé 2 or 3 minutes until bubbly and golden brown. Serve with mushrooms sautéed in butter and wine.

*Variation:* Not always do we have white bass when we want to show off this charming soufflé. We've found that walleye fillets or catfish steaks can be substituted quite well. Follow directions as given, brushing the fillets or steaks with butter and wine mixture. Broil for 5 minutes on each side, and continue with soufflé directions.

---

*I have laid aside business, and gone a-fishing.*

—*Izaak Walton (1593–1683),*
The Compleat Angler

---

## Baked Fish Provençal in Terra Cotta

*Serves 4 to 6*

This works well with almost any whole fish weighing 3 to 4 pounds. We have done catfish, trout, and red snapper this way. You must have one of the clay stoneware cookers, the kind whose bottom half is glazed and the top unglazed, large enough to accommodate the fish. Follow the manufacturer's directions for your clay cooker—ours advises us to soak the unglazed part in warm water for 10 minutes for clay to absorb moisture. This is what makes possible such moist, delectable, tender offerings from such clay cookware.

---

*DAIRY HOLLOW HOUSE FLOWERS: THE WHITE PITCHER*

*If you have one vase, make it a clean-lined white china or porcelain pitcher. Anything looks lovely in it—a mixed bouquet, a grouping of one type of flower. It works beautifully in a formal or informal room, with any period or style of furnishings, in a farmhouse or a penthouse. Some people collect white pitchers—a row of differently shaped ones is very pretty even without flowers.*

---

Preheat oven to 300°. Lightly Pam the inside of bottom of stoneware cooker. In it, place

*1 whole 3- to 4-pound fish, washed, patted dry*
*(you can use either 1 whole fish or boneless fillets)*

Combine

*2 cups canned tomato sauce*
*4 cloves garlic, pressed*
*¼ cup finely minced fresh parsley*
*2 tablespoons finely minced fresh sweet basil*
*salt and freshly ground pepper to taste*

Spoon this over and around the fish, and sprinkle with

*½ cup dry breadcrumbs*
*¼ cup grated Parmesan cheese*

Bake, covered, for about 1 hour, or until fish is tender and firm and breadcrumbs are lightly browned. Serve with a simple rice or noodle, a green salad, and plenty of French bread to mop up the sauce.

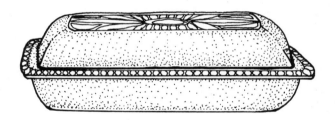

## A Provence-inspired Birthday Dinner

*Feta Cheese Tartlets in Crepe Cups with Sage and Onions*
*Dairy Hollow House Supreme of Vegetable and Olive Soup Eureka*
*Jan's Pleasures of Summer Salad*
*In a Breadbasket: Assorted Breads—Angel Biscuits,*
*Whole Wheat Butterhorns, Oatmeal Bread Supreme*
*Baked Fish Provençal in Terra Cotta*
*Lemon Rice*
*Stir-Fry of Zucchini and Eggplant with Garlic*
*Grand Marnier Chocolate Decadence*
*Coffee, Very Strong and Dark*

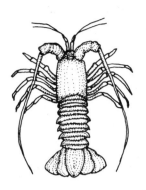

## Shrimp Margarita

*Serves 4*

This tequila, cream, and avocado-enriched shrimp dish of Jan's is a knockout! We only get good fresh shrimp here very occasionally anyway, when someone comes through from the Gulf with a refrigerated truckful, so they are always a treat, and this way they are simply indescribably good.

Shell and devein

*1 pound medium-size shrimp (about 24)*

Place shrimp in a small bowl and add

*juice of 1 lime*
*salt and pepper to taste*

Let stand, refrigerated, until a few minutes before serving time, because, as you will see, it goes together very quickly. Make sure you have the accompaniment, cooked rice, ready before you begin. Now, melt in skillet

*3 tablespoons butter*

Add shrimp and cook over medium heat until shrimp turn pink—about 2 minutes. Sprinkle them with

*3 green onions, finely chopped*

and pour over them

*¼ cup tequila*
*1 cup heavy cream*

Cook for 1 minute, and add

*1 avocado, ripe but not overripe, peeled and sliced*

Cook *just* until the avocado is warmed, no longer, then quickly scoop out the shrimp and avocado from the sauce and place them on the plate(s) from which you intend to serve, on a bed of

*hot cooked rice*

Turn up the heat under the sauce and bring it to a full rolling boil for about a minute. Then add

*1 tablespoon chopped fresh cilantro,*
*also sometimes called coriander or Chinese parsley*

Remove sauce from heat, spoon sauce over the shrimp and avocado in their rice nest, and sprinkle with

*paprika*
*additional chopped cilantro (optional)*

Serve with an outrageous green salad with fresh orange slices, red onion, black olives and vinaigrette, and your favorite hot bread.

## Broiled Catfish Steaks with
## Red Pepper–and-Herb Butter

*Serves 4*

When Crescent's father, Maurice, first came to the Ozarks, long before we had Dairy Hollow House, he was eager to try the local fresh catfish. He was deeply disappointed to discover, wherever he went, only deep-fat fried catfish.

*(continued)*

When we make him catfish now, this simple way, at the inn, however, he is very, very pleased. The herb-garlic–sweet-red-pepper butter does not interfere with the good catfish flavor but enriches it subtly, as do the assorted vegetables that we ring around it.

First, make the seasoned butter by softening to room temperature

*¹/₂ cup butter (1 stick)*

Place the butter in a food processor with

*1 small clove garlic*
*rind of ¹/₂ lemon, grated*
*¹/₂ of 1 sweet fresh red pepper, seeded and chopped*
*¹/₄ cup chopped fresh sweet basil*

Buzz in the processor till smooth; scoop out into a bowl. Meanwhile, cut into julienne strips

*1 zucchini*
*2 large carrots*

Wash and de-string

*1 handful of fresh pea pods (Chinese sugar snap edible pod peas)*

Steam the carrots, zucchini, and pea pods together for 1 minute only. Now, Pam a baking dish and place in it a few

*romaine lettuce leaves*

Atop them, place

*4 catfish steaks, each large enough for 1 serving*

Dot each piece with ¹/₂ tablespoon of the prepared butter. Broil for about 6 minutes, remove from broiler, and turn catfish steaks. Scatter all around them the lightly steamed vegetables as well as

*2 or 3 mushrooms, sliced*
*4 scallions, cut into tiny slivers*

Top each steak with an additional ¹/₂ tablespoon of herbed red pepper–garlic butter, and broil for another 6 to 8 minutes, or until catfish is cooked all the way through. Serve each piece with some of the vegetables surrounding it, sitting on one of the romaine leaves, and top with a pat of the remaining prepared butter.

*Fish dinners will make a man spring like a flea.*

—*Thomas Jordan (1612–85)*

## Baked Trout in Grape Leaves

*Serves 4*

This unusual dish combines two of the treasures the Ozarks yield: trout and grape leaves.

Gather and prepare

*16 grape leaves, as in Hollow-Mades (p. 153)*

Preheat oven to 350°. Wash, de-bone, and cut into 16 small rectangular pieces

*2 pounds trout*

Each piece should weigh approximately 2 ounces. Lay out grape leaves, and on each grape leaf place a piece of the trout. Dot each piece of trout with

*½ clove garlic, pressed*
*1 teaspoon butter*
*1 tablespoon fresh breadcrumbs*
*½ teaspoon finely chopped fresh mint*
*salt and pepper to taste*

Fold grape leaf around each piece of trout, wrap tightly, and place seam-side down on Pam-ed baking sheet. Brush with

*olive oil*

(continued)

Bake for 20 minutes. Squeeze over the stuffed leaves the juice of

*½ lemon*

Remove the leaves from the baking sheet and serve immediately, with rice and acorn squash puree.

◆————————————————◆

*Oh, the gallant fisher's life!*
*It is the best of any;*
*'Tis full of pleasure, void of strife,*
*And 'tis beloved by many.*

—*John Chalkhill,*
*"The Angler" (1683)*

# A Harvest of
# Vegetarian Entrées

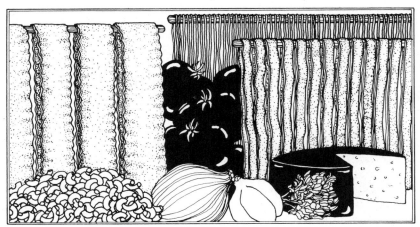

$D$o you suffer from the "pork chop syndrome"? Do you, when you think about vegetarian food, picture a bland plate with a pile of mashed potatoes, a pile of green beans, and a big blank space where the pork chop belongs?

Today's vegetarian plate does not have that big blank spot. It probably doesn't have plain old mashed potatoes and boiled green beans on it, either. Today that plate is not just not empty in parts but full to overflowing with interesting, sensuous, satisfying, totally varied food.

The plate contains vegetables, of course, but not just the familiar, tried-and-true ones, cooked by the same tired old methods. If there are mashed potatoes sometimes, there are also potato latkes at others; there are also spaghetti squash, eggplant, chayote, a half-dozen varieties of mushrooms and a dozen of greens, to name just a few that might appear from time to time. Corn might be served not just on the cob but as a pudding, or souffléed, or cut fresh from the cob and beautifully stir-fried with zucchini and onions and red and green peppers, and seasoned to a T with fresh herbs out of the garden.

Besides this wide range of interestingly prepared vegetables, the vegetarian plate also contains, most likely, eggs and milk and yogurt and sour cream and cheeses, glorious cheeses, often from around the

215

world: salty feta from Greece, sharp Gloucestershire and Cheshire from England, fontina and Parmesan and gorgeously creamy marscarparone from Italy, Gouda from Holland, Gjetost from Norway, Rocquefort and Brie and Camembert and wonderful *chèvres*, goat cheeses, from France (we are starting to have some great American-made goat cheeses, too), and many more. The plate contains, sometimes, pasta—perhaps homemade, very, very fresh, perhaps flavored with fresh spinach or tomato or even something like artichoke, simply done or sauced in any of a thousand ways. It may contain rice, or cracked wheat, or cornmeal (perhaps in the form of polenta, perhaps as spoonbread or Corn Muffin, pp. 68–70), to say nothing of millet and kasha and triticale—grains from the world over. It contains other foods of national origin: tofu from China and tempeh from Indonesia; sesame seeds and cashews from India; it contains nuts and seeds of all kinds, in fact, and nut and seed butters from everywhere.

Vegetarians may one night dine on crepes with broccoli and mushroom and a white-wine-and-cheese sauce, the next on lasagna and garlic bread and salad, the next on cheese enchiladas with guacamole and Spanish rice, the next stuffed grape leaves and eggplant and artichokes, the next grits soufflé with cheese and fried okra, and the next good old beans and rice.

In short, most vegetarians today are not deprived but, on the contrary, enjoy, in general, far more variety in their diets than do most of the rest of us. They are, as a rule, adventurous and sensual eaters, and often good cooks (they have to be, because, still, few restaurants offer much they can eat). They may well turn out to be healthier than meat eaters, too; study after study indicts excessive red meat intake as a contributing factor in various diseases. Yet we think the average vegetarian makes choices about what to eat not out of fear or negation but out of a more positive attraction: to health benefits, yes, for ethical reasons, yes, but also just because attentively prepared meatless food is so very, very good—as is the way eating it leaves a person feeling.

If our guests are any indication, many, many people who have no great interest in becoming strict vegetarians are leaning toward a semi-vegetarian diet: fish, and chicken, and shellfish, and nonflesh dishes, and red meat only once in a while. These guests, in general more adventurous eaters than the old meat-and-potatoes types, while they get excited about our chicken and fish dishes, also seem to enjoy our thick soups, pasta dishes, and vegetarian entrées almost as much as those who specifically request "No meat" at the time they place their dinner reservations.

A look at the recipes in this chapter will tell you why; a taste will convince you.

Enjoy this plentiful "Nouveau'zarks" harvest.

216

*Many of our hors d'oeuvres can easily be vegetarian entrées. Consider:*

- *Jenelle's Tomatoes Rockefeller, in full-size tomatoes*
- *Tidbits in Phyllo Dough, made as large triangular turnovers*
- *Mushrooms Diablo, as the main item on a luscious vegetable plate*
- *Feta Cheese Tartlets in Crepe Cups with Fresh Sage and Onions*

# Gougère

*Serves 4*

We will begin with probably our best-known vegetarian entrée, an incredible dish: Pâte à Choux, the classic French pastry from which cream puffs are made, is here used as a puffed, savory cheese topping, blanketing and enclosing all manner of steaming-hot wonderful stuff. This has charmed many a Dairy Hollow House guest. We still love it, though we've made it probably hundreds of times by now. There are several parts to this recipe, though it's far more showy than complicated.

First, prepare the filling. In

*4 tablespoons butter*

sauté

*1 medium onion, finely chopped*

with

*1½ teaspoons Tamari soy sauce*

When onions are nearly done, add

*½ cup sliced fresh mushrooms*

Stir mushrooms to coat well. Cook over medium heat for 1 minute. Add

*4 tablespoons finely chopped parsley*

Stir well and set aside. Meanwhile, steam the following vegetables, each separately

*(continued)*

*3 small carrots, thinly sliced*
*1 zucchini, thinly sliced*
*1 spear broccoli, finely chopped*
*1 cup cabbage, finely shredded*
*1 cup corn (fresh is best, frozen will do)*

As each vegetable finishes steaming, layer it into a buttered 10-inch casserole. Season each layer with

*salt, freshly ground black pepper, herbs such as 1 teaspoon basil or tarragon*

though we think this works beautifully when the vegetables are pretty straightforward, so rich is what is to come. Add

*a few drops white wine, brandy, or sherry (optional)*

Spoon over steamed vegetables

*1 ripe tomato, diced*

Now spoon onion-mushroom mixture over tomato, and prepare

## Pâte à Choux

Preheat oven to 400°. Place in a medium-size bowl

*1 cup sifted unbleached white flour*

Boil together

*½ cup butter*
*1 cup water*

Stir well and quickly pour over flour, stirring very quickly. Dough will become smooth and gather into a ball. Let mixture cool slightly. Then add

*5 eggs*

one at a time, beating well with a wooden spoon after each egg. (This step is very critical to the puffing of the pastry.) After the last egg is added, stir in

*1 cup grated sharp Cheddar cheese*

Now spoon Pâte à Choux around the edges of the filling in the casserole, or press it through a pastry tube with a large star tip, for extreme showiness. Sprinkle the center with

*1 cup grated sharp Cheddar cheese*
*a sprinkling of paprika*

218

Bake for about 30 to 35 minutes, until pastry is puffed and golden. Remove from heat and serve immediately.

*Note:* One can be very creative with fillings. Nonvegetarians can add a cup of julienned ham or turkey, cooked shrimp, or fresh crab-meat.

# February Dinner Before a Eureka Springs Guild of Artists and Craftspeople Board Meeting

*Jan's American Borscht*
*Mediterranean Vegetable Pie*
*Garlic Slaw*
*Jan Brownies*
*Jimmy Fliss's Homemade Vanilla Bean Ice Cream*
*& Home-Canned Peaches*

## Crescent's Mushrooms Stroganov

*Serves 4 to 6*

Rich and simple, this voluptuous vegetarian entrée can be prepared in 10 to 15 minutes, yet—served over rice and noodles—is a feast. In tiny portions, it's a nice accompaniment to a simple chicken or fish entrée; it can also fill Tidbits in Phyllo Dough (p. 160) for an irresistible starter.

In

*4 tablespoons butter*

*(continued)*

219

sauté

*1 large onion, chopped or sliced into crescents*

When onion begins to soften, add,

*4 cloves garlic, pressed*

Add, also, a few at a time, stirring to coat with butter

*¾ pound sliced mushrooms (slice these by hand, into little "trees" about ⅛ inch thick—don't use a food processor)*

Raise heat if necessary, stirring the mushrooms often and adding more butter if necessary. One wants the mushrooms to fry but not to exude a great deal of liquid. Season, as they cook, with

*a lot of freshly ground black pepper (fresh ground is essential here; it's one of the primary seasonings)*
*freshly grated nutmeg (3 or 4 or 5 scrapes of a whole nutmeg on a nutmeg grater over the skillet)*

Continue stirring. When the mushrooms have shrunk slightly and deepened in color to a rich, butter-glossed brown, stir into them

*1 Morga broth cube, preferably unsalted*
*1 cup (8 ounces) sour cream or Alta-Dena brand kefir cheese (this thick, creamy concoction, made from yogurtlike kefir, is delectable, like sour cream only better)*

Stir this in, again tossing to coat the mushrooms, and lowering the heat. From this point on—the point of the sour cream or kefir cheese addition—the dish must not be allowed to reach a full boil. The sauce is now turning a lovely brown, from the mushrooms mingling with the tart creaminess that has just been poured in. Stir well. Heat through and serve.

For *Vegetable and Mushroom Stroganov,* use ½ onion, cut into crescents, and stir-fry with it the following: ½ *each* slivered green and red bell pepper; 1 large carrot, cut on the diagonal; 1 stalk broccoli, most of the lower stalk removed and the remaining stalk, with florets, sliced into thin "trees." Use ½ pound mushrooms. I once served this to my mother, over artichoke pasta, and she said, "Oooh, I think this is *better* than beef stroganov." We think so, too. There's also *Mushroom Stroganov over Pan-fried Tofu or Tempeh,* which is just what it says —the mushroom mixture served as a thick sauce over pan-fried tofu or tempeh. We use about 10 ounces of tofu to serve 4 people, or two 8-ounce packages of tempeh for 4. Or, alternatively, the prepared tempeh or tofu may be stirred into the mushroom mixture. And just what is pan-fried tofu or tempeh? I'm glad you asked that question . . .

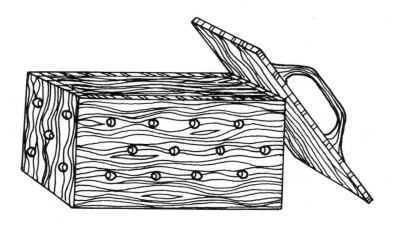

## Pan-fried Tofu or Tempeh

*Serves 4 to 6, when mixed into a multi-ingredient casserole, as above*

*Tempeh* is pronounced "tem-pay." This book is not the place to go into at length our love, in private life, of two delicious nonmeat protein foods, each very distinct but both derived from soybeans. See the Glossary for a full description, and know that there are a thousand ways with these wonderful foods. However, since they do not seem to us "Dairy Hollow House-y," and since we serve them only very, very occasionally at the inn, we are offering just this listing of a few basics with them, which can be added to any number of the dishes in this or other chapters. Do read the Glossary first; then what follows will make sense.

Cut into cubes or strips

> *1 drained block of tofu* or *1 package tempeh*

Prepare the following marinade/presauté dip:

> *1 tablespoon Tamari soy sauce*
> *2 tablespoons water*
> *3 tablespoons cider or balsamic vinegar*
> *a few shakes of Pickapepper and Tabasco sauces*

*(continued)*

Pour this mixture over the prepared tofu/tempeh chunks. Toss. Now, prepare a breading mixture made as follows:

*3 tablespoons nutritional yeast*
*2 tablespoons each unbleached white flour and whole wheat flour*
*⅓ cup crisp cracker crumbs (optional; if you omit these,*
*use a little more flour and/or yeast)*
*1 teaspoon sesame seeds (optional)*
*seasonings: black pepper, plenty of paprika, pinch of sweet basil*

Now, bread the tofu/tempeh, premoistened by its bath in the Tamari-vinegar mixture, in the yeast-crumb-flour mixture. Tempeh is quite sturdy; crumbs and tempeh can be shaken together in a paper bag; tofu, tenderer, should have its crumb mixture in a small saucer and be dipped gently, piece by piece. Heat a skillet, Pam-ed, with

*2 or 3 tablespoons light vegetable oil*

Not until oil is hot (but long before it reaches the point of smoking), add the breaded tofu/tempeh chunks, a few at a time. The oil should sizzle as they go in. Brown, flip with spatula, brown on other side. Drain the pan-fried tofu/tempeh on a paper towel.

Tempeh or tofu can also be done minus the breading mixture, stir-fried directly with vegetables, the tofu going in at the very last (it is so delicate it will crumble if not tossed with extreme care), the tempeh sooner.

Or you can make a particularly crispy version—this is perfect for tempeh—by omitting the breading mixture and dipping each piece of tofu/tempeh first in flour, then in beaten egg, then in finely ground cracker crumbs, then frying in the hot oil. This is the way to do tempeh, with some sort of wonderful concoction like Crescent's Mushrooms Stroganov, page 219, spooned over it, for those who have never eaten soy foods before.

Or you can make *Roxanne's Herb-Butter Sautéed Tofu.* Serves 2 to 4, depending on accompaniments. This would probably work with tempeh as well, but we think the delicate flavor and texture of tofu are beautifully enhanced by this simple and fragrant method of sauté-ing that was invented by Roxanne Harlowe, fine cook and real kitchen trouper. This method results in cubes of tofu that are quite saturated with delicious, buttery flavor, light brown and slightly chewy—deli-cious. Sprinkle them atop a plate as a final touch, incorporate them into stir-fries, get ready for people saying, "Uh, are there any more of those little brown, uh, whatever they were, those little, kind of, those really *good* things?"

Dice the tofu, well-drained but not dipped in marinade, into chunks the size of board-game dice.

Melt butter over low heat in a large skillet. Allow 4 tablespoons butter per 8 ounces or so of tofu. When the butter is gently bubbling but not anything like hot enough to burn, add the tofu cubes. Let them cook in the melted butter, simmering, almost, rather than frying as such. Then mince together, again per 8 ounces tofu, 3 or 4 cloves pressed garlic and a good tablespoon finely minced assorted fresh herbs —basil, rosemary, sage, etc. Sprinkle this over the tofu simmering in butter, along with several shakes of Tamari soy sauce. Stir, flip with a spatula every once in a while to distribute tofu and herbs and to turn it—but, again, you are not trying to brown it to crispness, you are trying to almost saturate it in the flavors of butter, garlic, herbs. The herbs and garlic make this inclined to burn if you don't watch it closely—do so. Cooked over a very low heat, these tender morsels of tofu will be done in about 20 minutes.

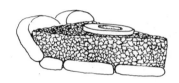

# Elegant Russian Dinner When the First Snow Flies

*Tidbits in Phyllo Dough: Tiny Phyllo Triangles*
*Stuffed with a Mixture of*
*Feta, Grated Cheddar, Garlic, Sautéed Onions, and Fresh Dill*
*Crescent's Winter Borscht à la Vielle Russe*
*Two Sisters Russian Black Rye*
*Crescent's Mushrooms Stroganov over Rice*
*Steamed Carrots and Peas Marinated in Vinaigrette on*
*a Bed of Red Leaf Lettuce, Minced Hard-boiled Egg*
*Buckwheat Crepes with Cherry Preserves*
*Vodka in which Buffalo Grass has Marinated*
*Hot Black Tea in Glasses with a Spoonful of Cherry Preserves*

# CREPES

In the words that were the title of one of the first books on the subject, *You Can Do Anything with Crepes.* (This book is by Virginia Pasley, a fine cook and a personal friend of ours; her seminal book on crepes was first published in 1958, and a reissue may be in the offing; she has since done another glorious cookbook, the 1974 *In Celebration of Food.*) Anyway, crepes, those thin, almost noodle-y French pancakes, have become so popular that today they are almost a cliché. They got that way for a good reason: they're delicious and totally versatile. We like them a lot, but we try not to overuse them. Here is a basic recipe, and several variations. In the first series, the crepes are used simply in the ordinary way one uses crepes, as lovely pancake-containers, with vegetables and cheeses and the like rolled up in them and sauce spooned over the top. In the second series, they are presented as a layered torte, a kind of crepe cake, with several variations. Third, we use them as tart shells, as we did in the Hors D'oeuvres chapter (see Feta Cheese Tartlets in Crepe Cups with Fresh Sage and Onions, p. 167), by pressing them into well-greased muffin tins. These little tart shells are then filled with any one of several interesting fillings, most on a quiche-filling line. But first:

## The Basic Crepe

*Makes 15 to 18 crepes*

As you will see, this is simplicity itself. Simply beat together till smooth

*3 eggs*
*1 cup milk*
*1 cup unbleached white flour*
*¼ teaspoon salt*
*1 tablespoon butter, melted and cooled*

Now, a most important step: *let batter stand for an hour.* This allows the flour particles to absorb the milk, making for a tender crepe. (If it is convenient to let it stand overnight, it will not harm the batter at all, but the flour-absorbing work is done within that first hour.)

Anytime after batter has rested (within reason), the crepes may be cooked. One of the charms of crepes is that they keep extremely well after they are made—for two or three days refrigerated or for a month or two frozen. Thus they are perfect make-in-advance food, and a package of them waiting in the freezer for an unexpected special occasion is like a twenty-dollar bill hidden in the bottom of the jewelry box.

To cook the crepes, have ready some

*soft butter*

Heat a crepe pan—any 5½- or 6-inch skillet, cast iron or nonstick or cast aluminum; we like to use a pan with rounded sides, the same kind we use for omelette making, and we usually spray it with Pam first. Brush with the softened butter, and, as it sizzles, pour in just enough batter to barely cover the pan—about 2 to 2½ tablespoons batter to a 6-inch pan. (We use a small ladle to scoop the batter into the pan.) Shake the pan to distribute the batter evenly, and cook over medium heat for 30 seconds to 1 minute, or until the top surface of the crepe has a slightly dulled, drier finish and, when you lift a corner of the crepe, you can see that its underside is a pleasantly mottled golden brown. Flip the crepe with a spatula, and cook for about 20 seconds on the second side (this side never cooks as attractively as the first and is usually used as the inside or bottom side of the completed dish, hidden from public scrutiny).

Arrange the crepes, as they come off the heat, on a cake rack to dry and cool for a few minutes. When they are dry but not brittle, stack the crepes on top of each other and wrap the stack in foil. Alternatively, you can place each crepe as it comes off the heat on a piece of wax paper, building a stack as you go: wax paper, crepe, wax paper, crepe.

For freezing, package the crepes in stacks of no more than 10. Thaw at room temperature, and use in any of the ways we'll shortly get into. But first, some simple variations on this basic crepe batter:

- Instead of milk, use a mixture of 1 cup beer and ⅓ cup half-and-half; this makes an extremely light and tender crepe.

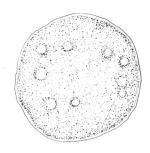

- Substitute buckwheat flour for the unbleached white; this makes a toothsome and distinctively flavored crepe that we like a lot, especially stacked for breakfast with butter and maple syrup, just as you would an ordinary pancake.

- Or substitute whole wheat pastry flour, for a crepe that is tender yet substantial with that good whole grain taste.

- Or skip over to page 227 and check out Wanda's Soft Corn Tortillas, a delicious Mexican cornmeal crepe.

- And the tenderest crepe of all is made with cornstarch, ideal for those with a gluten allergy. But be forewarned: cornstarch crepes do not hold up well when frozen and thawed (as I found out, to my dismay, when doing Ratatouille in Crepes Gratinée for thirty for a brunch some years back).

What to do with your treasure trove of crepes? Consider:

### Simplest Vegetable Crepes

Preheat oven to 400°. Fill crepes with any good stir-fried vegetable mixture or perhaps with Roxanne's Herb-Butter Sautéed Tofu, p. 222). Roll and place filled crepes, seam-side down, in a greased or Pam-ed baking dish. Sprinkle with grated cheese and bake just till cheese melts.

### Still-Simple Sauced Crepes

Make up a medium-thick basic white sauce: 2 tablespoons butter, melted; 2 tablespoons flour, whisked in; 1 cup milk (or, depending on how all-out you want to go, half-and-half or even heavy cream), also whisked, gradually, into butter-flour amalgamation; salt, pepper, and other seasonings as called for. Follow the preceding recipe for Simplest Vegetable Crepes, but pour the white sauce over them before baking, seasoned with one of the following:

- ½ cup finely grated sharp cheese and 1 teaspoon *each* Pickapepper sauce and dry mustard

- 1 Morga cube and sherry or brandy to taste (excellent over a mushroom-and-spinach stir-fry moistened with cream and sherry)

### Crepes with Sunset Sauce

Follow proportions on the white sauce, but use a good tomato juice from the health food store instead of milk or cream, and, when it is thickened, stir in grated Cheddar and Parmesan cheeses. Stuff the crepes with a well-seasoned stir-fry that includes just a bit of tomato, basil, and oregano; toss the vegetables, before stuffing the crepes, with a bit of grated cheese. Bake as directed.

## Wanda's Soft Corn Tortillas

*Makes about 20*

Because Arkansas borders Texas, Mexican food is probably the average Arkansawyer's favorite foreign food. These are somewhat Mexican in flavor, but they have a delicacy of texture and a subtlety of texture that is close to a French crepe.

We were introduced to these by Wanda Ross, a fine painter who raises goats, grows all her own food and flowers, and still finds time to philosophize. These oh-so-good thin pancakes are made with masa harina, a Mexican-style cornmeal. They can be used in any of our other crepe recipes. But we most often eat them by themselves, hot with a smear of butter, rolled up next to any good bean or vegetable soup, or dunked into Arkansalsa (p. 246). Don't miss these.

Blend well in blender or processor

*1 egg*
*1 cup milk*
*½ cup good fresh masa harina (available in the baking section of most groceries or at health food stores)*
*1 heaping tablespoon flour*
*½ teaspoon salt*

Let stand for 1 hour, and proceed as for cooking crepes (p. 225).

## CREPES AS A TORTE

We confess this is our favorite way with crepes: showy; good served hot, cold, or lukewarm; capable of infinite variation; as at home on the dressiest of buffets as it is on a very special picnic out by Beaver Lake, and, wherever and however served, totally delicious. Crepes line a skillet, in which are placed layers of savory vegetables and cheeses of contrasting flavors, colors, and textures. Over each layer is poured a rich but neutral in flavor binding cream, an eggy-cheese-y custard not unlike a quiche filling. Crepes separate the filling layer and top the whole, which is baked. After baking, it's turned neatly out of the skillet and sliced as one would slice a layer cake, artfully revealing the glorious layers of color.

We do three major variations on this theme. One, Crepe Torte Mediterrranée aux Arcs, features the sun-drenched Mediterranean flavors of Provence and Greece: tomatoes (just out of the garden, all summer long) and herbs and olives and feta cheese. Just a few changes in seasoning and method and, lo and behold, there's Italian Crepe Torte aux Arcs. Then, a simpler version—Garden Crepe Torte. It's that one we'll start with.

## Garden Crepe Torte

*Serves 18 to 20 as an hors d'oeuvre, 8 to 10 as an entrée (depending on accompaniments)*

Make up and have ready

*1 batch crepes (p. 224), made either with unbleached white or whole wheat pastry flour*

Now you will make up three fillings, of contrasting flavors and colors. We offer here a bright carrot layer, a green pea-onion-zucchini layer, and a dark brown mushroom layer. But be aware that the orange-red layer could also be made with red pepper or tomato; the green layer could be broccoli, zucchini, or green beans; and the brown could be eggplant.

*Carrot Filling:* Cut

*1 pound carrots (about 7 small to medium ones) into julienne pieces about the size of wooden matchsticks, neatly squared off*

Steam them quickly—no more than 30 seconds—and then give them the quickest of sautés—2 minutes, if they have been cut meticulously enough—in

*1 tablespoon butter, melted in a skillet*

They should be tender, but barely so, and not browned. Season them to taste with

*salt, pepper, and 2 tablespoons finely diced fresh parsley, plus a few drops fresh lemon juice*

Set aside. (For tomato filling, see either of the two Crepe Torte variations that follow; for red pepper filling, substitute 5 or 6 julienned red peppers for carrots and proceed with the same quick stir-fry.)

*Green Pea–Onion–Zucchini Filling:* Melt

*3 tablespoons butter*

Sauté in it

*1 small onion, finely diced*

As you stir it, remove from the freezer

*two 9-ounce boxes frozen peas*

Place the peas in a colander and set aside. Quickly grate

*2 small zucchinis*

Squeeze the grated zucchinis in handfuls over the sink to drain them of excess water and, when the onion has wilted, toss the zucchini into the skillet. Continue sautéing over medium heat, meanwhile running hot water over the frozen peas in the colander for about 30 seconds. Toss the peas into the zucchini-onion mixture (the grated zucchini should now have wilted, too) and remove from heat. Toss all together, and season to taste with

*salt, pepper, possibly a dab more butter*

*(continued)*

229

Set aside.

(A different green layer, of broccoli, is made as follows: Prepare

*1 nice bunch of broccoli*

by cutting off the tough end, then peeling the stem and julienning it into pieces about the length of a matchstick but slightly fatter. Separate the top into florets. Steam the broccoli just until its color intensifies, no longer. Remove from heat, run under cold water, and season with

*salt and pepper, about 1 tablespoon butter, again, and a bit of lemon juice*

Set aside.)

*Mushroom Filling:* In

*4 tablespoons butter*

sauté

*4 scallions, finely diced*

As they soften, add

*4 good-size double handfuls of sliced fresh mushrooms*

Sauté the mushrooms, stirring, until they darken in color, shrink slightly, and look buttery-glisten-y. Season with

*salt, freshly ground black pepper, and a touch of nutmeg*

Set aside. You now have three bowls of filling and a batch of crepes, ready and waiting. Grate, and also set aside, in separate bowls

*⅓ cup grated Swiss or Jarlsberg cheese*
*⅔ cup grated sharp Cheddar cheese*
*6 tablespoons Parmesan cheese (measure after grating)*

Preheat oven to 350°. Just one more step remains before you can do the actual assembly and baking, and that is to make the

*Custard for Binding:* This is simply done by combining in a food processor

> 4 ounces cream cheese or unflavored Boursin
> 3 eggs
> ½ cup milk, half-and-half, evaporated skim milk, or, to go all-out, heavy cream
> salt and freshly ground black pepper to taste, and another dash of nutmeg
> ½ teaspoon Pickapepper sauce

Buzz till smooth; it will be foamy, but never mind.

*Assembly and Baking:* Spray with Pam a 9-inch cast-iron skillet and grease it very, very well with

> *plenty of softened butter*

Now, line the skillet with the prepared crepes, the prettier side down, as follows: Overlap the crepes around the edges of the skillet first, so that there is some overhang over the top edge and some on the bottom. There should also be a spot about the size of a smallish saucer in the middle of the skillet where the black is still clearly visible. Over that spot, on top of the first ring of crepes that you have already laid, place another crepe, again with the good side down. The skillet is now lined with crepes.

Turn the Carrot Filling into the lined skillet, and over it sprinkle half the grated Cheddar cheese and a third of the Parmesan. Press the mixture down gently with your hands, and pour or ladle over it a third of the custard mixture. Set 1 crepe atop the carrots, in the center (there will be a border of carrots visible, un-crepe covered, but don't worry about them). Now, spread the layer of Mushroom Filling, sprinkle with all the grated Swiss or Jarlsberg and a third of the Parmesan, again press down lightly, again pour the custard over, again center a crepe atop the mushrooms. Now, spread the final layer, the Green Pea–Onion-Zucchini Filling, and sprinkle with the remaining cheese; press; pour over custard.

You now wish to seal the filling securely into the crepes. At this point, we usually have about 3 to 5 crepes left. Put one in the center of the broccoli and fold the overhang from the crepes lining the side of the skillet down over it, overlapped petal-style. Place the remaining 2 or 3 crepes overlapped atop these, to enclose the whole thing well. Smear some more

> *softened butter*

on the top. Place the filled skillet in a larger baking dish, place the

*(continued)*

whole thing in the oven, and pour hot water into the larger pan so that it comes halfway up the exterior of the skillet. Bake thus, uncovered, for about an hour. Then turn up the heat to 400° and bake for another 15 minutes; this makes it puff up a bit. By this time, it will be deliciously fragrant.

Remove from the oven. Let cool for about 10 to 20 minutes, run a knife around the edge, then reverse onto a serving plate. We have never had a problem with it sticking because of custard leakage, but this could conceivably happen if one either did not (a) grease the skillet thoroughly enough or (b) seal the fillings very securely with the crepes that lined the skillet. If you did have such a problem, just do the best you can, perhaps serving it from the skillet, or repairing the individual pieces and garnishing each plate prettily. It will taste wonderful in any case, but truly, if you've followed the directions, there should be no problem.

Let the torte, de-skilleted, cool for another 15 mintues, then cut into wedges, like a cake.

This and the variations that follow are quite possibly the ultimate vegetarian entrées, but, as we mentioned, they're equally great as hot or cold hors d'oeuvres or lukewarm on a buffet, or taken to a picnic.

Once you have got the hang of it, we know that you, like us, will be tempted to try these variations on this glorious theme.

## Italian Crepe Torte aux Arcs

*Serves 18 to 20 as an hors d'oeuvre; 8 to 10 as an entrée, depending on accompaniments*

The orange carrot layer described in the previous recipe is replaced by a

*Tomato Filling:* In

> *3 tablespoons olive oil*

sauté till softened

> *1 red onion, finely diced*

Add

> *8 large fresh tomatoes, diced*

Raise heat and cook quickly, stirring frequently, till almost all liquid is evaporated; you want a thick, almost dry paste of the tomatoes and onions. Remove from heat and season with

> *salt, pepper, basil, a touch of honey, oregano*

Now, replace the mushroom layer with a

*Ricotta Filling:* Make by simply combining

> *1½ cups ricotta cheese*
> *5 tablespoons grated Parmesan cheese*
> *3 cloves garlic, pressed*
> *1 egg yolk plus 1 whole egg*
> *salt, white pepper, and nutmeg to taste*

And instead of zucchini, onion, and green peas, make a

*Zucchini-Spinach Filling:* In

> *1 tablespoon each olive oil and butter*

sauté

> *1 bunch green onions, sliced*

When the onions tenderize a bit, stir in

> *4 medium zucchinis, cut in juliennes*
> *2 cloves garlic, pressed*

Toss around in the butter for 2 minutes, then add

> *3 handfuls well-washed chopped fresh spinach*

Pop a cover on and steam for 30 seconds, or until spinach wilts. Let cool in a colander, reserving any liquid that drips out. Combine that liquid, mushing in with the fingers, with

> *1 teaspoon cornstarch*

Recombine spinach-zucchini mixture with cornstarch mixture and

> *2 tablespoons minced parsley*

Set aside.

For cheeses with these fillings, we suggest ½ cup *each* mozzarella and provolone, grated, mixed with 2 tablespoons Parmesan. This mixture goes atop the zucchini and tomato layers, but not the ricotta. The binding custard, too, is divided two ways; the ricotta filling, in the middle, is self-binding.

Other than these changes, follow the same basic assembly and baking instructions given earlier, using the variations given. The tomato goes in first, then cheese, custard, crepe; then ricotta, then crepe,

233

then zucchini-spinach, cheese, custard, and seal the whole thing in.
Then, there's also our

## Crepe Torte Mediterranée aux Arcs

*Serves 18 to 20 as an hors d'oeuvre; 8 to 10 as an entrée, depending
on accompaniments*

With layers of eggplant, tomato, and green beans with olive,
spiked with feta and Parmesan, seasoned with . . . well, read on. The
first time we actually made this, from our mental hypothesis, Jan
turned to me and said, "You know, this *may* be the best thing we've
ever made."

*Tomato Filling:* Follow the Italian version, page 232, but season lightly
with a jot of cinnamon, basil, and oregano.

*Eggplant Filling:* In

> *3 tablespoons olive oil*

sauté

> *½ eggplant, skin included, cut into tiny dice*
> *2 cloves garlic, pressed*

Cook over medium-low heat, stirring often. When eggplant dice is a
tender, thick, fragrant mass, remove from heat and season with

> *salt, freshly ground pepper, oregano, and fresh dill*

Set aside.

For the *Green Bean and Black Olive Layer*, steam till tender-crisp

> *½ pound fresh green beans, cut in 1½-inch pieces*

Remove from heat and quickly finish them in

> *1 tablespoon each butter and olive oil*

After this sauté, add to them

> *⅔ cup sliced black olives*

Toss gently with

> *salt, freshly ground pepper, and oregano*

The order of the layers of this: Green Bean and Black Olive is the first layer to go in the skillet, and instead of the grated cheese it is covered with ⅓ cup or so

*crumbled feta cheese*

then the custard, crepe, and so on. In the middle, the eggplant layer, then a little feta, then custard, then crepe. At last, tomato, binding custard, top crepes. Then, bake.

Then, eat. This last suggests, as Middle Eastern–style foods always do to us, rice and artichokes for accompaniments.

This is as perfect to us as an hors d'oeuvre as it is a meatless entrée. The same is true of the Feta Cheese Tartlets in Crepe Cups with Fresh Sage and Onions, which is in the Hors D'oeuvres chapter. This basic recipe (see p. 167) is so versatile that we conclude our section on crepes with an elaboration on the theme.

### DAIRY HOLLOW HOUSE FLOWERS: FALL

*Fall arrangements: wild purple asters, goldenrod, and white chrysanthemums; branches of red and gold fall leaves (dogwood or maple) with rust-colored mums and goldenrod; a basket piled high with gourds and Indian corn and stalks of deep red-berried wild sumac, with a central vase or piece of florist's oasis into which rust and yellow chrysanthemums are placed, dried wild grasses placed here and there among the crevices between gourds; the same arrangement done with a basket of apples or pears and/or walnuts in the shell; a small hollowed-out pumpkin, water-filled, absolutely stuffed with chrysanthemums in rust and yellow and white, branches of changing leaves, vining clouds of blooming virgin's bower, set in a loosely twirled circle of entwined bittersweet; the first of the pink-berried, arching buckbrush combined with the last of the pink cosmos and lilac and wine chrysanthemums, dotted with wine-red roses (like the ones Ned sent me on our anniversary this year—not just a dozen on the day, but one a day for a week thereafter—male readers, are you taking notes?!).*

# CREPES AS TARTLETS

*Makes 15 to 18*

These are a far, far simpler thing than the hors d'oeuvres version. These tartlets are nothing more than crepes cunningly tucked into (with the good side down) well-greased, large-ish muffin tins. You will have to fold and tuck to get them to fit, but that is part of their charm. Have ready a Filling to pour in once the tartlets are in place, plus, if desired, a Savory Sauté.

## A Filling

Whip till smooth the following in a food processor:

*4 ounces cream cheese, softened*
*2 eggs*
*¼ cup sour cream*
*¾ cup half-and-half*
*¼ teaspoon salt*
*freshly ground black pepper to taste*
*few drops Pickapepper sauce*

and a selection of two or three of the following:

- ½ cup finely grated Cheddar or Jarlsberg cheese

- 2 tablespoons *each* minced fresh parsley and scallion

- 2 cloves garlic, pressed

- 1 teaspoon assorted dry herbs (thyme, basil, sage)

Savory Sauté possibilities:

- Mushrooms sautéed with butter and garlic

- Onions sautéed with butter

- Red onions sautéed in olive oil, with 1 finely diced tomato and some fresh sweet basil; cook till nearly dry.

## Assembly and Baking

Preheat oven to 350°. If you made a Savory Sauté, spoon a bit into each crepe cup. Then pour on filling, a bit in each, dividing evenly among the crepe cups. Bake for about 25 minutes.

We would like to mention again a close cousin of the crepe, Wanda's Soft Corn Tortillas, a delectable thin corn pancake made with masa harina (Mexican-style cornmeal). Much closer in texture to a crepe than to a tortilla, these are too good to miss. You'll find them on page 227.

Crepes are built around that miracle of culinary architecture, the egg, so it is natural to progress from crepes to egg dishes. Omelettes, in the Breakfast chapter, can serve as fine supper dishes, and so can soufflés. They often do, here—but because we feel space limitations hovering and because so many good soufflé recipes are available in other books, we will leave out the conventional ones.

## Grits Soufflé

*Serves 6 as an accompaniment, 4 as an entrée*

This Jan Brown specialty uses the good flavor and heft of corn grits, sparked with pale gold Monterey jack cheese. A kind of spoonbread, we like this as an accompaniment for simpler fish or chicken dishes, or any tomato-y entrée. In and of itself, it can serve as a meatless main dish (but serve it with something spicy).

In the top of a double boiler, bring to a boil

> *1½ cups milk*
> *1½ cups water*

Stir in slowly until mixture thickens

> *¾ cup grits, yellow or white, preferably stone-ground (but instant*
> *will do if you're in a pinch)*
> *½ teaspoon salt*

Cook, covered, stirring occasionally, for 30 minutes. Then add

> *3 tablespoons butter*

*(continued)*

Beat in till butter melts, and let cool for 30 minutes. Toward the end of that period, preheat oven to 350°. Then separate

*4 eggs*

Beat the whites till stiff and set aside. Beat the yolks till glossy. Stir the yolks into the grits gently yet thoroughly, and then fold in the stiffly beaten egg whites. Pour half the mixture into a Pam-ed 9-inch soufflé dish. Then sprinkle with

*½ cup grated Monterey jack cheese*

Pour the remaining mixture over cheese. Bake the Grits Soufflé for 45 minutes, or till puffed and lightly browned. Serve immediately.

*If he's content with a vegetable love
  which would certainly not suit me,
Why what a most particularly pure
  young man this pure young man must be!*

—W. S. Gilbert, Patience

# OTHER VEGETARIAN DISHES

Any of these are fancy vegetarian cooking at its best. But not all our vegetarian dishes, or, for that matter, all our egg dishes are rich and dripping with cream and cheeses. Some of our favorite meatless entrées are homey, down-to-earth peasant dishes, hearty and satisfying. You've run into plenty of them throughout this book already—

Ozark-Style Tuscany Bean Soup (p.103), for instance, is a great meat-less supper, coming as it does with bread and cheese included and accompanied by The Salad (p. 125). Jan's Pleasures of Summer Salad (p. 129), Crescent's More-or-Less Greek Salad (p. 126), Salade Park-hurst (p. 130)—any of these could be a light meal by themselves, a full meal if served with a cup of good hot soup (any of the potato soups are great with any of these salads). Here are some of our favorite simpler meatless dishes.

First on our Greatest Vegetarian Hits list of less elaborate vegetarian dishes are a few that deal with the egg in a style closer to its own natural and inherently satisfying form than those we have dealt with so far. Consider:

## Crescent's Eggs in Hell

*One skilletful, which will feed 3 or 4 to 6, depending on how many eggs each person wants*

I have been making this glorious dish since the age of sixteen, when I first read about it in M. F. K. Fisher's *How to Cook a Wolf.* It has never been anything less than enthusiastically received. M. F. K. Fisher is a *great* food writer. And these eggs—poached in a seasoned tomato sauce, which I spice up a bit more than Fisher—are great, too, as straightforward and evocative and sensuous as Fisher's writing about food. Simple, hearty peasant fare, Eggs in Hell makes you happy to eat.

In

*4 tablespoons olive oil*

sauté

*1 onion, chopped*
*1 green pepper, diced*
*2 cloves garlic, pressed*

When they soften, stir in

*one 20-ounce can tomatoes and their juice,*
*the tomatoes broken up*
*a bit*
*4 tablespoons tomato paste*
*1 teaspoon basil*
*½ teaspoon oregano*
*a few needles rosemary, 1 bay leaf, 1 teaspoon honey*

*(continued)*

Simmer the sauce for about 10 minutes, then make indentations in it insofar as possible, with a spoon and break into it

*4 to 6 eggs*

Spoon sauce around and over them, pop on a cover, and let the whole thing simmer gently till eggs are poached; the whites should be medium firm, the yolks still runny. Lift each egg out with a spatula onto a serving plate in which you've placed

*a bed of cooked spaghetti*

or

*a thick slice of toasted French bread*

or

*a pile of steaming hot rice*

Spoon extra sauce around each golden-eyed egg, and sprinkle with

*grated Parmesan cheese*

## Mexican-Style Eggs in Hell

Arkansans, because of their proximity to Texas, in general have a penchant for Mexican food. This dish is kin to Huevos Rancheros but a bit more sophisticated and less oily. Sauté 2 teaspoons cumin seed, whole, with the onion and green pepper. Cut the basil and oregano by half, and add a dash of chili powder and a little bit of juice from a jar of jalapeño peppers. Lift the cover before the eggs are through poaching and sprinkle them with a blanket of grated sharp Cheddar. Serve with any of the starches just listed, or with corn or flour tortillas, or Wanda's Soft Corn Tortillas, page 227. For an extra fillip, garnish each egg with a few slices of avocado, a dab of sour cream, a puff of alfalfa seed sprouts, some chopped onion—all your favorite Mexican "fixings."

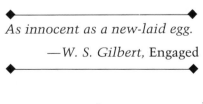

*As innocent as a new-laid egg.*

—*W. S. Gilbert*, Engaged

## Eggs Poached in and on Stir-fried Vegetables

*One skilletful, to feed 2 or 3 to 6, depending on how many eggs each wants and the accompaniments*

A delicious brunch or lunch or late-night supper, quick and easy and very, very good. Sauté in a large skillet enough vegetables for the number of people you're serving. (The morning I wrote this we had a combination of onions, green peas, carrots, broccoli, and mushrooms.) Sauté vegetables until they are nearly done. Season with Tamari soy sauce and fresh herbs. Make an indentation in the vegetables with a wooden spoon and crack an egg into each space. Gently crowd the vegetables around the eggs, nestling them but being careful not to break the yolks. Cover the skillet with a lid and let the eggs poach for about 3 minutes. Remove cover and check doneness. When eggs are still on the runny side but approaching doneness, cover with piles of grated cheese, cover again and let cheese melt, remove from heat, and serve.

Then there's the whole subject of pasta—a subject that is of endless interest to us. We do pasta in a thousand different ways—but rarely at the inn, because it doesn't seem Dairy Hollow House-y. However, we must make an exception to the rule for a dish that is truly exceptional, and that is

## The Great, The One and Only, Garlic Spaghetti

*Serves 2 to 4 as an entrée*

If The Salad is the most important recipe in this book, Garlic Spaghetti is the one we have been asked for most often over the years. We would never serve it at the inn without knowing the guests extremely well; it is too bold, too assertive a dish, and, again, it doesn't quite fit the inn's ambience. But it is simply too good to leave out. Jan and I one day were talking about how, if this book reflected the way we actually ate while working on it, it would be three hundred pages of garlic spaghetti!

As far as I can tell, I must take credit for the invention of this glorious dish. It is basically an adaptation of Spaghetti à la Carbonara, made vegetarian and with a whole lot more garlic. Yes, the garlic and the egg are both raw. Don't be fainthearted about this, or about the amount of garlic, or you will miss one of the best dishes known to man or woman. What happens is the butter melts, the egg cooks ever

241

so slightly, the cheese melts, and an indescribably heavenly amalgamation takes place.

Put on a pot of boiling water and prepare

*8 ounces dry spaghetti*

While spaghetti is cooking, prepare the "sauce"—a thick paste, really, that you will toss over the cooked hot spaghetti.
Into blender or food processor, place

*1 raw egg*
*5 to 8 cloves garlic, peeled and pressed—not less!*
*4 tablespoons butter*
*¼ to ⅓ cup grated Parmesan cheese*
*1 teaspoon dried sweet basil*

Whirl all together, until smooth and well blended. One can also do this by hand, if the garlic is put through a press. When spaghetti is cooked, but not overcooked, and drained, place it in a large bowl or pan and spoon over it the garlic-cheese paste and

*¼ cup finely chopped parsley*
*fresh coarsely ground black pepper to taste—a lot!*

Toss well. Mound this glorious concoction onto plates and serve. Pass at the table

*red pepper flakes*
*vegetarian bacon bits*
*more Parmesan and black pepper*

Eat this and swoon.
In the years since making the acquaintance of Garlic Spaghetti, I have tried various embellishments of this. I have sautéed onions and mushrooms, stir-fried green peppers, added cream. But nothing—nothing—except the optional red pepper flakes and veggie bacon bits adds anything special to the unadulterated blissful purity of this.
You will know you used enough garlic if you wake up the next morning tasting it on your breath.

◆——————————————————◆

*THE GARLIC LADY IN FEBRUARY*

*I am the garlic lady, six*
*pressed cloves on my spaghetti, and*
*those bulbs as raw as myself on*
*this blustery day*

*which I shall spend at home, entertaining*
*myself. I find my jokes*
*enormously funny, and I know*
*about herbs and botanicals, too.*
*Take the pungent healing tuber*
*I love to chew: it's allium,*
*an errant member of the lily family*
*and you'd sweat it through your pores*
*if you wore it in your shoe.*

*For just today I've ten good books*
*and wood and food and fire. Only*
*sleet and gust are welcome guests;*
*who'd dare drive this windy way, to knock*
*at my steamy kitchen, who would*
*intrude? I am the red-wine one-woman*
*gypsy-coven, and I dance*
*and dance and dance*
*my smell is strong and my taste*
*is strong and you say*
*I am wild, yet never begin*
*to see me dance and dance and dance.*

*Now if you should see me walking the town*
*if you dare, watch for my eyes:*
*they'll catch you like a dime in the sidewalk.*
*Put this meeting in your pocket; now add*
*your chilly fingers. Now, now,*
*though you may not see me again 'til April,*
*your hands are warm for the rest of the winter.*

—Crescent Dragonwagon,
Message from the Avocadoes

◆————————————————————◆

## "Ark-Mex" Lasagna

*Serves 8*

This hearty, spicy dish, officially called Chilequiles and closely
resembling enchiladas, is not exactly what we'd call Dairy Hollow
House-y, but it is so good and so enthusiastically received whenever
we do serve it (usually as a winter supper to nonmeat eaters) that we
simply had to include it. Again, the general love of Mexican food

243

throughout the state, and our own enjoyment of this dish, compelled us to include it.

Like lasagna, it is a bit of a production, involving making up several components and then assembling them in layers in a casserole, which is then baked. The components, as in so many international dishes, are analogous yet highly distinctive in seasoning. The sauce used in real Italian lasagna is generally a basil-and-olive-oil–scented tomato sauce; here we use "Arkansalsa," our vigorous version of Mexican-style picante, or hot, sauce. (The directions for it follow this recipe.) The fillings, which in a traditional lasagna might be ricotta and spinach for one and ground beef for the other, here are a cheese filling and a bean filling (their how-tos are included in the body of this recipe). And the place that broad noodles fill in conventional lasagna —that of adding a sink-your-teeth-into-it starchy layer, as well as de- lineating the sauce and various fillings, is occupied here—and occu- pied well—by corn tortillas.

Make up

*1 recipe Arkansalsa (recipe follows)*

Make up, also, a simple Cheese Filling, as follows. Grate

*4 cups assorted cheeses (either one or a combination of sharp Cheddar, Monterey jack, hot pepper jack, mild Cheddar, mozzarella)*

Set aside.

Now make a Bean Filling: Chop and set aside

*2 large onions*

Season

*3 cups cooked pinto beans*

with

*2 cloves garlic, pressed*
*1 teaspoon cumin*
*salt to taste*

Mash half of the beans with a potato masher, or whirl in blender. Stir mashed and whole beans together.

*Jan on Jalapeños:*
*Jalapeños are among our favored garden treasures. We pick them fresh from the garden, wash and dry them, and then pop them whole into clean fruit jars, putting the jar in the freezer. When we need 1 or 2 peppers for a recipe, they are easily removed from the jar and thawed.*

*Sometimes we have dehydrated them fresh from the garden. Always be extremely careful in handling jalapeños—their oil leaves an essence that can be quite painful and easily spread. Once, after arranging pepper slices on the dehydrating trays, my hands began to ache and burn. Even washing them in salt water did not remove the sting. Since that time, I've kept a pair of cloth gloves in my kitchen linens, just for handling peppers.*

## Assembly and Baking

Grease or spray with Pam a 12-inch casserole or large cast-iron skillet. One by one, dip into Arkansalsa and begin layering into casserole

*corn tortillas (uncooked; you will need about 20 in all)*

Preheat oven to 350°. Line the bottom of the casserole with one layer of dipped tortillas. Spread tortillas with some of the bean filling. Now another layer of Arkansalsa-dipped tortillas, sprinkled with the cheese mixture, and another layer of Arkansalsa-dipped tortillas. Sprinkle each layer with a little of the chopped raw onion. Keep layering in this fashion until you've used all the tortillas and fillings. If you have extra Arkansalsa, pour it over the entire casserole. Top with

*1 cup grated cheese*
*3 tablespoons minced parsley*
*a sprinkle of paprika*

Bake for 35 to 40 minutes, or until cheese is bubbly and tortillas are browned. Remove from oven and cut into lasagnalike portions. (You can top each portion with a dollop of sour cream and a dash of cayenne.) Serve with The Salad, page 125, or Garlic Slaw, page 134. For dessert, fresh chilled pineapple, and maybe Elsie Freund's Incredible Spanish Flan, page 298.

## Arkansalsa
*Makes 2 cups*

Into a food processor or blender container, place

*4 tomatoes, chopped*
*¼ cup tomato paste*
*1 whole jalapeño pepper, stem removed*
*1 medium-size onion, finely chopped*
*6 to 8 cloves garlic*
*juice of 1 lemon*
*3 tablespoons minced fresh parsley*
*1 teaspoon minced fresh cilantro (optional)*
*½ teaspoon minced fresh oregano (or ¼ teaspoon dried)*

Blend together well.

## A Simple Dinner for Billy

*The Salad with Avocado*
*"Ark-Mex" Lasagna*
*Rice*
*Flan with Fresh Fruit Garnish*

# Baked Cheshire with Almonds

*Serves 6*

Another great cornmeal-based dish, this can easily serve as a vegetarian entrée, but it's also a great accompaniment. It's a fragrant dish that gives cornmeal a whole new slant—a tasty casserole with almonds, melted cheese, and hot chilies.

In a dutch oven, bring to a boil

*3 cups water*
*1 teaspoon salt*

Whisk into the boiling water, stirring constantly so that it does not lump

*1½ cups yellow cornmeal*

Simmer over low heat for about 3 minutes, or until mixture begins to thicken. Remove from heat.

Preheat oven to 350°. In a small skillet, sauté together until onions are tender

*3 tablespoons butter*
*1 small onion, chopped*
*1 fresh jalapeño, very finely sliced*
*3 cloves garlic, finely minced*
*1 teaspoon Tamari soy sauce*

Just before removing from heat, stir in

*1 cup chopped raw almonds*

Stir to just coat almonds. Add onion-almond mixture to cornmeal in Dutch oven. Stir in

*4 well-beaten eggs*
*3 cups grated cheese (try one of the Cheddars or Monterey jack or a combination with mozzarella)*

When all ingredients are well blended, top with

*1 more cup grated cheese*
*a sprinkle of paprika*

Bake for 45 to 55 minutes, or until cheese is melted and casserole is golden brown.

If you are serving this with an especially spicy, rich, or highly seasoned entrée, you might wish to make this a bit more neutral in flavor by omitting the almonds and jalapeños.

# Mediterranean Vegetable Pie

*Makes 1 pie, serving 6 to 8*

This spicy main-dish pie is excellent in the fall, when eggplant and squash are at their height and the cool fall days suggest that the warming presence of the oven is in order.

Preheat oven to 350°. Prepare a single whole wheat pie crust, page 340, adding to the flour mixture

*4 tablespoons sesame seeds*

Roll out crust and place in pie pan. Bake for 10 minutes. Remove from oven and cool slightly. Add the filling, made as follows: In

*2 tablespoons olive oil*

sauté

*5 or 6 cloves garlic, minced*
*1 medium onion, finely diced*
*1 green pepper, finely diced*
*1 teaspoon each oregano and basil (triple the amounts if fresh herbs are available—and count yourself lucky!)*
*1 teaspoon Tamari soy sauce*

When onions are tender, stir well and add to sauté

*1 cup peeled and diced eggplant (in ½-inch pieces)*
*1 cup each ⅛-inch-thick rounds zucchini and yellow summer squash*

Cover and steam over low heat for 4 minutes. Remove from heat and let sautéed vegetables cool for 5 minutes. Pour vegetable mixture into cooled pie crust. Layer on top of vegetables

*1 tomato, finely sliced*
*6 mushrooms, finely sliced*

Top with

*1 cup grated mozzarella cheese*

Place in oven and bake for 45 minutes, or until crust is lightly browned and cheese is golden. Serve in pie wedges.

❖

# A Late-Afternoon Vegetarian June Wedding Feast for 25 in the Garden

*"Hollow-Mades"*
*Crepe Torte Mediterranée*
*Theda's Chilled Stuffed Artichokes*
*Roquefort Wafers, Parmesan Olive Balls*
*Tidbits in Phyllo Dough: Small Triangles with Ratatouille Filling*
*Large Crudités Table: Vegetables in Season with*
*Lemon Tahini Dressing in Pumpkin Shell*
*Savory Onion and Herb Dip in Hollowed Cabbage Shell*
*Ample and Interesting Cheese Tray*
*(Vermont Cheese, Herb-Garlic Boursin, Gruyère,*
*Gouda, Camembert, Gorgonzola, Chèvre, a Marinated Mozzarella)*
*Two Overflowing Breadbaskets: In the First:*
*Land of Milk and Honey Whole Wheat Bread, Dairy Hollow*
*Oatmeal Bread Supreme, Two Sisters Russian Black Rye Bread*
*with Butter • Assorted Mustards*
*And in the Second:*
*Strawberry Bread, Pannetone, Bountiful Blueberry Muffins*
*with Butter • Strawberry Butter • Assorted Jams and Jellies*
*Wedding Cake*
*Fresh Fruit Platter • Platter of Assorted Cookies*
*Hot Coffee • Alcoholic and Nonalcoholic Punch Bowls*

*On the table:* Everywhere, fresh daisies and clouds of babies' breath, rose petals and mint leaves sprinkled on the tablecloths

*A note on this menu:* Although it seems huge, this would be an ideal menu for a self-catered wedding or any large affair. Virtually everything can be done in advance. Virtually nothing needs to be served hot-hot or cold-cold. You do need a trusted assistant laying all this out during the ceremony, obviously, and the wedding cake is one item that could be farmed out professionally or to a dear, dear friend (we like the lemon pound cake, with lemon filling, as a wedding cake very much, and the carrot cake or apple-spice also works well as a wedding cake, and both have become classics in the last ten or fifteen years). Friends can make the sweet breads and the cookies for the platter ahead of time—or at least store those *you* make in their freezers. Make ahead, also, and freeze unbaked phyllo triangles.

# Picnics: The Portable Repast

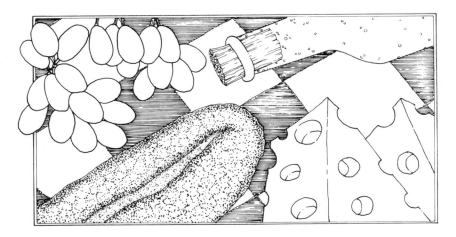

## Jan's Recipe for a Perfect Picnic

*Serves 1 or 2 or more*

You'll need

*1 good-size Ozark basket (handmade split oak is ideal)*

Line basket with

*1 nice thick red-and-white checkered towel (you can use blue and white if your fellow picnicker has blue eyes)*

Begin now by layering in all the things you'll need for your picnic:

*plates: allow 1 per person (this is one time that a respectable plastic or paper is acceptable)*
*eating utensils: forks, soup spoons, dessert forks or spoons, dinner knives, 1 good sharp knife, serving spoons*
*a can opener, a corkscrew, salt and pepper shakers*
*cups, sometimes paper, usually genuine champagne glasses*
*napkins (we prefer red or blue bandannas, or small thirsty hand towels in an appropriate color)*

(It is essential for cold things to be *very* cold and hot foods to be piping hot. In hot weather, be particularly careful with salads containing mayonnaise or dishes with dairy products.)

In an adjacent basket, be sure to bring along insect repellent and suntan lotion.

When you've gathered and basketed all the accoutrements, add

## The Picnic Food

● *a chilled soup, poured into a chilled Thermos bottle (we suggest Cascadilla, p. 112, or Chilled Strawberry Soup with Mint, p. 113, or Chilled Caraway Squash Bisque, p. 115)*
● *a prepared salad, well chilled, sealed in a container, a heartier one that will travel well (like Salade Parkhurst, p. 130, with the marinated components each traveling in separate containers, and the green leaves left whole and well washed, also in a separate bag; or Confetti Slaw, p. 133)*
● *an entrée, well dished and wrapped, perhaps traveling in a lidded casserole dish (like a sumptuous Crepe Torte, pp. 228–235, or Chicken Breasts in Phyllo with Dijon, p. 195, or Vegetable Terrine, p. 169)*
● *home-baked bread (maybe a Two Sisters Russian Black Rye, p. 82, or Crescent's Favorite Whole Wheat Butterhorns, p. 85); don't forget the butter!!!!!!*
*(For a less formal affair, the two previous items can sometimes be combined in the form of a glorious sandwich or a giant stuffed bread . . . recipe to follow.)*
● *dessert (some Jan Brownies, p. 326, Crescent's Classic Chewy Brownies, p.327, Brown Sugar Brownies, p. 328, Virginia's Lemon Bars, p. 324, or Chocolate-dipped Oatmeal-Walnut Drop Cookies, p. 329)*
● *fruit (an assortment of what's in season—apples, peaches, bananas, grapes, blueberries, strawberries, slabs of melon . . . )*
● *beverage(s): some bring chilled wine or chilled sparkling cider, an insulated jug of iced tea or herb tea punch or lemonade; some, a Thermos of hot coffee.*

Arrange the foods well in the basket, stacking where necessary. Garnish the entire picnic basket with

*1 homemade quilted picnic cloth (the Aunt Sukey's Choice pattern would be nice)*

A perfect accompaniment is a chilled jug of Ozark spring water or

251

a bottle of wine. You'll also need

*a beautiful picnic site (we like the overhang at Hogscald Hollow, the cliffs out by Beaver, or a rowboat at Lake Lucerne)*

When you arrive at the site, enjoy it. This may include such activities as

*a.* swimming

*b.* talking

*c.* kissing

*d.* reading trashy magazines

*e.* suntanning (have someone else apply the lotion)

*f.* examining geological or other natural formations

*g.* playing musical instruments (recorder is more suitable than tuba) (but never, never a radio!)

*h.* identifying wildflowers from a book

When enjoying is partially done, spread out the picnic cloth, arrange the foods, set out the plates and utensils, pour the wine (or other beverage).

Eat.

Enjoy some more.

You may wish to finish with a nap in the sun: especially enjoyable.

## Variation

Pack the basket into a canoe. Tie in place. Get into the canoe. Float down

*a.* The White River

*b.* The King's River

*c.* The Buffalo River

Depending on the time of the year and the water levels, you may wish to pack the basket into a very, very securely knotted heavy-duty plastic garbage bag.

Stop to eat at some point along your float, a sitting-down place that permits as many of the enjoying activities just listed as possible. You should stop some time after you get hungry and before you get sleepy.

## Another Variation: Winter Picnics

Here in the Ozarks, warm, springlike weather alternates with cold, foggy damp days and the occasional spell of bitter cold. But people less lucky than we—New Englanders, to wit—have introduced us to the joys of winter picnics, eaten along a vigorous hike or cross-country ski trek. One must be dressed very warmly; the menu must include hot, hot soup from a Thermos; one must bring a waterproof cloth to go under the blanket—but with these provisos, a picnic lunch during a winter walk in the woods is a special and unusual pleasure.

Of course, you can always wait till one of those 70-degrees-in-January Ozark days, and take off then.

*A special note:* Whenever and however you take off, if you are a guest with us, we can prepare an absolutely glorious picnic lunch or dinner basket for you on advance notice; we will also be happy to arrange a float trip for you, with or without a guide. Ozark float trips, whether an hour long or a week long, whether your first or your hundredth, whether white water or placid, are always, always peak experiences. I have never had one, even when it was pouring down rain and I was cold and soaked to the bone, that did not have moments of pure joy.

◆——————————————————————————————————————————◆

*DAIRY HOLLOW HOUSE FLOWERS: SPRING SWEETNESS
IN WINTER*

*You can have the sweetest touch and fragrance and form of spring in
the dead of winter, with just a little advance planning. In the fall,
purchase paper-white or soleil d'or narcissus bulbs for "forcing"—
that is, growing indoors in the winter months. These exquisitely
scented flowers can be started anytime from November into late January. Nothing could be easier: Fill a pot with good drainage one-third
of the way full with pebbles. Place the onion-y looking bulb or bulbs
in the pebbles, root side down, sprout side up. Sprinkle more pebbles
around the bulb, until only the upper quarter of it shows. Water; the
water should be visible around the top layer of the pebbles. As the
green stalks shoot up, check them for water often. Some people swear
by a tablespoon of gin—yes, gin—added to each cup of water poured
on the bulbs, saying it helps the stalks stand straighter, preventing
legginess. From the time you settle the bulb in its pebbles to full
bloom is only about four weeks (this short duration makes narcissus
growing an excellent indoor gardening project for kids).*

*For a most beautiful holiday table, plan your guest list early and
start a single paper-white in a single clay pot for each guest, placing
it in front of each table setting. Naturally, the flowers can be carried
home—a special party favor which, if planted outdoors, foliage and
all, as soon as the ground can be worked, will bloom year after year.*

◆——————————————————————————————————————————◆

# ELEGANT, UNFORGETTABLE
# PICNIC ENTRÉES

Here are a few more recipes that we think are just perfect for very
special picnics.

Quick! Creep back to the Hors d'oeuvres, to the entrées! We
think Jenelle's Tomatoes Rockefeller (p. 155) are wonderful to take
on a more formal, sedate picnic, and we just love any of the Crepe
Tortes (pp. 228–235) served lukewarm or cool. Lemon-Pepper Chicken
(p. 176) is as good cold as it is hot, and chicken with John S. Cross's
Great Southern Barbeque Sauce (p. 200) is perfect at sites with a grill.

Some of our other special picnic entrées include a Chilled Trout
that is an incredible, dreamy picnic entrée for the more civilized out-

door meal (obviously, a chilled trout is not something you take back-packing up Petit Jean Mountain).

Mediterranean food, it seems to us, often does well served hot, cold, or lukewarm, and is thus just right for a picnic. Consider our "Hollow-Mades" (p. 153), stuffed grape leaves, perhaps rounded out by Crepe Torte Mediterranée (p. 234) and pita breads . . . Oh! Delicious-ness! And somewhat in the same idiom, this glorious creation:

# Italian Spinach Torte

*Serves 6 to 8*

This is elegant picnic fare—layers of mushrooms, spinach, and cheeses enfolded in a rich pastry crust. One of its secrets is that it's baked in a springform pan, which allows for a much taller than usual "pie."

*Mushroom Filling:* Sauté together

> *2 tablespoons butter*
> *½ pound fresh mushrooms*
> *1 teaspoon Tamari soy sauce*

over medium heat until mushrooms are golden. Remove from heat and set aside.

*Spinach Filling:* Grind or finely chop and stir together

> *1 pound washed and chopped fresh spinach*
> *1 small onion, finely chopped*
> *4 cloves garlic, minced*
> *½ cup finely chopped parsley*

Add to spinach mixture

> *1 egg, beaten*

Stir together well and set aside.

*Ricotta Cheese Filling:* In a small bowl stir together

> *15 ounces ricotta cheese*
> *1 teaspoon minced fresh oregano (or ½ teaspoon dried)*
> *1 teaspoon Tamari soy sauce*
> *¼ teaspoon cayenne pepper*

*(continued)*

255

Prepare

*a pastry for a 9-inch double crust pie (see p. 337),*

adding

*2 tablespoons grated Parmesan cheese to the flour*

Roll out two-thirds of the pastry and ease it into a 9-inch springform pan. Brush the bottom and sides of pastry with

*1 egg white, beaten*

Spread the fillings over the pie crust: first the mushroom filling, then the spinach filling, the ricotta cheese filling, and finally sprinkle with

*½ pound mozzarella cheese, shredded*

Preheat oven to 400°. Roll out the remaining pastry and cover the top of the pie. Seal and crimp edges together. Brush entire top with more unbeaten egg white. Bake for 10 minutes; then lower heat to 375° and bake for 25 to 30 minutes more, until crust is golden. Cool slightly before serving. Release the springform pan, removing the cylindrical piece, and keep the pie on the bottom of the pan, setting it onto a pretty serving platter. Or you can chill the entire pie and carry it in the springform pan to the picnic site, where it can be unpanned, sliced, and served. Rhapsody!

# Seduction by a Waterfall Picnic

*Vegetable Terrine with Assorted Crudités*
*Cold Lemon-Pepper Chicken*
*Jan's Pleasures of Summer Salad*
*French Bread • Two Sisters Russian Black Rye Bread*
*Brie • Grapes on the Stem • Perfect Pears*
*Virginia's Lemon Bars*
*May Wine • Coffee in a Thermos*

# Chilled Poached Trout

*Serves 4*

Serve *this* on your next fishing trip and you will be inspired to catch even more (though the fish, of course, may not be so inspired to bite). Here, small trout are poached in a flavorful broth, chilled, and well garnished.

We might well serve this at a secluded picnic spot if we had seduction in mind . . .

Simmer in a large pan for about 30 minutes

*2 quarts water*
*1 cup apple cider vinegar*
*1 onion, quartered*
*1 carrot, sliced*
*1 stalk celery, sliced*
*juice of ½ lemon*
*½ teaspoon grated lemon rind*
*2 bay leaves*
*1 teaspoon whole cloves*
*1 teaspoon salt*

Poach in this broth

*4 small whole cleaned trout*

for 5 to 7 minutes, or until they are cooked through. Remove gently, drain, and refrigerate to chill. Arrange to serve on individual plates, with the following for each trout

*1 hard-boiled egg, sliced*
*a sprinkle of paprika*
*a portion of Cucumber-Dill Cloud, page 203*
*a dill weed garnish*
*salt and pepper to taste*

Bring these items to the picnic site each in their separate containers. Asparagus vinaigrette and a French-style potato salad or French bread would be a natural with this, as would some meltingly ripe Brie, some crisp apples, a stem of perfect green grapes, some sparkling cider, or a nice Vouvray to drink . . . Ah.

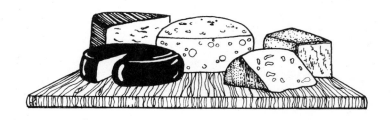

257

# San Francisco Cross-to-the-Ozarks Chicken Salad

*Serves 4 to 6*

One of the all-time best chicken salads, which takes its name from a perfect holiday Jan once had in this loveliest of cities and on which she experienced the revelation of chicken and fruit together, cold and delicious, for the first time. This salad is a meal in itself. Note that the chicken is left in large chunks, not minced as in most most chicken salads.

Make sure this, like any salad with mayonnaise, stays well chilled to prevent spoilage.

Blend together in a large bowl

*½ cup sour cream*
*½ cup mayonnaise*
*½ teaspoon Tamari soy sauce*

Add the following:

*4 cups cooked chicken chunks, cut into 1-inch cubes*
*2 apples, unpeeled, cut into small pieces*
*3 stalks celery, finely chopped*
*2 tablespoons finely diced cucumber*
*1 teaspoon grated orange rind*
*1 cup walnut halves*
*1 cup golden raisins*

Stir until all ingredients are coated with dressing. Chill thoroughly.

## Crescent's Variation

Instead of apples, add 1 cup diced fresh pineapple and ½ cup halved green grapes. Omit celery, cucumber, orange rind, raisins; use ¼ cup walnuts and add 3 tablespoons very, very, very finely minced onion. Use the bare minimum of mayonnaise; season with salt and black pepper, freshly ground of course.

---

*DAIRY HOLLOW HOUSE FLOWERS: THE GRAND
COMMANDER LILY*

*The Grand Commander lily—with huge glorious trumpet-shaped
blooms, pink and white and large as a salad plate, deep maroon
speckles on its delicate throat, deep, burnt-orange stamens which
poke proudly out, and a heavenly, indescribably sweet nutmeglike
fragrance—are as close to a religious experience as one can get in
flowers. When the Grand Commanders bloom, usually in late June
and early July, you can hardly pry us away from Dairy Hollow, where
the sweet scent permeates the air. We clip off individual blooms to
send to some of our favorite people around town (like Jan Watson, at
the Bank of Eureka Springs); we wish we had long black hair down to
our waists so we could wear these magnificent things. Grand Commanders fill us with wonder and joy. Everyone should grow them.
Our best bulbs came from Van Bourgondien Brothers, Box A, Babylon, New York 11702.*

---

# SATISFYING SANDWICHES

## World's Best Pimento Cheese

---

*Makes 2½ cups cheese for 4 to 6 sandwiches*

We had never liked pimento cheese until we ate it at Papa Robin's,
a now-defunct restaurant in Jasper, Arkansas. Our re-creation of their
marvelous pimento cheese:

Puree till smooth in processor

*4 tablespoons mayonnaise*
*3-ounce package cream cheese, softened*
*3 cloves garlic*
*handful fresh parsley*
*several vigorous shots of Pickapepper and Tabasco sauces*

Turn into a bowl. Now, in food processor, process just till coarsely
chopped

*1 cup pecans*

*(continued)*

259

Add to mayonnaise mixture with

*1 small jar diced pimentos and all juice*

Now, grate, in food processor

*12 ounces extra sharp Cheddar cheese*

Turn into bowl with remaining ingredients. Stir well to combine. Let stand, refrigerated, at least 1 hour. Even better the next day.

Great on thick slices of Land of Milk and Honey Whole Wheat Bread (p. 80) with sprouts and thick juicy tomatoes. Oh, boy! Let's have some now!

## A Simple and Wonderful Sandwich

We often use this at teatime, on thin-sliced bread:

*herb-garlic Boursin*
*thinly sliced peeled cucumber*
*alfalfa seed sprouts*

## A Quick-Run-Out-to-Lake-Leatherwood-for-Lunch-with-the-Kids-Picnic

*Peanut Butter, Banana, Honey, and Date Sandwiches*
*on Whole Wheat Pita*
*New Wave Carrot-Pineapple Salad*
*Oranges • Apples*
*Chocolate-dipped Oatmeal Walnut Cookies*

## THE STUFFED POCKET À LA 1890'S DELI

The 1890's Deli, tucked into tiny Center Street in Eureka Springs, is a family-owned operation, several times chosen the best deli in Arkansas by the readers of the *Arkansas Times Magazine.* The sandwiches are good, the desserts range from an excellent baklava to an imported-from-New-York cheesecake to homemade chocolate chip and oatmeal cookies. But we think the real secret of 1890's success lies in its genuinely warm, friendly atmosphere: the matrilineal conviviality of Edna, Sandy, Rose, and Robbi (mother/grandmother, daughters/sisters/mother, and granddaughter/daughter, respectively). This clan with assorted husbands and brothers and fathers lived in Texas until opening the deli here in 1980.

Sandy, who has always liked to cook and is a big reader of cookbooks, brought me this recipe for the 1890's Stuffed Pocket, a pita bread sandwich that is a cornucopia of good things. It's also the deli's single most requested recipe, and one that we stop in for when we're halfway through a busy day of in-town erranding. "You'd think *anyone* could just figure this out," she told me, "but people ask for it all the time." The sautéed mushroom mixture makes it extra-good, and also indefinable to the average eater.

That mixture is the starting point.

## Mushroom Sauté for Stuffed Pocket à la 1890's Deli

*A batch of it suffices for about 4 stuffed pockets, but if you are only making 1 or 2 sandwiches, it keeps, refrigerated, for a couple of days*

In a skillet, melt

*4 tablespoons butter*

and in it sauté

*1/3 cup chopped onions*
*1 cup sliced mushrooms*
*1/4 cup Tamari soy sauce*

Stir-fry for about 5 minutes, then add the following spices to taste (but no salt, as the Tamari is quite salty):

*garlic (the 1890's Deli uses granulated; we'd go with fresh, being the garlic fiends we are here)*
*dried dill weed*
*parsley, fresh and finely minced (or dried)*

Let cool and use in the next step.

*Assembly and Filling of Stuffed Pocket 1890's:* (Directions and ingredients are for 1 sandwich, but you could easily set up an assembly line and do 3 or 4 in a row for a picnic.)

Open fully, all the way around

*1 large pita bread*

(continued)

261

Spread mayonnaise on both insides of pita (or do like I do and go for mustard instead; they are very nice at the Deli about exceptions to the rule—and of course everyone in Eureka Springs believes he or she is the exception to the rule). Now, designate one half of the pita bread as the bottom, on which you will construct this bountiful creation. Begin by piling on it

> *2 to 3 ounces of your favorite sliced cheeses (Sandy recommends a*
> *combination of mozzarella and sharp Cheddar)*

and follow with

> *¼ cup of the mushroom sauté, drained of any juice*
> *another 2 to 3 ounces cheese*

Close pita and butter both outsides, and toast in a broiler oven until cheese is barely melty, turning so both sides get toasted. Do *not*, Sandy warns, toast too long or the pita bread will become so crisp it breaks and you will not be able to continue with the next phase of the stuffing. This begins when you remove the pita from the broiler, open it again, and on top of the melted cheese, pile

> *1 ripe avocado, peeled, pitted, and sliced*
> *(if the avocado is very large, use only half)*
> *several sliced black olives ("Greek would be great!" notes Sandy)*
> *a dollop of your favorite dressing or sour cream, optional (The 1890's*
> *uses Marie's Avocado Dressing cut 50–50 with plain yogurt)*
> *plenty of shredded lettuce, sliced tomato, alfalfa seed sprouts*

"At this point, for the meat lover, crisp bacon can be added," Sandy notes on the recipe, adding, "Close with top of bread. Now here comes the skill! *Gently* cut in half with bread knife . . . If you are generous with your portions, as we are, you will find half a Stuffed Pocket will be plenty for the average appetite."

# By Beaver Lake on a Crisp Day in October

> *Downtown Black Bean Soup in a Thermos*
> *Corn Bread Baked with Cheese and Jalapeños*
> *Garlic Slaw*
> *Dixie Fried Pies*
> *Cinnamon Coffee in a Thermos*
> *Red Bandanna Napkins*

## Full Moon Blue Cheese and Artichoke Pocket with Mushrooms

For 4 sandwiches, make up

*the mushroom sauté mixture on page 261*

Also, cream together

*8 ounces cream cheese, softened*
*4 ounces sharp blue cheese, crumbled*
*3 scallions, finely minced*

Lightly toast

*4 pita breads, preferably whole wheat*

Split them and spread each with a fourth of the blue cheese mixture, a fourth of the mushroom mixture, and

*3 or 4 well-drained marinated artichoke hearts, chopped*

Top with

*alfalfa seed sprouts*
*sliced tomato*
*paper-thin slices of red onions*

Close the sandwich back up.

## Piedmont Park Sandwiches

*Makes 2 sandwiches*

Pit and chop

*24 Greek Kalamata olives*

Open

*2 lightly toasted pita breads*

Spread each with

*½ ripe avocado, mashed in with fork*

Top with the chopped olives and

*1 ounce each sliced provolone, Cheddar, and Swiss cheeses*
*2 sliced, drained marinated artichoke hearts*
*sprouts, tomato, red onion, as above*

*(continued)*

263

Now, sprinkle each sandwich lightly with

*oregano*
*a few drops* each *olive oil and vinegar*

Close sandwiches. Oooo-ooo.

Here are some of our other favorite sandwich ideas:

- Peanut butter, banana, honey, and chunks of date on whole wheat–sesame pita bread. This is a sandwich kids love, as you would expect, but adults also find it immensely satisfying. The date chunks really elevate this.

- Crescent's More-or-Less Greek Salad (p. 126) stuffed into a pita.

- A good egg salad sandwich with sprouts, tomato, etc., on Dairy Hollow Oatmeal Bread Supreme (p. 81).

- Swiss cheese, with or without ham, with mustard and lettuce, tomato, sprouts, onion on Sweet-Sour Rye (p. 84).

- Avocado, tomato, cheese, and sprouts on Crescent's Land of Milk and Honey Whole Wheat Bread (p. 80).

- Ramu's Tuna Pâté (p. 148) on Two Sisters Russian Black Rye (p. 82) with sprouts, tomato, slice of red onion.

- Lentil Pâté (p. 149) on Two Sisters Russian Black Rye.

- A simple sandwich that works *only* if all the ingredients are the best of the best: best-quality roast beef, rare, sliced paper thin, on perfect French bread, split (the kind with a supremely crisp crust), the bread spread lightly with mayonnaise and the roast beef peppered liberally with freshly ground black pepper.

- Softened cream cheese on any sweet bread.

And then there's . . .

## The Ultimate Sandwich

A big sandwich—just one—that can feed four hungry picnickers very, very satisfyingly. First you need

*a large round loaf of good bread*

In larger cities, good bakeries will have a multiplicity of round loaves for you to choose from: crispy, dark, caraway-sprinkled ryes, light golden French breads, and so on. Here, we just make our favorite yeast bread of the moment in a round loaf rather than a bread pan.

Slice it across to make four layers. Butter the bread between on either side of the first layer. As filling for the bottom layer make

*a 4-egg Farmer's Omelette (p. 28)*

The omelette goes in opened out flat—it should just about fit the dimensions of the average round loaf of bread. Let it sit in the pan till it has cooled slightly, then lift onto the bread. Now, sprinkle the bread surfaces on either side of the next layer with a little

*oil, vinegar, oregano*

And fill that layer with

*a layer of finely chopped Kalamata olives*
*a layer of marinated artichoke hearts, sliced*
*a layer of sliced tomatoes*
*a layer of paper-thin slices of red onion*

And, in the next cavity, spread the cut surfaces of the bread with

*mustard*

and layer in

*slice after slice of assorted cheeses*

Close the bread. Wrap the whole loaf tightly in aluminum foil. Take to the picnic, and don't forget a good knife to cut thick wedges of this great concoction of flavors, as well as a cutting board.

# Picnic for Maurice's First King's River Float

*Lentil Pâté with Assorted Crudités*
*Assorted Crackers, Sharp Cheddar, Brie*
*Smoked Turkey Slices*
*The Ultimate Sandwich*
*Jan Brownies*
*Granny Smith Apples*
*Coffee in a Thermos*
*Sparkling Apple Cider*

Where would any picnic be without potato salad? Here are two great ones.

# Mama Murray's Potato Salad

*Serves 8 to 10*

"Over the years, after jillions of buckets of potato salads for family feeds and neighborhood gatherings, Mama has developed one totally wonderful potato salad," says Jan. "It has a unique, dill-y, unsweet flavor, and can be made with or without boiled eggs."

Cook "with their jackets on" in boiling salted water, for about 30 minutes, or until done

*7 or 8 medium-size potatoes*

Cool, peel, and chop the potatoes into ½-inch pieces. In a large mixing bowl, whisk together

*1 cup mayonnaise*
*3 tablespoons yellow prepared mustard*
*1½ tablespoons celery seed*
*1 cup finely grated dill pickles*
*1 cup finely chopped green olives, plus*
*1 tablespoon juice from the green olives*
*1 teaspoon paprika*

Add the potatoes to the mayonnaise mixture. Add

*5 or 6 stalks celery, finely chopped*
*4 or 5 hard-boiled eggs, finely chopped (optional)*
*salt and black pepper to taste*

Stir gently until all ingredients are well blended. Sprinkle with more paprika, garnish with boiled egg slices and fresh parsley, chill well, and serve.

# Holiday Island Fourth of July Picnic Before the Fireworks

*Mama Murray's Potato Salad*
*Confetti Slaw*
*Cold Fried Chicken*
*Sliced Tomatoes Marinated with Fresh Sweet Basil*
*Whole Wheat Butterhorns with Butter*
*Watermelon*
*Fallen Angels • Creole Chocolate Cake*
*Iced Tea in a Thermos*
*Hot Coffee in a Thermos*

## Crescent's Nouveau'zarks Baby Potato Salad with Red Wine

*Serves 4 to 6*

Because the potatoes cook in a rich broth before their final bath in a sophisticated sharp-smooth dressing, they are saturated in layers of good, good flavors. Very special, both earthy and sublime.

Combine and bring to a simmer

*1 to 2 cups good chicken or vegetable stock*
*1 Morga broth cube*
*several shakes Pickapepper sauce*

Drop in

*1½ pounds small new potatoes, preferably red-skinned and not much larger than a marble, unpeeled*

Cover tightly—the stock won't cover the potatoes completely—and let simmer for 20 minutes, or till cooked through but not mushy. Lift potatoes from stock, reserving stock for another purpose (see our Soup chapter for many delicious other purposes), and let cool to where you can handle them. Slice potatoes fairly thickly into a glass, enamel, or ceramic bowl, with

*½ bunch scallions, finely chopped*
*¼ cup heavy cream*

*(continued)*

In a separate bowl, whisk together

> *3 tablespoons Dijon mustard, the coarsely ground kind*
> *3 tablespoons good hearty red wine, like a Beaujolais*
> *1 tablespoon olive oil*

Toss this mixture over the potatoes, adding

> *salt and plenty of fresh ground pepper to taste*

Adjust the seasonings with more mustard, cream, red wine, or olive oil, to taste. Bear in mind that the flavors intensify as they chill, so be careful not to oversalt (particularly if the Morga cube has been salted). Chill for several hours or overnight.

*Variation:* Add 1 tablespoon each finely minced fresh parsley and fresh basil. A lower-calorie version, not as good but still plenty tasty: use plain yogurt instead of heavy cream.

## Last-Day-of-July Luncheon for Bob Penquite

*Cascadilla in Chilled Cups*
*Spinach Salad with Mushrooms*
*Crescent's Nouveau'zarks Potato Salad*
*Sliced Chicken, Garden Tomatoes, and Red Leaf Lettuce*
*with Homemade Mayonnaise*
*on*
*Dairy Hollow Oatmeal Bread Supreme*
*Arkansas Peach Turnovers in Phyllo*

# Fruitpoem

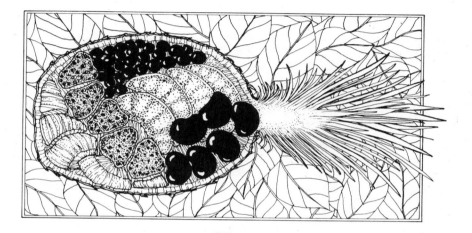

The poetry that seasons this book is here because poetry seasons our lives and because, to us, cooking is an intensely poetic activity. Both poetry and cooking have as their essence *connection*; both strive for that connection on common paths.

To cook or to write poetry, for example, one must observe, both sensually and emotionally, and one must remember what one has observed. One must study scrupulously the world of form and the rules governing that world, yet with the knowledge that greatness begins only when those strictly grasped rules are discarded and a bold, risky surge—which may or may not work—is taken. The cook and the poet, when they are working best, understand least: through some interior, intuitive, spiritual leap not fully understood by the cook or poet himself or herself—in fact, not understood at all—the most specific and earthy of ingredients—*a* particular pear, say, and the way the sunlight slants over it on *a* particular October morning—are somehow transformed into a poem or a pie that mysteriously connects here-and-now with the Ultimate.

That cooking is more evanescent than poetry makes it art no less; it is simply an art which succeeds more readily and quickly in what all art strives for: to become part of its audience (its reader, listener, seer, eater)—forever.

We were not at all surprised, when we began to hunt for poems that fit our purposes here, to discover that there was far more poetry written about fruit than virtually any other food. Fruit is sublime: in its shape and scent, in its sweetness, in its shower of blossoms, in its power to evoke, and, perhaps, in its poignancy—what else on earth simply drops off, ready to let go when ripe, offering itself freely to be eaten? That is "the sacrifice that all things make each other," as I wrote in one of my own poems—and yet it seems that fruit *doesn't* sacrifice; it goes willingly, insistently offering itself and through that offering assuring its own continuity. If it is true, as Christ said, that we must give up our life to have it, fruit illustrates this truth—and even quietly enlists our glad participation. Is it this willing submission that also makes fruit a symbol of love, over and over, in poetry?

Here are our poems, written from the earth transmogrified into fruit: the juicy cleavaged flesh of a peach, the rounded contours of a pear, the dark glossy globe of a cherry, the round orange a small sun on the breakfast table, the misted blueberries we gathered ourselves, getting sunburned on our backs but staying pale on our faces, bent under those fragrant bushes abuzz with bees. Connections: the earth, the fruit that grows from it, us, you, cooking, eating, sustaining, matter into spirit . . . here are our poems.

◆————————————————◆

*What wondrous life is this I led!*
*Ripe apples drop about my head—*

*—Andrew Marvell,*
*"The Garden"*

◆————————————————◆

## APPLES

Every October finds us, like thousands of other visitors, making our annual pilgrimage to Banta's Apple Orchard in Alpena. Frieda Banta once told me, years ago when I did a story on them for the now-defunct *Arkansan Magazine,* "Back when we started, we really thought we'd set the world a-fire if we sold two pies in a day." Now, Banta's goes through several hundred pies on a busy fall weekend.

The orchard is famous for the Quindell, an apple variety Ralph Banta himself discovered and bred. But we personally prefer the Bantas' Arkansas Blacks. This old, old apple variety is a late-ripening, very dark red beauty, tart, and not seen much these days. My uncle Joe, who grew up on a rice farm in eastern Arkansas, remembered these

270

apples with pleasure all his life. The Arkansas Blacks and the tart, crisp, savory Stayman Winesaps, which indeed have a wine-y undertone in their flavor, are our favorites of Banta's beautiful crops. A nonlocal apple we love is the Granny Smith, and its cousins the Pippin and Newton apples, all three green, firm, and deliciously tart. Here are some of the ways we use any good apple.

### Raw Apples

Raw apples are our first choice for a simple dessert.

- A child's good-night snack: raw apple slices, fanned out in a half-circle, delicately sprinkled with just-plain cinnamon.

- Spread for apple slices: combine 3 parts good peanut or almond butter to 2 parts honey, add a drop of vanilla and—yes—1 part powdered milk. Stir quickly into a thick, delicious paste. Spread on crisp apple slices.

- A Light Apple Lunch While Working at Home: slices of a good tart apple topped with a thin strip of cream cheese, with a walnut half pressed on top. This simple and delicious combination is perfect with Hefty Bran Muffins, page 72.

- Apples and cheese: apples, like pears and grapes, seem made for this divine pairing. We love crisp apples with a good, very sharp New York Cheddar or a Brie ripened to meltiness. Add two varieties of good crackers—Ak-Maks from the health food store and stoned wheat thins, say—and you have an equally wonderful start or finish to a meal.

## An Apple Harvest Feast

*Walnut Wings with Apple Butter*
*Butternut Squash and Apple Soup II*
*Waioli Carrot (substitute apples) Bread • Butter • Apple Jelly*
*The Salad with Blue Cheese and Julienne of Red Delicious Apple*
*Chicken Breasts in Cider with Sautéed Apple*
*Rice • Country Spinach with Sour Cream*
*George and Starr's Apple-Spice Wedding Cake with Apricot Filling*

## Cooked Apples

- Baked Apples: we like these a lot, a homey wintertime staple for a dessert. The simple way: core, allowing 1 apple per person, place in Pam-ed baking dish, sprinkle with brown sugar, dot with butter, sprinkle with cinnamon, stick 3 whole cloves in each apple, place a twist of lemon peel in each core and ½ inch of water or apple juice with a drop of vanilla added in the bottom of the dish. Bake at 350° (or at any temperature from 300° to 450° if you have something else going in the oven) till done, soft but not mushy. Baste once or twice while cooking. These can also be done with maple sugar or honey replacing the brown sugar.

    Serve this, or the variation that follows, with a Custard Sauce (p. 376) to which you've added any pan juices, cooked down if necessary, from the apples, the apples still a little warm, the custard cold.

    Or serve with cold unwhipped heavy cream.

- Baked Stuffed Apples (for 4 baked apples): Before baking, stuff apple cores with the following mixture: 3 tablespoons each butter, brown sugar, whole wheat pastry flour, oatmeal; dash salt; ½ teaspoon vanilla; ½ teaspoon cinnamon; dash each nutmeg, cloves, ginger. Toss this together with a few raisins till crumbly.

- Apple Croissants: a great late-night snack when you're in the mood for apple pie but don't want to fuss. Carefully split croissants and toast. Meanwhile, sauté thinly sliced apples in butter. As they soften, drizzle a little honey and cinnamon over them. Remove from heat. Toss with a couple of tablespoons sour cream and a few walnuts. Fill toasted croissant.

# Jan's "Appl'ava"

*Makes about 20 servings*

Almost a strudel, the Jan Brown magic worked with apples and phyllo: follow our phyllo directions on pages 160–164, particularly the Diamonds-in-a-Pan version.

For the filling, lightly sauté together

*3 tablespoons butter*
*3 apples, finely chopped*

When apples are tender, add

*1½ teaspoons cinnamon*
*½ teaspoon nutmeg*
*½ cup honey*

For the syrup, melt together

*½ cup butter*
*½ cup honey*
*½ cup finely chopped walnuts*

Follow the directions for Diamonds-in-a-Pan, substituting the apple-honey mixture for the filling and using the walnut-y syrup in place of the butter between phyllo. Use a 9-×-13-×-2-inch pan. Be very sure to follow prebaking cutting directions, and don't forget the Pam. Bake in a preheated 350° oven for 35 to 40 minutes. Cool and serve.

## Crescent's Earth Angel Apple Pie

*Serves 6 to 8*

This is definitely not the apple pie you grew up with! It's hearty, wholewheat-y, and not too sweet. I think it is the best apple pie I ever ate, but would only serve it to people who have some previous acquaintance with natural foods.

Make up the dough for Whole Wheat and Butter Crust (p. 340). Toss together

*at least a dozen good apples, washed but unpeeled, cored, of several*
*different varieties, and sliced about ⅛ inch thick*

with

*cinnamon*
*nutmeg*
*a little ground clove*
*a tiny fleck of black pepper*

Drizzle the apples with

*about ⅓ cup honey*
*the juice of ½ lemon (unless apples are fairly tart)*
*3 or 4 tablespoons whole wheat pastry flour*

Toss again. Fill pie shell—it should really be heaped high, because the apples cook way down—put on top crust, slash decoratively. Bake in a preheated oven at 450° for 10 minutes, lower to 350° and bake until done—perhaps 45 minutes to 1 hour total. Serve warm, with vanilla ice cream. The leftovers, with very sharp Cheddar cheese, make a very special breakfast the next morning.

A friend of ours had a woman in his past named Carla Diekie, against whom he measured excellence in all things. When he said to me one day, solemnly, "This is the only apple pie I've ever eaten that was *better* than Carla Diekie's," we knew his broken heart was healing. In fact he married, happily and well, a few years later. Hey, George, we're talking about you, buddy!

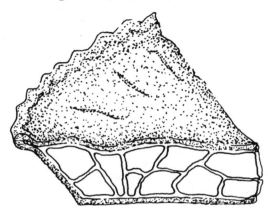

## DIXIE ORCHARD

*It's our custom, during the cold winter months, to have hot apple cider with a cinnamon stick and a few cloves ready and waiting when our guests arrive. Late on a chilly grey October afternoon, Jane Mc-Gehee of Little Rock arrived with her friends Babs Pennick and Elsie Pugh. They eagerly accepted the proffered cider, and then someone—I think it was Elsie—said, "Mmmmmm . . . I wonder how this would taste with a little bourbon in it?" and she pulled out a flask in a handsome leather case. Thus was born the Dixie Orchard: good hot spiced cider spiked with bourbon. Try it!*

# APRICOTS

We dearly love good fresh apricots but have yet to find any for sale around here that have a decent flavor and texture, so we make do with the dried. We use them in Elsie's Winter Fruit Compote (p. 46), which we sometimes serve as a dessert, dressed up with a shot of Frangelico or other good liqueur, or we make

- Apricot Mousse (serves 4 to 6): This is very, very simple, yet elegant and rich. Soak 6 ounces dried apricots overnight by pouring boiling water, enough to just barely cover, over them and letting them stand till cool. In the morning, puree them and any juice they may have in the food processor. It should be a thick paste, almost a butter. An hour or less before serving time, whip 1 cup cream till stiff and fold in the thick apricot puree, with a drop of vanilla and even less than a drop of almond extract. Taste. Sweeten, if desired, with powdered sugar—but it really isn't necessary. We have done this many times for people on a sugar-free diet. Those who do eat sweets may enjoy this with a good cookie: Rum Raisin Shortbreads (p. 316), Viennese Nut Crescents (p. 331), or Penuche Lace Cookies (p. 330).

# BANANAS

They aren't at their best until very ripe, the skin speckled deeply with black spots. Avoid under- or overripe bananas.

Of course we eat 'em on our cereal, but we really prefer to take them to extremes, as follows:

- Frozen Bananas: peel and freeze ripe bananas. Use them, still frozen, in any sort of instant sorbet (see Deluxe Ambrosia, p. 298). They add, besides their flavor, a wonderful creamy smoothness.

- Bananas Flambé: choose bananas a bit firmer than usual, allowing ½ banana per person. Sauté as for the Banana German Baked Pancake Filling (p. 38) except that when the bananas are almost done, pour over them ½ cup light or dark rum, brandy, or bourbon. Give it about 10 seconds to heat, and ignite, either by tipping pan down into burner flame or by setting a match to it. Of course you want your guests to ooh and ahh. As it flames, spoon the liquid over the bananas. When the flames die down, serve, immediately, over good vanilla ice cream (possibly in a meringue shell) or with crepes and whipped cream and/or fresh sliced strawberries. Spoon pan juices (*oh* they're good!) over each serving.

There is nothing much to doing flambés, but boy, do people get excited about them!

● Orange Bananas Flambé: when doing the preliminary sauté of the bananas, sprinkle them with a little orange juice and/or orange liqueur, and grate the rind of an orange over them. Then proceed as above.

# BLUEBERRIES

Blueberries are among our favorite fruits, in part because they can be grown with such great success in the area. Every June we go out to Blueberry Hills Farm for lunch at their blueberry café and an afternoon of picking that results in blueberry pancakes, blueberry muffins, blueberry pies, and so on for our guests—and us!

● Raw, we like blueberries with sweet or sour cream or crème fraîche, and brown sugar. We like them combined with any other berry, or with bananas.

● Serve Blueberry–Sour Cream Coffee Cake (p. 65) with whipped cream and it becomes dessert.

● In a stemmed goblet, with Honeyed Zabaglione Napoleon (p. 296) over them.

● Deep-Dish Blueberry Cobbler *(serves 6 to 8):*
Pam a deep casserole dish and fill it with 4 to 5 cups washed fresh blueberries. Reach your hand down in and squish one handful of them to make some juice. With the other hand, scoop up about ⅓ cup flour and sprinkle it over the berries, along with ½ cup or so of honey, or to taste (you can use brown sugar instead, if you like). Stir well, with the blueberry-embedded hand. Now wash hands. Roll out any pie crust and top the blueberries with it, slashing decoratively. Bake as for apple pie. Serve hot, with whipped cream or ice cream.

To make a biscuit-topped cobbler, cook the blueberries—with flour and honey added—on top of the stove first. After the berries are good and hot and have thickened nicely, pour them hot into the Pam-ed casserole. Top with any of our biscuits, to which you've added a bit of extra sugar, or our shortcake biscuit, see under Strawberries, page 294. Bake till the biscuits are done.

- Blueberry Sauce for Sundaes or . . . : cook them ever so slightly as follows: mash a cup of the blues and put them on to cook, along with 2 cups of the whole berries. Mush 2 tablespoons cornstarch into 3 tablespoons cold water and mix with another cup of mashed blueberries. When the berries on the stove have come to a good simmer, stir in the cornstarch mixture and cook, stirring, till juice is clear and thickened. Remove from heat. Sweeten to taste with a bit of honey. Serve hot over ice cream, topped with whipped cream, for a delicious blueberry sundae. Or, serve over pancakes . . . or crepes . . . or waffles . . . or French toast . . .

- Blueberry Shortcake: see Strawberries.

## CHERRIES

We love these dark, round beauties with their sweet burst of flavor, their spurt of juice, their round, bone-hard pit. We mostly eat them as is, out of hand. But occasionally we make:

- Marinated Cherries: halve and pit sweet Bing cherries. Marinate for several hours in Cherry Heering, Cherry Kijafa, or kirsch, Frangelico, amaretto.
  *Variation:* Marinate with orange sections.

## Cherry Clafouti

*Serves 6 to 8*

We had read about this in Colette and were pleased to unearth a recipe for it. It is a very plain and simple little cake, but fully as wonderful as she describes it, and it must be eaten straight from the oven to be appreciated fully. Served so, studded with red-ripe cherries and dusted with powdered sugar, it is very special. It bears a family resemblance to our German Baked Pancake (p. 36).

*(continued)*

277

Preheat oven to 400°. Combine

*1 cup unbleached white flour*
*½ teaspoon salt*
*2 tablespoons sugar*

Make a well in these ingredients and pour into it

*2 eggs, lightly beaten*
*1 cup milk*

Stir until well blended but do not beat. Now, combine

*2 cups pitted fresh Bing cherries*
*1 tablespoon kirsch*
*1 drop—no more!—almond extract*

Turn half the batter into a Pam-ed 8-inch cake pan or a 9-inch pie pan; sprinkle evenly with the marinated cherries; top with remaining batter. Bake until puffed and golden—about 35 minutes. Remove from oven and dust lightly with

*powdered sugar*

Serve hot.

- We also like fresh cherries, whole, unpitted (but warn guests about the pits!) floating in a bowl of cold, creamy, rich custard sauce, a bit on the thin side. Or, sliced in half, pitted, and topped with Honeyed Zabaglione Napoleon (p. 296).

## LEMONS

We love the spark of flavor lemon gives to so many dishes, from soup, to chicken or fish, to cookies. And we love the scent of fresh lemon; the sweetness, when one knows the fruit itself is so sour. We

love Lemonade: ½ lemon, sugar or sweetener to taste, fill the glass with water, add ice—the taste of summer. And we love this

## Simply Incredible Lemon Mousse

*Serves 4 or 5*

In a large bowl that you can firmly set over/in a saucepan of hot water, beat

*3 whole eggs*
*3 egg yolks*

Add, and beat hard with a whisk for about 20 seconds

*⅔ cup fresh lemon juice (seeds picked out, pulp left in)*
*2 teaspoons grated lemon rind*

Very gradually beat in

*¾ cup sugar*

Now, set the bowl over the saucepan of very hot—but not boiling—water, the heat on medium-low. Whisk vigorously until mixture is foamy on top and starting to thicken—about 3 to 5 minutes. Continue whisking, occasionally stirring up from the bottom of the bowl with a spoon, until mixture is quite thick—about 7 minutes more. Immediately remove from heat and whisk another minute, to stop further cooking and to continue aerating the mousse. Pour into 4 or 5 stemmed glasses, cover, and refrigerate.

Serve very cold, with a puff of

*lightly whipped cream*
*a sprig of fresh mint*

to garnish.
Or make

## Simply Incredible Lemon Mousse Pie

*Serves 7 or 8*

Yes, this is the pie that is the darling of the nouvelle cuisine restaurants, but actually it has been around for some time. You can make this even more splendiferous by doing it in individual tart shells.

Make up a Pastry Brisée Sucre (p. 341), but add to the flour a teaspoon of grated lemon rind and ¼ cup finely ground almonds or hazelnuts or walnuts. Line a 10-inch pie pan with the pastry. Chill for at least 1 hour. Bake, unfilled, in a preheated 400° oven for 10 to 15 minutes—till golden. Do not overbake! Let cool completely.

Filled cooled shell with lukewarm lemon mousse, spreading with spatula to smooth top. Refrigerate. Garnish with whipped cream put through a piping tube, a twist of a paper-thin lemon slice, and fresh mint.

Prepare to ascend into heaven.

# MELONS

*Stumbling on melons as I pass,*
*Ensnared with flowers, I fall on grass.*

—*Andrew Marvell,*
*"The Garden"*

For our thoughts on melons, please see the fruit section in the Breakfast chapter (pp. 45 to 50). Any melon selection makes a perfect dessert, either for a simple, hot-summer-night dinner or, conversely, a light touch at the end of a more elaborate meal.

- Marinate assorted balls of firmer melons—cantaloupe, Santa Claus, Crenshaw, honeydew—in melon liqueur and the juice of ½ lemon. Serve very cold, garnished with fresh mint. Port, no lemon added, is also a time-honored and delicious marinade for melon.

- Charlotte's Melon: a wedge of cantaloupe with a scoop of very good chocolate ice cream resting in the middle.

- Quick Melon Sorbet: this works as a dessert or, in a very very very fancy dinner, as the "palate-clearer" between dinner and dessert. We think it far surpasses more elaborate frozen concoctions. One simply purees, in a food processor, frozen unsweetened melon balls, the kind that come in the freezer case in a plastic bag, with just a bit of liquid: melon liqueur, apple juice, or yogurt (which makes a most refreshing sorbet and no, you would never guess that it's yogurt). Taste. Add, if necessary, a touch of sweetness (honey, maple syrup, artificial sweetener—sugar would be too grainy here) and perhaps a bit of lemon or lime juice.

# ORANGES

When they are good, they are very very good; when they are bad, they are horrid. We think the best eating oranges are the large, beautiful California navel oranges that come in in December, January, and February. We also have had smaller oranges in Europe, called blood oranges because their flesh is a bright, vibrant, incredible blood-red, that are absolutely divine in color, fragrance, and taste. They are starting to be available in some of the pricier metropolitan fruit markets; we think the day will come when, like kiwis, one can buy them anywhere. That will be a happy day!

- Marinated Oranges: fresh orange slices, layered in a stemmed glass with fresh or even semithawed frozen raspberries, with a bit of Napoleon, Grand Marnier, or Frangelico over them, is a truly ambrosial dessert. For lily-gilding, you can add whipped cream and a crisp cookie.

# PEACHES

*The nectarine, the curious peach,*
*Into my hands themselves do reach—*

*—Andrew Marvell,*
*"The Garden"*

How we love peaches in that fleeting time when they are perfect, soft-ripe, fuzz-skinned, rich yellow flesh with its tender blush of pink dripping with juice! We eat peaches fresh, in pie, in cake, in ice cream, baked and stuffed, raw and stuffed, plain, fancy, as shortcake, with cream and sugar, and, again, fresh out of hand. Since peaches and almonds are in the same family, they seem to us a natural together, and we often pair them with either amaretto or amaretti, the wonderful Italian almond liqueur and cookie, respectively.

It seems to us that each year it gets harder and harder to find really perfect peaches in the big supermarkets; perhaps the tastier varieties do not ship well, or the growers are more and more reluctant to ship when the peaches are *a point*, and so they send us underripe, underflavored ones. The good ones are still to be found, but often only on the outskirts of town, at the smaller markets, with the hand-lettered signs.

Clingstones, the peaches whose flesh, naturally enough, clings to the stone, are the tastier. Freestones, whose flesh pulls away easily from the pit, are less delectable but much easier to cook with, especially to can. We do not think white-fleshed peaches have half the flavor of yellow-meated ones.

- Peach Shortcake, see Strawberries.

- Sour Cream Peach Pie, see page 346.

- Fresh sliced peaches topped with peach ice cream, covered with fresh raspberry or strawberry puree.

- Fresh sliced peaches topped with Honeyed Zabaglione Napoleon (p. 296).

- Fresh peaches, peeled, marinated in amaretto. Serve as is or over ice cream, or over ice cream in a meringue shell.

# Italian Peaches Stuffed with Chocolate Mousse Cream

*Serves 8*

Peel

*4 peaches*

by dipping them into boiling water for 3 minutes, then slipping off the skin (perhaps *slipping* is an overly optimistic word; it depends on the variety of peach—some you have to use a knife and they still come out all raggedy-looking; some do indeed slip). Halve the peaches, and marinate them in ½ cup of white wine to which you've added a bit of brandy. Turn them occasionally to coat. Let them soak, refrigerated, while you combine in a double boiler over hot water

*2 ounces semisweet chocolate, chopped*
*1 tablespoon butter*

When both are melted, whisk in

*2 egg yolks*

Whisk over heat for about 30 seconds, then remove from heat and whisk for another 2 minutes, till smooth, thick, and cooled. Whisk in

*2 teaspoons brandy*
*1 drop—no more—almond extract*
*tiny fleck of salt*

Whip till stiff

*¾ cup heavy cream*
*2 tablespoons sifted powdered sugar*

Fold cooled chocolate mixture into cream, and refrigerate. Have ready

*8 large amaretti cookies, crumbled*
*8 tiny amaretti cookies, called amarettini*

Up to an hour before serving, put the chocolate cream into a pastry bag with a large star tip. Place each peach half on a serving plate and sprinkle the cavity well with the amaretti crumbs. Now pipe into the cavity a lovely swirled puff of the Chocolate Mousse Cream. Put a tiny amarettini on the peak of the puff, and serve, garnished with, perhaps, fresh cherries.

- A Simpler Stuffing for Peaches: this also involves amaretti. Preheat oven to 350°. Halve peaches; this time, unpeeled. Pit them, enlarging hole with a serrate-edged grapefruit spoon. Combine finely crumbled amaretti (allow 1 per peach—and, really, you could substitute any good cookie, crumbled, here), a dash cinnamon, and a teaspoon *each* of butter and brown sugar per peach. Fill the cavities of the peaches with this, and bake for about 25 minutes. Drizzle a bit of brandy over the baking peaches and return them to the oven for another 15 minutes. Serve hot, with ice cream.

# PEARS

There is something in the contours of the Ozarks that reminds us of the curves of pears, an anatomy both sculptural and human in its purity of form, both austere and sensual.

Pears for eating *must* be ripe-ripe; the flesh should give with a gentle prod from the thumb. Whether the tiny, very sweet Seckels of midsummer, the beautiful late-summer Bartletts, or the green-skinned, pink-blushed Anjous, probably our favorites, we enjoy them. Kiefer pears grow vigorously, half-wild, throughout the area; we use these brown-skinned, firm pears for cooking and marmalades.

- Raw Pears: like apples, pears are perfect with cheese. Our favorite combinations are creamy-ripe pears with Vermont cheese or Gje-tost or Camembert or Stilton.

- Sliced Pears à la Miss Kay: sliced, perfectly ripe pears in a bowl, with heavy cream poured over them, served with a buttery cookie, such as Rum Raisin Shortbreads (p. 316) or Holsteins (p. 321). (We would never do this at the inn, but you can: cheat deliciously here with some Pepperidge Farm Bordeaux cookies.)

- Pears in Salad: another trick from Miss Kay, the woman who first showed me the wonders of kitchen alchemy, when I was a small girl. Put sliced, perfectly ripe pears in a salad. Finish with crumbles of blue cheese.

## Cocoa-stuffed Pears in Custard

*Serves 8*

I have forgotten where I learned the following trick, but it is a neat one—one might even say spectacular. It doesn't look nearly as lovely as all those poached pears one sees all the time with some nouvelle chef posing beside—but it tastes much, much better.

Select

*4 very ripe, juicy pears—Anjous, Bartletts, or Boscs*

Halve but do not peel them, and core them, enlarging the core cavity with a melon baller. Now, combine

*4 tablespoons sifted unsweetened cocoa*
*1 tablespoon sifted powdered sugar*

284

Pack this mixture carefully into the pears and let them sit overnight, covered, in the refrigerator. This is when the magic happens: the powdered cocoa gradually soaks up and becomes saturated with the juice of the pear.

The next day, make

*Custard Sauce, page 376*

Chill it deeply. Also, whip

*1 cup heavy cream*
*4 tablespoons powdered sugar*
*½ teaspoon vanilla*

Serve each cocoa-stuffed pear half floating in a placid golden pool of custard, a puff of whipped cream concealing the cocoa, and a sprinkle of

*shaved semisweet chocolate*

on the cream, hinting at the hidden treasure.

## Honeyed Tarte aux Poires

*Serves 6 to 8*

Preheat oven to 400°. Prepare a 9-inch pie crust, using the Pastry Brisée Sucre, page 341. Bake for 5 minutes. Remove from oven and set aside. Wash, core (using a melon baller), and slice in half

*5 or 6 Anjou pears*

Place them carefully in a large Pam-ed skillet with

*1 cup water*
*½ cup apple juice*
*1 inch of vanilla bean*

Simmer for 15 minutes; then add

*⅓ cup honey*

Simmer for another 10 minutes. Very carefully remove the pears from the poaching liquid and let them cool. Remove the vanilla bean and continue simmering the poaching liquid, cooking it down until it is very thick. Set aside; this will make the glaze for the tarte.

*(continued)*

And now for the custard. In a separate saucepan, stir together and warm

*½ cup sugar*
*1½ cups milk*

Beat together

*2 egg yolks*
*2 tablespoons unbleached white flour*

Whisk the egg-flour mixture into the honey-milk mixture. Add

*1 drop almond extract*

Stir well. Now arrange the pear halves in the pastry crust, skin sides up, in a circle around the crust's edge, with one pear nestled in the middle. Gently pour the custard liquid around the pears. Bake at 400° for 35 to 40 minutes. Both the pears and the custard will be lightly golden. Remove from the oven and let cool for 10 minutes. Now pour the thickened glaze over the top of the pears and custard. Smooth and let cool to room temperature before serving.

## PERSIMMONS

In fall, along the hedgerows and back-country lanes, one can see a rangy tree, usually short in stature—though we have seen a few very tall ones. Leafless, yet with small round globes of fruit clinging to the branches, they resemble nothing so much as stylized Shaker Trees of Life, and they are lovely.

This enchanting sight is the native persimmon tree, *Diospyros virginiana*, and those strange small fruits of purple-y orange brushed with a pale white mist (as blueberries are) are persimmons. Eureka Springs has its own bona fide persimmon queen, Muriel Schmidt, who has been working on and off with the upgrading, through grafting, of these native trees for the past two decades. She's developed dozens of persimmon recipes over the years; she's also taught local high school conservation-ecology classes about persimmon culture (persimmons, according to Muriel, have an extra long taproot, need little water, are not persnickety about soil, and thus are ideal erosion-control plants and often introduced for that purpose.) Through Muriel's recent efforts, Arkansas Governor Bill Clinton has recognized November as "The Month of the Persimmon," while, on a local level, our mayor, Don Thurman, has declared Eureka Springs the Persimmon Capital of the World.

And, in 1985, Muriel staged the First Annual Persimmon Bake-Off, where none other than our own Jan Brown took Grand Prize, with a Persimmon Chantilly Cream Pie. This celestial dessert has a filling loosely based on the recipe below, swirled into a rich cookielike crust originated by David Old, a fine chef and the owner of The Spring Street House, one of Eureka's finest restaurants.

When persimmons are most edible, they certainly don't look it. Earlier in the fall, they are lovely little lanterns of bright orange—but if you bite into them then, the alum makes your mouth pucker unpleasantly. But once they soften to dead-ripeness, mottled with bruised colorations, sheened white, they're ready . . . and ambrosial. Every trace of the puckery alum is gone, their overripe appearance belying the succulent and bright crimson-orange flesh that lies within, its flavor sweet and intense and indefinable—something like a cross between a date and an apricot, yet more perfumed than these, softer and richer, melting-textured. They are small—perhaps two-thirds the size of a walnut in the shell—and their vivid flesh is marred by several seeds (Muriel's grafting is gradually breeding persimmons with fewer seeds). But size and seeds don't stop us from eating dozens out of hand if we come up on a loaded-down persimmon tree with just-right persimmons, a snack nature has thoughtfully provided for us on an autumn day's hike.

Because of their numerous seeds, cooking with these native persimmons is a lot of work. We've done it and will continue to do so, but what patience it takes to put enough of those things through one

of the triangular cone sieves, the type that stands on its little tripod, or a Foley food mill, to get enough to get even a cup of persimmon puree!

So, we sometimes settle for the Japanese persimmons, Kaki, the larger kind you see at the market. Though their flavor is less intense than the wild persimmons, they are still delicious. They, too, must be dead-ripe, although their flesh retains more of the crimson to it at ripeness than does our native variety. The Kakis, besides being larger, are also seedless. One cuts off the four-pointed stem end, and there it is, ready to

- Eat as is, an intensely delicious experience.

- Puree and cook with, as in Jan's Persimmon Bran Bread, page 61, or Persimmon Cookies, page 333, or the Persimmon Mousse, which follows.

- Freeze. Freeze them whole, and eat them frozen. Their high natural sugar content keeps them from freezing solid-hard, and their flavor is just sublime.

## Persimmon Mousse

*Serves 6 to 8*

A tricolored extravaganza of flavors, textures, and shades, this can be made from wild or domestic persimmons. It is superlative either way.

Have ready

*3 cups persimmon puree, either wild ripe or domestic ripe persimmons, seeded and prepared in a food processor or sieved*

Make up

*Custard Sauce, page 376, using ⅓ cup cornstarch instead of 2 tablespoons*

This will result in an alarmingly thick, weird-looking pudding, but have no fear. Combine this custard with 1½ cups persimmon puree in the food processor. Buzz till smooth. Turn out into a bowl. Have the remaining 1½ cups puree in another bowl. In a third, whip till stiff

*1 cup chilled heavy cream*
*2 to 4 tablespoons sifted powdered sugar*
*½ teaspoon vanilla*

288

Have ready 6 to 8 stemmed glasses. Carefully spoon in alternate scoops of the persimmon custard, the persimmon puree, and the whipped cream. Finish with whipped cream on the top, and a garnish of

*a thin slice of frozen persimmon*

Serve with Penuche Lace Cookies (p. 330).

# PINEAPPLE

This fruit, so very delicious when perfectly ripe, was the symbol of hospitality and welcome throughout colonial America, especially in the South. Getting a perfectly ripe one may be a bit difficult, however. Sniff the base of the pineapple; it should exude pineapple-ness. Squeeze it; it should give a bit. Its color should have golden-brown tones to it, not be strictly greenish. A leaf that pulls out easily from the center of a small, compact crown is another sign of ripeness.

- Marinated Pineapple in the Shell: cut pineapple lengthwise and scoop out flesh, leaving two shells, each with half the leaves attached. Discard tough core of pineapple; dice the meat. Marinate it, in a separate bowl, in kirsch, Grand Marnier, Napoleon, or Frangelico. It may be mixed, with great success, with any kind of melon ball, fresh strawberries, blueberries, and sectioned orange pieces. After an hour's refrigerated marination, return the fruit to the pineapple shells and serve at once.

- Pineapple Flambé: sauté thick cored rings of fresh pineapple in butter. When they soften slightly, spoon a little orange marmalade over them, allowing it to melt down but (of course) not burn. It'll take about ⅓ cup marmalade for the rings of 1 pineapple. When marmalade is liquid, pour over the pineapple ¼ cup dark rum, let heat for a moment, and ignite. Serve with any of the options listed under Bananas Flambé (p. 275).

- Our good old Honeyed Zabaglione Napoleon (p. 296) is excellent on pineapple.

## RASPBERRIES

I know we've just been raving about one fruit after another, but if we had to pick one, our very very favorite fruit, raspberries would be it, hands down, no contest. Perhaps it is the brevity of their season, and their soft crushable-ness—which makes them virtually unavailable commercially—but they knock us out. The bright, sweet, undiluted berry flavor, those tiny bursts from the little pocket of flesh surrounding each minuscule seed—we just love them. We love the domestic red raspberries; we love the smaller wild black raspberries we gather along Dairy Hollow Road each spring. Any way we can get them, we'll take them:

- Plain.

- With heavy cream, whipped or not.

- As an ecstatic shortcake, versions I, II, or III (pp. 294 and 295). At least one of each, each raspberry season.

- Over ice cream, in a meringue shell, topped with whipped cream. This is my favorite dessert in the whole world, one I was introduced to as a child by Miss Kay.

- With crepes and whipped cream, or waffles and whipped cream.

- With a cloud of Honeyed Zabaglione Napoleon (p. 296).

- Over good homemade vanilla ice cream, resting on a peach half, resting on a slice of good homemade pound cake (like our delectable Sour Cream Pound Cake, p. 358). Hey, somebody ought to come up with a snappy name for this, like, how about, Peach Melba?

- In

# Poppy Seed Torte with Raspberry Sauce the Randolph House

*Serves 10 to 12*

When Ned and I were sojourning in Atlanta, one of our favorite getaways was the Randolph House in Bryson City, North Carolina, run as an inn by Bill and Ruth Randolph Adams. Ruth, besides being a direct descendant of the attorney who built the 1895 mansion that is now the inn, is a fine cook. She shared this excellent recipe with us.

Soak

*⅓ cup poppy seeds*

in

*¾ cup milk*

As the seeds soak, cream together

*¾ cup butter, softened to room temperature*
*1½ cups sugar*

When butter and sugar are fluffy, beat in the soaked poppy seeds and their milk, and

*1½ teaspoons vanilla*

Sift together

*2 cups sifted cake flour*
*2½ teaspoons baking powder*
*¼ teaspoon salt*

*(continued)*

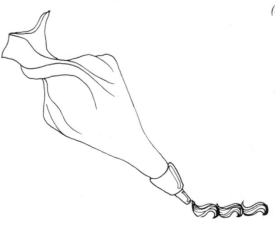

Beat this into the creamed mixture. Preheat oven to 375°. Separate

*4 eggs*

Reserving the yolks, beat the whites until very stiff and fold them into the flour mixture. Divide this batter evenly among four well-Pam-ed and flour-dusted cake pans. Bake for about 15 to 20 minutes, or until cake tests done. Let cool for a few minutes in pans, then turn out onto racks.

Meanwhile, make the following Walnut-Custard Filling by combining

*½ cup sugar*
*1 tablespoon cornstarch*

with

*1½ cups milk*

Heat, stirring constantly, till milk thickens slightly. Remove a bit of the hot thickened milk and beat it into the reserved 4 egg yolks, then add the yolks to the pot and continue to cook, stirring, till the custard thickens further—a matter of a few minutes. Remove from heat, and stir a minute or two to halt cooking and begin the cooling process.

Cool custard thoroughly in the fridge, then stir in

*1 teaspoon vanilla*
*¼ cup chopped walnuts*

Spread this filling between the layers, and chill the torte for 2 to 3 hours. Sift powdered sugar over the top, and serve with a thickened raspberry sauce, made as for the Blueberry Sundae Sauce, page 277, except using raspberries.

# RHUBARB

*I'm proud*
*of my rhubarb, its fine and crumpled brilliant*
*leaves which poke up, its rosy stems*
*poking up and through*
*the earth*

—Crescent Dragonwagon,
Message from the Avocadoes

It's strange-looking and it has a funny-sounding name, but this fruit that looks like rose-colored celery is a springtime favorite. Our heart leaps the first time we see it reappearing in the garden or at the market.

We like rhubarb stewed (oh, very much), we like it in pies. And we like

# Rhubarb Scrounge

*Serves 8 to 10*

It's called by many names: buckle, betty, crumpet, crisp, cobbler, grunt, dowdy—depending on where you grew up and what your grandma called hers. It's a sweetened fruit, baked with a crunchy battered topping, served slightly warm, with heavy cream poured over the top, and it might be your all-time favorite dessert. We like the word *scrounge* to describe ours, mostly because it describes *us* as we rummage in the garden or catch our clothes on blackberry brambles or search through the cellar or pantry to find a particular home-canned fruit to use for such a dessert. Use any of your favorite fruits, and be sure to try our version with rhubarb.

Preheat oven to 375°. Into a Pam-ed 9-inch-square baking pan, stir together

*4 cups rhubarb, washed, peeled, and cut into ½-inch pieces*
*⅔ cup honey*
*1 teaspoon vanilla*

Pour over the rhubarb mixture

*1 cup water* or *fruit juice*

In a mixing bowl, blend together

*1½ cups unbleached white flour*
*½ teaspoon salt*
*⅓ cup brown sugar*
*2 teaspoons cinnamon*

Cut in

*½ cup butter, softened*

When butter and dry ingredients are well blended, sprinkle it evenly over the fruit mixture. Bake for 30 to 35 minutes, or until rhubarb is tender and topping is well browned.

*(continued)*

*Variations:* This scrounge is good made with any fruit and juice combination—apples with apple juice, blueberries in orange juice. The topping may be made with half whole wheat flour, or half oatmeal, especially with apples. The topping is also good with the addition of ½ cup walnuts.

# STRAWBERRIES

Like rhubarb, like asparagus, the taste of strawberries means spring to us. When the local berries are in season, we can't get enough of them, and we make jam by the case (no matter how much we make, our guests eat it up; by September, it's always gone). The combination of strawberries and cream is surely one of the most ecstatic mixes known to man or woman. We like it so much that we make strawberry shortcakes three different ways.

## Strawberry Shortcake I

*Makes one 9-inch biscuit crust*

Traditionally Southern, this is a rich sweetened biscuit dough sliced into layers, spread with fruit and whipped cream.

Combine in a mixing bowl

> *1 cup sifted unbleached white flour*
> *2 teaspoons baking powder*
> *½ teaspoon salt*
> *1 tablespoon brown sugar*
> *a dash of nutmeg*

Cut in

> *3 tablespoons butter*

until mixture is crumbly. Blend together

> *1 egg, well beaten*
> *4 to 6 tablespoons milk* or *cream*

Pour into flour mixture, making a soft dough. Turn onto lightly floured board. Roll or pat out to a ½-inch-thick round, and place in a 9-inch cake pan. Bake for 12 to 15 minutes.

As soon as it comes from the oven, brush the top with

> *melted butter*

To assemble the shortcake, just before serving, stack one layer of this crust on a serving plate. Top with fresh strawberries and whipped cream. Add a second crust and more whipped cream, with strawberries and mint leaves for garnish.

### Shortcake I Variation:

After rolling out the dough to ½-inch thickness, cut it with a heart-shaped cutter, to make little individual shortcakes. When baked, slice each little shortcake in half and spread with melted butter. Then stack with fruits as directed, garnishing the top with 1 whole berry and a mint leaf. We served these for a late-winter wedding once; they were lovely.

### Strawberry Shortcake II

This is the French version.

Prepare a Pastry Brisée Sucre, page 341. Remove crust from oven and cool. For each serving of this delight, break off a portion of the crust, place it in a small serving dish, top it with lightly sweetened crushed strawberries and a very generous dollop of whipped cream, piped, if you wish.

For other versions of a French Shortcake (taught to us, incidentally, by Arkansas' celebrated, kind, and knowledgeable Larry Loman, naturalist and Parks Service man at Village Creek State Park—the only person ever to tap sugar maples and make syrup from them in Arkansas!), we find the fruit must be heated first and thickened with a little cornstarch, as in the recipe for Blueberry Sundae Sauce, page 277.

### Strawberry Shortcake III

The Jewish-American version. Jan grew up eating the first shortcake and I this one, at my grandmother's house. I still remember eyeing the tall, white, string-tied bakery box in which, I knew, this was hidden.

Prepare the Geranium Cake, page 367, omitting the geraniums— but you could use any very good sponge cake or yellow or white layer cake. You need at least two layers, which, when the cake is baked and cooled, you torte into four layers.

Between each layer, spread lots of fresh, lightly sweetened sliced berries, and lots and lots of thick whipped cream. On the top, frost with even more whipped cream; pipe little rosettes around the edge.

*(continued)*

Into each rosette, stand 1 whole, perfect, pretty little berry, its tip pointing proudly up.

## Strawberry Binge in Celebration of the Season's First

*Chilled Strawberry Soup with Mint*
*Angel Biscuits • Strawberry Bread*
*Butter • Strawberry Jam*
*Salade Parkhurst with Asparagus Vinaigrette*
*Italian Spinach Torte*
*Three Strawberry Shortcakes: Southern, French, Jewish*

# MISCELLANEOUS FRUIT-RELATED THOUGHTS AND RECIPES

## Honeyed Zabaglione Napoleon

*Serves 4 to 6*

Zabaglione is a thick, sweet, very rich Italian custard, usually made with marsala. We use Napoleon, an orange liqueur we love, or Grand Marnier, instead. This is lightened by the addition of some whipping cream and is very close to the way the women who wrote *The Political Palate* (The Bloodroot Collective: Betsey Beaven, Noel Giardano, Selma Miriam, Pat Shea) do theirs.

Cook over, but not in, hot water, as for Lemon Mousse (p. 279)

*5 egg yolks*
*¼ cup honey*

Whisk constantly, till sauce becomes extremely thick—about 10 minutes. Remove from heat and whisk in

*¼ cup orange Napoleon liqueur or Grand Marnier*
*½ teaspoon vanilla*

Chill deeply. Whip until stiff

*1 cup heavy cream*

Fold the cream into the Napoleon custard. And there you have it. And with one taste, it will have you. Very very very rich, and good over almost any fruit in season.

## Jan's Fruited Cheeseball for the Deavers

*Serves 2 or 3, with assorted fruits*

Ken Deaver of Fayetteville, Arkansas (one of our frequent Dairy Hollow House guests), eats no sugar. He loves fruit, so we offered him this delicate, tenderly sweet cheeseball. A short freezing before serving gives it a most pleasurable texture.

Bring to a boil in a small saucepan

*½ cup water*

Add

*6 to 8 pitted dates*

Remove from heat and let mixture sit for 15 to 20 minutes, until dates are softened and mixture has cooled. Drain the dates and puree them in a blender or food processor. Add

*4 ounces cream cheese, softened*
*½ teaspoon cinnamon*
*½ teaspoon vanilla*

Place this mixture in the freezer for 30 minutes. Remove from freezer and gently scoop cheese-date mixture onto a piece of wax paper that is sprinkled with

*⅔ cup chopped walnuts* or *pecans*

Roll the mixture in the nuts, nutting its entire surface and forming a cheeseball. Place in the freezer for 45 minutes before serving. Serve it encircled with slices of apples, pears, and tangelos, with a hyacinth garnish.

# Deluxe Ambrosia

*Serves 4*

Try this glimmering beauty as a light dessert on a hot summer's night. And in the deep South, it's traditional at Christmastime. Ours is enhanced with ruby-red raspberry juice. You'll *know* why it's the food of the gods.

Press the juice from

*4 large oranges*

Place the juice in the freezer for 45 minutes, until the juice is partially frozen and will break easily with a fork—slushy. While the orange juice is in the freezer, prepare individual servings in chilled brandy glasses with the following fruits

*orange wedges, cut into 1-inch pieces*
*fresh pineapple chunks*
*banana slices, about ¼ inch thick*
*a sprinkle of coconut*

Immediately before serving, remove the orange juice from the freezer. Stir gently to break it up some. Add

*4 tablespoons chilled raspberry juice*

Give another quick stir and spoon over fruit. Garnish with a geranium bud and a mint leaf.

# Elsie Freund's Incredible Spanish Flan

*Serves 6 to 8*

I have eaten Elsie's flan, a baked Spanish-style custard along the crème caramel line, for years, and I swear it gets better as she keeps refining the cooking process. It is a simple recipe but amazingly delicious when carefully made, so pay close attention to Elsie's tips. What is this doing with fruit? Well, it is spectacularly beautiful when garnished with fresh fruit, and that is why. I have seen people fight over the last bite of Elsie's flan.

Flans are best made hours before serving. They must be deeply chilled to reach the ultimate heights of flan-hood.

Preheat oven to 350°. Caramelize

*1 cup sugar*

by putting it in a small skillet over a low flame, stirring *constantly* until the sugar melts and turns a golden color. Pour this caramelized syrup into a shallow heatproof bowl with at least a 6-cup capacity. Now, beat together

*3 egg whites*
*8 egg yolks*
*two 15½-ounce cans of evaporated milk*
*¾ cup sugar*
*2 teaspoons vanilla*

Mix well; strain into the bowl coated with the caramelized syrup. Place this bowl in a larger pan containing *hot* water well up the sides of the flan bowl. Cover the flan loosely and bake for an hour or so, until knife inserted in the center of the custard comes out clean. Cool the flan and refrigerate it.

When ready to serve, run the blade of a knife around the edge of the flan to loosen the custard. Place the serving plate atop the flan bowl and reverse bowl onto the plate, so the flan and the wonderful caramel sauce are revealed in all their splendor.

## Fruit Kuchen

*Serves 6 to 8*

A kuchen is a kind of pastry, usually yeast-leavened and topped with fruit. This is a particularly good one, something like a Danish, something like a cheesecake. It makes a perfect dessert, too delicious to be as healthful as it actually is, very pretty with the jewellike colors of fresh fruit in season shimmering atop it over a delicious custard-y, cheesecake-y filling. It can be varied unto infinity.

Heat together till the butter melts
*¼ cup each milk, honey, and butter*

Turn into a bowl, and let stand till lukewarm, then add

*1 tablespoon yeast*
*1 teaspoon ground cardamom*
*1 teaspoon vanilla*
*the rind of 1 lemon, grated*
*1 whole egg, at room temperature, beaten*

Let sit till the yeast gets bubbly, then stir in

*2 cups whole wheat pastry flour*

*(continued)*

299

Knead about 5 minutes, adding flour, perhaps as much as ½ cup, if necessary. Let rise, covered, until doubled in bulk. Meanwhile, mix up the following filling by combining in food processor and buzzing till smooth

*2 cups ricotta cheese (or cottage cheese)*
*2 egg yolks*
*½ cup honey*
*¼ teaspoon almond extract*
*1 teaspoon vanilla*

When the dough has risen, spread it out in a Pam-ed 9- × -13-inch pan, pulling it out to the edges and up just a bit higher there. Spread the cheese filling over the dough, and let kuchen rise, covered, 30 minutes. Preheat oven to 400° in the last 15 minutes of the kuchen's second rise. Then, when kuchen has completed its rise, bake for 25 minutes, or until the crust is golden and the filling firm. Let cool.

After filling is cool, make the Fruit Topping. Select one of the fruit/juice combinations listed below this general recipe, then proceed as follows. Into

*⅔ cup fruit juice of your choice*

smush until lump-free

*2 tablespoons cornstarch*

Then add

*2 tablespoons honey*
*flavoring as suggested (following)*

Bring this to a boil, stirring constantly, and cook until thick and clear. Remove from heat. Pour/spoon a little of this thickened juice glaze over the cheese on the baked kuchen, just enough to be a thin layer. Arrange

*1½ to 2 cups fruit of your choice*

over kuchen. Pour the remaining thickened juice glaze over the arranged fruit. Serve chilled or at room temperature.

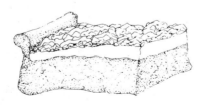

## Possible and Delicious Fruit/Juice Combinations
## for Kuchen Toppings:

- Apple-Strawberry Juice/Fresh sliced strawberries/1 drop almond extract

- Orange Juice/Very thin fresh orange slices/1 drop orange extract/1 drop vanilla extract

- Apple-Strawberry Juice/Fresh whole blueberries/1 drop almond extract

- Pineapple Juice/Canned crushed pineapple (cook with the cornstarch instead of arranging separately)

- Cranberry Juice/Fresh sliced purple plums (with skins)

- Cranberry Juice/Fresh cherries, sweet, halved and pitted/1 drop almond extract (this is divine!)

- Apricot Nectar/Canned apricot halves/1 drop almond extract

- Peach Nectar/Fresh sliced peaches, peeled/1 drop almond extract

*Note:* This kuchen doubles, triples, or quadruples with great success. It's fun to do a great big one, if you have a pan large enough, and do bands of different colors of fruit, each with their appropriate juice. Glorious!

# Love
# and Chocolate

$W$hat *is* it about chocolate?

What *is* it about that substance, derived from the tree whose genus name, *Theobroma*, literally translates to "food of the gods"?

It is more, we think, than the beautiful darkness, mysterious and rich, hinting of rain forests and exotic places, deep as the nighttime of dreams and desires. And it is more than the aroma, totally distinct among scents, evocative, permeating. So, then, it must be the flavor. But if so, *which* flavor? For chocolate is not one flavor but many: a number of flavors, felicitous and perverse in their strange, perfect combination.

In the forms in which we eat chocolate, there is in the flavor the sweetness, of course, as a top note, dominating, apparent. But there is a bass line of oily richness as well, for the literal essence of chocolate is in its fat, its "butter," a harmony often enriched by the addition of dairy butter or heavy cream to the cocoa fat.

But if the sweet carries the tune and the rich deepens it, it is the bitterness that is the final element, the percussion. Insistent and driving, perhaps at first not readily evident, we think it is the bitterness that is the essential element of chocolate, the nucleus. It may not always be registered by the taste buds as such, but the bitterness is

302

that always and deeply present drumming, perverse and primitive and sensuous, the heartbeat of chocolate.

And so it is, finally, the bitterness that does it; that sets chocolate apart; that cuts, yet deepens, the sweetness in any particular recipe; that causes people to get up in the middle of the night for it. It is that bitterness, cloaked in sweet, that contradicts, pleases, and titillates; that, in a perfectly prepared chocolate recipe, reflects the pairs of opposites harmonized: the harsh and the gentle, the overt and the hidden, the wild and the refined. Chocolate is about desire, satisfaction, and guilt (for in these days of calorie and cholesterol consciousness, on top of the basic equation that our culture makes with pleasure and inevitable dire consequences, hasn't the decision about when and how much and whether to eat chocolate become a moral decision for most of us, not just a simple matter of food choice, of what do we feel like eating? And haven't we, thus, given the substance even more power than it had?). Chocolate today is about sin, suffer, repent (which we at Dairy Hollow House don't think it should be); but it is also, as it always has been, about unity, about the perfection of melded opposites. In both these, it reflects life itself.

We've read, as you may have, about that polysyllabic substance scientists have recently isolated in chocolate, a substance that is supposedly identical to one the brain emits on its own when the subject is in love. That is why, the theory goes, we (a) give chocolate to those we love and (b) crave it when we are feeling low. To us, this obscures the central point about chocolate—and yet echoes it. For what but love and chocolate combine so perfectly the bitter and the sweet? What but love and chocolate are so sublime when perfect, and so disappointing when counterfeit?

The chocolate recipes that follow are not counterfeit. Being real —rich and deep and dark—we find them so totally satisfying that just a bit goes a long, long way. We find there is a kind of postperfect chocolate satiety like only one other (the parameters of which are inappropriate to discuss in a cookbook) in which one feels, "That was it, that was the ultimate, I will never want to eat chocolate again." Of course, one does eventually want to. Yet just as nothing can drive one to chocolate faster than a few weeks of just plain healthy, low-calorie foods, so nothing can make one crave salads like an occasional chocolate indulgence—the more so if that indulgence is total. It is the guilt, we feel, that undermines so many eaters in this country, where slimness is the ideal and yet where there are more overweight people than in any other nation in the world. Guilt sets off that obsessive overeating mechanism, not just of chocolate but of anything. Get rid of the guilt, and eat your chocolate like a good girl (boy) and then, tomorrow, you can have some vegetables. Subtract guilt, remorse, fear; add a self-accepting kind of open indulgence; and one will be led directly back to the path of moderation. Here goes.

## Dairy Hollow House Mocha Dream Torte

*Serves 12 to 15*

A smashing, spectacular party dessert in which the dark and bitter of chocolate in several forms is intensified by the dark and bitter of coffee, and the whole set off by the sweetness and light of whipped cream. The cream, chocolate-enriched but not too much so, is in thick, fluffy clouds between four layers of a thin, dark chocolate cake, chocolate-syrup drenched, that is almost more soufflé than cake. A wondrous and unusually put-together creation, this was featured in the Spring, 1985, issue of *Chocolatier* magazine. Time-consuming and worth it.

First make up the individual components: Thin Cake Layers, Rich Chocolate Syrup, Mocha Cream Filling.

*Thin Cake Layers* (you'll note this is flourless):
Pam a 10- × -15-inch jelly-roll pan, line it with wax paper, grease and flour the wax paper. Preheat oven to 350°. Melt over low heat, in a small heavy saucepan

*3 squares (ounces) semisweet chocolate*

in

*3 tablespoons strong coffee*

Stir until smooth, remove from heat, and let cool. Meanwhile, beat to soft peaks

*5 egg whites*
*a dash of salt*

With the beater going, add, ¼ cup at a time

*¾ cup sugar*

The egg whites should be stiff and glossy. Add, beating on low speed until just blended

*1 teaspoon vanilla*
*⅛ teaspoon almond extract*
*5 egg yolks*

304

Beating by hand, fold cooled chocolate mixture into whites-sugar-yolks. Pour the batter into the prepared pan, bake for 10 minutes at 350°, then 5 minutes at 300°. Cake will have sunk; it will be quite thin —⅛ inch to ¼ inch high—and a little cracked on the surface, but it will test clean with a toothpick. Remove from the oven. Sift

*powdered sugar*

over a large piece of wax paper and, after running a knife around the edge of the cake, invert cake onto sugared paper and peel off the paper that the cake baked on. Sift powdered sugar over cake and let cool under a dish towel.

Slice cake crosswise into four even slabs—use a ruler if necessary to get each piece even. (Once cake has cooled, layers may be stacked with wax paper between and frozen to be thawed and filled another day.)

*Rich Chocolate Syrup:* Melt over low heat

*5 squares (ounces) semisweet chocolate*

in

*5 tablespoons strong coffee*

Stir. Add more coffee if necessary to make a thick syrup.

*Mocha Cream Filling:* Bring to a boil

*2 cups whipping cream*

Pour cream, hot, over

*4 ounces semisweet chocolate chips*
*1 tablespoon instant coffee*
*2 tablespoons sugar*

Whisk until chocolate melts; refrigerate until cream is cold. Whip cold, chocolated cream until peaks form. Refrigerate until ready to use.

*(continued)*

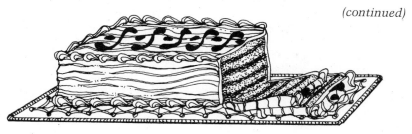

*Assembly:* Put one slab of cake on a serving platter; brush with ¼ cup syrup, spread with some mocha cream. Repeat, layering, until cake is used up. Frost the top and sides with mocha cream. Cover and refrigerate at least overnight. Cake will keep for three to four days refrigerated, and freezes well.

## Creole Chocolate Cake

*Serves 8 to 10*

A buttermilk chocolate cake, coffee in the batter, brown sugar instead of white, and a distinctive buttermilk-and-dried-fruit-and-nut filling, rich as all get-out, are what begin to make this cake so outstanding. But then add the element of whipping cream floated above that rich filling, and the most marvelous bittersweet European-style icing, and you have something very special. Good with New Orleans–style coffee, too, naturally. Preheat oven to 350°.

Pam and dust with unsweetened cocoa two 8-inch cake pans. Pour

*¾ cup very hot brewed coffee*

over

*3½ squares (ounces) unsweetened chocolate, chopped*
*½ cup butter, cubed*

Stir well to melt chocolate and butter, then add

*½ cup mild vegetable oil*
*1 teaspoon vanilla*

Set aside. Now, sift together

*2 cups unbleached white flour, unsifted*
*¾ teaspoon baking soda*
*¼ teaspoon baking powder*
*¼ teaspoon salt*

Set this aside, too, and beat till smooth and thick

*2 eggs*
*¼ cup white sugar*
*1¾ cups dark brown sugar, packed*

Beat half of the chocolate mixture into the eggs; add half the flour and

*¼ cup buttermilk*

Repeat: the remainder of chocolate, the remainder of flour, and another

*¼ cup buttermilk*

Stir by hand till well blended. Transfer to prepared cake pans and bake
for about 30 to 35 minutes, or till cake tests done. Meanwhile, make
up Creole Chocolate Icing (p. 307) and Creole Buttermilk-Date Filling,
herewith.

*Creole Buttermilk Date Filling:* In a small heavy saucepan, bring to a
boil together

*1 cup buttermilk*
*⅔ cup sugar*

Buttermilk gets a little curdly and weird-looking when it heats, but
don't worry about it. When it reaches a boil and the sugar is dissolved,
turn down heat slightly and add

*1 cup chopped pitted dates*

Stir constantly till mixture thickens—about 5 minutes. Remove from
heat. Stir in

*1 teaspoon vanilla*
*1 cup chopped walnuts or pecans*

*Assembly:* Have ready the cake layers, "torted" into four; the filling,
the icing, and

*1 cup heavy cream, whipped stiff*

Put together the cake as follows: cake, a layer of filling, a layer of
whipped cream (it is supposed to be unsweetened, by the way), cake,
repeating until you reach the top layer. Ice with the Creole Chocolate
Icing.

For professional assembly, use a cake board. Use filling dam of
Creole Icing. Pipe ruffled vertical stripes at intervals on the side of
cake; do shell borders at base and top.

## Creole Chocolate Icing
*Enough icing for two 8- or 9-inch layers*

Our favorite chocolate icing, this is incredibly simple to make,
yet with a richly elegant European bittersweet flavor and glossy sheen.
Rich and smooth, this is a perfect icing to pipe with.

*(continued)*

Melt, over hot water

*12 ounces semisweet chocolate chips*

When smooth, remove from heat and stir in

*1 cup sour cream*
*½ teaspoon vanilla*

Beat by hand till smooth. Let cool, stirring occasionally, till of spreading consistency—about 5 minutes.

## Chocolate-Orange Cake

*Serves 8 to 10*

Orange is another of those flavors that have a strange and wonderful synergy with chocolate, as coffee does, cutting the sweetness yet playing up the essential chocolate-y-ness at the same time. We took elements of the Creole Chocolate Cake (p. 306) and following recipes and added oranges, in several forms, to produce this winner.

Make up Creole Chocolate Cake layers, but using all white sugar and no brown, substituting orange juice for the coffee, and adding the grated rind of an orange to the batter. Torte the two layers into four.
Make up Rich Chocolate Custard filling, in following recipe, but omit peppermint extract and use instead orange extract.
Make up a batch of Creole Chocolate Icing, preceding recipe.
Make up a batch of Orange Buttercream by omitting the crème de menthe in Créme de Menthe Buttercream, in following recipe, and replacing it with 1 tablespoon Grand Marnier, 2 tablespoons orange juice, the grated rind of ½ orange, and ½ teaspoon orange extract.

Have ready a bottle of Grand Marnier or Napoleon liqueur (you'll just use a bit).
Melt

*1½ cups orange marmalade*

Strain out peel, and remelt.

Put together the cake as follows: Place a layer on the serving plate. Sprinkle lightly with liqueur. Spread with custard filling. Repeat, spreading with Orange Buttercream till you reach top layer. Brush entire cake with melted marmalade. Let stand for 30 minutes. Ice sides with Creole Icing. Top with Orange Buttercream. Pipe on additional icing, if desired.

Garnish each slice at serving time with a twist of fresh orange.

## Chocolate-Peppermint Layer Cake

*Makes one 8-inch cake, 6 inches high; 8 to 10 servings*

Certain flavors set off chocolate just right. Coffee, as discussed, is one. Peppermint is another. Peppermint is distinctive enough that one doesn't find many recipes for it; having found this one, search no further. This same good Creole Chocolate two-layer cake is "torted" into four layers. Between two, and on top, lurks a creamy green crème de menthe buttercream filling; between the other two is the most amazing rich, peppermint-scented chocolate custard you can imagine. A third icing, again our favorite Creole Chocolate Icing, of straight, nonminted chocolate, covers the sides of the cake and may be put through a piping tube as well. To gild the lily, bittersweet chocolate is dribbled, Jackson Pollock–style, over the smooth pale green canvas of the top. We always make this cake at the Christmas holidays, and throughout the year as requested.

Have ready

*cake layers, torted, from Creole Chocolate Cake, page 306*

Make the *Rich Chocolate Custard* as follows: In a heavy saucepan, heat, stirring constantly

*2 large egg yolks*
*⅓ cup half-and-half*
*2 squares (ounces) unsweetened chocolate, chopped*
*⅔ cup sugar*

(continued)

Do not allow it to boil. After about 8 minutes of faithful stirring, this will thicken up beautifully, at which point remove from heat and stir in

*½ teaspoon vanilla*
*1 teaspoon pure peppermint extract*

Keep stirring, off the heat, for 2 more minutes, then let cool.

While it cools, make Creole Chocolate Icing, page 307.

White *it* cools, make the *Crème de Menthe Buttercream* as follows: Beat till creamy

*3 tablespoons each softened butter and cream cheese*

Beat in, a bit at a time

*3 cups sifted powdered sugar*

When all sugar has been added, the mixture should be very, very thick, but smooth and creamy. Stir in, to make it of spreading consistency, and to color and flavor it

*3 tablespoons green crème de menthe*
*½ teaspoon vanilla*

Beat. The icing needs to be thick but beautifully, spreadably creamy. If it isn't, add more sifted sugar to thicken, a few drops of cream to thin.

For assembly, have ready the cake layers, both fillings, and the icings. For professional assembly, you will also need

*a jar of mint jelly*

as well as the ingredients for Chocolate Dribble, following.

For homey assembly: Stack the first layer on the plate, cover with half of the chocolate custard filling, stack second layer on top of it, and spread with half the Crème de Menthe Buttercream. Stack third layer atop that, and cover with remainder of chocolate custard, and stack fourth and final layer atop that. Ice the top with the remaining Crème de Menthe Buttercream, and do the sides in the Creole Chocolate Icing.

For professional assembly: Start out with layer on a cake board. Do a filling dam with Creole Chocolate Icing, fill with chocolate custard, stack another layer of cake, repeat filling dam and fill with Crème de Menthe Buttercream. When cake is entirely filled, brush well all over with melted, strained (if necessary) mint jelly (we make a lime-mint jelly here that is totally perfect for this). This is your crumb coat.

Let cake stand for ½ hour or even overnight. Then ice top with remaining buttercream. Lift cake to serving plate. Do sides in Creole Chocolate, and, if desired, do vertical lines of rippled icing through a star tip, or go all-out and basketweave the sides. Before you do borders, however, prepare *Chocolate Dribble* by melting together in the top of a double boiler

*½ ounce each semisweet and unsweetened chocolate*
*½ tablespoon butter*

When butter and chocolate have melted and are very very liquid, dribble them carefully from the tip of a spoon across the top of the cake—the pale green part. If desired, draw a toothpick carefully across the dribbles to make a marbled pattern, or do it free-form. Do not drip down sides.

Finish the cake with star-tip borders at base and top rim. Garnish each slice with a fresh mint sprig.

When professionally assembled, this cake is gorgeous. It would not be out of place on a pastry cart in any great restaurant.

## Augusta's Fall-down Chocolate Cake

*Serves 8 (maybe!)*

From Virginia Pasley's *In Celebration of Food* and Augusta Dabney, as warm a woman and as gifted a hostess as she is a talented actress. Everything from Augusta's kitchen always has a touch; it's not only delicious but ever so faintly offbeat, and always just lovely to look at. This is an exceptional cake, really more a baked chocolate mousse/fallen soufflé, moist and dense and like no other you have ever tasted.

Melt together over simmering water in the top of a double boiler

*½ cup butter*
*1 six-ounce package semisweet chocolate pieces*
*1 cup sugar*

(continued)

Remove from heat and cool the chocolate mixture to room temperature. Stir in

*8 egg yolks*

Place chocolate-egg mixture in the refrigerator for a few minutes. Preheat oven to 375°. Beat until stiff

*8 egg whites*

Remove chocolate mixture from the refrigerator and add to it

*1 teaspoon vanilla*

Gently fold the stiffly beaten egg whites into the chocolate mixture. Pam an angel food cake pan, and pour the batter into it. Bake for 45 minutes.

Now, pay attention to the following pointers from Virginia. "This cake will rise high like a soufflé. When the top cracks and starts to fall, it's time to take the cake out. Let it cool in the pan for a few minutes and turn it out onto a serving plate. (If you put it on a cake rack, it's likely to go right through.) When cool, put it in the refrigerator. It will look ugly, fallen in the middle and rough in places, but don't worry, it will taste divine, and the whipped cream covers all."

Whip until it forms peaks

*1 cup whipping cream*

Sweeten it with

*1 teaspoon sugar (or more to taste)*

Spread it over the top of the cake. Keep it in the refrigerator until ready to serve, and, of course, refrigerate any leftovers (hah!).

## Grand Marnier Chocolate Decadence

*10 small, rich servings*

This is not a cake at all but an incredibly rich dessert composed of Homemade Ladyfingers (p. 334), crushed amaretti cookies soaked in Grand Marnier (we offer two variations as well, or invent your own), and an unbelievable mixture that is a cross between mousse and a buttercream, with a serious chocolate wallop. Sectioned pieces of fresh orange interspersed here and there cut the almost obscene chocolate with their fresh innocence—yet somehow that only makes the whole affair seem more debauched! If the orange pieces are omitted, this can be done as a cake that is unmolded from a springform pan. But we much prefer it done up in tiny individual serving dishes, preferably glass, so one can view the various elements.

It should sit for at least six hours, and preferably overnight, before serving, so it is the ideal do-ahead chocolate dessert for a special party.

Unwrap and crumble slightly

*12 papers of amaretti cookies (these wonderful crisp, flavorsome Italian cookies, a very special macaroon, are available at any fine food store or good deli, or sometimes a liquor store; we buy them here at Austin's. Since there are 2 cookies per paper, this will mean you have 24 cookies in all)*

Drizzle over the amaretti

*½ cup Grand Marnier (or Napoleon)*

Set aside. Separate

*6 eggs*

and set both whites and yolks aside, too. Now, cream together till soft and fluffy

*1 cup butter, softened*
*¾ cup sugar*

Beat into this the reserved 6 egg yolks and

*3 squares (ounces) unsweetened chocolate, melted*
*½ teaspoon vanilla*
*grated rind of ½ orange, optional but good*

Then fold in

*½ cup chopped English walnuts*

and, lastly, the 6 egg whites, beaten to stiffness. You may have to use more of a stirring motion with the egg whites than is usual in folding; just be as gentle as you can and still get everything incorporated.

Line up ten individual serving dishes, and place in each

*a split ladyfinger*

Fill the dishes carefully, pressing up to the sides so the different colors and textures show through the glass, spoonfuls of the chocolate mixture, spoonfuls of the soaked amaretti, additional pieces of ladyfinger, and

*sections of fresh orange, seeded and peeled*

(continued)

313

Finish off with a layer of chocolate, leaving ¾ inch or so of space till the top of the serving dish. Cover and refrigerate these dishes for at least 6 hours, preferably overnight.

Just before serving, whip to stiffness

*1 cup chilled heavy cream*
*2 tablespoons sifted powdered sugar*

Pipe, or dollop, if you must, onto each of the Grand Marnier Decadences. Garnish with

*chocolate curls or an orange section half-dipped in melted chocolate*

*Variation:* Omit Grand Marnier, rind, fruit. Substitute Irish whiskey for Grand Marnier, and use pecans instead of walnuts. Or, for a roughness that is surprising and mighty pleasing in the midst of all that sweet, soak the amaretti in bourbon and use black walnuts instead of English walnuts.

I served this to a party of four one night, one gentleman of which said, "This is not chocolate decadence, this is chocolate *orgasm!*"

The following night I served it to a second party of four. There was a moment of silence as they all savored their first bites. Then— well, I can't even approximate the sound, but I am told it was a rebel yell. From one of the ladies.

Be forewarned.

For fabulous chocolate pie, see Jan's Mexican Chocolate Pudding, page 351.

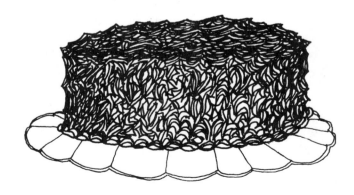

# Come for Cookies

There is a special smell at Dairy Hollow House. It hits you when you first walk in the parlor: a mixture of fresh, clean scents, indefinable and pleasant. Part of it's a faint flowery undertone, which we finally figured out emanates from the rose and lavender potpourri we store with the linens. It took us longer to pinpoint the other aroma, which is even more vague, yet definitely present: the faintest ghost of the sweet fragrance of a warm kitchen on baking day. A trace of it is always there, even if it is a cold day and we haven't baked in a week. We've finally decided that it must be, simply, the accumulated smell of years of breads rising, cookies in the oven, cinnamon and nutmeg stirred into batters and doughs, hundreds of rollings out and pattings and kneadings and bakings and, finally, servings to guests.

We do love to bake, all of us, and at the holidays especially we go a little bit wild in the cookie department. Besides the cookies we make year-round, there are always Pipparkakut, Finnish ginger cookies, cut into hearts and snowflakes and appropriately decorated with white icing. Often there are Rum Raisin Shortbreads, and delectable Ruge-lach, filled cream cheese pastries that are a happy Hanukkah nod to Crescent's Russian-Jewish heritage. And there are always Holsteins, our own invention: a rolled-out butter cookie with random patches of chocolate and vanilla, cut out in cow shapes, also piped in icing. Several other types of cookies, up to a dozen or so varieties, may get made as well over the month as we have time, to wait in readiness for guests, drop-ins, and friends.

The rest of the year, though, we mostly stay away from rolled cookies; they are, after all, a bit fussy. Two exceptions are our two pie-dough cookies, Grandmother Fuller's Jelly Tarts and cinnamon roll-ups, delicious ways to use up the scrips and scraps always left over when one makes a pie dough and is rolling out anyway. See pages 342–343 for the how-tos.

Other than these, we generally prefer drop cookies, and, most especially, bar cookies, above the roll-out kind. Bar cookies, being baked in one pan and then cut into pieces, are the simplest of cookies to make. As a rule, too, they're the most luscious, moist, chewy, and interesting. We have quite a few bar cookies that are, as Jan says, *"too good."* Many include chocolate, like the devastating Jan Brownies, the Fallen Angels, and peppermint-filled Afternoon Delights from my friend Anne Breedlove. But two of the best bar cookies we know, Decadent Date Delights and Virginia's Lemon Bars, do not contain even a trace of chocolate. Try them all . . . bar none.

# ROLLED COOKIES
## Rum Raisin Shortbreads

*Makes one dozen cookies*

Note from Jan: These elegant shortbreads are the all-time favorite of my father, John Murray, who loves them for their rich buttery flavor. If you're like Crescent (who isn't fond of raisins), simply leave the raisins out. Note from Crescent: Well, wait a minute, Jan, I might try these with chopped apricots instead of the raisins . . . and add some chopped black walnuts or maybe toasted hazelnuts . . . I could relate to that kind of Rum Raisin Shortbread real good!

Bring to a boil

*¼ cup rum*
*1 cup raisins*

Remove from heat and let soak for 1 hour. Drain raisins. (You may discard the rum at this point, or reserve it for your next rum recipe—remember, it will be slightly sweetened from the raisins—or be a very good cook and simply drink it down!) Preheat oven to 375°. Cream together

*1 cup butter, softened*
*½ cup sifted powdered sugar*

Sift together

*2 cups unbleached white flour*
*¼ teaspoon baking powder*
*a pinch of salt*

Add sifted ingredients to butter mixture. Add raisins and

*½ teaspoon vanilla*
*a pinch of nutmeg*

Stir well. Roll out dough to ½-inch thickness. Cut with cookie cutter (hearts and star shapes are prettiest, we think) and bake for 15 to 20 minutes.

## DAIRY HOLLOW HOUSE FLOWERS: WINTER

*Winter arrangements: a few red mini-carnations from the florist tucked in among branches of spruce or cedar; red roses done the same way; holly branches, cedar, and red carnations; a bowl of pomegranates with holly sprigs tucked in here and there; the same with buckbrush; buckbrush, evergreens, baby's breath, and three pink sweetheart roses from the florist; a stark, bare branch, branches of any evergreen, daisy mums from the florist, and tiny gold Christmas balls hung over all.*

## A Sumptuous February Birthday Tea

*Pastry Tray: Anne Breedlove's Afternoon Delights, Viennese Nut Crescents,*
*Rum Raisin Shortbreads, Rugelach*
*Sandwich Tray: Cucumber and Boursin Cheese on Thin-sliced White;*
*Pimento Cheese, Tomato, and Sprouts on Thin-sliced Pumpernickel*
*Fruit Kuchen*
*Chocolate-Orange Cake*
*Hot Scones • Butter • Raspberry Jam • Crème Fraîche*
*Ceylon Tea • Cream • Sugar*
*Sherry*

## Pipparkakut: Finnish Ginger Cookies

*Makes about four dozen small cookies, fewer large ones*

If you are a Dairy Hollow House guest in early December, odds are that when you check in, you will be handed a large, crisp gingerbread heart with your name piped on it in white icing. Come after the tenth or so, and your cookie will be hanging on our tree. Most Decembers we run through several batches of these before all holiday guests, and the merchants we do business with all year, and the friends who drop by, have received their heart cookies. How they're done: this simple recipe.

Most cookies suitable for hanging on a holiday tree are not that tasty to begin with and quickly grow stale and unpleasantly hard. Not so these spicy, delicious cookies, which start out and stay crisp and flavorful, every bit as pleasing to bite into as to look at, their deep brown color a perfect foil for the white icing.

Cream together

*2/3 cup butter, at room temperature*
*3/4 cup brown sugar*

Blend in

*2 teaspoons cinnamon*
*1 teaspoon each ginger and cloves*
*1/4 teaspoon nutmeg*
*dash or two each cardamom and coriander*
*1 1/2 teaspoons baking soda*

318

Add

*2½ cups unbleached white flour*

with

*¼ to ⅓ cup water or enough water to make a smooth, pliable dough*
*1 teaspoon cider vinegar*

Chill for 30 minutes.

Preheat oven to 375°. Roll dough out ⅛ inch thick. Cut out cookies, using your favorite shapes. (We do our hearts freehand; after all, you need a larger heart for "Eureka Flower Shop" or "The Gillilands," than you do for simply "Joe.") We also have a cookie cutter (see following), which makes, with later white-icing embellishment, the most perfect snowflakes; they look just great on the tree.

Place the cookies on ungreased baking sheets. If you intend to use them for ornaments, make a hole on the top of each cookie for the hanging string with a toothpick. Be sure to make the hole large enough so it will not bake shut, as the cookies rise and spread, just a bit, during their oven sojourn; wiggle the toothpick around to be sure. Bake for 7 to 10 minutes—until the cookies are crisp and lightly browned. Let cool on racks. After cooling, if you wish, embellish with Decorative Icing, following. This is not an absolute must—the cookies taste quite good with or without the icing—but they do look charming.

## Decorative Icing

*Enough to pipe decoratively one batch of Pipparkakut*

A fairly stiff icing that works beautifully in a pastry tube and dries crisp and hard and keeps well.

In a large bowl, beat until stiff

*1 egg white*

Gradually beat in

*3 cups unsifted powdered sugar*
*1 to 2 tablespoons water*
*1 drop vanilla*

Beat, adding water until icing has reached a consistency that can be easily put through a pastry tube. (See pp. 365 and 366 on piping and pastry tubes.) This icing should not be so thin that it is at all drippy;

on the other hand, it must be thin enough so it can be pressed through without undue strain on the hand. Fill a pastry bag fitted with a fine writing tip two-thirds of the way, and go to it with names, greetings, sentiments, and designs.

# Rugelach

*Makes three dozen*

From the Finnish Christmas cookies to these buttery rich, wonderful Russian-Jewish pastries is quite a leap; a world of difference in flavors and textures as well as origins and method; a world of delicious contrasts.

Soften to room temperature

*1 cup each cream cheese and butter*

Cream together till smooth and thoroughly blended. Beat in

*1 teaspoon vanilla*
*4 tablespoons sugar*
*dash or so salt*
*1 cup unbleached white flour*

When smooth, stir in

*1 additional cup flour*

Turn dough out onto lightly floured board and knead just a few times, till dough just comes together. Divide dough into thirds and pat each third into a thick, flattened circle. Refrigerate, wrapped, for about an hour. Toward the end of the hour, preheat oven to 350°. Combine, tossing together

*½ cup sugar*
*1¾ tablespoons cinnamon*
*⅔ cup very finely chopped walnuts or almonds*

Working with the dough circles one at a time, remove one from the refrigerator and roll out into a circle about 14 inches in diameter and about ⅛ inch thick. Dough will be deliciously soft and smooth, with the texture of a baby's bottom. Leaving a 1-inch border at the perimeter of the dough "blank," spread the circle very lightly with

*jam (favorites for this are raspberry or plum, or apple butter)*

and then sprinkle with a third of the nut-cinnamon mixture. Cut and roll up the dough round as described and pictured with Crescent's Favorite Whole Wheat Butterhorns, page 85, allowing 12 pie-shape wedges per dough circle. Repeat the rolling out, the filling with jam and cinnamon-y nuts, the rolling up, for each of the remaining rounds, placing cookies, as you complete them, on well-greased or Pam-ed baking sheets. Bake for about 15 to 20 minutes, or until Rugelach are pleasantly golden brown. They do have some tendency to stick, and to edge toward burning, because of the jam, so keep an eye on them. Let cool on rack. Sprinkle the cooled Rugelach with a generous drift of

*powdered sugar*

Great with hot coffee or tea!

## Holsteins

*Makes about three dozen cow cookies*

Completely and totally our own invention. Our guests love these! Two rich butter cookies, chocolate and vanilla, rolled into one and cut out with a cow-shape cookie cutter.

Several hours before commencing, take out and let soften to room temperature

*2 cups butter*

When you're ready to get cracking, and the butter is quite soft, divide the butter, placing 1 cup in one bowl and the second cup in another. Pour over each cup butter

*⅔ cup sugar (in other words, 1⅓ cups sugar altogether)*

Using an electric beater or by hand, cream each bowl of butter-sugar until light and creamy. Then break into each bowl

*1 egg (2 eggs total)*
*1 teaspoon vanilla (2 teaspoons total)*

(continued)

Cream each egg into each butter-sugar bowl. Now, set

*1 square (ounce) semisweet chocolate*

to melt over hot water, while you sift

*unbleached white flour to equal 5 cups sifted*

Now, to the first bowl of butter-sugar-egg-vanilla, stir in 2½ cups of the sifted flour with

*½ teaspoon salt*

This dough is quite stiff; you may have to knead the last bit of flour in by hand. You have now made rich vanilla butter cookie dough. Now, turn your attention to bowl two. Add to it the melted chocolate and

*⅓ cup sifted unsweetened cocoa*
*½ teaspoon salt*

plus 2 cups of the previously sifted flour. Again, you will have to knead in the flour toward the end. You may need to use a little more flour than the 2 cups to achieve a consistency of the thickness of the rich vanilla cookie dough.

At any rate, divide the finished doughs into four balls, two light and two dark. Take about 1 heaping tablespoon of each of the chocolate and vanilla doughs and firmly press the two together. Keep doing this, building up tablespoon by tablespoon of the mixed doughs, adding each teaspoon to the first two, until you build up a large ball of marbleized dough. Divide dough into four portions and place in four plastic bags. Let dough chill for 30 minutes. Then roll out and cut into cow shapes, using a cow-shape cookie cutter (of course, you could cut this dough into other shapes, but then these wouldn't be Holsteins!). Preheat oven to 375°. Place cookies on ungreased cookie sheets and bake for 8 to 10 minutes, until cookies are lightly browned. Transfer cookies to rack; cool completely. If you wish, use pastry bag and Decorative Icing, page 319, to draw in features.

MOOOOOOOO!!

# BAR COOKIES

## Decadent Date Delights

*Makes 18 bar cookies, about 1½ × 3 inches*

A truly great bar cookie recipe, rich and buttery and provocative, one we always like to include on a tray of assorted cookies, as with the Lemon Bars which follow. In both cases, a pastry crust is topped with a sweet, toothsome mixure containing eggs, and the whole thing, after baking, is covered with sifted powdered sugar. Still the two are very different.

Preheat oven to 350°. For the *Pastry Layer*, combine

*1¼ cups unbleached white flour*
*⅓ cup sugar*
*½ cup butter*

Blend to fine crumbs. Press into bottom of Pam-ed 9-inch square pan (it works with a larger pan, too; crust will be thinner, crisper). Bake this pastry for about 20 minutes—until edges are very lightly browned. As it bakes, mix up the

*Top Layer* — combine and beat together well

*½ cup brown sugar*
*¼ cup white sugar*
*2 eggs*
*1 teaspoon vanilla*
*2 tablespoons unbleached white flour*
*1 teaspoon baking powder*
*½ teaspoon salt*
*¼ teaspoon nutmeg*
*1 cup chopped walnuts*
*1 cup chopped pitted dates*

Spread mixture over hot pastry layer in pan. Bake for another 20 minutes. Cool in pan. Sprinkle top with

*¼ cup finely sifted powdered sugar*

and cut into bars.

## Virginia's Lemon Bars

*Makes one 9-×-13-inch panful*

These delicious sweet, chewy, lemony bars were given to me by my dear friend Virginia Carey, who died in 1979, leaving a space that can never quite be filled by anyone else, for me and many other Eureka people. Virginia always used to say, "One of these days I'm just going to get on my broomstick and fly off"; she died on Halloween.

Preheat oven to 350°. Mix and press into bottom of pan

*½ cup butter*
*1 cup unbleached white flour*
*¼ cup powdered sugar*

Beat

*2 eggs*
*1 cup sugar*
*2 tablespoons flour*
*½ teaspoon baking powder*
*juice and rind of 1 lemon*

This mixture will be thin. Pour it over first layer. Bake for 30 to 35 minutes. Let cool slightly and sift over them

*¼ cup powdered sugar*

Let set for a while, then set into squares.

## Late-Afternoon-in-June Treat for Arriving Guests

*Fresh Lemonade*
*Virginia's Lemon Bars*

# Anne Breedlove's Afternoon Delights

*Makes one 10-×-14-inch panful, to be cut into tiny squares*

Sweet Anne Breedlove brought these for Ned's birthday party, even when she herself was going to be out of town for the occasion. These are wonderful! Rich, with a knockout flavor, they are delicate cookies, really more like a tea cake or petit four than a cookie, with a thin chocolate cakelike layer, a rich creamy green peppermint layer, and a shiny chocolate glaze on top. Cut them into *tiny* squares; they are very rich. Most distinguished on a tea tray.

Preheat oven to 350°. In top of double boiler, melt together

> *3 squares (ounces) semisweet chocolate*
> *¾ cup butter (1½ sticks)*

Beat together

> *3 large eggs*
> *1½ cups sugar*
> *1 teaspoon peppermint extract*

Mix chocolate-butter mixture and egg mixture with electric mixer for 30 seconds on medium speed. Sift together

> *¾ cup unbleached white flour*
> *¼ teaspoon salt*

Add to other ingredients and blend until smooth. Add

> *¼ cup chopped walnuts*

Line a 10-×-14-inch cookie sheet with aluminum foil and spray foil with Pam. Pour in mixture and bake for 20 to 25 minutes. As soon as cake comes out of oven, spread Peppermint Icing on top while cake is still hot.

*Peppermint Icing:* Mix together

> *4 tablespoons butter, softened*
> *1¾ cups sifted powdered sugar*
> *1 teaspoon peppermint extract*
> *3 tablespoons green crème de menthe*

Let the icing sit on cake for 25 mintues before putting on Glaze.

*(continued)*

*Glaze:* Melt in top of double boiler

> *3 squares (ounces) semisweet chocolate*
> *4 tablespoons butter*

While glaze is hot, pour it on top of cake and icing. Keep in refrigerator until the  glaze is hard—approximately 2 hours. Remove from refrigerator. Cut into bite-size pieces and remove from foil.

# Jan Brownies

*Makes 18 brownies*

Jan took all the things she liked best in sweets and combined them in this incredible, *very* chocolate-y marvel, which is somewhere between chewy and cakey. She often bakes a batch of these for people having grump days, for which they are a perfect antidote. And, because they are known to travel with her often to picnics, her basket is always the first raided.

Preheat oven to 350°. Melt

> *½ cup butter*

Add

> *1 cup brown sugar*
> *2 tablespoons instant coffee powder*

Beat together until well blended. Add

> *3 eggs*
> *1 teaspoon each vanilla and baking powder*
> *½ teaspoon salt*

Stir well. Combine with

> *1¼ cups sifted unbleached white flour*
> *6 tablespoons cocoa*
> *½ cup brewed coffee, cooled*

Fold in

> *1 cup chopped walnuts*
> *1 cup semisweet chocolate chips*

Pour batter into 13- × -9- × -2-inch pan. Bake for 25 to 30 minutes. Cool and cut into squares.

## Crescent's Classic Chewy Brownies

*Makes one 9-×-13-inch panful*

Rich and chewy, this is a brownie to dream of, utterly wonderful as is, with a glass of cold milk, or topped with homemade vanilla ice cream or peppermint ice cream. Straight, unadulterated chocolate—a lot of it—goes into these, along with plenty of nuts and butter. These have an oddly dulled surface; don't be put off by it.

Preheat oven to 375°. Melt together over very low heat, stirring constantly

*8 ounces—yes, that's 8 full squares—unsweetened chocolate*
*1 cup butter*

Remove from heat and cool for a few minutes while you beat together until very light, using an electric mixer

*5 eggs*
*3 cups sugar*
*2 teaspoons vanilla*
*¼ teaspoon salt*

This beating should take at least 8 minutes at high speed. Long beating is one of the secrets of this simple gem. At last, beat in the semicooled chocolate mixture, and remove beaters. From here on, you proceed with a wooden spoon. Stir in, beating just enough to blend well but no more

*1½ cups unbleached white flour*

After flour is blended, stir in

*1 to 2 cups chopped nuts—pecans or English walnuts*

Transfer to a Pam-ed 9-×-13-inch pan, and bake for about 35 minutes, being careful not to overbake.

I like to bake a batch of these while playing Scrabble with Ned and assorted friends. The delightful aroma makes itself more and more evident throughout the game. Eaten afterward, even the sorest of losers has an easier time with the gloating party who won with *quixotic* on a triple-word score.

327

## Brown Sugar (or Blond) Brownies

*Makes one 9- × -9-inch panful*

How can anything so simple be *so* good? These delicious bars, made from ingredients you are almost sure to have, can be mixed up in 10 or 15 minutes. Really ridiculously easy, these, and always pleasing. Sublime with pecans.

Preheat oven to 350°. Melt

*4 tablespoons butter*

Stir into it

*1 cup dark brown sugar*

Stir well, so all the lumps dissolve. Let this mixture cool while you sift together

*½ cup sifted unbleached white flour*
*½ teaspoon salt*
*1 teaspoon baking powder*

Into the brown sugar–butter mixture, beat

*1 egg*
*1 teaspoon vanilla*

Combine this with the sifted flour mixture and

*½ to 1 cup chopped pecans (or any nut you like—but pecans are made for brown-sugary things!)*

Transfer to a greased 9- × -9-inch pan and bake for about 20 minutes. Let them cool, if you can, before cutting them.

## Fallen Angels

*Makes one panful; about 18*

We call these Fallen Angels because, despite our insistence on no shortcuts, no convenience foods, and doing everything from scratch (invariably the most complicated and time-consuming way, though the way that generally yields the finest results), there comes a time in every cook's life when she has to give herself a break. These cookies are *easy*, require almost no cleanup, and are, in the words of an old Mose Allison blues song, "as sweet and pure, pure and sweet, as homemade sin."

Preheat oven to 350°. In a 13- × -9-inch baking pan, melt

*½ cup butter*

Sprinkle over butter

*1½ cups graham cracker crumbs (or stale cake crumbs, or stale breadcrumbs plus 1 tablespoon brown sugar, or oatmeal which you have ground to crumbliness in a food processor, or any combination of these to equal 1½ cups)*

Pour

*one 14-ounce can sweetened condensed milk*

evenly over crumbs. Top with

*3½ ounces flaked coconut*
*1 cup chopped nuts*

Press down lightly. Bake for 25 to 30 minutes, or until lightly browned. Cool thoroughly before cutting.

Insult-to-Injury Variation: Add butterscotch chips to the above. Oh, Lord!

# DROP COOKIES

Only nominally more complex than bars, many of our favorite cookies are dropped from a spoon or piped through a tube.

## Chocolate-dipped Oatmeal-Walnut Drop Cookies

*Makes about 30 cookies*

One thinks of oatmeal cookies as plain, wholesome after-school fare. Not these!

Preheat oven to 325°. In a bowl with an electric mixer, beat

*2 large eggs, lightly beaten*
*½ cup each brown sugar and granulated sugar*

until the mixture is thick and pale. Add

*2 cups old-fashioned rolled oats*
*¼ teaspoon salt*
*1 teaspoon vanilla*
*2 tablespoons melted butter, cooled*
*¾ cup medium-fine-chopped walnuts*

Stir the mixture until it is combined well. Drop the batter by level teaspoons 3 inches apart onto baking sheets lined with Pam-ed foil. Flatten each mound with the back of a fork dipped in water and bake for 10 minutes, or until golden around the edges. Let the cookies cool on the baking sheets and peel them gently off the foil.

In the top of a double boiler, over gently boiling water, melt

*8 ounces semisweet chocolate chips*
*2 tablespoons boiling water*

Dip one edge of each cookie in the melted chocolate, and then dip immediately in

*very finely crushed walnuts*

Put the cookies on racks to cool while the chocolate hardens.

## Penuche Lace Cookies

*Makes about four dozen cookies*

A most delicately textured cookie, fragile and attractive, crunchy with just a hint of chewiness in the middle of a delectable robust brown-sugary flavor. Great with any lighter dessert; a fruit marinated in liqueur, a mousse. Dedicated to Katie Mehlburger, age nine, who told me I should write the recipe in a book "so my mother can make them for me."

Preheat oven to 375°. Bring to a boil in a saucepan

*½ cup each butter and light corn syrup*
*⅔ cup light brown sugar*

Remove from heat. In a bowl, combine

*1 cup flour*
*1 tablespoon plus 1 teaspoon cocoa*
*½ cup finely ground pecans (or black walnuts would be good)*

Combine dry ingredients with hot mixture. Add

*¼ teaspoon vanilla*

Mix well. Mixture will be the consistency of thick syrup. Drop by level measuring teaspoons about 2 inches apart onto well Pam-ed cookie sheets, pushing batter from teaspoon with the fingers. Bake for 5 to 6 minutes. They will look bubbly in the middle and underdone when you remove them. Let them sit on the baking sheet for a couple of minutes, then transfer them, with care, using a spatula, to a cooling rack.

These can be chocolate-dipped, as in the previous recipe, but are a bit fragile for this treatment to be entirely successful. They can also be put together in pairs with melted chocolate in between.

You need to play with the baking time on this a little. Underbaked just a bit, these come out chewy in the middle but crisp at the edges, and they are good this way, as they are baked to the point of through-and-through crispness, which takes about a minute more. If they are chewy all the way through, though, and droop a bit when you lift them, they are definitely too underbaked.

## Viennese Nut Crescents

*Makes four to five dozen cookies*

I was taught how to make these shaped drop cookies when I was a child by Miss Kay, who probably was the single most influential person in my love of cooking. Later I ran across these buttery, rich, sophisticated marvels in *The New York Times Cookbook*, where Craig Claiborne says that when the recipe was published in the *Times*, "A noted cookbook authority wrote that, in her opinion, this was the greatest cookie recipe ever devised." You may well agree. Although I learned them with almonds and have listed them that way here, they are equally wonderful with pecans, and either English or black walnuts.

Preheat oven to 350°. With your fingers, combine

*2¼ cups sifted unbleached white flour (or half unbleached white and half whole wheat pastry flour)*
*1 cup butter, at room temperature*

(continued)

Add

*1½ cups granulated sugar*
*1 cup almonds, chopped fine (or ground in food processor)*
*1 teaspoon vanilla*

Mix well. Shape dough, 1 teaspoon at a time, into small balls or crescents. Bake on ungreased cookie sheet for 15 to 20 minutes. Cool for 5 minutes or so. While still warm, sprinkle liberally with

*about ½ cup sifted powdered sugar*

## Marla's Penultimate Peanut Butter Cookies

*Makes three dozen cookies*

Jan says, "The best peanut butter cookies you ever ate, even better than your mother made. Almost shortbreadlike in texture." She received this recipe in a letter dated January 31, 1979, from her friend Mimi, a weaver, craftsperson, and mother of three. In Jan's opinion, these are the world's absolute best PB cookies. In Crescent's, the recipe as written was too good to pass by, so we are breaking format to present it as it appeared in that fateful letter on brown paper.

*1 cup butter*
*1 cup brown sugar*
*1 cup white sugar*

*Cream butter and sugars (boy, that's a lot of sugar).*

*1 cup peanut butter*

*Add peanut butter.*

*2 cups flour*
*2 teaspoons baking soda*
*1 teaspoon vanilla*

*Add flour, soda, and vanilla.*

*½ teaspoon salt*
*2 eggs*
*1 tablespoon milk*

*Roll into balls on ungreased sheet. [Hey, what about adding the eggs, salt, and milk?] Smash with fork [crosshatch-wise, in the universal symbol for peanut butter cookies], bake at 325° for 15 to 20 minutes. [We add the eggs, lightly beaten, to the creamed butter, sugar, PB mixture. Next, stir in the milk. Blend flour, salt, and soda and add to creamed mixture. Add vanilla last.]*

*Variations (ours, not Marla's):* Peanut butter cookies can attain new heights of glamour and tastiness when either (a) chocolate chips are added to them or (b) a chocolate glaze, as in Chocolate-dipped Oatmeal-Walnut Drop Cookies (p. 329), is applied to them, with a few crushed unsalted peanuts pressed into it.

## Persimmon Cookies

*Makes about three dozen*

Another favorite made from 'Ozark dates'' (see pp. 286–288 for a full description of the persimmon). This is a soft cookie, perfect for fall and after-school-with-milk. Sweet but not too much so.

Preheat oven to 375°. Thoroughly cream together

*½ cup honey*
*4 tablespoons butter*
*¼ cup vegetable oil*
*2 tablespoons brown sugar (you may omit sugar, or substitute 1 tablespoon molasses)*

Beat lightly and add

*1 egg*

Dissolve

*1 teaspoon baking soda*

in

*1 cup persimmon pulp*

Combine honey and persimmon mixtures. Stir in

*1 cup chopped black walnuts*
*2 cups whole wheat flour*
*1 teaspoon cinnamon*
*½ teaspoon each ginger, ground cloves, and allspice*

Drop by heaping teaspoonfuls onto Pam-ed cookie sheets. Bake for 15 to 18 minutes, or until golden around the edges.

## After-School Snack in October

*Persimmon Cookies*
*Milk*
*Crisp Apple*

## Homemade Ladyfingers

*Makes 20 to 25*

Far more delicate and flavorsome, less spongy, than the commercially made ones. For use at tea, or in a million desserts you already have the recipe for, or in our Grand Marnier Chocolate Decadence, page 312.

Preheat oven to 300°. Pam a large cookie sheet (14 × 17 inches). Separate

*3 eggs, at room temperature*

Beat egg whites until foamy. Add

*pinch of salt*
*⅛ teaspoon cream of tartar*

Beat until soft peaks form. Beat in

*¼ cup sugar*

adding a spoonful at a time, and beat for 1 minute at high speed. In a separate bowl, beat

*3 egg yolks*

Add

*1 teaspoon vanilla*
*large pinch of grated nutmeg*
*⅛ teaspoon almond extract*
*¼ cup sugar*

and beat until very light and thick. Pour gently over beaten egg whites and fold together.
  Sift together

*½ cup less 1 tablespoon flour*
*2 tablespoons cornstarch*

Sprinkle gradually over egg mixture. Fold in gently—very gently—with a rubber spatula, so that mixture remains light and airy. Proceed from this point gently—ever so gently—with batter; it is very delicate. Use a pastry bag with a ½- to ¾-inch plain tube. Put half the batter into pastry bag. Pipe the batter onto prepared pan, making ladyfingers about 1½ inches wide and 4 inches long. Sprinkle

*½ cup sifted powdered sugar*

evenly over ladyfingers. Bake for 20 minutes, until ladyfingers are lightly golden. Turn off oven and leave ladyfingers in for another 5 minutes. Remove from baking sheet and cool on rack.

## Holiday Cookie Exchange and Tasting Party

*(Everyone brings a cookie tin and a double recipe of a favorite cookie, tastes others' offerings, and brings home an assortment.)*
*Decadent Date Delights*
*Crescent's Classic Chewy Brownies*
*Blond Brownies*
*Chocolate-dipped Oatmeal-Walnut Drop Cookies*
*Rugelach*
*Coffee • Tea • Hot Cider • Milk*
*Favors: A Pipparkakut Heart Tree Ornament with Each Guest's Name*

# City Pies,
# Country Pies

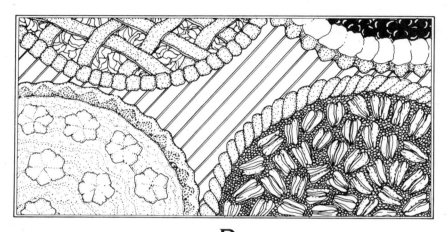

$P$ies are love letters: the pastry dough a scented envelope that, even without opening, one knows encloses something special, something worth anticipating; the filling the sweet words, the particularizing substance daintily hidden from view. Who can resist opening a love letter? Who can resist cutting into a pie?

"Oh me Oh my," wrote Bob Dylan a few years back, "Love that country pie." We do, too—those pies that are simple, down-home straightforward, all-American: fruit pies (most of which are in the Fruitpoem chapter), custard pies (like Choo-Choo's Buttermilk Pie), and a few other miscellaneous simple-but-good delights.

But we also love our city pies—those pies with a foreign accent, like Jan's Mexican Chocolate Pudding Pie or our Three Golden Fruits Italian Ricotta Tart of Italian ancestry.

How you gonna keep 'em down on the farm after they've seen Paree? Well, how you gonna keep 'em down in Paree after they've seen the farm? And, more important, why can't they—and you, and me—have the farm *and* Paree?

Have a slice of country pie. Have a slice of city pie. Tear into a culinary love letter—or write one. Oh me, oh my.

# CRUSTS

You may well have a favorite pie crust recipe or method. We suggest you read ours through anyway—if only to shock yourself at some of the heretical suggestions we make, some of which fly in the teeth of age-old crust-making clichés.

In the Dairy Hollow House family, Jan is undisputed pie crust queen. She does them quickly and beautifully every time, with an incredible amount of ease. I can turn out a pretty good crust if I do say so myself, but never with her ease and speed and nonchalance. That girl even makes tart shells before breakfast without blinking an eye! I have gotten better, though, in my crust adventures since watching her —and you will, too, through her words on the subject.

## Jan's Basic Pie Crust

*Makes one 9-inch crust*

"They'll eat *anything* if you put a crust on it," Jan's mama used to say. They would if it was this crust—basic, good, fail-proof. We think this crust is especially appropriate for open-face pies, like the Mexican Chocolate Pudding Pie (p. 351) or Avocado-Lime Pie (p. 349). It is also ideal for tart shells; the other two are much more temperamental.

But, for all its being so agreeable, this is a delicious crust. Correctly made, it achieves heights of flakiness, ease, and attractive handling undreamed of by many crusts.

From here on, in Jan's words: "I grew up as the oldest girl in a family of nine children, nine happy kids, who loved their desserts *almost* as much as they loved their mama. Mama made a lot of pies, and many of my earliest days were spent at her elbow, standing on a chair by the cupboard, watching, smelling, sampling, watching some more. I think watching is most important in pie crust; recipes for crust don't quite tell it all. So watch a good pie crust maker in action. And don't 'worry' the crust; as you make it, see it pretty, round and whole.

"Mama never measured much for her pies; she just made them. When I was ready to make my own pies, we devised a little formula: 'one/one-third/one'—1 cup of flour, ⅓ cup shortening, 1 teaspoon of salt. Today I still think of that little formula when I start to mix the pie dough, though I vary it a bit according to the flour I am using. Here are my latest versions."

*(continued)*

Place in a mixing bowl

*1 cup flour (unbleached, whole wheat, a combination of both,*
*or sometimes rice or millet flour)*
*½ teaspoon salt (less salt these days)*

Blend together. Then cut in

*⅓ cup vegetable shortening*
*1 tablespoon butter, softened*

The *mixture* of these two fats, the butter and the shortening, is all-important. The butter adds its special flavor, the vegetable shortening gives texture—that essential flakiness. Also most important is the flour-shortening-butter alchemy: here's where you simply have to *feel* if it's right. With certain flour mixtures, you will need to use a bit more of the shortening-butter mixture. For example, whole wheat or some combinations can absorb a little more shortening-butter than straight unbleached white, so when using these whole grains, I might add another tablespoon of butter. But with unbleached flour, increasing the shortening-butter at all might well be too much—the crust will shrink and pull as it bakes, which is not good.

To mix—or "cut"—the shortening-butter mixture into the flour, I use a fork to scrape back and forth across the shortening-butter, blending lightly with the flour, forming little crumbles "about the size of peas," as the classic cookbooks say. This should be a light, quick mixing. The less you fuss and stir the dough, the flakier your crust. *(Note from Crescent:* I have found that using a pastry cutter enables me to work the shortening into the flour more quickly and with less fussing than a fork; it might be true for other less experienced crust-makers as well.)

After the shortening-butter mixture has been cut in, begin adding

*water, 1 tablespoonful at a time*

with your left hand, while stirring the dough with the fork in your right hand, until the dough forms a ball. Knead the ball with your hands, quickly and lightly, including the remaining crumbles in the bowl. (Do not refrigerate the dough.)

Roll out the dough on a lightly floured surface. Fold it in half and lift it into the pie pan. Gently press the dough to the bottom and sides of the pan. Trim it around the edges, leaving an inch overhang. Fold the overhang under, leaving no raw edges. Crimp the crust all the way around, with your fingers.

For a *Prebaked Pie Shell*, preheat oven to 400°. Prick the crust with a fork, thoroughly, across the bottom and around the sides. It is especially important to poke holes with the fork at the juncture of the bottom surface and sides of crust. Bake for 12 to 15 minutes, or until golden (*Note from Crescent:* Jan is one of the only people in the world who can bake a crust this way and not have it collapse in on itself, shrivel, and die during baking. The usual recommendation is to lay a piece of foil in the crust and fill it with a ½ cup or so dry beans as it bakes to prevent this. Unless you have Jan watching over you, you might want to do it this way the first few times, but pricking the holes *just so,* as she says, really helps.)

For a *Filled Fruit Pie,* make a double recipe of the crust. Roll out the bottom crust as directed, place in the pie pan (but do not crimp edges), and pour/spoon/place the fruit filling in it. Now roll out the top crust, but before you place it on the top, carefully brush the bottom crust around its top edge, where the crusts will join, with water or egg white—this helps seal in the juices. Now place the top crust on the pie, pressing gently around the top edge, trim and turn under as directed, and crimp. Prick holes in the top crust with a fork now, or cut slashes or shapes before placing it on the pie.

Place the filled fruit pie in a preheated 400° oven for 15 minutes; reduce heat to 350° for about 30 more minutes—until crust is lightly browned.

## Further Crust Variations

To the "one," the 1 cup of flour, add the following:

- for a *nutty* crust, perfect with a chocolate pie, add 3 tablespoons finely chopped or ground walnuts, pecans, almonds, hazelnuts, or peanuts

- for a *sesame* crust, excellent with a vegetable pie or cheese or some fruit pies, add ¼ cup sesame seeds

- for a *cheese* crust, also good with vegetable pies and, sometimes for variety, with apple pie, add ¼ cup grated Cheddar, Swiss, or Parmesan cheese

- for a *sweet* crust, fine with almost any open-face fruit tart, add 1 tablespoon brown sugar and/or 1 teaspoon cinnamon

- for an *herb* crust, lovely with quiches, add 1 teaspoon fresh (or ½ teaspoon dried) herbs—basil, oregano, sage, thyme, chives

*An Un-shortening Variation:* I've experimented with many ways, and simply haven't found any combination as flaky and good as the basic recipe. Some people, for health reasons, would prefer using a good refined oil, though, rather than shortening. An oil crust can be good, it can be crisp, but it will never, ever be flaky. Given these parameters, here is a good one: For a two-crust pie, use 2 cups flour, ⅓ cup oil mixed with 1 well-beaten egg and ½ teaspoon apple cider vinegar. Again, handle as little as possible. The egg will reduce the amount of water that you add to knead the dough. Follow the directions given for a basic pie crust.

## Crescent's Whole Wheat and Butter Crust

*Makes two 9-inch crusts or 1 double crust*

Be forewarned: This is a difficult crust to handle. It will never, ever look as beautiful as the first crust; you'll probably have to patch here and there. Also, not everyone will like it; it is different from the pie crusts most people have known. But those who love it will adore it. We ourselves love it.

This crust's flavor is intensely wonderful. The whole wheat gives it that distinctive grainy flavor, as well as a very special texture—a texture with that delicious crisp flakiness that every pie crust worth the name ought to have (but many don't), and yet with a pleasing solidity, a crunch, a sense that there's something really *there* between your teeth, not disintegrating pasty mush. And 100 percent butter, while making it trickier to handle, gives an unmatched flavor. I wouldn't dream of using anything else on apple, blueberry, or many other fruit pies.

Combine

*2 cups whole wheat pastry flour*
*½ teaspoon salt*

Cut in, using a pastry cutter

*¾ cup butter (1½ sticks)*

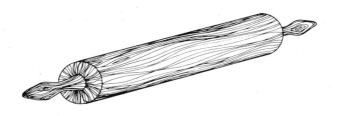

Keep cutting in till the mixture is the texture of coarse cornmeal. Have ready

*ice water*

Sprinkle over the dough

*a few drops of fresh lemon juice*

and gradually start adding the ice water. The woman who taught me how insisted that it should take absolutely no more than 4 tablespoons of water, but I find it usually does; it seems to depend on the flour. You want just enough water, but no more than it takes for the dough to come together. Form it into a ball.

This is the point at which virtually every recipe I've ever seen for pie dough tells you to chill the dough. Well, Jan and I do not agree. In the case of this pie dough, for instance, chilling would harden the butter to where it would be downright unrollable.

So we divide the dough in two and roll it out immediately on a lightly floured board, with a lightly floured rolling pin. Again, there are always dire warnings about what happens if you use too much flour in rolling it out—how it will toughen the dough, etc. Well, I am here to tell you that there are worse consequences to using too *little* flour: the dough will stick to your board and you either have to kiss that crust good-bye or reroll it, with more flour and more handling, and that really *will* toughen it.

When your dough is rolled out in its neat round, transfer it to pie shell as follows: fold it over itself once, and then again. You now have the dough folded in quarters, in a sort of triangle with the wide edge of the triangle rounded. Lift the folded dough and place it so the point of the triangle is in the center of the pie pan. Unfold the dough out from there; it will be perfectly centered. Patch if necessary, pressing together with fingertips any tears here and there.

Bake as the recipe suggests, or by the guidelines Jan has given in the basic recipe.

## Pastry Brisée Sucre

*Makes one 9-inch crust*

This third crust is a rich, sweet, cookielike pie dough that can be further enriched by the addition of crushed nuts. It's good for cheesecakes and some other really world-class fillings: Honeyed Tarte aux Poires (p. 285), for instance.

*(continued)*

341

In a mixing bowl, place

*1 cup unbleached white flour*
*¼ cup sugar*
*a pinch of salt*

Cut in with a pastry cutter

*½ cup butter*

until it resembles coarse meal. Add

*1 egg, well beaten*
*1 drop vanilla or almond extract (optional)*

stirring dough into a ball. Add water, 1 tablespoon at a time, if necessary, until dough sticks together. Press mixture into the bottom and sides of a 9-inch round pan and bake as recipe directs. For a prebaked shell, follow the directions Jan has given (p. 338).

## On the uses of pie crust scrips and scraps:

Jan says, "At home we always used to roll the scraps back up into a ball, roll out the ball, and place it in a small pie pan or skillet—whatever it fit. Then we'd sprinkle it with sugar, pour heavy cream or evaporated milk over it, and sprinkle it with cinnamon. We'd bake it until it was done, and cut it into small tastes for a snack—one that preceded the evening's pie and helped us anticipate it."

What we do here is, again, ball up the scraps and roll them out into circles no more than 5 inches in diameter. Dot circles with butter, sprinkle with cinnamon and sugar, and cut and roll up as for Whole Wheat Butterhorns (p. 85), but tiny. Bake in preheated 350° oven till browned and crunchy.

We also do the following with leftover bits and pieces of dough, but every so often we make up a whole pie crust's worth of these little morsels: tiny tart shells filled after baking with jewel-like jelly. Nobody can make these look as pretty as Ruth Eichor, from whom we got this recipe and who has helped us in so many ways in the completion of this book. Ruth's jelly tarts are perfect, uniform little stars; ours are a bit more chaotic-looking. but they all taste very good!

◆───────────────────────────────────◆

*Madam, you flavour everything, you are the vanilla of society.*

—*Sydney Smith (1771–1845),*
Lady Holland's Memoir

342

## Grandmother Fuller's Jelly Tarts

*Enough for a one-crust pie will make 75 of the tiny ones
we use for holidays, teas, etc.*

Use your favorite pie crust recipe. Roll as for a pie; cut with a 1¼-inch round cutter. Pinch four corners, like a cocked hat. Prick the bottoms a couple of times. Bake on ungreased cookie sheet until lightly brown in a preheated 450° oven (about 8 minutes). Remove from oven, cool and fill with about ¼ teaspoon plum or red currant jelly.

For larger tarts, use a 3-inch round cutter and proceed as for the small ones. Makes about 3 dozen of this size.

*When the pie was opened,
the birds began to sing—
Wasn't that a pretty dish
to set before the King!*

*—Mother Goose Rhyme*

# COUNTRY PIES

## Choo-Choo's Buttermilk Pie

*Makes one 9-inch pie*

A country classic, this delectable treat is something like a custard pie, but with more zing and sweetness. It's another one of those how-can-something-this-easy-be-so-good recipes, sure to become a regular part of your dessert repertoire. Choo-Choo, whose real name is Marcia, is our dear friend and fellow Eureka businessperson; she owns a charmingly decorated guest cottage, replete with her own special style of antiques, loads of stencils, wallpapers, calicoes, lace, and what have you. We often swap referrals with her cottage, Sweet Seasons, on Spring Street. Have ready

*1 unbaked 9-inch pie shell*

Preheat oven to 350°. Cream together

*½ cup butter, softened
1½ cups sugar*

*(continued)*

343

Beat in

*3 rounded tablespoons flour*
*3 eggs, beaten*
*1 cup buttermilk*
*1 tablespoon vanilla*
*the grated rind of 1 lemon (optional, but good)*

Pour this into the unbaked pie shell and sprinkle liberally with

*nutmeg*

Bake for 45 minutes. It should be slightly browned, though still a little liquid. Don't worry; it will set deliciously as it cools; please don't overbake! Serve chilled. No whipped cream, no adornment; just perhaps a glass of cold milk or a cup of coffee. We love this as the finale to a Peasant's Feast.

◆────────────────────────────────────────◆

*DAIRY HOLLOW HOUSE FLOWERS: ON THE CARE OF VASES AND BOUQUETS*

*Nothing's more beautiful than a perfect arrangement, perfectly placed —and nothing's more foul than the water in the vase after a couple of days. First line of defense: Strip all leaves from flower stalks below the point where they enter the water. Then, after two or three days, even if your bouquet still looks perfect, remove it from the vase, discard the water, and wash the vase out with hot soapy water. Rinse a couple of times, then shake in a couple of shots of cheap white vinegar, and rinse again. The white vinegar kills off the unpleasant-smelling bacteria which slimes up the inside of flower vases after several days use. Go over your bouquet, picking out any dead flowers or flowers whose stalks are rotten and recutting stem ends that are softening. Replace in vase, adding fresh flowers.*

◆────────────────────────────────────────◆

# Dairy Hollow House Sweet Potato–Black Walnut Pie for a Peasant's Feast

*Makes one 10-inch pie*

We enjoy this combination of two old-fashioned favorites. We use black walnuts rather than pecans because we have a black walnut tree just across from the inn, but English walnuts, pecans, or even broken almond pieces could be used with equal success. This recipe was featured in *Innsider Magazine*.

You'll need:

*1 unbaked 10-inch pie crust, with a bit of sugar added to the dough*

*Sweet Potato Filling:* Beat until smooth, for 1 to 2 minutes

*1½ cups cooked, mashed fresh sweet potatoes*
*(bake or steam sweet potato, peel and mash)*
*⅓ cup firmly packed brown sugar*
*1 egg*
*2 teaspoons vanilla*
*a dash each of salt, nutmeg, allspice, and ground cloves*
*½ teaspoon cinnamon*

Set aside.

*Black Walnut Glaze:* Beat together for 1 minute

*¾ cup brown sugar*
*⅔ cup honey*
*¼ cup dark molasses*
*2 eggs*
*2 teaspoons vanilla*

Stir in gently

*½ to 1 cup black walnut pieces*

Preheat oven to 325°. Into dough-lined pie pan, spread sweet potato filling, smoothing the top. Carefully pour black walnut glaze over that. Bake for 1½ hours, or until crust is slightly brown and glaze is no longer runny. Cool. Serve with real whipped cream, piped on each piece after it has been placed on its serving plate, or with ice cream.

## Kansas Sour Cream Peach Pie

*Makes one 9-inch pie*

Here's another delectable pie that uses sour cream, this time in a partnership with peaches.

Preheat oven to 375°. Prepare

*one 9-inch pie crust*

Wash, peel, pit, and slice

*6 to 8 peaches*

Place the peaches in a bowl. Add

*¼ cup unbleached white flour*
*¾ cup brown sugar*
*a dash of nutmeg*
*1 tablespoon lemon juice*
*1 teaspoon vanilla*

Stir well and pour into crust. Spread over the top of the peaches

*1 cup sour cream*

In a small bowl, stir together

*¼ cup sugar*
*2 tablespoons unbleached white flour*
*1 teaspoon cinnamon*

Stir in until crumbly

*2 tablespoons butter*

Blend together well and sprinkle over the sour cream. Slide the pie into the oven and bake about 40 minutes, until crust is golden and sour cream lightly browned.

## Dixie Fried Pies

*Makes 12 to 15 hand-size fried pies*

Margaret Conner is a warm and energetic woman here in town who operates a B-and-B in her own Victorian home. At Harvest House, Margaret's B-and-B, guests are treated royally, not only to breakfast but to late-night snacks such as these melting, fruit-filled fried pies.

Sift together

> 2 cups unbleached white flour
> 2 teaspoons baking powder
> ½ teaspoon salt

Cut in

> 3 tablespoons shortening

Add gradually

> ¾ cup milk

Stir with a fork, and press dough into a ball. Roll to ⅛-inch thickness and cut into 5-inch circles. On each circle, put 2 tablespoons of Cooked Fruit Filling. Fold the dough over to make a half-circle. Seal the edges with a fork and carefully transfer to deep fat at 375°. Fry until golden brown and drain on paper towels. Dust with powdered sugar. Serve warm. Or omit powdered sugar, place on a dessert plate, and top with ice cream or whipped cream.

*Cooked Fruit Filling:* Cook dried apricots, peaches, or apples in water to cover, with sugar and seasonings, until tender and most of the liquid is absorbed.

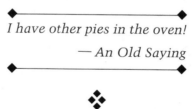

*I have other pies in the oven!*

*— An Old Saying*

# CITY PIES

## Savannah Peanut Butter Pie

*Makes one 9-inch pie*

In Georgia, the nation's largest peanut producer, great peanut and peanut butter recipes abound. This is one, from beautiful Savannah, where they really know their stuff historic-preservation-wise (we in Eureka could take some lessons—but don't get me started). Anyway, in this luscious creation, peanut butter crumbles are buried under a delectable thick custard, topped with whipped cream and more peanut butter. It's superb, and a big favorite of Ned's.

*(continued)*

Have ready

*1 prebaked 9-inch pie shell*

Blend together till crumbly

*½ cup good, unhydrogenated smooth peanut butter*
*⅔ cup powdered sugar*
*½ teaspoon vanilla*

Set aside. Meanwhile, make up a custard as follows: Heat

*1¾ cups milk*

As it heats, mush together with fingers till lump-free

*¼ cup cornstarch*
*¼ cup cold milk*

Whisk cornstarch mixture into hot milk, adding, when it starts to thicken

*3 egg yolks, beaten*
*½ to ⅔ cup sugar*
*dash of salt*

Continue cooking over low heat, stirring constantly, until the egg yolks further thicken the mixture. Remove from heat and beat in

*2 teaspoons butter*
*1¼ teaspoons vanilla*

Now, to assemble pie: in pie shell, sprinkle half of the peanut butter mixture, and pour the hot custard mixture over it. Refrigerate until completely cool. Then whip

*1 cup chilled heavy cream*
*2 tablespoons sifted powdered sugar*

Cover, or pipe, the top of the chilled pie with the whipped cream. Sprinkle each piece with some of the reserved peanut butter crumbles. Just for fun, you may also garnish each slice with

*a mint sprig and one whole, in-shell, peanut*

## Avocado-Lime Pie

*Makes one 9-inch pie*

Back when Bill King made this delicacy at the Pita Hut, people in Eureka would line up and zoom in for a slice. Sitting at a blue picnic table in the open air, under the polomia tree, with a piece of this pie and a fresh-squeezed lemonade, was a bright spot in any summer's day.

Combine in a blender or food processor

*1 cup honey*
*3 large or 5 small ripe avocados*
*1 cup cashew cream (½ cup raw cashews and ½ cup spring water whirled in the blender)*

Blend until smooth. In a small saucepan, combine

*½ cup lime juice*
*1 teaspoon agar-agar (in powder form)*

Bring to a boil and boil for 3 to 5 minutes, or until mixture begins to thicken. Remove from heat and cool slightly—5 to 10 minutes. Stir the thickened lime juice into the blended ingredients. Line

*one 9-inch baked pie shell (Pastry Brisée Sucre, p. 341, would be divine, or any good pie crust)*

with

*banana slices*

Pour avocado-lime custard into the banana-lined crust, and chill the pie thoroughly.

*Note:* Although this pie is dairy-free and perfect as it is, one could gild the lily with whipped cream!

## Three Golden Fruits Italian Ricotta Tart

*Makes one 9-inch pie*

We have read, and tried, many, many versions of this pie, which in Italy is usually served in the spring, around Eastertime. Many versions are baked. One was scented with rosewater. One contained wheat kernels cooked in milk for hours and hours, which, when stirred into the pie, added a wonderful flavor and texture, a bit like some indefinable dried fruit. Another used barley the same way. We liked these; but this simpler, lighter, unbaked version, studded with the jewels of apricots, pineapple, and golden raisins, is our favorite.

You will need to have ready

*one 9-inch Pastry Brisée Sucre shell (p. 341), baked and chilled*

but don't prepare it until the day after you soak

*¾ cup each golden raisins and finely chopped dried apricots*
*½ cup dried pineapple, diced*

in

*⅓ cup good brandy*

Cover, and let stand overnight. The next day beat together till creamy

*1 pound ricotta*
*½ cup powdered sugar or honey*
*dash of salt*
*1 teaspoon vanilla*
*1 teaspoon grated lemon rind (optional)*

Fold into this the soaked dried fruits and

*3 tablespoons sour cream or Alta-Dena kefir cheese*

Turn into baked pie shell. Smooth top. Cover and chill deeply. Before serving, garnish each piece with piped-on

*whipped cream*
*shelled pistachio nuts*
*additional dried fruits*

# Mexican Chocolate Pudding Pie

*Makes one 9-inch pie*

Here's one unbeatable combination—chocolate, coffee, cream, and cinnamon, with a thick pudding-y texture that is divine either in a pie shell or stemmed glasses. This is a chocolate pie for grown-ups: bittersweet.

In a large saucepan, mix together

*½ cup brown sugar*
*¼ cup unbleached white flour*
*1 teaspoon cinnamon*
*dash of salt*
*1 teaspoon instant coffee or coffee substitute (Pero or Postum)*

Add

*½ cup butter (1 stick)*
*2 cups milk*
*3 squares (ounces) unsweetened chocolate, grated or chopped*

Heat over medium flame until chocolate melts and the mixture is slightly thickened and begins to boil. Stir.
 Place in a separate bowl

*1 egg, well beaten*

Remove ½ cup of the chocolate mixture from the saucepan and slowly whisk it into the well-beaten egg. Now whisk the chocolate-egg mixture back into the saucepan, stirring constantly. Cook over low heat until mixture thickens—about 2 minutes. (Do not boil.) Remove the saucepan from the heat. Add

*1½ teaspoons vanilla*
*½ cup chopped pecans*

Cool the pudding some and pour it into

*one 9-inch baked pie shell*

Chill the pie. Pipe with whipped cream, garnish with pecan halves, and dust the cream with a shake of powdered chocolate.

# A Celebratory Covey
# of Cakes

$J$an and I have both been baking
cakes since girlhood: chocolate cakes, white cakes, cakes using fresh
fruit, cakes using dried fruit, natural foods cakes sweetened with
honey, decadent cakes laden with enough sugar and butter to sink a
battleship (yet, paradoxically, feather-light). Cakes for Christmas,
cakes for birthdays, Easter cakes, wedding cakes, anniversary cakes,
and more.

Nothing a cook makes says *celebration* more clearly, or is so
much appreciated and rejoiced over, as a cake.

And, if you like to cook, nothing is more fun than baking a cake.
The alchemy of shortening, flour, liquid, sugar or honey, and leavening
interacting to make something of totally different form than any of its
ingredients; the element of suspense (will it bake evenly? Will it come
out of the pan?); the artistry of the final stacking, filling, icing, and,
sometimes, decorating—all these combine to make cake baking a special pleasure for those who enjoy kitchen work. Of course we have
fond feelings about virtually every dish we make. But our mind-set is
entirely different on those occasions when we say, "I think . . . I'll
bake a cake," from those days we say, "I think . . . I'll make some
soup." To undergo cake baking takes a certain lightheartedness, yet at

352

the same time a definite determination (a good cake is a much bigger deal), and, for sure, the sense of a special undertaking. Cakes are frivolous—they aren't essential to the diet, they aren't one of the four basic food groups—and yet, at the same time, they're serious; they take lots of work, lots of good intentions, and a certain amount of skill.

I once offered to do a wedding cake for some friends of mine who were getting married, blithely assuming (oh, the trouble assumptions get us into!) that theirs was to be a fairly smallish wedding and the cake for no more than thirty or forty. Imagine my astonishment—and horror—when they said, "Oh yes—we'd *love* to have you do our wedding cake!"—and then informed me that 150 guests were expected! Never one to duck out of a challenge, however, I was galvanized into taking an action I had long wanted to do, anyway—attending a ten-session course on cake decorating, with pastry tube and all.

Piping with a pastry tube, which I had always been overawed by before, is a skill I have used hundreds of times since the wedding, and it is not difficult at all; with even a little practice you can turn out highly impressive, glamorous creations; and only the cook need know that under all that beauty the guests are oohing and ahhing over, lies a cracked cake, a cake with crumbs in the icing, or numerous other errors that would otherwise have been very visible. As Phyllis Ashley, my cake-decorating instructor, used to say sagely, "You can hide your sins." Besides decorating with a pastry tube, Phyllis also taught me a number of tricks of the trade that have really improved my cake-baking skills. I pass them on to you in Seven Baker's Secrets to a Truly Spectacular Cake.

By the way, the wedding cake for my friends did turn out beautifully. I had been so much with the durn thing for the previous week that I couldn't bear to eat a bite of it at the wedding reception, but they kindly saved me a piece in the freezer. They served it to me almost six months to the day later, on my birthday!

*A note to chocolate fans:* Chocolate Cakes are in the chapter entitled Love and Chocolate, page 302.

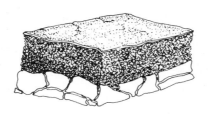

# SIMPLE CAKES

First, a few simple cakes: not iced, not stacked, not fussed with.

## Elsie's Gingerbread

*Serves 12 to 16*

There is no doubt in our minds that this is the world's best gingerbread. Moist and sweet and dark, tinged with molasses but not *too* molasses-y, sprinkled with a crisp streusel topping, this is outstanding, perhaps one of our ten all-time favorite recipes. Try it plain, with ice cream, with whipped cream, accompanying a baked apple or pear; make it, with a few variations, as muffins (p. 73); try it as upside-down cake. A wonderful, can't-go-wrong dessert, perfect for fall.

Preheat oven to 350°. Combine

*1½ cups unbleached white flour*
*1 cup sugar*
*2 teaspoons ginger*
*1 teaspoon cinnamon*

Cut in

*½ cup butter or shortening*

Reserve ¼ cup of crumbled mixture for topping. Add to the remaining flour mixture

*1 egg, well beaten*

Stir in

*3 tablespoons molasses*

Dissolve

*1 teaspoon baking soda*
*1 scant teaspoon salt*

in

*1 cup buttermilk*

Add to the other mixture. Pour into a Pam-ed 9-inch square pan, sprinkle with the topping, and bake for 30 minutes.

*I like my coffee with sugar, I like my sky filled out with clouds.*

—*Bill Haymes*

## Evelyn Cross's Very Special Carrot Cake

*Serves 20 to 24*

Carrot cakes seem to go in and out of fashion: they were rediscovered in the seventies and people took to them by the drove; they were on almost every menu. Now they seem to be fading once again from favor. We don't think they should; a good carrot cake is a wonderful affair—moist, tender, sweetly flavorful, delicately spiced. This is such a carrot cake, given to me in my first few years in Eureka Springs by Evelyn Cross. It is also easy and of natural foods, but doesn't taste health-food-y. Like a string of good pearls, this recipe is always in style.

Preheat oven to 300°. Combine, beating or whizzing in food processor till emulsified

*1 cup vegetable oil (corn or peanut)*
*1 scant cup honey, topped off by 1 or 2 tablespoons molasses*

Add, one at a time

*3 eggs*

Sift together

*1⅓ cups whole wheat flour*
*1 teaspoon salt*
*1⅓ teaspoons each baking soda, baking powder, and cinnamon*
*dash of nutmeg (no more; cinnamon should dominate)*

Stir the dry ingredients into the oil-honey mixture with

*1 teaspoon vanilla*

Then, fold in

*2 cups grated carrots (raw)*
*¾ cup dark raisins*
*½ cup coarsely chopped walnuts*

Transfer to a Pam-ed rectangular 9-×-13-inch pan. Bake for 1 hour. Serve warm or cool, plain or with whipped cream. Or you *can* ice it (although it's very good as is). The classic carrot cake icing is Cream Cheese Buttercream Icing (p. 360).

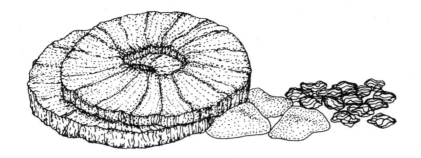

## Ruth's Lemon Bread That Is Really the Best White Fruitcake You Ever Ate in Your Life

*Makes three medium-size loaves*

When we were in the mad throes of last-minute deadlines on this book, many of our friends undertook our care and feeding. Jim and Sherree Smedley brought us a breakfast basket one day, and, another day, they collaborated with Choo-Choo/Marcia on a wintery picnic that we ate crouched on the floor while the word-processor printer typed crazily in the other room.

And Ruth Eichor brought us this—well, she calls it a bread and it looked like a bread, loaf-shape in its neat aluminum foil, and I remember thinking (we had just been doing final recipe-testing on the Sweet Breads section), Oh, no, not *another* bread! But I politely thanked her and forgot about the bread until, ranging around the kitchen for something easy the next day, I rediscovered it. Pulled back the foil. Tasted it. Wow! I called Jan. She tasted it. Oh boy! This was the elusive Perfect White Fruitcake we had been hunting for! You see, she and I both despise traditional heavy dark fruitcakes, and we had been talking about what we preferred—something like a pound cake, but studded with dried fruits and nuts; close-textured, dense, but not sticky-moist like those yucky traditional fruitcakes everybody gives each other at Christmas but nobody really eats.

Except we didn't have a recipe. Until Ruth came along—the gift horse I blushingly admit secretly looking in the mouth—only to find a perfect set of teeth!

Thank you, Ruth.

Preheat oven to 350°. Cream together

> *1½ cups butter*
> *2⅓ cups sugar*

Add

*6 eggs, well beaten*
*4 cups unbleached white flour*

stirring until well blended. Stir in

*1 pound raisins (when we make this next year, we will probably use*
*a pound of assorted golden fruits—yellow raisins, dried chopped*
*apricots, dried pineapple from the health food store;*
*Ruth uses dark raisins)*
*1 pound pecans, broken into pieces*
*1 ounce lemon extract (2 tablespoons)*

Pour into three medium-size Pam-ed loaf pans. Bake for 1 hour or until loaves are a deep golden brown and toothpick inserted in center of each loaf comes out clean. Please note: there is no leavening of any kind in this recipe, and no salt.

## Helen's Carob-Yogurt Cake

*Makes one 9-×-13-inch cake, about 20 to 24 servings*

This, like Evelyn Cross's Carrot Cake, is another natural foods delight that doesn't taste that way. From Helen Cummins, who used to live up the road from me, this is dense, sweet, dark, and delicious. We admit the combination of ingredients sounds strange, but it all comes together beautifully.

Preheat oven to 300°. Beat together, using an electric mixer or food processor

*3 eggs*
*1½ cups honey*
*6 tablespoons butter*

(continued)

Sift together in a separate bowl

*2½ cups unbleached white flour*
*1 teaspoon each baking soda and salt*
*¾ cup carob powder*

Measure out and have ready

*½ cup sorghum*
*1 cup plain yogurt*

Stir half the carob-flour mixture into the egg-honey-butter mixture with all the sorghum and a bit of the yogurt. Add remaining flour with the rest of the yogurt and

*2 teaspoons vanilla*

Do not overbeat. Turn into Pam-ed 9- × -13-inch pan, and bake for 45 minutes.

## Sour Cream Pound Cake

*Makes two large loaves or two 10-inch layers*

Luscious. Look no further for *the* pound cake.

Make sure all ingredients are at room temperature before you start. Preheat oven to 300°. Cream till fluffy

*1½ cups butter*

Gradually add, ½ cup at a time

*3 cups sugar*

After sugar has been added and mixture is very light and fluffy, add, one at a time

*6 eggs*

and

*2 teaspoons vanilla*

In a separate bowl, sift together

*3 cups unbleached white flour*
*¼ teaspoon each salt and baking soda*

Add the flour mixture to the butter-sugar-egg mixture alternately with

*1 cup sour cream*

Bake in two well-Pam-ed medium-size loaf pans, until cake is deeply golden, cracked on top, and a toothpick inserted in the crack comes out clean—about 1 hour and 15 to 30 minutes. Cool cake in pan for half an hour before turning out on rack. Serve as is, or with any embellishment you can imagine (from fresh fruit to vanilla ice cream and fudge sauce). Or follow the recipe for Charla's Birthday Cake, page 369, for a spectacular variation.

Now, before we get into the more elaborate cakes, we will pause to digress for a filling, and an icing.

*Milk in the batter! Milk in the batter!*
*We bake cake, and nothing's the matter!*

*—Maurice Sendak,*
In the Night Kitchen

## Fresh Lemon Filling

*Will fill a two-layer 10-inch cake*

Mush together with the fingers until lump-free, in the top of a double boiler

*2½ tablespoons cornstarch*
*¼ cup water*

When smooth, gradually stir in

*⅔ cup sugar*
*dash of salt*
*3 more tablespoons water*
*4 tablespoons fresh lemon juice*
*finely grated rind of 1 lemon*
*1 tablespoon butter*

Put the double boiler on top of its base, which should be filled with boiling water. Cook the filling, stirring constantly, over the boiling water for about 5 minutes, or until mixture thickens. Then lower heat and cook, covered, without stirring, about 8 to 10 minutes more. Remove 2 tablespoons of the filling and combine with

*3 egg yolks, lightly beaten*

(continued)

359

Then beat the yolks into the pot of filling. Raise heat again, to bring water under the filling back to a boil, and cook 2 more minutes, again stirring constantly, until filling thickens further. Watch it very closely. Remove from heat and stir for 2 minutes to cool it without further cooking; then chill till ready to use.

A most delicious filling with any white or yellow cake.

# Cream Cheese Buttercream Icing

*Will frost and fill a two-layer 9-inch cake*

We prefer this basic quick icing to the classic French buttercream with the beaten egg whites and the cooked sugar syrup and all that nonsense. The French method results, in our opinion, in a too-sweet, too-buttery icing. This, besides being simpler, is a delicious icing. The cream cheese in it cuts a bit of the sweetness of the powdered sugar and adds a delightful flavor and body. There are many variations on this delicious theme.

Soften to room temperature

*6 tablespoons butter*
*one 8-ounce package cream cheese*

Cream together until fluffy. Sift in, a little at a time, while beating

*one 16-ounce package powdered sugar*

Beat till fluffy, adding

*1 teaspoon vanilla*
*dash of salt*
*1 to 4 tablespoons heavy cream, if necessary*

You may need to add extra powdered sugar or cream to get it to just the right consistency for piping. And, in hot weather, be aware that it will not hold well at room temperature if piped; the cream cheese may get a bit droopy.

## Variations:

- Orange: Add the grated rind of 1 orange; use orange juice or an orange liqueur instead of cream.

360

- Lemon: Add the grated rind of a lemon; use lemon juice instead of cream.

- Chocolate: Add 2 or 3 squares unsweetened chocolate, coarsely chopped and melted, to the butter–cream cheese mixture.

- Mocha: Follow the Chocolate variation, but use coffee as the liquid instead of cream.

# MORE ELABORATE CAKES

"A thing of beauty is a joy forever," wrote Keats. Not true if that thing is a beautiful cake, decorated with love and panache and care and attention (a pretty unbeatable combination, really) and is as wonderful to taste as behold. Like fresh flowers, celebration cakes are transitory, and that is their nature, and that is that.

So, if you are repelled or disheartened by the idea of spending hours in the kitchen to create something gorgeous that, if it is truly successful, will quickly be gone, then read no further. Instead, make one of the previous simpler cakes, or a pie, or serve fresh fruit with liqueur, or get out of the kitchen altogether and leave the job to a reputable bakery. Otherwise, pay close attention to the

## SEVEN BAKER'S SECRETS TO A TRULY SPECTACULAR CAKE

1. *"Diapering" the cake pan.* Have you ever had a cake turn out bumpy and lumpy, with high spots and low, for no apparent reason? Have you checked the obvious things—accuracy of oven temperature, levelness of stove, preheating of oven, and so on—and, having made corrections where necessary, still had your cakes turn out like topographical maps? Here is the reason you have had this problem, and the improbable but unfailing solution to it.

    *Reason:* Cakes, some more than others, tend to get done at the outer edges before the center. This causes an uneven rise.

*Solution:* Retard the outer edges' cooking time a bit, to give the middle time to catch up. Here's how: by "diapering" the cake pan. To make the diapers, you will need a couple of old cotton terry cloths, a good stapler or some safety pins, a scissors.

Cut a long strip of terry cloth triple the width of the outside of the cake pan and a little longer. What you are aiming for is a piece of cloth that, when folded in thirds, can be pinned or stapled around the exterior of the cake pans securely. Cut such strips for every size layer cake pan you possess. Put them in a labeled box or other people will throw them out, thinking they are rags, and you will have to go through the whole nonsense of destroying more towels, which may well cause a little teeth-gnashing.

When the oven is preheating, but before the cake is mixed up, prepare your pans for baking as follows: Pam the inside of the pan, then dust with flour or cocoa or whatever the recipe suggests. Take your terry cloth strip and rinse it in cold water until it is saturated *thoroughly.* Wring out only minimally; you don't want it damp, you want it wet—but not dripping wet. Pin the wet cloth, triple-folded, to itself, around the pan, or, if you have a stapled ring, simply pull it up around. Yes, we know it's a pain in the neck to do all this; we grumble too.

After cake batter is mixed, pour it into the prepared pan and put it in to bake, terry cloth diaper attached. No, the cloth will not burn, though it will be dry by the time you remove the cake from the oven—at which time you will see that you have a beautifully flat, picture-perfect cake, more level than most people's minds.

We know you are skeptical. We were too. But this *works.* Phyllis, my cake-decorating teacher, said, "This tip is worth the price of the course, and you won't find it in any book." Now we've made her wrong on that latter point, but on the efficacy of the diaper, she couldn't be more right, and we will be grateful to her forever.

2. *The proper cooling and removal from pans.* After a cake comes out of the oven, *leave it in its pan,* set on a rack, for at least 5 to 10 minutes, unless the recipe instructs otherwise. Then—and only then—reverse it onto a cooling rack. Racks are essential; the air must circulate around the cake. Let cake cool completely before attempting to "torte" it (see following), fill it, ice

it, or do anything else to it. In fact, cakes are often easier to handle if you try:

3. *The old freezer ploy (with "torting" option).* Wrap and freeze cooled cake layers. Their rigidity in the frozen state makes handling them a carefree affair and "torting" a breeze. Frozen cake layers can be filled, stacked, and iced with or without previous torting. At room temperature, a frozen-solid cake done in this fashion will thaw in 2 hours.

In most cookbooks, the word *torte* is commonly used as a noun and means any fancier filled cake. We use the word that way sometimes, but we also use it as a verb: "to torte" a cake. This simply means to slice each layer through the middle the long way, to make the one (thicker) layer into two (thinner) layers. We find it easier to torte a cake evenly when the layer is frozen and when, instead of trying to slice it straight through, we work our way *around* the cake, with a sharp knife, pushing the blade only as far as the center point, and turning the cake.

What are the advantages to torting a layer cake? First of all, no matter how good a cake itself is, it is the filling and frosting that, ultimately, make or break a cake. The more filling there is, the more rich, moist, and intensely flavored it will be. Torting a cake means more surfaces for filling application, thus a better-tasting cake. Looks are also improved: torting makes possible a nice high, elegant-looking layer cake, from only two layers.

4. *The use of cake rounds.* A cake round is simply a cardboard circle, cut ever so slightly larger than the dimensions of the cake by setting the pan down on a piece of cardboard, running a pencil around its perimeter, and cutting out the resulting circle. When you get ready to assemble the cake, place the bottom layer of the cake on this circle, dabbing the cardboard first with a bit of icing to "glue" the cake in place. Fill (see step 5), "crumb-coat" if desired (see step 6), and ice with your base layer of icing. If by any chance you wish to press finely chopped nuts into the sides and/or top of the cake, now is the time to do it, but do not do any further decoration. After cake is iced, and any drips have dripped, and any dribbles have dribbled, and any excess pressed-in crushed nuts have fallen by the wayside, get out your serving plate.

Place a dab of icing at its center and place the almost-completed cake, *on its circle*, on the plate, the icing again serving to anchor things a bit. Don't worry if a thin perimeter of the cardboard circle is showing.

Now and only now is it time to get out your pastry tube and decorate it (see step 7).

What the cardboard cake round, or circle, has thus permitted you to do is have complete access to every crevice of the cake you are icing, merely by turning the circle (you can set the circle on a lazy Susan to make this even easier). It has also enabled you to get on as much icing as you like without fear of messing up your serving plate.

5. *The proper way to fill a cake.* Have you ever had the experience of having a delicious filling between the layers of a cake, a filling different from that cake's icing, ooze out of the sides and break through into the surface of the icing? Besides ruining the surprise of the filling, such an occurrence badly mars the look of the finished cake.

It doesn't have to happen, if you proceed as follows: Have ready the cake layers, the filling, and the icing, as well as a pastry bag fitted with a ¼-inch plain tip. Fill the pastry bag halfway with the icing. Place the bottom layer of the cake on its cake circle, and carefully pipe a thick, fat "dam" of icing around the perimeter of the cake, the side facing up, in which you will spread the filling. Now spread the "blank" circle of cake encircled by the "dam" with the filling. Spread the filling right up to the "dam." Top with another layer of cake and repeat. Thus, the filling does not ever touch the exterior of the cake, where the icing will go; its proper position, hidden within the cake, is guarded by this ring or "dam" or moat of icing, which will make contact with the same icing when the cake as a whole is iced.

Savvy?

6. *Crumb-prevention technique.* You know those pesky little crumbs that insist on getting mixed into the icing instead of staying put on the cake, thus ruining the desired perfect finish of the cake? You can make them stay put with a thin layer of diluted icing, or melted jam or jelly, called a crumb coat. Here's how to do one:

Have ready the filled, stacked cake, on its cardboard cake round. Also have on hand about ¾ cup of icing—the same icing you intend to use on the cake, but diluted with a little cream or water to the point of almost but not quite runny.

Spread this diluted icing over the cake. The cake will—and should—look dreadful at this point, and crumbs will be misbehaving all over the place. Their moments of mischief-making, however, are numbered. Because what you are going to do now is let the cake just simply sit, as is, for half an hour or so, until dry to the touch. As the crumb coat dries, you see, it will "glue" all the wayward crumbs in place, and, when you spread on your *real* coat of icing, the crumbs will not break off into it.

You may use, instead of diluted frosting, jam or jelly heated to a boil and strained, brushed over the cake, as a crumb coat. (You won't need to strain jelly.) Choose a jam appropriate to the flavor of the cake; on our Chocolate-Peppermint Layer Cake (p. 309), for instance, we use mint jelly; on our Chocolate-Orange Cake (p. 308), strained orange marmalade. Apricot or peach jam goes with just about anything, however.

If you don't want to bother with a crumb coat, you have several other options available. You can diminish crumbiness by baking the cake the night before you intend to use it and leaving it out, uncovered, overnight. This dries the cake out a little bit, so any loose crumbs can be brushed off. You can also try the old freezer ploy (see step 3), which minimizes crumbiness.

Or you can let the crumbs fall where they may and hide your sins, as Phyllis Ashley used to say, by the use of:

7. *Magical piping.* We've made reference to piping throughout the book, sometimes referring to pastry tubes. Basically, you "pipe" (that is, put icing through) through a "pastry tube" (a triangular-shaped bag, usually of heavy plastic, cut on one end to allow insertion of a "tip," which can be changed to vary effects), with the result that the icing is squeezed out in decorative forms, depending on the serrations and shape of the particular tip.

Piping, like phyllo dough, is one of our favorite neat tricks for making almost anything look and taste special, and piping is not hard to master. Take a course, as I did, or simply get a book that details the process, and practice, practice, practice. Basically all you need to remember is that (a) you should fold down the edges of a pastry bag before you fill it; (b) you should never fill it more than two-thirds full; (c) assuming right-handedness, you should tightly close the top of the bag with several twists, secured in the crevice of your thumb (see illustration); (d) apply pressure with the fingers of the right hand, at the top of the bag only; and use the forefinger of the left hand, touched to the tip, only to direct and guide.

If you practice, using these guidelines, experimenting with a few different tips, and with perhaps a book at hand to guide you, such as the Wilton instructional books (available at many department stores), you will pick it up without much trouble. The main item of business is to learn how to do borders with a star tip; these borders, at the base of the cake (where a border covers the junction of the cake and the plate and also hides any visible cardboard cake round) and at the upper edge (the juncture of sides and top of cake) neaten and refine the appearance of any cake. A simple, homey iced cake takes on a very special elegance with just these two simple borders—actually there are at least eight or ten different borders one can do with a star tip alone, just by manipulating it in different ways.

Piping is a mechanical skill on about the difficulty level of learning to crochet, but far easier than learning how to drive a stick shift. And, with a minimum of effort, it will enable you to turn out cakes whose appearance simply flabbergasts those they are set before. And not only cakes: meringues and other cookies, whipped cream atop pies, gougère pastry, vegetable purees, mashed potatoes, the seasoned yolk mixture in deviled eggs, ad infinitum. All will take a quantum leap in elegance; although, like with anything else in cooking, you also have to know when to restrain yourself and hold back.

For anyone who truly enjoys cooking, though, piping is a skill well worth knowing.

# Geranium Cake

*Makes two 8-inch layers*

After all that, it seems like a bit of a letdown to offer this, which, though filled and stacked, is not iced and certainly not piped. It is, however, more elaborate than simple.

This is a very delicious old-fashioned cake, a dreamily good white cake made light by a four-times-sifted cake flour, and made interesting and piquant by the addition of—rose geranium leaves! The bottom of the cake pan is lined with the leaves before the delicious batter is poured in; the leaves are carefully peeled off after the cake has baked. They add an indefinable, delicate intoxicating flavor: a little bit lemon-y, a little bit herb-y, faintly perfumed. Then the whole thing is raspberry-jammed and whipped-creamed, and, well, the whole thing is great. Variations follow.

Preheat oven to 350°. Cream until light and fluffy

*½ cup soft butter*

Gradually add

*1⅓ cups sugar*

and continue beating until fluffy. Sift together three times

*2 cups sifted cake flour*
*¾ teaspoon salt*
*2 teaspoons baking powder*

Add sifted dry ingredients, half at a time, to creamed ingredients, alternating with

*⅔ cup half-and-half*

beating until smooth. Add

*1½ teaspoons vanilla*
*¼ teaspoon almond extract*

(continued)

Beat until stiff

*4 egg whites*

Fold lightly, mixing into batter very gently. Pour into two prepared 8-inch pans, which have been Pam-ed and lined with several perfect geranium leaves. Bake for 30 minutes, or until cake tests done.

Cool in pans for about 5 minutes, then reverse onto racks. After cake has cooled for 30 minutes on racks, very carefully peel off and discard the geranium leaves. You will not be able to avoid disrupting the smooth bottom of the cake with a few ragged crumbly spots where the leaves were, but don't worry.

Torte the layers.

For filling, whip

*1 cup chilled heavy cream*
*3 tablespoons sifted powdered sugar*

Fold into this

*½ cup raspberry jam (we use our own homemade)*

Assemble the cake as follows: On the bottom layer, spread half the raspberry whipped cream. On the second layer, simply spread

*some raspberry jam*

On the third layer, spread the rest of the raspberry whipped cream. On the fourth and final layer, lay a paper doily on top of the cake, sift onto it

*finely sifted powdered sugar*

and carefully remove the paper doily. (You should now have a "doily" of powdered sugar atop the cake.) Garnish with

*geranium blossoms (pink) and mint leaves*

*Variation:* If you like the taste of kiwi as much as we do, use it instead of raspberry as the filling. Make kiwi whipped cream by adding kiwi jam (also our homemade) to the whipped cream. Instead of the ribbon of raspberry jam, top the second layer with very thinly sliced kiwi atop a thin layer of more kiwi jam. Proceed as directed to finish the cake, garnishing with slices of kiwi and mint leaves.

*Another Variation:* We are so taken with the wondrous delicacy of the geranium that we plan to try other varieties of geranium to flavor our cakes. Like chocolate mint geranium leaves to flavor a chocolate layer cake, or lemon geranium leaves to flavor this same cake, filled with Simply Incredible Lemon Mousse (p. 279) or Fresh Lemon Filling (p. 359). We'll let you know how it comes out!

*Other Variations:* Without the leaves, we think this is a perfect basic white cake, to turn into whatever you please. We haven't tried this but are quite positive that it would make a marvelous orange cake (which, by the way, we intend to try soon), using fresh orange juice to replace the half-and-half, the grated rind of 1 orange, and ½ teaspoon orange extract to replace the almond extract, omitting the leaves, cutting the baking powder back to 1¾ teaspoons, and adding ¼ teaspoon baking soda. We plan, with this, to brush the torted layers with Grand Marnier or Napoleon, and either ice with an Orange Cream Cheese Buttercream (p. 360) or fill with whipped cream into which orange marmalade has been folded. We know this will be spectacular (come in the spring and we will personally make it for you!).

## Charla's Birthday Cake

*Makes two 8-inch layers*

Charla Weston, a former Dairymaid (who still occasionally substitutes for us when one of the regulars can't make it), is a warm and vivacious woman, mother of two nifty kids and a Eureka Springs native. Jan and I made a lunch for her on her last birthday, which was interrupted by the arrival of Nancy from Eureka Flowers with a dozen red roses for Charla from Brian, her husband.

This is the birthday cake we made for her.

Make the following:

> Sour Cream Pound Cake, page 358, baked in layers
> Fresh Lemon Filling, page 359
> Cream Cheese Buttercream, page 360

Have on hand

> coconut, either freshly grated or from a package

Torte the cake. Fill it with Lemon Filling, making a "dam" (see p. 364) if desired. Crumb-coat if you like, then cover with Cream Cheese Buttercream. Press into sides of cake with palm of hand as much coconut as the icing will hold. Transfer cake to serving plate. Pipe borders. Decorate further with mint leaves and yellow marigolds; use yellow candles (the sunshine-y yellow hints, but does not reveal, the delectable lemon filling hidden inside).

This is one of the very best cakes either Jan or I have ever tasted. The pound cake bakes up into delicious, unusually textured layers, with that slight, characteristically pound-cake-y crusted golden top, and, in combination with the lemon filling, is densely rich and intensely flavorful yet at the same time slightly refreshing. And the coconut sets things off just right.

## George and Starr's Apple-Spice Wedding Cake with Apricot Filling

*Makes two 8-inch layers*

This is a deep, dark, delicious, very moist apple cake. I found the recipe in 1982, on a scrap of paper in a drawer in the kitchen of the mansion at Ossabaw Island, then a writers' and artists' colony. When Starr told me she wanted "something sort of like a spice cake, with apricots in it or on it somehow," this is what I came up with. For their wedding—and yes, it was the infamous 150-guest affair mentioned earlier—I made it with a classic French buttercream, flavored with a bit of apricot brandy, but I have done it since, and prefer it, with Cream Cheese Buttercream.

Preheat oven to 325°. Beat until thick

> *1½ cups vegetable oil*
> *1 cup each brown and white sugar*
> *1¼ teaspoons vanilla*

Add, one at a time

> *3 eggs*

In a separate bowl, sift together

*3 cups sifted unbleached white flour*
*½ teaspoon salt*
*1 teaspoon each baking soda and cinnamon*
*½ teaspoon nutmeg*
*a couple of dashes ground cloves*

Stir this into the oil-sugar-egg mixture, and, when well combined, fold in

*3 cups chopped apples, peel left on*
*¾ cup chopped walnuts*

Pour into two Pam-ed 8-inch layer cake pans and bake until cake tests done—approximately 1 hour to 1 hour and 15 minutes. Let rest in pan a few minutes, then reverse onto racks to cool.

*Note:* I always like to torte cakes, and with the delicious apricot filling, this is excellent torted. *However,* with all the nuts and apples, one's torting job is likely to be extremely raggedy and torn up unless the layers have been frozen solid first. Caveat emptor.

*Assembly:* Have ready a very thick unsweetened Apricot Puree, a doubled recipe made according to the rule in Apricot Mousse (p. 275). Also have ready a batch of Cream Cheese Buttercream (p. 360) in which you have substituted apricot brandy for the heavy cream.

Torte layers or not, as you wish.

Stack them together with the apricot filling, using a "dam" or not, as you wish (see p. 364).

Frost with Cream Cheese Buttercream.

If desired, press

*finely chopped walnuts*

into the sides of the cake with the palm of your hand, brushing off any that do not adhere before setting the cake on its final serving plate.

If you wish, pipe borders.

For George and Starr, I decorated this with two small chickens in a canoe, made of hand-painted pottery by Mario Petririna, the canoes with a border of tiny hearts, the boy chicken wearing a tuxedo, the girl chicken holding a bouquet of flowers.

But that's another story.

And by now, you may have heard more than enough of our stories. Thank you for listening so patiently.

Come to Dairy Hollow House: we'd love to listen to yours.

# Miscellaneous Lagniappe

It was not until we visited New Orleans that we heard the word *lagniappe*—a little something extra, a gift, thrown in free. These recipes didn't quite fit elsewhere in *The Dairy Hollow House Cookbook.* From Celebratory Punch Bowls to Jimmy Fliss's Homemade Vanilla Bean Ice Cream to Dog Biscuits for Phaedrus, here are our Lagniappes, final farewell gifts from us to you.

## THREE CELEBRATORY HERBAL PUNCH BOWLS

Iced herb tea and *wine* in a punch bowl? Oh, yes, we're the first to admit the combination seems incongruous, but not when the herb tea in question is one with a delicate, flowery bouquet, such as the chamomile and hibiscus we use in the two versions that follow. And also consider that May wine, a light fresh spring wine, traditionally has fresh sweet woodruff, an herb, steeped in it. In fact, these two punches are among our favorite beverages for a crowd—sweet and fruity, yet with the twinkle of wine. Wine purists may sneer, but there's never *anything* left at the bottom of the punch bowl when the party's over!

# Golden Punch Bowl

*Makes thirty-two 1-cup servings*

Chamomile and white wine; sweetness and light.

Bring to a boil

*2 quarts water*

When water is boiling well, drop in

*2 cups chamomile flowers, enclosed in a homemade tea bag, made by tying the dried chamomile flowers securely in a cheesecloth package*

Turn off the flame under the boiling water, cover the pot with a lid, and let the tea steep for 5 to 10 minutes, making a very strong tea. Remove the tea bag from the tea while it is still hot, and add to the tea

*1½ cups honey*

Stir well to dissolve the honey. Let the tea cool completely, pour it into a glass gallon jar, and fill the jar with spring water. Stir well. To serve the punch, mix the tea half-and-half with

*a white Chablis*

in a punch bowl over ice. Float

*lemon slices and mint leaves*

on the top. Serve well chilled. (You'll mix 1 gallon of tea with 1 gallon of wine, making 2 gallons, or thirty-two 1-cup servings—but everyone will want several servings.)

## Rose-Pink Punch Bowl

Substitute 2 cups hibiscus tea and 3 sticks cinnamon for the chamomile tea, steeping as directed. Substitute a rosé wine for the Chablis. Serve over ice. Float pink rose petals, thin orange and lime slices on the top. Serve well chilled.

## Crescent's Summer Fruit Punch Bowl for a Crowd

*Makes forty 1-cup servings*

I have done this a lot for casual, informal weddings, often ones where budget was an issue; I did this at the Dairy Hollow House open house. Cheap champagne is pretty loathsome when drunk as such, but it works just fine in this festive mixture, covered up as it is by all the fruit and simply adding a pleasant celebratory effervescence. Or, you can just use your favorite inexpensive white wine.

I never ever measure when I make this, but people always ask me for the recipe. It is very very fruity indeed; you almost wouldn't know it has alcohol in it (and, in fact, it is excellent made without, too). Have ready a large punch bowl—I usually mix this up on site, then do refills in the kitchen, pouring them into the punch bowl from a pitcher. Since it keeps getting refilled, the amount of alcohol in it waxes and wanes depending on what was last added, and, in fact, the entire thing undergoes continuing subtle alteration as the party continues.

Pour into the punch bowl

*two 6-ounce cans frozen pineapple juice concentrate, thawed*
*one 12-ounce can frozen orange juice concentrate, thawed*
*1-quart bottle unsweetened apricot nectar from the health food store*

Stir to blend, and then stir in

*maybe ½ gallon apple juice (hold the rest back for refills)*
*½ cup fresh lemon juice*
*white wine or champagne, inexpensive (I usually use just 1 bottle per mixing up)*
*1 bottle of either sugar-free ginger ale or club soda*
*plenty of ice*
*2 to 4 cups fresh sliced fruit: thin half-slices of orange, sliced fresh oranges, sliced bananas, sliced peeled kiwi fruit, etc.*

## Elsie's Sangría

*Makes two quarts*

Another simple and wonderful recipe from Elsie Freund, this Sangría is wonderful with all things Mexican or Spanish, and, interestingly, Mediterranean. Use the lesser amount of limeade if you want a wine-ier sangría, the greater if you prefer it fruity.

Dilute according to the directions

*one or two 6-ounce cans frozen limeade concentrate*

Combine with

*1 bottle good rich red wine—Elsie uses a burgundy*

Pour into pitcher, over ice, floating

*thin slices of orange and lime*

Celebration of a different kind is sure to take place any time you bring out or announce plans for

## Jimmy Fliss's Homemade Vanilla Bean Ice Cream

*Makes 1½ quarts*

Jimmy, affectionately known to us as "Uncle Cookie," is not only one of the town's best cooks; he is also a stained-glass artist extraordinaire, a business manager, a math teacher, a fixer of anything, and Judith's boyfriend. (We like him *almost* as much as she does.) Here is one of his best recipes; he often shows up at a potluck or picnic with his ice cream freezer in hand. The tiny flecks of vanilla seed give this ice cream a heightened dimension. This is the *ultimate* in vanilla ice cream.

Make a custard by scalding together

*1 cup heavy cream*
*1 cup milk*

*(don't boil it!!!).* Stir in

*¾ cup sugar*
*1 vanilla bean, left whole*

Take out about ½ cup of the hot mixture, and beat into it

*4 egg yolks*

Combine the eggs slowly with the hot mixture, whisking all the while. Cook slowly until it thickens and coats the spoon. Remove the vanilla bean and scrape the seeds into the custard. Don't forget to add

*a pinch of salt*

(continued)

Chill until it's good and cold. Add

*1 cup heavy cream*
*1 cup milk*

Freeze in an ice cream freezer, following manufacturer's directions.

*Variation—Mocha Supreme Ice Cream:* Make a custard, using *all* the milk and cream in the beginning. Add 2 or 3 squares melted unsweetened chocolate and ¼ cup more sugar. Add 2 or 3 tablespoons instant coffee when you put in the sugar.

## Crème Fraîche

This is one of the most versatile items in a good cook's repertoire of tastes and textures.

Into an enamel pan with a lid, or a glass bowl, pour

*1 cup heavy cream*

Whisk in

*2 tablespoons buttermilk*

Cover tightly and let the mixture sit at room temperature for 24 hours. Stir well and refrigerate. (You can successfully refrigerate crème fraîche for about a week, but you'll use it up long before that!) It is wonderful spooned over steamed vegetables, served with fresh fruits, or cooked in sauces.

## Custard Sauce / Crème Anglaise

*Serves 2 to 4 as a sauce*

A delicious basic that can dress up any fruit or simpler dessert with great success. We love it with baked apples especially, or over fresh sliced peaches, and it is a must with Cocoa-stuffed Pears, page 284.

Put on to heat in a heavy saucepan

*1¾ cups milk*

Meanwhile, blend another

*¼ cup cold milk*

with

*1½ teaspoons to 2 tablespoons cornstarch (less for a thinner, sauce-
ier sauce, more for a puddinglike sauce)*

Stir the cornstarched milk into the hot milk and cook, stirring constantly, over extremely low heat, adding

*¼ cup sugar or, for a different and delicious taste, brown sugar
⅛ teaspoon salt*

When the milk thickens, scoop out 1 cup of it and beat it with

*1 whole egg and 1 or 2 egg yolks*

Return the egg-enriched custard to the pot, continue cooking till custard thickens further, and remove from heat. Stir in

*1 teaspoon vanilla*

Chill.

You have no doubt seen the many references to this throughout
the book, but we must call your attention to two more:

- *Custard-Fruit Pie.* Prepare any good baked pie shell. Fill it halfway
  with sliced fresh fruit or berries—strawberries, bananas, raspberries, whatever. Pour custard, made with the larger amount of cornstarch, over the fruit. Chill deeply. Serve, garnished with
  additional fresh fruit and a few mint sprigs. Top with whipped
  cream if you like. Homey, but mighty good.

- *Trifle.* Serves 6 to 8. Have on hand any good sponge cake, pound
  cake (see p. 358 for ours), white cake (see Geranium Cake, p. 367),
  or Ladyfingers, bought or homemade (p. 334). Layer the following
  in a glass dish for a delectable do-ahead dessert, rich, with a sock
  to it

  *cake or Ladyfinger pieces, sprinkled well with sherry
  dabs of good jam—raspberry or strawberry preferred
  sliced fresh fruit of a single kind: any berry, bananas
  cooked custard made with 1 tablespoon cornstarch,
  2 yolks, whipped cream*

This English dessert is wonderful. It travels successfully to a potluck.
Beautiful made in a glass dish so that its multicolor layers are revealed.

## Dog Biscuits for Phaedrus

*Makes three dozen*

*Note:* not intended for human consumption, though there's nothing in them that would hurt you in the least, or even taste too offensive.

Phaedrus is Jan's golden retriever, a real stick-chasing fool. He may have happily greeted you when you first arrived at Dairy Hollow House, thinking that you came just to throw sticks for him. Jan makes him his very own dog cookies for his morning coffee break and afternoon snacks: you've heard the phrase "lucky dog"?

Preheat oven to 275°. Dissolve

*1 tablespoon dry yeast*

in

*1 cup warm water*
*2 tablespoons honey*

Add

*3 cups whole wheat flour*
*1 cup cornmeal*
*1 cup cracked wheat*
*¼ cup nutritional yeast*
*1 teaspoon salt*
*1 teaspoon garlic powder*
*1 egg, well beaten*

Blend together well, and knead in additional flour, if necessary, to make a stiff dough. Roll out to ½-inch thickness and cut into bars or bone shapes. Brush the tops with

*1 egg, well beaten*
*1 tablespoon milk*

Place on Pam-ed baking sheets. Bake for 1 hour. Let biscuits stay in oven to dry out until oven is completely cool. Serve anytime.

# GLOSSARY OF
# WEIRD AND UNUSUAL FOODS

*Agar-agar:* A tasteless, gelatinlike substitute, derived from seaweed, which, when softened in and heated with liquid, can jell dishes. It is somewhat less predictable than gelatin, in part because it comes in several forms—powder, flakes, and "bars" which are then crumbled—each of which is measured differently. The powder is most closely analogous to gelatin, the jelling power of 1 tablespoon of plain, unflavored gelatin being equal to about 1½ teaspoons of agar-agar. Follow the recipe directions for the specific form of agar-agar requested; if that form is not available, try to estimate, what with the information given here, in the recipe, and on the agar-agar package.

Why put up with all this "agar-vation"? Because gelatin is derived from animal hooves, and most vegetarians will not eat it. Because of its derivation, it also causes problems for anyone on a kosher diet. If you fall into either of these categories—or are cooking for someone who does—it's worth your while to play with it a bit.

Agar-agar is available in most natural foods stores.

*Alta-Dena: The* brand of dairy products to purchase whenever you can. This California-based dairy ships to natural foods and gourmet stores all over America, and the quality is excellent. I once did a story about them and was as impressed by the cleanliness of their facilities and the mountains of organic carrots set aside to feed those beautiful cows as I always had been by their dairy products. Unless you yourself have a cow, or live in an area where there is a really special local dairy (such as Mathis in Atlanta, Georgia), you can't get any fresher, better dairy products.

*Amaretti/amarettini:* Wonderful cookies from Italy, made by the same people who make Amaretto di Saronno liqueur. They taste like a crisp almond macaroon, yet they are made with apricot kernels, not almonds, as well as sugar and egg white. Amaretti are the larger size of the cookie, about the size of a silver dollar and much plumper, and they come wrapped, two to a package, in a charming printed tissue paper, twisted at the ends. These packages are in turn packed in a beautifully decorative red-and-orange tin. Amarettini are a tinier version of the same, only about the size of a dime and not individually wrapped. The manufacturers recommend them with "vino, caffé, il whisky, il the, lo champagne, il gelato" (the two you might not have been able to figure out are *tea* and *ice cream*). We like them every one of these ways we've tried, and we also crush them for use in a couple of desserts. Pass a basket of the larger ones, wrapped in their clever papers, at the conclusion of an Italian dinner.

These are available at any specialty food store and some liquor stores as well.

*Black mustard seed:* Used in Indian cooking, black mustard seeds are tinier and milder than the yellow mustard seeds we commonly use here. Available at your local spice/herb emporium, or write to Stamps' Apothecary (see Resources).

*Boursin:* Very creamy cheeses from France, these have become widely available in the last few years. While those with access to a really good cheese shop may prefer the triple crèmes such as Saint-André, we are pleased to be able to find something like a Boursin so easily. Plain Boursin is like a superrich yet lighter, smoother cream cheese. Herb-and-Garlic Boursin is what it says, and is great as an omelette filling, especially with sautéed mushrooms. Black Pepper Boursin is that same creamy cheese pressed into cracked peppercorns, which give a definite, delicious bite. We like this a lot on cheese boards.

*Cilantro/coriander/Chinese parsley:* This herb, which looks like a broad-leaved parsley, is used in Indian, Chinese, and Mexican cooking and consequently goes under a multitude of names. It has a crisp, assertive flavor, pungent and lemony and not quite like anything else. People generally love it or hate it. All in the Dairy Hollow House bunch love it, with the exception of Ned, who despises it. Know where you stand on it before you toss it into the general guacamole.

*Crème fraîche:* A thick, delicious cultured cream; we flipped when we first tasted this in Paris. We now make it ourselves, by the method given on page 376. It is best if you can make it with heavy cream that has *not* been *ultrapasteurized* (horrible word, and what, exactly, does it mean, anyway?), but it will work with the U.P. if that's all you can get. Not only does it have a delicacy of flavor unmatched by sour cream, it is less prone to curdling when heated. Much loved by the nouvelle cuisine people.

*Feta:* A salty Greek cheese we love—although there are many good fetas now made outside Greece as well. It can be made from cow, sheep, or goat milk. We like to alternate them; they're all good. The freshest comes in blocks which float in a salty brine. If the feta you've purchased is very salty, rinse it quickly before using.

*Kasha:* Also called groats, this is whole grain buckwheat, available from a natural foods store.

*Kefir:* A cultured milk product, like yogurt, and, like yogurt, available plain or in flavors. Also available, a product we're very excited about, is

*Kefir cheese:* A thick, white substance, like sour cream but with more body and freshness, like cream cheese but much creamier and lower in fat. It's absolutely delicious; from Alta-Dena.

*Masa harina:* Ground corn that has been soaked in lime water. Its texture resembles flour, and it has a cornmeal color. It is most often used to make corn tortillas and tamales. It is available in most grocery stores, packaged by The Quaker Company, or it is also available in bulk from many natural foods stores.

*Miso:* A wonderful salty paste made from fermented soybeans that serves much the purpose that bouillon cubes do in Western kitchens: diluted with water, it makes a magically tasty broth, or a bit can enliven numerous sauces or gravies. It is considerably more healthful than most bouillon cubes, too, lacking as it does all those chemicals whose names are either ominously short initials or ominously polysyllabic. It has a distinctive and delicious flavor you may recognize from Japanese restaurants. The dark version is a little heartier and stronger, the golden almost chickenlike in color and flavor. From natural foods stores.

*Morga broth cubes:* These Swiss-made broth cubes are the one exception to the rule of chemical-laden bouillon cubes. Vegetarian, derived from the cooked-down essence of onions, garlic, carrots, potatoes, herbs, and much more, they are available salt-free or with salt, at any natural foods store. We use them a lot, probably even more than we do the misos, as flavor enhancers. In any given recipe, adjust salt up or down, depending on whether your Morga cube is salted or unsalted.

*Pero:* A caffeine-free grain-derived coffee substitute.

*Pickapepper:* This is a savory sweet-salty-spicy bottled sauce, similar to Worcestershire, to which we much prefer it. Not only is it purely vegetarian (Worcestershire contains anchovies), not only is it very delicious, but it has a wonderful label with a parrot on it. Specialty food stores or the exotic food section of a good supermarket has it.

*Postum, Coffee-flavored:* See Pero.

*Phyllo:* We have described the commercially made Greek pastry dough, with every particular of using it, on pages 160–164.

*Rice flour:* Flour derived from rice, available at natural foods stores. Very fine-textured, utterly different in handling properties from any wheat flour, it is delicious added to muffins or breads, and, all by itself, makes a most superior waffle (see p. 34). Ideal for those with a gluten allergy.

*Sesame oil, toasted:* This Oriental oil lends an exquisite, indefinable flavor to many different dishes when used in small quantities. It's used as a flavoring agent more than as shortening. It is pressed from the sesame seeds after the seeds have been toasted, and it is much darker than the pale yellow untoasted sesame oil (which is perfectly acceptable for cooking or frying but lacks the special taste of the other). Available at Oriental markets, some natural foods stores, some exotic food sections of supermarkets. Keep refrigerated after opening.

*Spike:* A seasoned herb mixture, salt-free, available at natural foods stores.

*Tahini:* With a texture like slightly runny peanut butter, tahini is made from ground sesame seeds and is available at natural foods stores. We use it in salad dressings.

*Tamari soy sauce:* A strong, dark, naturally fermented, full-bodied soy sauce that makes the supermarket varieties look disgustingly pallid. Once you've experienced the magic of Tamari, especially in combination with butter in stir-fries, it will be a regular part of your seasoning repertoire. From natural foods stores.

*Tempeh:* A traditional Indonesian food, tempeh ("tem-pay") is cakes of compressed cultured soybeans. We know it sounds loathsome, but it is delicious. We almost never serve it at the inn, it being too far beyond the pale for most people's sensibilities at present, but we predict that within five years, it will be widely used and widely loved. See the Vegetarian Entrée chapter for further discussion. Available at natural foods stores.

*Tofu:* A milder, softer white soybean "cheese," usually described as being similar to cottage cheese, but that's not quite accurate. It's difficult to describe, delicate and obliging, traditionally used in sukiyaki. It is purchased in blocks, which are covered with water. If one changes the water every other day, tofu will stay fresh for a week. Like tempeh, it is an Oriental food still having to overcome a certain amount of prejudice in America—but remember how yogurt caught on? We almost never serve it to guests, for the reasons given for tempeh, but love it ourselves and foresee its future as rosy. Buy stock in tofu futures. Experiment with it, too. Available in natural foods stores and many supermarkets now, too, as well as Oriental food stores.

We have experienced a wonderful soft-frozen ice cream called Tofutti, and are sure it will knock your socks off when it comes to your hometown.

*Vege-Sal:* An herbed vegetable salt from the natural foods store.

*Wonton wrappers:* Pastalike squares of dough, available at Oriental markets and in the produce sections of many supermarkets, these were designed to hold bits of meat and vegetable and be boiled in chicken stock to make wonton soup. But many innovative cooks have pushed these handy squares far beyond their original application as the outside of dumplings. See our Walnut Wings, page 168, for one delicious example.

*Yeast, baking:* This is the yeast that rises the bread, and it needs heat in some form, and sugar in some form, to do it. Yeast comes in granules and fresh; fresh is just a bit quicker acting, and the granules are available both in individual packages and in bulk. One tablespoon bulk yeast equals 1 packet instant dry yeast (like Fleischmann's). An individual bread recipe will give you further details.

*Yeast, nutritional:* This is a yeast that is *not* used for baking and will *not* cause anything to rise, except possibly your spirits if you eat it often enough. A dry, golden powder, this yeast is grown especially for use as a highly nutritious food, rich in the B vitamins and various minerals. Yeasts vary; try to find a natural foods store that carries several different types of nutritional yeast in bulk so you can sample a few. Our favorite, called Good Tasting Nutritional Yeast, reminds us a lot of the flavor of Parmesan cheese. We use it in and on lots of foods but rarely tell people what we're doing, knowing of the prejudice against things that are healthy. Well, try it for yourself. Even if you hate the flavor (we doubt you will), you can always add a bit to bread. No one will be the wiser, but everyone, the healthier.

# RESOURCES

Some by Mail, Some for When You Visit Eureka Springs

Dairy Hollow House
Route 4 Box 1
Eureka Springs, Arkansas 72632
501-253-7444

Call or write for a brochure or reservation, or stop by when you're in town. For sale at the inn: jams, jellies, preserves, and a complete selection of all Crescent's books—including this one. Of course, why thank you, we'll be pleased to autograph it for you!

Jacqueline Froelich
Springs Graphics
34 North Main
Eureka Springs, Arkansas 72632
501-253-9048

Jacqui did all the beautiful graphics in this book, as well as the design and logo. She can do design work or printing for you, too.

Jan Brown
P.O. Box 494
Eureka Springs, Arkansas 72632

Jan is as superlative a seamstress and designer as she is a cook. A quilt of hers was recently featured in the *Arkansas Times,* and she was written up years ago in the *Wichita Eagle* for her quilting. She will design a custom-made quilt or garment for you you will treasure forever. She has no home phone, but write her at the address above or leave a message at Dairy Hollow House.

## CATALOGS BY MAIL

Eureka Springs Tobacconist
19 Spring Street
P.O. Box 690
Eureka Springs, Arkansas 72632
501-253-8272

Free catalog mailed to you on request includes a very special selection of tobaccos, coffees, teas, and accessories thereof, including pipes, teapots, coffeepots, mugs, etc. Visit the shop in town, too.

Jerry Stamps
Stamps' Apothecary
33 Van Buren
Eureka Springs, Arkansas 72632
501-253-9175

Catalog, $1 (applicable to first order), mailed on request, includes culinary and medicinal herbs, spices, homeopathic remedies, essential and massage oils, children's remedies, and other goodies. Stop by and visit Jerry when you're in Eureka.

Muriel Schmidt, the Persimmon Lady
Route 4, Box 420
Eureka Springs, Arkansas 72632

A free brochure describes mail-order persimmon puree, persimmon-oriented T-shirts and sweatshirts, and more. Includes 70 persimmon recipes.

# WHEN YOU VISIT EUREKA SPRINGS

Baskets and Such
Danny Abraham • Tom Strauss
87 Spring Street
Eureka Springs, Arkansas 72632
501-253-6120

Baskets and Such is a very special place: a wonderland of baskets from down the hollow and around the world, as well as antiques, quality reproductions, and fine country wares. They also stock a fine selection of jams, jellies, and preserves and gourmet food items. In addition to the Dairy Hollow House line, they carry Crabtree & Evelyn and The Silver Palate.

Beau Troutt
Sidereal Jewels
81 Spring Street
Eureka Springs, Arkansas 72632
501-253-9820

Fantastical, one-of-a-kind jewelry, masks, sculpture, prisms.

Eureka Art Company
67 Spring Street
Eureka Springs, Arkansas 72632
501-253-9522

Beautiful, elegant locally made art pottery, gorgeous hand-blown art glass. They will ship.

# OTHER BED-AND-BREAKFASTS/GUEST COTTAGES IN EUREKA

For information on availability of rooms at any of our town's numerous fine B-and-B's call or write:

The Association of Bed and Breakfasts,
Cabins and Cottages of Eureka Springs
P.O. Box 27
Eureka Springs, Arkansas 72632
501-253-6767

For information about Eureka's many attractions call or write our excellent Chamber of Commerce, P.O. Box 551, Eureka Springs, Arkansas 72632, 501- 253-8737.

*Go, little book, and wish to all*
*Flowers in the garden, meat in the hall,*
*A bin of wine, a spice of wit,*
*A house with lawns enclosing it,*
*A living river by the door,*
*A nightingale in the sycamore!*

*—Robert Louis Stevenson (1850–94),*
*"Underwoods"*

# INDEX